# THINKING CRITICALLY

## JOHN CHAFFEE
**LaGuardia Community College, City University of New York**

**HOUGHTON MIFFLIN COMPANY** Boston

**Dallas   Geneva, Illinois   Hopewell, New Jersey   Palo Alto**

*For Jessie*

*Acknowledgments*

Cover: SKY AND WATER by M. C. Escher, © BEELDRECHT, Amsterdam/V.A.G.A., New York, 1984. Collection Haags Gemeentemuseum, The Hague.

Old woman/young woman and dog in Chapter Five: From *The Dynamics of Human Communication* by Myers and Myers, copyright © 1973, McGraw-Hill Book Company. Reproduced with permission.

*Satire on False Perspective,* engraving by L. Sullivan after Hogarth. The Metropolitan Museum of Art, Gift of Sarah Lazarus, 1891. Reproduced with permission.

Photograph in Chapter Five: © Janice Fullman/THE PICTURE CUBE

''The Investigation'' cartoon: © John Jonik. Reproduced with permission. This cartoon first appeared in *Psychology Today,* February 1984.

Photography in Chapter Eleven: © Christian Delbert/THE PICTURE CUBE

Barbara Lewis, ''The Cook,'' from PATTERNS: A SHORT PROSE READER, Mary Lou Conlin, Copyright © 1983 Houghton Mifflin Company. Used with permission.

From THE AUTOBIOGRAPHY OF MALCOLM X, by Malcolm X, with Alex Haley. Copyright © 1964 by Alex Haley and Malcolm X. Copyright © 1965 by Alex Haley and Betty Shabazz. Reprinted by permission of Random House, Inc.

Nissan Stanza ad: © 1984 Nissan Motor Corporation in U.S.A. Used with permission.

Godiva chocolate ad: Used with permission of Margeotes Fertitta & Weiss, Inc.

Flemming/Mansbach: READING FOR RESULTS, Second Edition, Copyright © 1983 Houghton Mifflin Company. Used with permission.

Cynthia Roberts, ''We Must Reinstate the Draft'': This article appeared in *The New York Times,* February 25, 1982. Copyright © 1982 by The New York Times Company. Reprinted by permission.

Copyright page continued on page 457.

# Contents

## Chapter Twelve   Constructing Arguments   411

# Preface

THINKING is the way we make sense of the world—to solve problems, work toward our goals, interpret information, understand ourselves and others, and make informed decisions. *Thinking Critically* is based on the conviction that thinking is an ability that can be improved and developed through guidance and practice. This book has grown out of my experiences over six years in teaching a course entitled "Critical Thought Skills" at LaGuardia Community College. Viewed in retrospect, that course and this book respond to three general purposes: first, to develop students' reading, writing, listening, and speaking abilities along with their thinking ability; second, to address basic problem-solving and reasoning abilities; and third, to encourage students to explore their basic attitudes toward life and education and to foster qualities like initiative, maturity, and responsibility.

The approach of this book is significantly different from others in the field. In the first place, it systematically and organically presents the fundamental skills of critical thinking that are usually presupposed, ignored, or dealt with in a fragmentary way. Also, this book continually relates critical thinking to the life experiences and situations of the people using the text, rather than focusing on abstract or contrived situations to illustrate the concepts and processes being explored. This text further recognizes that thinking is an active process. It transforms readers from passive observers into active participants by creating a dialogue with readers and by stimulating them to think through situations and apply concepts to their own experiences. Write-on lines are provided at certain junctures in the text and for many of the exercises to encourage this active interaction. However, readers should not feel limited by these lines and should probably use a notebook in conjunction with this text, where they can develop ideas more fully. Finally, this book integrates thinking and language abilities through writing assignments, challenging readings, and activities that encourage meaningful class discussions.

*Thinking Critically* has been carefully sequenced. However, individual instructors may want to adapt the text to the particular circumstances and needs of their students and courses. The first three chapters lay a foundation by raising readers' awareness of how they think and of how to examine their thinking and the thinking of others. Chapter One, "Thinking," presents the various ways our thinking enables us to make sense of the world and decide what we should do. Chapter Two, "Thinking About Thinking," introduces the idea that we can improve our thinking by carefully examining the thinking process and working systematically through situations. This activity of thinking about the way we make sense of the world is continued in Chapter Three, "Thinking Critically." As explored in this chapter, thinking critically is not simply one way of thinking, but a total approach to the world that includes a variety of thinking skills and attitudes.

The next three chapters engage readers in examining and developing major areas of thinking in their lives. Chapter Four, "Solving Problems," presents an organized approach to dealing with complex problems. Sense experience provides the basis for much of our information about the world, and Chapter Five, "Perceiving," examines how thinking critically can clarify what we are experiencing through our senses. In addition to evaluating information based on personal experiences, we also form beliefs based on information provided by others. Chapter Six, "Believing & Knowing," explores strategies for thinking critically about the information provided by others so that we can develop the most informed beliefs possible.

While the entire book integrates thinking and language abilities, the next four chapters focus on the integral relationship between language and thinking. Chapter Seven, "Language," explores how developing our language abilities helps us sharpen our thinking abilities. Chapter Eight, "Symbolizing & Map-Making," explores the way we use symbols—including language symbols—to represent and communicate our experiences. This chapter also develops the technique of mapping as a way of aiding our thinking, writing, reading, listening, and speaking. The activities of symbolizing and map-making are made possible by our ability to form and apply concepts. Chapter Nine, "Forming Concepts," explores in detail the interactive process of forming and applying concepts, a process that enables us to organize and relate our experiences into meaningful patterns. Several of the fundamental concepts we use in forming, relating, and organizing our experience and ideas in writing are examined in Chapter Ten, "Composing," which presents an organic model of the composing process.

The final two chapters introduce students directly to the processes, concepts, and pitfalls of reasoning. Chapter Eleven, "Reporting, Inferring, Judging," focuses on another group of fundamental concepts used in making sense of experience and examines the significant role that each plays in this process. Chapter Twelve, "Constructing Arguments," draws together various dimensions of reasoning presented in previous chapters and introduces the primary forms of deduction and induction, as well as some common, illogical ways of reasoning.

This book knits together critical thinking with the fabric of students' experience—past, present, and future; daily and academic. From our experience at

LaGuardia, critical thinking learned in this way becomes part of who our students are—how they perceive and understand themselves, others, and their world. Our success at LaGuardia supports my conviction that teaching thinking *is* accomplished through this synthesizing process.

Although this is a published book, it continues to be a work in progress. In this spirit, I invite you to share your experiences with the text by sending me your comments and suggestions. I hope that this book serves as an effective vehicle for your own creative and critical thinking resources.

Many people from a variety of disciplines have contributed to this book at various stages of its development. I would like to give special thanks to the following colleagues for their thorough scrutiny of the manuscript and their incisive and creative comments: Nancy Nager (Wheaton College), Thomas Fink (LaGuardia C.C.), Janet Lieberman (LaGuardia C.C.), Karsten Struhl (Adelphi University), Diane Ducat (LaGuardia C. C.), Daniel Lynch (LaGuardia C. C.), Susan Lowndes (Rockland C. C.), James Friel (SUNY at Farmingdale).

The following reviewers also provided detailed and systematic evaluations that were of great help in preparing the final manuscript:

Ronald P. Drucker, University of California, Berkeley

Robert D. Hackworth, St. Petersburg Junior College (Florida)

Sharon K. Hahs, Metropolitan State College (Colorado)

Mary Kay Harrington, California Polytechnic State University

James L. Litwin, Bowling Green State University (Ohio)

Frank Louis Mauldin, University of Tennessee at Martin

Curtis Miles, Piedmont Technical College (S. C.)

Magdalena M. Rood, University of Texas at Austin

Special acknowledgment is given to Curtis Miles, Director of the Center for Reasoning Studies at Piedmont Technical College, who generously provided both materials and guidance when I first began working in the area of critical thinking. His pioneer work in problem solving provided the original basis for Chapter Four, "Solving Problems." I am also indebted to Professor Eric Lindermayer of Suffolk County Community College for his work in the area of concept development. His teaching materials provided a basis for key ideas in Chapter Nine, "Forming Concepts."

I would also like to thank the following colleagues for their valuable contributions: Anita Ulesky (Sussex C. C.), Harriet Schenk (Caldwell College), Ana Maria Hernandez (LaGuardia C. C.), Joan Richardson (LaGuardia C. C.), Daniel Kurland (Johns Hopkins University), Mary Beth Early (LaGuardia C. C.), Neil Rossman (LaGuardia C. C.), Robert Millman (LaGuardia C. C.), Gilbert Muller (LaGuardia C. C.).

This book grew out of the Critical Thought Skills program at LaGuardia Community College. My grateful acknowledgment is extended to the National Endowment for the Humanities for their generous support of this program. In addition, I would like to offer my deepest gratitude to the faculty members who have participated so creatively in the Critical Thought Skills program; to the administrators at LaGuardia for their steadfast support of the program's development; and to the countless students whose enthusiasm and commitment to learning are the soul of this text.

I have been privileged to work with very special people at Houghton Mifflin Company who have respected the purposes of this book while giving it the kind of wise and imaginative attention that every author hopes for.

Finally, I want to thank my wife Heide, my daughter Jessie, and my parents Charlotte and Hubert Chaffee for their ongoing understanding and support.

J. C.

# Chapter One
# Thinking

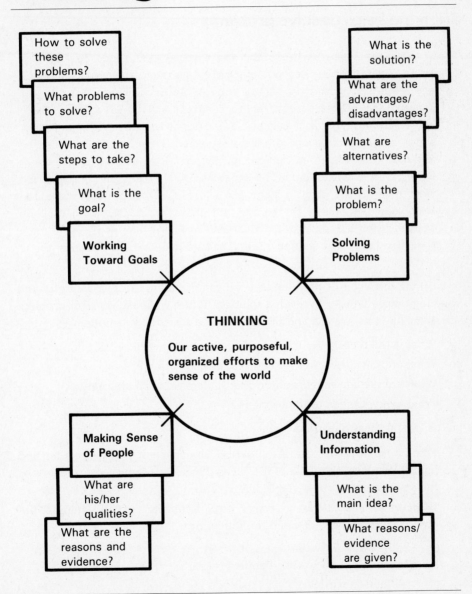

How to solve these problems?

What problems to solve?

What are the steps to take?

What is the goal?

**Working Toward Goals**

What is the solution?

What are the advantages/disadvantages?

What are alternatives?

What is the problem?

**Solving Problems**

**THINKING**

**Our active, purposeful, organized efforts to make sense of the world**

**Making Sense of People**

What are his/her qualities?

What are the reasons and evidence?

**Understanding Information**

What is the main idea?

What reasons/evidence are given?

THINKING is the way that we make sense of our world. Successful thinking helps us solve problems, work toward our goals, comprehend information, and understand people. Because thinking helps us make sense of the world in these and other ways, it is an activity that is crucial for living.

## Thinking helps us solve problems

> One day I was baby-sitting for a young girl named Jessie. While I was helping her put a puzzle together, the phone rang, and I went to answer it. A few minutes later, I heard a loud scream, and I immediately ran to Jessie's aid. I discovered that her hands were red and burned. I looked around the room, and saw steam coming out of one of the radiators. I ran to the kitchen to get some ice to put on her hands. My next step was to call her parents at a dinner party. I explained the situation to them, and they gave me the phone number and address of their doctor's clinic. I carried Jessie to the car and drove her to the clinic. They examined her burns, applied a cream, and gave her aspirin. I then took her home, put her to sleep, and waited for her parents to arrive.

In working through this problem, the babysitter had to think in a careful and systematic way in order to reach a solution. When we make sense of problem situations like this, we ask and try to answer a series of questions.

1. What is the *problem?*
2. What are the *alternatives,* or choices, available to me?
3. What are the *advantages* and/or *disadvantages* of each alternative?
4. What is my *solution* to the problem?

Let us look at these questions further.

1. *What is the problem?*  In this situation, the problem was Jessie's burned hands. What was the cause of the burns? Probably either the hot radiator or the steam coming out of the radiator.
2. *What are the alternatives, or choices, available to me?*  In this situation, the possible alternatives included the following:
   a. Panic and do nothing.
   b. Get ice to put on Jessie's hands.
   c. Call Jessie's parents.
   d. Take Jessie to the clinic for treatment.

Can you think of any additional alternatives a person might consider in this situation?

e. _____

f. _____

3.  *What are the advantages and/or disadvantages of each alternative?* In this situation, the various alternatives might include these advantages and disadvantages:

a.  Panic and do nothing.
    *Advantage:* ?
    *Disadvantage:* Doesn't solve the problem.

b.  Get ice to put on Jessie's hands.
    *Advantage:* Helps reduce the pain from the burns.
    *Disadvantage:* ?

c.  Call Jessie's parents.
    *Advantage:* Informs them of the problem, and I find out the best place to take her.
    *Disadvantage:* ?

d.  Take Jessie to the clinic for treatment.
    *Advantage:* Provides professional care.
    *Disadvantage:* Costs money.

What are the advantages and/or disadvantages of the additional alternatives you listed?

e. _____
    *Advantage:* _____
    *Disadvantage:* _____

f. _____
    *Advantage:* _____
    *Disadvantage:* _____

4.  *What is my solution to the problem?* In this problem situation, the person arrived at a solution by taking the various steps we just listed:

a.  Get ice to put on Jessie's hands.

b.  Call Jessie's parents.

c.  Take Jessie to the clinic for treatment.

Can you think of other possible steps that would have helped solve the problem?

d. _____

e. _____

As this problem illustrates, we spend much of our lives trying to figure out what is going on in our experience. Once we make sense of what is occurring, we can then make the appropriate decisions. In the situation above, figuring out that Jessie had burned her hands led the person to a series of decisions to deal with this problem. This is what the thinking process is all about—trying to make sense of what is going on in our world. When thinking is used to solve problems like this one, our thinking process often follows the same general approach that we just explored:

1.   What is the *problem?*
2.   What are the *alternatives* available to me?
3.   What are the *advantages* and/or *disadvantages* of each alternative?
4.   What is my *solution* to the problem?

   Read through the following problems. Select *one* problem to work with and explore how the problem was solved by answering the questions that follow the problem descriptions.

Damon

The problem that I solved recently deals with my 9-year-old son Damon. He is a very bright child in the 4th grade. He has a reading score of 8.3 and a math score of 7.3. He's always been in a one class since starting school. The problem is: He gets bored very fast when the class is moving at a slow pace. He starts to clown around, fight with other children, and leaves the room when he gets too bored. I was constantly going to the school every other day, meeting with the teachers to discuss Damon's behavior.

The teachers suggested that Damon had an emotional problem and asked me to have him tested. I took him to be tested. They found that he was way above average, but they didn't have a placement for gifted children in his grade. The principal and his teachers continued to call me up from the school saying that Damon was emotionally disturbed. I knew Damon knew the work, and so did the teacher. She often told me that Damon can do the work but just won't participate.

So I solved the problem by going to my district office to discuss what was going on. We came to the conclusion that Damon needed to be placed in a class that specializes in dealing with children who are bright. We have decided to have him tested again. If he meets the requirements, he will be eligible for monies for a private school where he can get the kind of work he needs.

## Going Back to School

A problem that I recently solved was a decision about whether or not I should go back to school and further my education. This has been a bigger problem to solve now than it was when I first graduated from high school in 1976. Now I think I am mentally prepared to do a lot of work and not get paid until I eventually graduate. It was not a problem to decide back then because I knew in my mind that there was no possible way I could cut it. I was fed up with school work, and all I wanted to do was get a job and start making money. I knew that I could always find a job because I was always good with my hands.

My alternatives were:

1. To stay at my old job (plumbing) getting dirty every day.
2. To stay at a job that is not as rewarding now as it was a few years ago.
3. To get a good education in business and try to get a job that I could look forward to going to every day.
4. To become financially wealthy.

My steps for solving this problem were:

1. To move back in with my family to save money.
2. To get back into reading.
3. To get a good part-time job at night.

1. What is the problem? _____

_____

_____

_____

_____

2. What are the alternatives available?

a. _____

b. _____

c. _____

d. _____

Can you think of additional alternatives?

e. _____

f. _____

3. What are the advantages and/or disadvantages of each alternative?

a. _____

*Advantage:* _____

*Disadvantage:* _____

b. _____

*Advantage:* _____

*Disadvantage:* _____

c. _____

*Advantage:* _____

*Disadvantage:* _____

d. _____

*Advantage:* _____

*Disadvantage:* _____

e. _____

*Advantage:* _____

*Disadvantage:* _____

f. _____

*Advantage:* _____

*Disadvantage:* _____

4. What is the solution? _____

_____

_____

Can you think of another possible solution to this problem?

_____

_____

Describe a problem that you solved recently. Then explain *how* you went ➤•◄
about solving the problem.

Reread your explanation, and explore *how* your thinking through this problem answered the following questions:

1.  What was the problem?
2.  What were the alternatives available to me?
3.  What were the advantages and/or disadvantages of each alternative?
4.  What was the solution to the problem?

## Thinking helps us work toward our goals

As we have just seen, thinking helps us make sense of the world by giving us the
means to solve problems in a careful and organized way. Thinking also helps us
make sense of the world by enabling us to identify *goals* in our lives and then
plan ways to reach these goals. Goals are those aims in life that we are striving
to achieve. Consider the following activities:

A person running for a bus

A person trying to throw a ball through a metal hoop

A student studying for an exam

In each of these activities, a person is behaving in a certain way for a specific purpose. This purpose is the goal that the individual is working to achieve.
Most of our behavior has a purpose or purposes, a goal or goals, that we are trying to reach. We can begin to discover the goals of our actions by asking the
question *Why?* of what we are doing or thinking.

Answer the following question:

*Why* did you come to school today? _____

_____

_____

This question may have stimulated any number of responses:

Because I want to pass this class.

Because I felt I should.

Because I couldn't think of anything better to do.

Whatever your response, it reveals at least some of your goals in attending
class. We attempt to make sense of what people, including ourselves, are doing

by figuring out the goal or purpose of the behavior, by asking the reason *why* they or we are doing it.

*Why* is that person running for a bus?

*Why* is that person trying to throw a ball through a metal hoop?

*Why* is that student studying for an exam?

In answering the question *Why,* we often find that our answer leads us to ask *Why?* again:

*Why* is that person trying to throw a ball through a metal hoop?

Because he/she wants to score points.

*Why* does he/she want to score points?

Asking *Why* about our goal usually leads to additional *Why?* questions because a specific goal in our lives is part of larger goal patterns. For example, the person throwing the ball through the metal hoop is pursuing the goal of scoring points, which is part of the larger goal of winning the game, which is part of the larger goal of keeping the team in first place, and so on.

| Throwing the ball through a metal hoop | Winning the game | Keeping the team in first place | Winning the championship |
|---|---|---|---|

Therefore, one approach we can use to try to discover our goal patterns is to ask *why* we did something, then to ask *why* about the answer, and so on.

---

►•◄     Using your response to the question "Why did you come to school today?" (p. 7) as a starting point, try to discover part of your goal patterns by asking a series of *Why* questions.

*Why* did you come to school today? _____

_____

_____

*Why* do you want to _____

_____

_____

*Why* do you want to _____

_____

_____

*Why* do you want to _____

_____

_____

*Why* do you want to _____

_____

_____

**Reaching our goals**

Goals—and our efforts to reach them—play very important roles in our lives. In the following passage, a cook describes how goals function in her work.

## The Cook
*by Barbara Lewis*

Preparing food for the sauté line at the restaurant where I work is a hectic two-hour job. I come to work at 3:00 P.M. knowing that everything must be done by 5:00 P.M. The first thing I do is to check the requisition for the day and order my food. Then I have to clean and season five or six prime rib roasts and place them in the slow-cooking oven. After this, I clean and season five trays of white potatoes for baking and put them in the fast oven. Now I have two things cooking, prime ribs and potatoes, at different times and temperatures, and they both have to be watched very closely. In the meantime, I must put three trays of bacon in the oven. The bacon needs very close watching, too, because it burns very easily. Now I have prime ribs, potatoes, and bacon all cooking at the same time—and all needing constant watching. Next, I make popovers, which are unseasoned rolls. These also go into an oven for baking. Now I have prime ribs, baking potatoes, bacon, and popovers cooking at the same time and all of them needing to be closely watched. With my work area set up, I must make clarified butter and garlic butter. The clarified butter is for cooking liver, veal, and fish. The garlic butter is for stuffing escargots. I have to make ground meat stuffing also. Half of the ground meat will be mixed with wild rice and will be used to stuff breast of chicken. The other half of the ground meat mixture will be used to stuff mushrooms. I have to prepare veal, cut and season scampi, and clean and sauté mushrooms and onions. In the meantime, I check the prime ribs and potatoes, take the bacon and the popovers out of the oven, and put the veal and chicken into the oven. Now I make au jus, which is served over the prime ribs, make the soup for the day, and cook the vegetables and rice. Then I heat the bordelaise sauce, make the special for the day, and last of all, cook food for the employees. This and sometimes more has to be done by five o'clock. Is it any wonder that I say preparing food for the sauté line at the restaurant where I work is a very hectic two-hour job!

For the student who wrote this passage, the goal of preparing food at her after-school job stimulates her to plan and carry out a complex sequence of steps. Her experience illustrates the way goals help organize our thinking, giving our lives order and direction. Whether we are preparing food, preparing for an exam, or preparing for a career, goals suggest courses of action and influence our decisions. By performing these functions, goals help make life meaningful. They give us something to aim for and lead to a sense of accomplishment when we reach them—like the satisfaction this student enjoys in winning her two-hour race with the dinner-bell. It is our thinking abilities that enable us first to identify what our goals are and then to plan how to reach these goals.

---

➤•◄        Reread "The Cook" (pp. 9–10), and then answer the following questions:

1.  The *overall goal* that the cook is working to achieve is to have all the dishes completed by 5:00 P.M. What are the *specific goals* that make up this overall goal?

    a.  Prepare the various dishes.

    b.  _____

    c.  _____

    d.  _____

2.  The cook has to plan very carefully in order to make sure all of the dishes are completed by 5:00. List the main steps she must take to prepare the meal. Try to organize the steps in the order that she must take them.

    a.  Check the requisition for the day and order any food that is needed.
    b.  Clean and season rib roasts, then place in oven.

    c.  _____

    d.  _____

    e.  _____

    f.  _____

3.  What problems do you think might come up that the cook will have to solve?

  a.  Miscalculating the amount of ingredients needed

  b.  _____

  c.  _____

3.  How could the cook deal with these potential problems?
    a.  Double-check the amounts needed and the ingredients on hand

    b.  _____

    c.  _____

The cook's thinking process enables her to (1) identify her goals, (2) plan the steps needed to reach these goals, and (3) solve the problems that might arise. This thinking process operates in our own lives.

---

Describe an activity in your life that you must carefully plan and organize.  ➤•◀
Make sure your description is very specific and mentions *all* of the things you must do.
    After writing your description, reread it and explore your thinking process in this activity by answering the following questions:

1.  What is the *overall goal* of the activity? _____

    _____

    _____

    What are some of the *specific goals* that make up this overall goal?

    a.  _____

    b.  _____

    c.  _____

    d.  _____

2.  List the main steps you must take in reaching these goals, organized in the order that you must take them.

    a.  _____

    b.  _____

    c.  _____

    d.  _____

    e.  _____

3.  What problems do you have to be prepared to solve that may come up while you are pursuing these goals?

    a. _____

    b. _____

    c. _____

4.  How might you deal with each of these problems?

    a. _____

       _____

    b. _____

       _____

    c. _____

       _____

Goals help us to organize our daily activities. Goals also act as the structure and the incentive for the larger projects in our life, such as our career choices, our decisions regarding marriage and children, our friendships, and so on.

In the following passage from his autobiography, Malcolm X, a civil rights activist and black Muslim leader who was assassinated in 1965, describes his concentrated pursuit of a significant goal while serving time in prison. During his stay at Norfolk Prison Colony, Malcolm X began writing letters to former friends as well as various government officials. His frustration in trying to express his ideas led him to a course of self-education.

## The Autobiography of Malcolm X
*by Malcolm X with Alex Haley*

I became increasingly frustrated at not being able to express what I wanted to convey in letters that I wrote, especially those to Mr. Elijah Muhammad. In the street, I had been the most articulate hustler out there—I had commanded attention when I said something. But now, trying to write simple English, I not only wasn't articulate, I wasn't even functional. How would I sound writing in slang, the way I would *say* it, something such as, "Look, daddy, let me pull your coat about a cat, Elijah Muhammad—"

Many who today hear me somewhere in person, or on television, or those who read something I've said, will think I went to school far beyond the eighth grade. This impression is due entirely to my prison studies.

It had really begun back in the Charlestown Prison, when Bimbi first made me feel envy of his stock of knowledge. Bimbi had always taken charge of any conversation he was in, and I had tried to emulate him. But every book I picked up had few sentences which didn't contain anywhere from one to nearly all of the words that might as well have been in Chinese. When I just skipped those words, of course, I really ended up with little idea of what the book said. So I had come to the Norfolk Prison Colony still going through only book-reading motions. Pretty soon, I would have quit even these motions, unless I had received the motivation that I did.

I saw that the best thing I could do was get hold of a dictionary—to study, to learn some words. I was lucky enough to reason also that I should try to improve my penmanship. It was sad. I couldn't even write in a straight line. It was both ideas together that moved me to request a dictionary along with some tablets and pencils from the Norfolk Prison Colony school.

I spent two days just riffling uncertainly through the dictionary's pages. I'd never realized so many words existed! I didn't know *which* words I needed to learn. Finally, just to start some kind of action, I began copying.

In my slow, painstaking, ragged handwriting, I copied into my tablet everything printed on that first page, down to the punctuation marks.

I believe it took me a day. Then, aloud, I read back, to myself, everything I'd written on the tablet. Over and over, aloud, to myself, I read my own handwriting.

I woke up the next morning, thinking about those words—immensely proud to realize that not only had I written so much at one time, but I'd written words that I never knew were in the world. Moreover, with a little effort, I also could remember what many of these words meant. I reviewed the words whose meanings I didn't remember. Funny thing, from the dictionary first page right now, that "aardvark" springs to my mind. The dictionary had a picture of it, a long-tailed, long-eared, burrowing African mammal, which lives off termites caught by sticking out its tongue as an anteater does for ants.

I was so fascinated that I went on—I copied the dictionary's next page. And the same experience came when I studied that. With every succeeding page, I also learned of people and places and events from history. Actually the dictionary is like a miniature encyclopedia. Finally the dictionary's A section had filled a whole tablet—and I went on into the B's. That was the way I started copying what eventually became the entire dictionary. It went a lot faster after so much practice helped me to pick up handwriting speed. Between what I wrote in my tablet, and writing letters, during the rest of my time in prison I would guess I wrote a million words.

I suppose it was inevitable that as my word-base broadened, I could for the first time pick up a book and read and now begin to understand what the book was saying. Anyone who has read a great deal can imagine the new world that opened. Let me tell you something: from then until I left that prison, in every free moment I had, if I was not reading in the library, I was reading on my bunk. You couldn't have gotten me out of books with a wedge. Between Mr. Muhammad's teachings, my correspondence, my visitors—usually Ella and Reginald—and my reading of books, months passed without my even thinking about being imprisoned. In fact, up to then, I never had been so truly free in my life.

The Norfolk Prison Colony's library was in the school building. A variety of classes was taught there by instructors who came from such places as Harvard and Boston universities. The weekly debates between inmate teams were also held in the school building. You would be astonished to know how worked up convict debaters and audiences would get over subjects like "Should Babies Be Fed Milk?"

Available on the prison library's shelves were books on just about every general subject. Much of the big private collection that Parkhurst had willed to the prison was still in crates and boxes in the back of the library—thousands of old books. Some of them looked ancient: covers faded, old-time parchment-looking binding. Parkhurst, I've mentioned, seemed to have been principally interested in history and religion. He had the money and the special interest to have a lot of books that you wouldn't have in general circulation. Any college library would have been lucky to get that collection.

As you can imagine, especially in a prison where there was heavy emphasis on rehabilitation, an inmate was smiled upon if he demonstrated an unusually intense interest in books. There was a sizable number of well-read inmates, especially the popular debaters. Some were said by many to be practically walking encyclopedias. They were almost celebrities. No university would ask any student to devour literature as I did when this new world opened to me, of being able to read and *understand*.

I read more in my room than in the library itself. An inmate who was known to read a lot could check out more than the permitted maximum number of books. I preferred reading in the total isolation of my own room.

When I had progressed to really serious reading, every night at about ten P.M. I would be outraged with the "lights out." It always seemed to catch me right in the middle of something engrossing.

Fortunately, right outside my door was a corridor light that cast a glow into my room. The glow was enough to read by, once my eyes adjusted to it. So when "lights out" came, I would sit on the floor where I could continue reading in that glow.

At one-hour intervals the night guards paced past every room. Each time I heard the approaching footsteps, I jumped into bed and feigned sleep. And as soon as the guard passed, I got back out of bed onto the floor area of that light-glow, where I would read for another fifty-eight minutes—until the guard approached again. That went on until three or four every morning. Three or four hours of sleep a night was enough for me. Often in the years in the streets I had slept less than that. . . .

---

After reading the excerpt from *The Autobiography of Malcolm X* (pp. 12–15), answer the following questions:

1.  As described in this passage, what is the overall goal that Malcolm X de-cides to pursue?

    _____

    _____

    _____

2.  What are the reasons for his decision to work toward this goal?

    a.  _____

    b.  _____

    c.  _____

3.  List the steps he takes to reach his goal in the order in which he takes them.

    a.  _____

    b.  _____

    c.  _____

    d.  _____

    e.  _____

4.  Describe some of the problems he encounters while working toward his goal.

    a.  _____

    b.  _____

5.  Explain how he deals with each of these problems.

    a.  _____

    b.  _____

➤•◄        In his *Autobiography*, Malcolm X recounts how he taught himself to read
and write while in prison. His thinking about racism led him to a determined
course of self-education.

By answering the following questions, explore your present educational
planning for a larger, future goal of a career:

1.   Identify what your current career goal is. If you are not certain what career
     you are aiming for, identify a career that interests you.

     _____

     _____

     _____

2.   Review the college catalogue and list the courses that you will have to take
     in your major for graduation.

     a.  _____

     b.  _____

     c.  _____

     d.  _____

     e.  _____

     f.  _____

     g.  _____

     h.  _____

     i.  _____

     j.  _____

     k.  _____

     l.  _____

3.   Next to each course, identify the semester or quarter in which you plan to
     take the course. For example:

     Introduction to COBOL: fall semester, sophomore year

4.   List some of the problems that you think might occur between now and
     graduating with a degree in your major.

     a.  _____

     b.  _____

5.  Explain how you might approach solving each of these problems.

    a. _____

    _____

    b. _____

    _____

## Thinking helps us understand information

A third area of our lives where thinking plays a central role involves information. Locating the right information is necessary for solving problems and for working effectively toward our goals.

Consider the problem you described on page 7. As you were trying to solve that problem, did you have to locate any information? If so, list the information that you needed to gather.

1. _____
2. _____

Where did you locate the information you needed?

1. _____
2. _____

Review your exploration of your career goal on page 16. As you try to decide whether this is a career you want to pursue, what information will be useful?

1. _____
2. _____
3. _____

Identify the sources (places or people) you can use to locate the information.

1. _____
2. _____
3. _____

Thinking not only aids us in locating the information we need to solve problems and work toward our goals but also helps us to make sense of the information that we find or that is being presented to us by other people. When we are trying to make sense of information, the first thing to do is figure out the *main idea* of the information being presented. Read carefully the advertisement for the following product:

> This is the new Nissan Stanza GL. A family car that seats 5 with room to spare. Room that includes luxuries like 6-speaker stereo with cassette, power windows and door locks, and plush upholstery. Now you're talking major value.
>
> And when a family sedan has Nissan technology going for it, you get even more than room and luxuries. You also get performance. Performance from a semi-combustion engine with two spark plugs per cylinder, fed by electronic fuel-injection. Go ahead, step on it, and feel your Stanza come to life.
>
> Another nice thing about owning a Nissan Stanza, you don't have to feel guilty every time you step on the gas. Because Stanza's highly developed Nissan engine is as gas efficient as it is responsive.
>
> So before you buy your family's next car, compare its specs to that of a new Stanza. Stanza thrives on comparison. After all, Stanza has Nissan technology behind it. And that takes it way beyond transportation; all the way to Major Motion.

The *main idea* of this advertisement is that we ought to compare the qualities of Nissan Stanza with those of other cars before deciding what kind of car to buy. In addition, if we make such a comparison, we should decide on a Stanza.

Along with determining the main point, making sense of information involves identifying the *reasons* or *evidence* that supports the main idea. Evidence that supports the main point is designed to encourage us to believe that the information is accurate. In the advertisement above, what evidence is offered to support the idea that if we are looking to buy a car we should seriously consider the Nissan Stanza?

1.   It seats 5 people with room to spare.

2.   _____

3.   _____

4.   _____

5.   _____

Read carefully the following advertisement.  ➤•◄

At Godiva, we take great pride in our renowned Belgian heritage. Many of our luscious milk and dark selections, with their enrapturing fillings, owe their graceful flavors and consistencies to exclusive Belgian recipes. Even our gracefully sculptured shapes reflect the patience of Europe's artisans of pleasure. It's no wonder why Godiva Chocolates bring moments of elegance to people throughout the world.

1. What is the main idea of the advertisement?_____
   _____ *Belgian Tradition* _____
   _____

2. Identify the reasons or evidence with which the advertisement supports its main idea.

   a. _____

   b. _____

   c. _____

Making sense of information is a crucial aspect of thinking, whether the information is being presented by advertisers, newspeople, college professors, or our friends. Read each of the following five paragraphs. Then identify the main point of the information being presented and the evidence or reasons that support the main point.  ➤•◄

Soap operas, the dramatic serials shown on afternoon television, are extremely popular, and every day millions of viewers tune into their favorite serial to discover the fate of a beloved hero or a hated villain. Soap operas, however, although they lay claim to realism, cannot be considered realistic; they do not show what really happens in the world outside the television studio. In soap operas people who commit vicious crimes are quickly punished, or else they die an untimely death. Even when suicide or murder enters the story, there's usually a happy ending. Problems, which in real life have no solution, are always solved on television.

1. What is the main idea of this passage? *Soap operas are a Reality*
   _____
   _____

2.  Identify the reasons or evidence with which the passage supports its main
    idea.

    a. _____

    b. _____

    c. _____

     A growing number of scientists are worried about the destruction of
wildlife. The most outspoken among them seem to be the zoologists (people who study animals) who warn that continued hunting and slaughtering
of wildlife will endanger humanity. Zoologists claim that people can learn
much about their own lives by studying other species and that useful
knowledge is lost when animals are carelessly destroyed. Perhaps even
more dangerous, according to the scientists, is the way the careless destruction of wildlife disturbs the balance of nature.

1.  What is the main idea of this passage? _wildlife Extinction Endangers_
    _Humanity_____

    _____

2.  Identify the reasons or evidence with which the passage supports its main
    idea.

    a. _____

    b. _____

    c. _____

    d. _____

     In World War II while America was at war with Japan, more than
100,000 Japanese people living on the Pacific Coast were rounded up and
put into special camps. During this same period many Japanese were
forced to give up their jobs because fellow employees were convinced that
anyone who was Japanese must be on the side of the Axis powers (Germany, Italy and Japan). Families were forced out of their homes because
constant threats made life unbearable. For some Japanese men and
women, it was not even safe to be seen on the street because the color of
their skin was liable to arouse hostile feelings.

1.  What is the main idea of this passage? _Jap Segregation_____

    _____

    _____

2.  Identify the reasons or evidence with which the passage supports its main idea.

    a. _____

    b. _____

    c. _____

    d. _____

    In the seventeenth century the emotionally disturbed suffered more from their treatment than they did from their illness. Since the devil was thought to be the cause of mental illness, brutal attempts were made to drive him out. Patients were whipped and beaten, and scalding liquids were poured over them. If the treatments failed, and they usually did, the patients were simply locked away in hospitals that were little more than jails. There they were left to the mercy of attendants who were underpaid and not much more emotionally stable than the patients.

1.  What is the main idea of this passage? _Historical abuse of Mental patients_

    _____

    _____

2.  Identify the reasons or evidence with which the passage supports its main idea.

    a. _____

    b. _____

    c. _____

    d. _____

    It is commonplace to hear outrage expressed at the callousness (lack of feeling) with which some Americans can view violence. We are, it seems, shocked to hear that five people can walk by while an old woman is beaten senseless because she refused to give up her handbag. It is similarly unbelievable that crowds can gather and wait in fascinated expectation for a young man or woman to jump from the top of a high building. Years ago when a young woman called Kitty Genovese was murdered in New York City, the American public could not believe that more than twenty people had heard her screams and seen her attacked without trying to help her. Yet after the countless hours of blood and gore that have filled our television screens and the numerous movies that have presented violence in glorious Technicolor, how can we claim to be shocked or even surprised?

1. What is the main idea of this passage? *By passer syndrome*

   _____

   _____

2. Identify the reasons or evidence with which the passage supports its main
   idea.

   a. _____

   b. _____

   c. _____

   d. _____

## Thinking helps us make sense of people

We are interested in getting to know people, understanding why they behave
the way they do, and predicting how they will act in the future. Making sense of
both other people and ourselves can help us to achieve our goals and solve problems. Understanding ourselves and others is a complicated process and involves our thinking abilities.

► • ◄      Listed below are words or phrases that a student used to describe herself.

1. Sensitive
2. Independent
3. Good friend
4. Love for life and people
5. Open and honest
6. I like myself

Now list five words or phrases that you think describe the kind of person
you are.

1. _____ *Introspective* _____

2. _____ *Honest* _____

3. _____ *Fastidious* _____

4. _____ *Slim* _____

5. _____ *Wealthy* _____

Listed below are words or phrases that a student used to describe a friend of hers.

1. Dedicated to school
2. Concerned mother
3. Willing to help
4. Wise
5. Strong character

Now list five words or phrases that describe a friend of yours.

1. _cheap dresser_
2. _Honest_
3. _loyal_
4. _gives up easily_
5. _negative outlook_

Listed below are words or phrases that a student used to describe a teacher of his.

1. Cares about the students
2. Well prepared
3. Encouraging
4. Interested in students' ideas
5. Dedicated to his work

Now list five words or phrases that describe a teacher you have known.

1. _Self-disclosing examples_
2. _Efficient_
3. _Easy to talk to_
4. _Task oriented_
5. _altruistic_

In the preceding exercise, the words or phrases you selected reflect your attempt to make sense of the people involved—yourself, a friend, a teacher. Of course, these words and phrases are just shorthand descriptions for your understanding of these individuals. The way we make sense of people is usually much more complex—and the people even more so. Our understanding of others is not simply a listing of their personality characteristics; we must also understand how these characteristics are organized into the total person. One way to give a more complete picture of someone is to explain *why* you believe he or she is a certain sort of person, to give reasons or evidence that supports your view.

Individual characteristics can be used to form a more complete picture of someone by explaining the reasons or evidence that supports the views of that person.

The following passage was written by the student who listed on page 22 the words and phrases that describe her. For each word or phrase, she gave the reasons or evidence that she believes supports her viewpoint.

I am a very <u>sensitive</u> person, and it's good to a point. I feel everyone should be able to feel or understand what others are going through. But when you hurt, cry, or are unhappy for people you don't know, or a movie that is not real, then I think that's a little too sensitive. That's the way I am.

I am a very <u>independent</u> person. I must do things for myself. I don't like people doing things for me, or helping me, or giving me things. It's not that I don't appreciate it, because I do. I just feel that when someone does something for you that you owe them, and if there is one thing I don't like to feel it's that I owe anyone anything.

I think that I make a <u>good friend</u>. I would do almost anything for someone I like, to share or give anything I have. I'm very caring and understanding. People trust me with their secrets, and they're right for doing so because I never tell anything that is told to me. I'm always there to help in any way that I can. All you have to do is ask.

I have a <u>love for life and people</u> that makes me feel good. I find fun in almost everything I do (except housework). I love to watch people, talk to them, and be around them. It makes no difference whether I agree or disagree with what they feel or how they live or what they look like or what age they are. I just love learning and being aware of everything and everyone around me.

I believe in being <u>open and honest</u> with people, even if it does backfire on you sometimes. I feel it's the only way you can have a good relationship with people, and it's the only way you are going to be able to enjoy other people. I have never come across a phony that I enjoyed being with. People are going to like you for what you are or they're not.

I think I'm a person who likes my life and myself. I'm a very strong person who can handle just about anything life hands me. I will forever jump at the chance to learn something new or more about something I already know about. I used to be a closed and untrusting person, who was unhappy and lonely. I'm glad I was able to release the real person who was locked inside me.

---

Using the words or phrases you used to describe yourself on page 22, give a ➤•◄ more complete picture of the kind of person *you* are by explaining the reasons or evidence that supports the descriptions you chose.

1. I am introspective, I find answers from within myself

2. I am a lousy liar & believe that telling it like it is is the best policy overall

3.

4. _____

   _____

   _____

   _____

   _____

   _____

   _____

5. _____

   _____

   _____

   _____

   _____

   _____

The passage below was written by the student who, on page 23, listed the words and phrases that describe a friend of hers. For each word or phrase, she gave the reasons or evidence that she believes supports her viewpoint.

> Gerrie is a friendly and polite person. She is very <u>dedicated to school</u>, perhaps because she failed the first time around. She says that the first time she was sort of pushed into going, and wasn't really ready for it. But now she seems very involved with her education. As a matter of fact, Gerrie says: "Right now college is the most important thing to me."
>
> Gerrie is also a very <u>concerned mother</u>. She is devoted to her two children and is very proud of them. She wants to give her children a firm foundation on which they can build the rest of their lives. I think that she has a very relaxed and open relationship with her kids. Even though it is a disadvantage being a single parent, she is able to deal with it. And she really enjoys the challenge of handling the problems alone.
>
> Gerrie is the kind of person who you can't help but like. She's friendly, intelligent, and has an undying desire to always be there for someone who needs her. She is the type of person who is always <u>willing to help</u>.

Gerrie is a <u>wise</u> person, but wise in more than one way. She is "book wise" in the sense that she does well in her classes, makes thoughtful comments in class, and keeps up to date in her work. She is also "street wise" in the sense that she is very aware concerning people and life in general. She's not about to let someone put something over on her.

Gerrie has had many disappointments in life and she has overcome all of them. I think this is a tribute to her <u>strong character</u>. She is a remarkable person to have had so many things against her and yet be on top of things at this point in her life. Gerrie is a person who is making it good, and rocking the neighborhood while she's doing it.

---

Using the words or phrases that you used to describe a friend on page 23, ➤•◄ give a more complete picture of the kind of person your friend is by explaining the reasons or evidence that support the descriptions you chose.

1. _____

_____

_____

_____

_____

_____

2. _____

_____

_____

_____

_____

_____

3. _____

_____

_____

_____

4. _____

5. _____

The passage below was written by the student who, on page 23, listed words and phrases to describe a teacher of his. For each word or phrase, he gave the reasons or evidence that he believes supports his viewpoint.

This teacher works with us as a class and also as individuals. He seems to care about each one of us. He listens carefully to our questions and tries to answer them as best as he can. If a student is having trouble understanding the work, he gives him special attention or works with him after class.

The classes are always interesting and informative. The teacher has a clear idea of what he wants to accomplish and is always well prepared. Classes always begin on time, the lesson is organized (but flexible), and you never get the feeling that your time is being wasted.

This teacher is very encouraging. He wants each student to do the best he is capable of. He is very understanding but expects you to work hard and says: "There are no shortcuts to being excellent."

This teacher is very interested in students' ideas. He encourages you to ask questions and expects you to express your

views on what we are discussing. He always makes you feel that
your ideas are important and that we all learn from each other by
exchanging our ideas.

What impressed me the most and showed me his <u>dedication to
his work</u>, was when he gave the class his home phone number in
case we needed to talk to him. There are not many teachers who
would be willing to do this. It meant that he respected us and
trusted us not to abuse his faith in us.

---

Using the words or phrases that you used to describe a teacher on page 23,  ➤ • ◄
give a more complete picture of the kind of person your teacher is by explaining
the reasons or evidence that supports the descriptions you chose.

1. _____

_____

_____

_____

_____

2. _____

_____

_____

_____

_____

3. _____

_____

_____

_____

_____

4. _____

_____

_____

_____

_____

5. _____

_____

_____

_____

_____

## A working definition of *thinking*

At the beginning of this book we stated that thinking is the way that we make sense of the world. Throughout this chapter we have been exploring the different ways our thinking enables us to make sense of the world by

solving problems

working toward our goals

locating and understanding information

making sense of people

Of course, our thinking helps us make sense of the world in other ways as well. When we attend a concert, a movie, or a sporting event, it is our thinking that enables us to figure out what is happening. In fact, these attempts to make sense of what is happening are going on all the time in our lives, and they represent the heart of the thinking process.

However, as we have seen in this chapter, thinking is not simply *anything* that goes on in our head. If we review the different ways of thinking we have been exploring in this chapter, we see that

*Thinking is an active process:* Whether we are trying to solve a problem, reach a goal, understand information, or make sense of someone, in each case we are actively using our mind to figure out the situation.

*Thinking is directed toward a purpose:*  When we think, it is usually for a purpose—to solve a problem, reach a goal, understand information, or make sense of people.

*Thinking is an organized process:*  When we think effectively, there is usually an order or organization to our thinking. For each of the thinking activities we explored, we saw that there are certain steps or approaches to take that help us solve problems, reach goals, understand information, and make sense of others and ourselves.

Through the ways of thinking explored in this chapter, a working definition becomes

**Thinking** • Our active, purposeful, organized efforts to make sense of the world.

At this point, our definition of thinking is too general; it needs to *specify* more exactly what thinking involves. We will continue to define thinking as we work through this book.

---

As pointed out, the definition of *thinking* as "our active, purposeful, organized efforts to make sense of the world" is too general. What questions do you still have about what thinking is and how the process operates?

---

Think back on the different ways of making sense of the world that we explored in this chapter. In each case, list some of the questions that we found it was important to ask.

1. Solving problems
   a. What is the problem?
   b. _____
   c. _____
   d. _____

2. Working toward our goals
   a. _____
   b. _____
   c. _____
   d. _____

3.  Locating and understanding information

    a. _____

    b. _____

    c. _____

    d. _____

4.  Making sense of people

    a. _____

    b. _____

## Thinking can be developed and improved

In all of the situations we have been examining in this chapter, we have seen examples of people thinking in careful and organized ways as they attempted to make sense of what was going on in their world. We have been trying to figure out exactly what the thinking process is all about. This awareness, along with experience and practice, also works to improve our ability to think clearly and to think effectively.

Thinking develops with use over a lifetime, whether we are trying to decide what courses to take in school, which career to pursue, or simply how much to bet on a poker hand. By continuing to develop our thinking abilities, we become even better prepared to make sense of our world, to explore the choices available to us, and to make appropriate decisions.

# Chapter Two
# Thinking About Thinking

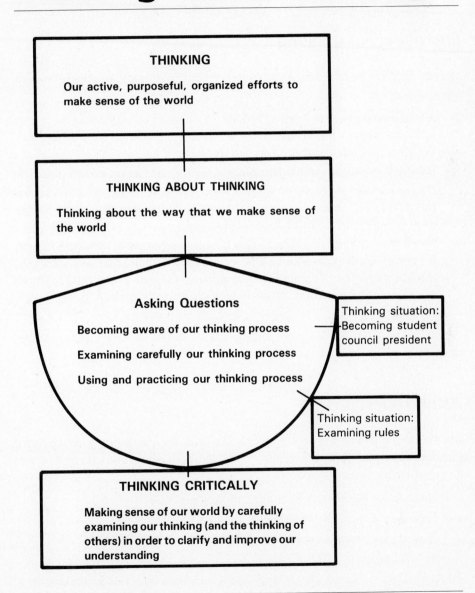

**THINKING**

Our active, purposeful, organized efforts to make sense of the world

**THINKING ABOUT THINKING**

Thinking about the way that we make sense of the world

**Asking Questions**

Becoming aware of our thinking process

Examining carefully our thinking process

Using and practicing our thinking process

Thinking situation: Becoming student council president

Thinking situation: Examining rules

**THINKING CRITICALLY**

Making sense of our world by carefully examining our thinking (and the thinking of others) in order to clarify and improve our understanding

AS WE WORKED through the last chapter, we found that thinking is the way that we make sense of the world. In this chapter we are going to explore a new step in thinking: *thinking about our thinking.* When we think about our thinking we are carefully examining the way we are making sense of the world so that we can do it as effectively as possible.

## Improving our thinking

We can improve our thinking in an organized and systematic way by following these steps:

1.  *Becoming aware of our thinking process.* We usually take thinking for granted and do not pay much attention to it. Developing our thinking means that we have to think about the way we think.
2.  *Carefully examining our thinking process and the thinking process of others.* In the last chapter we explored various ways in which our thinking works. By focusing our attention on these (and other) thinking approaches and strategies, we can learn to think more effectively.
3.  *Practicing our thinking abilities.* This means that we actually have to think for ourselves, to explore and make sense of thinking situations by using our thinking abilities. Although it is important to read about thinking and watch other people think, there is no substitute for actually doing it ourselves.

As we improve our thinking, we will be able to deal with new thinking situations more effectively.

## Asking questions

It's easy enough to identify the ways we can improve our thinking, as we have just done. The real challenge comes as we attempt to determine exactly *how* we go about taking these steps.

How do we *become aware* of our thinking process?

How do we *examine carefully* our thinking process?

How do we *practice* our thinking skills?

Asking questions is one of the important tools we have for improving our thinking. By asking questions we are developing a habit of mind which encourages us to explore, to investigate, to learn more than we already know. By developing the habit of questioning, we are taking an active role in trying to make sense of the world, as the following student passage illustrates.

### Questioning

I was always the type of student that did not ask any questions, and I made it seem like I knew everything. I have learned to be aggressive and active in asking questions. If we just sit back and wait for the answer to come to us, it's never going to happen. We have to be active and go out and ask questions, to be eager to learn new things. By asking questions we open our minds to new ideas and are able to comprehend new concepts. I am no longer ashamed to ask questions. I was able to pass my math and social science classes by asking the teachers to explain what I didn't understand and then learning from my mistakes. I felt more confident about myself when I did this. This has also helped me in my social activities because I now feel more free to ask questions of people I'd never dream of asking before. The only way you are going to learn is by asking questions when you are not sure or simply don't understand.

---

After reading the preceding passage, answer the following questions:      ➤•◄

1. What were the reasons why developing a questioning attitude was so important in changing the student's life both within school and outside of school?

   a. _____

   b. _____

   c. _____

   d. _____

   e. _____

2. What is your opinion of the student's experience and reasoning?

   _____

   _____

   _____

   _____

In the last chapter, asking certain questions was central in the various ways we make sense of the world—solving problems, working toward our goals, understanding information, making sense of people. In this chapter we will be using these and other questions to explore two thinking situations. Working through these situations will also give us the opportunity to continue thinking about *how* we make sense of things so that we can improve our thinking abilities.

## Thinking situation: becoming student council president

Imagine that you have just been elected president of the student council at your school and are determined that during your term in office some important goals will be achieved. How do you proceed?

In thinking about this situation, you will most likely use the various ways of making sense of the world that we discussed in the first chapter.

### Working toward our goals

As we found, working effectively toward our goals involves asking and trying to answer the following questions:

1.   What are my goals?
2.   What are the steps I will have to take to reach my goals?
3.   What problems do I have to solve?
4.   How will I solve these problems?

***What are my goals?***   In this situation, as president of the student council, one of our main goals will be to improve the quality of student life on our campus. To be more precise, we can ask ourselves to describe in clear and specific terms what we think is one of the most important problems facing students on our campus. A possible response to this problem might be the following:

> Many students on our campus get into academic trouble in their courses without realizing it. By the time these students understand that they are failing, it is often too late for them to catch up. They soon may get placed on academic probation or even suspended. This makes it very difficult for them to start over, improve their work, and eventually graduate. As a result, they often just give up and drop out. My first goal as Student Council president will be to try to do something about this problem.

Now describe in clear and specific terms what *you* think is one of the most ▶•◀ important problems facing students on your campus. Using clear and specific language is important in communicating our ideas effectively to others.

_____

_____

_____

_____

_____

_____

_____

_____

_____

***What are the steps I must take to reach my goal?***  The next move in working toward our goal is to identify the steps we will have to take in the order we will have to take them. In the case of the problem of student failure, some of the steps might include the following:

1.  Discuss this problem with other members of the student council, to gain their support in pursuing this goal. If they support this goal, we can discuss and examine their suggestions for how best to proceed.

2.  Discuss this problem with the appropriate faculty committees in order to explore what the faculty can do to reduce student failure.

3.  Discuss this problem with the school administration in order to explore what the administration can do to reduce student failure.

4.  Have the student council prepare a report evaluating the situation and suggesting specific ways to reduce student failure.

5.  Have the student council devise the means to see that these suggestions are carried out.

Can you think of an additional step that might be taken in order to work toward this goal?

6.  _____

    _____

    _____

➤•◄          Now describe what steps you think you will have to take in order to reach
the goal you identified on page 37.

1.   _____

     _____

     _____

2.   _____

     _____

3.   _____

     _____

     _____

4.   _____

     _____

5.   _____

     _____

***What problems do I have to solve? How will I solve these problems?***   The third aspect of working toward our goals is identifying the problems that might come up. After identifying the problems, we need to figure out how to solve them. With the goal of reducing student failure, one of the most important problems is to devise specific plans for reducing student failure. Everyone talks about a problem like this, but how can we really *do* something about it? Dealing with this problem effectively makes use of another way that our thinking can make sense of the world: solving problems.

### Solving problems

As we discovered in the last chapter, solving problems effectively involves asking and trying to answer the following questions:

1.   What is the problem?
2.   What are my alternatives?
3.   What are the advantages and/or disadvantages of each alternative?
4.   What is the solution?

***What is the problem?***   In trying to reduce student failure, we identified the following problem: What specific plans can we devise that will insure that something is actually done to reduce student failure, instead of merely talking about the problem?

Describe one of the important problems you might have to deal with in ➤•◀ working toward the goal you identified on page 37.

**What are the alternatives available to me? What are the advantages and/or disadvantages of each alternative?**  Once we have identified the problem, the next step in solving problems is to list each of the possible alternatives, and then to identify the advantages and/or disadvantages of each alternative. In order to devise specific plans to reduce student failure, we might consider the following alternatives:

1.  Teachers should describe clearly at the beginning of a course exactly what will be required and how much work will be involved.

    *Advantage:*  Students will have an idea how hard they will have to work in the course in order to be successful and can plan accordingly.

    *Disadvantage:* _____

    _____

2.  Teachers should give students progress reports that would inform the students how well they are doing.

    *Advantage:*  Students will know early in the course if they are having difficulties.

    *Disadvantage:* _____

    _____

3.  Students should request a conference with the teacher if they are not doing well.

    *Advantage:* _____

    _____

    _____

    *Disadvantage:*  Teachers may not have time for student conferences.

4.  The school should have an "early warning system" in which teachers must submit a midterm grade for each student. Students who are doing poorly are then asked to meet with a school counselor to identify the reasons for the difficulties the student is having. The counselor can then work with the student in arriving at a solution.

    *Advantage:* _____

    _____

    _____

    *Disadvantage:*  It will cost the school money to create such a program.

Can you think of an additional alternative to reduce student failure that should be considered?

5. _____

_____

*Advantage:* _____

_____

*Disadvantage:* _____

_____

---

►•◄        Now list some of the alternatives you might consider in trying to solve the problem you identified on page 39 and note the advantages and/or disadvantages for each.

1. _____

_____

*Advantage:* _____

_____

*Disadvantage:* _____

_____

2. _____

_____

*Advantage:* _____

_____

*Disadvantage:* _____

_____

3. _____

_____

*Advantage:* _____

_____

*Disadvantage:* _____

_____

4. _____

_____

*Advantage:* _____

_____

*Disadvantage:* _____

_____

***What is my solution to the problem?*** After carefully examining each of the alternatives to the problem, we should try to come up with a solution and a specific plan of action. Since each of the alternatives we listed in our attempt to reduce student failure seems promising, we have decided to pursue each of them. Our specific plan might be as follows:

1.  Speak with the administration to try to get it to adopt an early warning system. We can point out that the money spent in setting up such a system will be made up by reducing the number of students who drop out of school.
2.  Speak with the faculty to try to get it to (a) describe clearly what is expected of students in the course, (b) give students progress reports on how they are doing, and (c) schedule conferences with students who are having difficulties.
3.  Speak with students to encourage them to seek help when they are doing poorly. Students could contact the teacher, a counselor, or a tutor in the learning laboratory.

Can you think of any additional steps that might be taken to reduce student failure?

4. _____

_____

_____

Now describe your proposed solution to the problem that you identified on ➤•◄ page 39, based on the alternatives you listed on page 40. Be sure to list the specific steps you will take as part of your plan of action.

1.  *Solution:* _____

_____

_____

2.  *Specific steps:*

    a. _____

       _____

    b. _____

       _____

    c. _____

## Thinking situation: examining rules

As we continue our thinking about thinking, we need to examine the subject of *rules*. Rules are expressions of our thinking about human behavior; they are guidelines for how people are supposed to behave in certain situations. Rules play an important part in our relationships with other people. When we play a game such as poker or baseball with others, rules organize the way we can behave. (For instance, "A full house beats three of a kind," or "Three strikes and you're out.") Without these rules, which everyone agrees to follow, it would not be possible to play the game since it would become disorder. Traffic rules are another example:

A red light means we must stop.

A green light means we can proceed.

Suppose all of us decided on our own when to stop and proceed; we would have a giant case of bumper cars on the road. Before we can question whether rules are "right" or "wrong," we must question and discover whether there are important *reasons* for these rules.

➤•◄    List some additional traffic rules we are supposed to follow.

1.  People in the United States must drive their vehicles on the right side of the road.

2.  _____

    _____

3.  _____

    _____

Now describe the reasons why you think these rules exist.

1.  Asking people to drive consistently on one side of the road (whether the right or left) permits traffic to flow in two directions without cars running into each other.

2.  _____

    _____

3.  _____

    _____

It makes sense for us to use our thinking abilities to examine and try to understand the thinking behind the rules we are asked to follow. This understanding will affect our willingness to follow the rules. How do you react if someone asks you to obey rules that you do not believe are supported by good reasons? However, if you feel that the rules you are being asked to follow make sense and that there are good reasons for them, are you usually more willing to follow them?

---

In 1920 the Congress of the United States passed a law prohibiting the sale ➤•◄ of alcoholic beverages, beginning Prohibition. By the time the law was changed in 1933 to once again permit the sale of alcoholic beverages, a large number of people in the United States were simply ignoring the law.

Describe a rule or a law that you are supposed to follow and that you believe does not make sense.

_____

_____

_____

Now identify the reasons *why* you think this rule or law does not make sense.

_____

_____

_____

In situations where we are trying to work toward a common purpose with a group of other people—such as the class that you are in—it is usually necessary to have rules that we all agree to follow. Some of these typical rules for a class are listed below, followed by questions that attempt to explore whether the rules make sense and have good reasons backing them up.

*Rules*

1. Students and teachers should attend class and be on time unless a very good reason prevents them.

2. Students and teachers should come to class prepared, having completed the assigned reading and homework.

3. A class should include examinations and/or other ways of measuring students' understanding of the course work.

4. Students should ask questions and actively participate in class discussions.

1. Attendance

   a. What do you think are the main reasons for making class attendance required? _____
   
   _____
   
   _____
   
   _____

   b. What types of reasons should be considered acceptable for an absence? Why? What reasons should be considered unacceptable? Why?

   *Acceptable Reasons*                        *Unacceptable Reasons*

   _____        _____

   _____        _____

   _____        _____

   _____        _____

   c. What is your main purpose in taking a course? Explain your answer.

   _____
   
   _____
   
   _____
   
   _____

   d. Do you feel that you have any obligations to the other members of the class? to the teacher? to yourself? Explain your answers.

   _____
   
   _____
   
   _____
   
   _____

e.  What effect does someone walking in late to class have on the instructor? the student? the class as a whole?

_____

_____

_____

_____

f.  What types of reasons should be considered acceptable for lateness? Why? What reasons should be considered unacceptable? Why?

*Acceptable*                              *Unacceptable Reasons*

_____          _____

_____          _____

_____          _____

_____          _____

2.  Assignments
   a.  Does it make a difference whether you do the assigned reading for the class *before* or *after* the class for which it is assigned? Why?

_____

_____

_____

_____

   b.  What do you think are the purposes of homework assignments?

_____

_____

_____

_____

   c.  Does it make any difference to the teacher if your homework is handed in late? Why?

_____

_____

_____

_____

d. Does it make any difference to *you* if your homework is handed in late? Why?

_____

_____

_____

_____

e. Should you work hard at doing the homework well or just do enough to get credit for the assignment? Why?

_____

_____

_____

_____

3. Examinations

   a. List the reasons for examinations:

_____

_____

_____

_____

   b. If you were teaching a course, would you give examinations? Why or why not?

_____

_____

_____

_____

   c. If you were creating an examination for the class, what types of questions would you ask? Why?

_____

_____

_____

_____

d.  What standards would you use to grade the results of your examina-
    tions?

    _____

    _____

    _____

    _____

e.  If _no_ examinations were given, would this effect how much class mem-
    bers studied and learned? In what ways?

    _____

    _____

    _____

    _____

4.  Class participation
    a.  Do you think it is important for students to participate _actively_ in class
        discussions? Why?

        _____

        _____

        _____

        _____

    b.  Is active participation important for developing your thinking abilities?
        Why?

        _____

        _____

        _____

        _____

    c.  Why is it difficult for some students to participate in class?

        _____

        _____

_____

_____

d.  Why is it hard for some instructors to let the class actively participate?

_____

_____

_____

_____

e.  What advice would you offer them to help overcome these difficulties?

_____

_____

_____

_____

## Thinking critically

In Chapter One, we explored some of the different ways that we use our thinking to make sense of the world by solving problems, working toward our goals, understanding information, and making sense of people. In Chapter Two, we have seen that if we carefully examine the way we make sense of the world by thinking about our thinking, we can develop and improve the way we think. This in turn will help us deal more effectively with new situations, such as our project as student council president or our efforts to understand the purpose of rules and the way they operate. Thinking about our thinking involves developing the habit of asking questions, which in turn leads to

1.  becoming aware of our thinking process.
2.  carefully examining our thinking process and the thinking process of others.
3.  practicing our thinking abilities by working through thinking situations on our own.

These are the steps we followed as we tried to work toward the goals and solve the problems of being student council president. We also followed these steps as we explored the reasons that support (or fail to support) some of the rules in our lives. In both of these cases we were not only thinking, that is, trying to make sense of things; we were also carefully examining our thinking in order to clarify and improve it.

This ability to think for ourselves by carefully examining the way that we make sense of the world is one of the highest forms of human thinking. We are going to refer to this ability to carefully think about our thinking as the ability to *think critically.* We are able to think critically because of our natural human ability to *reflect*—to think back on what we are thinking, doing, or feeling. By carefully thinking back on our thinking, we are able to figure out the way our thinking operates and so learn to do it more effectively.

**Thinking Critically** • Making sense of our world by carefully examining our thinking and the thinking of others in order to clarify and improve our understanding.

Examining our thinking is a complex activity, and it is the subject of the next chapter, "Thinking Critically."

# Chapter Three
# Thinking Critically

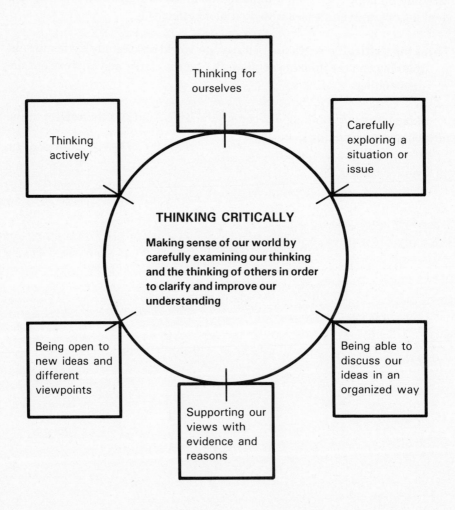

Thinking for ourselves

Carefully exploring a situation or issue

Thinking actively

**THINKING CRITICALLY**

**Making sense of our world by carefully examining our thinking and the thinking of others in order to clarify and improve our understanding**

Being open to new ideas and different viewpoints

Being able to discuss our ideas in an organized way

Supporting our views with evidence and reasons

**Thinking Critically** • Making sense of our world by carefully examining our thinking and the thinking of others in order to clarify and improve our understanding.

WE HAVE ARRIVED at this definition of *thinking critically* through our explorations of the thinking process. Thinking is the way we make sense of the world; thnking critically is thinking about our thinking so that we can clarify and improve it. If we can understand the way our minds work when we solve problems, work toward our goals, understand information, or make sense of people, then we can learn to think more effectively in these situations.

In this chapter we will be exploring exactly how we examine our thinking so that we can develop it to the fullest extent possible, that is, how we think critically.

The word *critical* comes from the Greek word *critic*, which means to question, to make sense of, to be able to analyze. It is by questioning, making sense of things and people, and analyzing that we examine our thinking and the thinking of others. These critical activities aid us in reaching the best possible conclusions and decisions.

The word *critical* is also related to the word *criticize*, which means to question and evaluate. Unfortunately, the ability to criticize is often only used destructively, to tear down someone else's thinking. However, criticism can also be *constructive*—analyzing for the purpose of developing a better understanding of what is going on. It is constructive criticism that we will engage in as we develop our ability to think critically.

---

In each of the following situations, describe how you could deal with the problem by thinking *constructively*.

*Example:*   You are discussing with a group of friends what you should do tonight. Someone suggests that you all go bowling, which you think is a poor idea.

*Constructive thinking*: You explain why you don't want to go bowling and then suggest something else for the group to do.

1.   You are approached by another student from your class, who suggests that you exchange homework assignments to check for mistakes. You're not interested in doing this, particularly since this student is not doing very well in the class and you don't expect to learn anything from the exchange.

*Constructive thinking:* _____

_____

_____

2.  You are the teacher of a class and you have just asked the following question: "What are the causes of poverty in the United States?" One of your students answers: "Poverty is caused by not having enough money."

    *Constructive thinking:* _____

    _____

    _____

3.  You are the parent of a child who spends a lot of time daydreaming, to the extent that his schoolwork is beginning to suffer.

    *Constructive thinking:* _____

    _____

    _____

## The qualities of critical thinking

Critical thinking is not simply one way of thinking; it is a total approach to understanding how we make sense of the world that includes many parts. In this chapter we will be exploring the various activities that are a part of thinking critically, including the following:

1.  Thinking actively
2.  Thinking for ourselves
3.  Carefully exploring a situation or issue
4.  Being open to new ideas and different viewpoints
5.  Supporting our views with reasons and evidence
6.  Being able to discuss our ideas in an organized way

### Thinking critically involves thinking actively

When we think critically, we are *actively* using our intelligence, knowledge, and skills to deal effectively with ourselves, others, and life's situations. When we are thinking actively, we are

1.  getting involved instead of remaining outside of the action.
2.  getting started on our own instead of simply waiting to be told what to think or do.
3.  following through on what we are involved with instead of giving up when we lose interest or encounter difficulties.

When we are thinking actively, we are not just standing on the sidelines, waiting for something to happen. Instead, we are in the game, trying to figure out how best to solve our problems and rech our goals. Imagine that you have just gotten back your midterm examination in a course. You thought you had done all right, but the grade on the exam is D. How do you react? One response would be to do nothing. You could explain the disappointing grade by suggesting that the exam was unfair, the teacher did not grade it properly, or you simply cannot do the work. But instead of seeing this grade as a reason to give up, you could also view it as a problem to solve, a challenge to overcome. Seeing it in this way, you can plan the steps you are going to take to solve the problem. List some possible alternatives to help solve this problem and reach your goal.

1. _____
   _____

2. _____
   _____

3. _____
   _____

From this example we can see that critical thinking involves taking an active attitude toward the situations encountered in life. Thinking critically does not mean simply having thoughts and waiting for things to happen. Such a response would be *passive;* we would be letting events control us or permitting others to do our thinking for us and determine our decisions. Critical thinking requires active use of our thinking abilities to solve problems and make sense of what is going on.

Your car breaks down far away from your home or public transportation. The road has little traffic and there are no houses or buildings in sight. The weather is cold, and night is fast approaching.

1. What are some of the alternatives available to you?

   a. _____

   b. _____

   c. _____

2. Which alternative do you think is most likely to succeed?

   _____

   Why do you think this? (What reasons support this choice?)

   _____
   _____

3.  Suppose you decide to try to stop someone for assistance. What sort of car
    or truck would you try to stop? (For example, would you try to stop a car
    filled with loud and rowdy people?)

    _____

    Why do you think this? (What reasons support this choice?)

    _____

    _____

    _____


➤•◄    You are not sure what field you want to work in for a living. A friend suggests that you do nothing until you get a clear idea of what you want to be. This
way you won't waste time and money studying in a field you might ultimately
decide is not for you.

1.  What are the advantages of following your friend's advice?

    a.  _____

    b.  _____

    What are the disadvantages?

    a.  _____

    b.  _____

2.  What are the advantages of enrolling in school or a training program even if
    you are not sure what you want to do?

    a.  _____

    b.  _____

    What are the disadvantages?

    a.  _____

    b.  _____

**Influences on our thinking**    As our minds grow and develop, we are
exposed to many influences that encourage us to think actively. However, we
also have many experiences that encourage us to think passively. Many people
believe that when we spend much of our time watching television we are being
influenced to think passively. Read carefully the following passage regarding
television watching.

## The Effects of Watching Television on Gorillas and Others

My four-year-old daughter has recently begun to appreciate jokes and riddles, although her understanding is not yet complete. Her latest effort goes something like this: "Why did the gorilla watch TV? Because he wanted to get dopey!" (followed by gales of laughter). This "joke" originated in my observation to her that, after watching several hours of television on Saturday morning, she usually becomes "dopey"—listless, unaware of anything going on around her, moody, and not interested in doing anything but watching more television. It doesn't matter much what show she is watching. What's important is only that she is *watching*. What is the power of this electronic box that will transform a lively, energetic, inquisitive little child into a hypnotized zombie in a matter of hours?

In the first place, watching television is an almost totally *passive* experience. We are being entertained, provided with images, characterizations, stories, and so on. Many other childrens' activities—like reading and playing imaginary games—require that children *create* images, producing a world of their own making. With television, we are not encouraged—or even normally permitted—to use our minds actively to create images, characters, or stories. That work has already been done for us. All we have to do is keep our eyes open and passively receive an experience that we have no control over.

Secondly, the television screen presents a world that in some ways is more fascinating and more visually intense than the world outside of television. Within the boundaries of the screen, we are usually offered an entire room, a complete landscape, a total panorama. If we were observing these scenes in real life, we would only be able to see a small part of them in a single glance. In addition, the action on television—unlike real life—is non-stop. The camera is constantly moving; the people and characters are always doing or saying something. Finally, the content of television shows and commercials has been carefully constructed to engage and hold our interest. All of these factors contribute to making television more visually entertaining than real life, and they also seem to have the effect of inducing a trancelike connection with the television that is difficult to break.

Thirdly, television is something that we have absolutely no control over, short of turning it on or off and switching the channels. We can't speed it up or slow it down. We can't ask questions, return to an earlier scene, or influence what we are experiencing. The television is immobile and can only be watched in a certain place at a certain time, sitting in furniture that is secured in place like movie seats. And unlike reading, which is composed of words that we ourselves can use for creative expression, the dynamic images of television are alien, completely beyond our power to produce. A television set is a controlling force, a technological god that demands the surrender of our imagination, our creative expression, and the control of our minds. It's no wonder that watching it can make gorillas—and others—a little dopey.

➤ • ◄        Reread the preceding passage about television and answer these questions:

1.   Does the author of this passage believe that watching television encourages active thinking or passive thinking?

_____

2.   What reasons does the author give to support his view?

a. _____

b. _____

c. _____

3.   Do *you* think watching television encourages active thinking or passive thinking?

_____

_____

_____

_____

_____

_____

4.   Give the reasons that support your view.

a. _____

b. _____

c. _____

Listed below and on page 57 are some of the influences we experience in our lives. As you read through the list, ask yourself whether you believe each item influences you to think *actively* or to think *passively*.

| *Activities* | *People* |
| --- | --- |
| reading books | family members |
| writing | friends |
| taking drugs | employers |

| *Activities* | *People* |
|---|---|
| dancing | advertisers |
| drawing/painting | schoolteachers |
| playing video games | police officers |
| playing sports | religious leaders |
| listening to music | politicians |

The passages below, written by students, analyze the effect of some of these influences on their thinking.

<u>Writing</u> is a skill that encourages us to think actively. When you are composing a letter, you first have to think about what you are going to say. Then you should check for your mistakes and make sure you are giving complete thoughts and sentences to the person you are writing to. I guess this form of communication was created so that we can use our heads.

<u>Advertisers</u> influence us to think passively. Advertisers are only out to make money and to try to think for us. For example, imagine that you want to buy a new pair of jeans. You are not naturally going to buy the name that is popular in the advertisements. Advertisements make you buy the product. They influence your thinking by telling you: "If you don't buy this brand then you will not be a part of the crowd. You will stand out with the rest of the people who have no-name jeans."

Our <u>parents</u> can help us to become both active and passive thinkers. Some parents tend to help their children become active thinkers by teaching them to express themselves clearly, make decisions for themselves, look at different points of view, and choose what they think is right for themselves. On the other hand, some parents can influence their children to be passive thinkers. They do this by not letting the child do things on his own. They tell the child when to do things, how to dress, and so on. They make his decisions for him; and then when he gets older he becomes dependent on other people. He cannot do anything unless he is being told what to do. The ideas of other people will become his escape.

---

Review again the list of influences on pages 56–57. Select one influence that you believe encourages you to think *actively* and one influence that encourages you to think *passively*. For each influence, give the reasons supporting your view.

1.  *Active influence:* _____

    *Explanation:* _____

    _____

    _____

    _____

    _____

    _____

    _____

2.  *Passive influence:* _____

    *Explanation:* _____

    _____

    _____

    _____

    _____

    _____

    _____

**Thinking critically means thinking for ourselves**
Answer the following questions, based on what you believe to be true.

                                                      *Yes    No*

1.  Is the earth flat?
2.  Is there a God?
3.  Will a college education lead to a satisfying career?
4.  Is abortion wrong?
5.  Was Michelangelo a great artist?
6.  Is democracy the best form of government?
7.  Should men be the breadwinners and women the
    homemakers?

In responding to these questions, we reveal aspects of our thinking—the way our mind works. How did we arrive at these conclusions? Our views on these and other issues probably had their beginning with our family, especially our parents. When we are young, we are very dependent on our parents, and we are influenced by the way they see the world. As we grow up, we learn how to think, feel, and behave in various situations. In addition to our parents, our "teachers" include our brothers and sisters, friends, religious leaders, schoolteachers, books, television, and so on. Most of what we learn we absorb without even being aware of it. Many of our ideas about the issues raised in the questions above were most likely shaped by the experiences we had growing up.

However, as a result of our ongoing experiences, our mind—and our thinking—continues to mature. Instead of simply accepting the views of others, we gradually develop the ability to examine this thinking and to decide whether it makes sense to us and whether we should accept it. As we think through such ideas, we use this standard to make our decision: Are there good reasons or evidence that support this thinking? If there are good reasons, we can actively decide to adopt these ideas. If they do not make sense, we can modify or reject them.

Of course, we do not *always* examine our own thinking or the thinking of others so carefully. In fact, we very often continue to believe the same ideas we were brought up with, without ever examining and deciding for ourselves what to think. Or, we often blindly reject the beliefs we have been brought up with, without really examining them.

How do we know when we have examined and adopted ideas ourselves instead of simply borrowing them from others? One indication of having thought through our ideas is being able to explain *why* we believe them. Such explanation involves telling how we arrived at these views and giving the reasons and evidence that support them.

---

For each of the views that you expressed at the beginning of this section, ➤•◄ explain how you arrived at this view and give the reasons and evidence that you believe support your view.

> *Example:*  Is the earth flat?
>
> > *Explanation:* The earth is round. I was taught by my teachers that the earth was round. I accepted it as a fact because of the training and knowledge of the people teaching me. Later, as an adult, I heard enough about the world being round that if ever there were any questions in my mind they disappeared.

1.  Is the earth flat?

    *Explanation:* _____

    _____

    _____

    _____

2.  Is there a God?

    *Explanation:*_____

    _____

    _____

    _____

3.  Will a college education lead to a satisfying career?

    *Explanation:* _____

    _____

    _____

4.  Is abortion wrong?

    *Explanation:*_____

    _____

    _____

    _____

5.  Was Michelangelo a great artist?

    *Explanation:* _____

    _____

    _____

    _____

6.  Is democracy the best form of government?

    *Explanation:* _____

    _____

    _____

    _____

    _____

7.   Should men be the breadwinners and women the homemakers?

     *Explanation:* _____

     _____

     _____

     _____

     The opposite of thinking for ourselves is when we simply accept the think-
ing of others without examining or questioning it. Imagine that a friend assures
you that a course you are planning to take is very difficult. Although the thinking of your friend may be accurate, it still makes sense for you to investigate the
evidence for that particular view yourself.

---

     For each of the following thinking situations, explain how you would re-   ►•◄
spond to the ideas that are being suggested to you. Then give the reasons that
support your views.

1.   A friend says that she thinks you are wasting your time in school. After all,
     there are places to get technical training where you would not have to take
     required courses in areas that you are not majoring in. How do you re-
     spond?

     *Response:* _____

     *Reasons that support your views:* _____

     _____

     _____

     _____

2.   One of your professors always wears blue jeans and sneakers to class. He
     says that the clothes you wear have nothing to do with how intelligent or
     how capable you are. Other people should judge you on *who* you are, not
     on the clothes you wear.

     *Response:* _____

     *Reasons that support your response:* _____

     _____

     _____

     _____

3.  You have had the same job for a year. During that time, you have not only improved your performance, but also taken on additional responsibilities. When you ask your employer for a raise, she replies: ''Why should I give you a raise? There are many people who would be happy to have your job at the salary you are earning.''

*Response:* _____

*Reasons that support your response:* _____

_____

_____

_____

***Thinking about our goals***   In Chapter One we found that one of the purposes of our thinking is to aid us in working toward our goals. Thinking critically plays a crucial role in helping us achieve our goals. Our ability to think critically gives us the means to (1) *identify* reasonable goals for ourselves, and (2) *achieve* these goals by devising plans and strategies. Naturally, the first step toward attaining our goals is identifying them. Not everyone is aware of what his or her real goals are. By real goals we mean goals that reflect *our* thinking, interests, and abilities. Often people have goals that are not really their own but have been borrowed from someone else. For example, we may be studying for a certain line of work because that is what our parents want for us—not necessarily what *we* want for ourselves. Or maybe we want to get married because ''everybody's getting married''—not necessarily because *we* want to get married. It is important that we try to make sure that our goals are *our own* goals, not someone else's.

When I first enrolled in college, I was majoring in engineering. I had selected this major not because I really wanted to go into this field or was particularly talented in this area, but because I had gone to a special engineering high school where *everyone* planned to be an engineer. In addition, we were told that there was a demand for engineers and that they had a bright future. While I was pursuing this goal, I felt like an actor who was living someone else's life.

➤•◄   Have you ever been in the position of pursuing a borrowed goal? Can you describe how it happened and how you felt about it?

*Example:*   The goal I borrowed was to be a nurse. Since my mother was a nurse, she wanted me to be one. In fact she wanted all of her daughters to be nurses. They had all tried it and didn't like it at all. She said I would be very happy. I tried it and hated it. It's not that I don't like helping others; it's just that it's not for me. I was very confused and didn't know what to do. I finally spoke to her and explained that being a nurse holds no future for me. I'm not happy in that field of work. She was hurt, but better her than me for the rest of my life.

Of course, our real goals do not necessarily remain exactly the same throughout our life. It is unlikely that the goals we had as eight-year-olds are exactly the same ones we have now. As we grow, change, and mature, it is natural for our goals to change and evolve as well. The key point is that we should keep examining our goals to make sure that they reflect our thinking and interests and not someone else's.

### Thinking critically involves carefully exploring a situation or an issue

When we are thinking critically, we carefully explore the situation we are in (or expect to be in) or the subject we are discussing. Our responses should be thoughtful and not simply whatever first comes into our mind. Imagine that you are trying to decide what courses to take next semester. As a critical thinker, you should carefully explore all the important aspects of the situation in order to arrive at a useful decision.

---

Identify some of the important questions that you need to answer before  making your course selections for next semester.

1.   Are there any courses that I am required to take next term?

2.   _____

3.   _____

4.   _____

Now go back and *answer* each of the questions that you identified. You may have to do some research in order to locate the information you need. You may want to ask yourself the following questions to help guide your search for information:

1.   Does the college catalogue contain this information?

2.   If not, who in the school would know this information?

3.   If there is someone who can help, how do I find and speak to him or her?

After answering the questions you identified above, make a list of the courses that you could take next semester.

1. _____

2. _____

3. _____

4. _____

5. _____

6. _____

Throughout the process that you just completed, you were using your mind to examine carefully the situation you will be in at the next registration period. Of course, you could have selected your courses in other ways. For example, you could have asked someone to tell you what courses to take. However, if we are really interested in thinking for ourselves, there is no substitute for carefully exploring the situation on our own.

 Identify something that you are planning to buy in the near future. It might be a radio, an article of clothing, a car, etc. Now list some of the important questions that you should answer before making your purchase.

1. How much can I afford to spend?

2. _____

3. _____

4. _____

Now answer each of these questions to the best of your ability. If you do not know the answer, do the research necessary to locate the information you need.

Of course, developing the quality of being thoughtful doesn't mean that we shouldn't be natural and spontaneous in many situations. We should be, and if we have developed the habit of being thoughtful in our attempts to make sense of things, our spontaneous reactions are more likely to be appropriate. But if our approach to life is typically thought*less*, then our spontaneous reactions are likely to be mistaken or even disastrous. Consider the difference between a person who has carefully prepared for a job interview and another who has simply decided to "play it by ear" and "trust his instincts." What would you predict would be the differences in their spontaneous reactions during the interview?

Imagine that you are scheduled for a job interview next week. List the ➤•◄
questions that you think may be asked.

1.  Why do you think you are qualified for this job?

2.  _____

3.  _____

4.  _____

5.  _____

Now go back and try to answer to the best of your ability each of the questions
you have identified. Make your answer as *specific* as possible since very general
answers are not usually very effective.

Imagine that you are involved in the problem situation described below:  ➤•◄

You have always been told that a certain ethnic group has some very un-
pleasant traits, and in fact the few members of this group that you have
encountered do seem to be like this.

1.  Describe your immediate reaction when you see or meet a member of this
    group.
2.  Do you think that this immediate reaction is a thoughtful response? If not,
    how would you go about investigating the situation further?
3.  Explain what you think is the danger with these sorts of "immediate reac-
    tions."

Describe an important decision you have made. In your description, try to  ➤•◄
reconstruct all the questions that you raised and the issues that your mind
weighed and balanced.

After re-examining your decision making, do you find that you would
change any part of the final decision? Which part? How would you change it?

*Example:*  I made a decision to go back to my ex-boyfriend. If I had really
thought it out, I would have asked myself these questions: Have things
changed? Is the reason we broke up and fought constantly resolved, and
do I understand the reasons for the problems we had? Have I changed?
Do I just feel secure with him or do I really feel things will be better? Am
I just scared to let go? Maybe if I had asked myself these questions, I

would not have been hurt a second time. It might not have resulted in an angry breakup and a lot of regretting.

*Example:*   I bought an expensive used sports car from the original owner. I didn't have a mechanic check it. I just bought it because I fell in love with it. Worst of all, I didn't know how to drive a standard transmission car. The first thing to go was the clutch. Then I noticed that the body was rusting badly, and it started having engine problems. After a few months and a lot of costly repairs, I sold it at a substantial loss.

### Thinking critically involves being open to new ideas and different viewpoints

A critical thinker is a person who is willing to listen to and examine carefully other views and new ideas. Nobody has all the answers. Our beliefs represent only one viewpoint or perspective on the problem we are trying to solve or the situation we are trying to understand. In addition to our viewpoint, there may be *other* viewpoints that are equally important and need to be taken into consideration if we are to develop a more complete understanding of the situation.

---

➤•◄      Imagine that you are living in your parents' house and that they give you a curfew that you think is much too early. They tell you that this is their right since you live under their roof and are supported by them. And anyway, they ask, don't you love them and want to make them happy?

1.   Describe how you would approach this situation, and identify the reasons that you think support your viewpoint that a curfew is unnecessary.

   *Example:*   "I think that a curfew is unnecessary *because* I'm old enough to decide when to come home."

2.   Now describe this situation from your *parents'* viewpoint. Identify the reasons that might support their idea that a curfew makes sense.

   *Example:*   "We think that a curfew is necessary *because* we are worried about your safety and won't be able to sleep until you get home."

3.   Can you think of any suggestions to help resolve this disagreement?

   *Example:*   "I have an idea that might help settle this problem. Suppose I tell you exactly where I am going and when I'll be home so you won't worry."

As children we only understand the world from our own point of view. As we grow, we come into contact with people with different viewpoints and begin to realize that our viewpoint is often inadequate, that we are frequently mistaken, and that our perspective is one of many. If we are going to learn and develop, we must try to understand and appreciate the viewpoints of others.

Imagine that your boyfriend or girlfriend tells you that while you were on vacation he or she got lonely and dated someone several times. He or she asks you to be understanding because "Everyone makes mistakes," "I couldn't help myself," and "To err is human, to forgive divine."

1. Describe how you would view this situation, and identify reasons that support your view.
2. Now describe this situation from your boyfriend's or girlfriend's standpoint, identifying reasons that might support his or her view.
3. Can you think of any additional steps the two of you might take to help resolve this situation?

Imagine that you are engaged in a discussion about religion. One of the people you are talking with tells you that he thinks your religious beliefs are completely false. Your first thought is to tell him that he will regret his words when he is burning in hell.

1. Describe how you would approach this situation, including some of the reasons that you think might support your beliefs.
2. Now identify some of the questions that this other person might reasonably ask about your views.
3. Can you think of any steps that the two of you might take to explore this situation?

Briefly describe a problem you are currently having that involves other people.

Now describe the situation as seen by each of the people involved. If possible, show your statements to the other people and get their reactions.

**Being open to other perspectives**   With most of the important issues and problems in our lives, one viewpoint is simply not adequate to give a full and satisfactory understanding. Thus in order to increase and deepen our knowledge, we must seek *other perspectives* on the situations we are trying to understand. We can sometimes accomplish this by using our imagination to visualize other viewpoints. Usually, however, we need to seek actively (and *listen* to) the viewpoints of others. It is often very difficult for us to see things from points of view other than our own, and if we are not careful, we can make the very serious mistake of thinking that the way we see things is the way things really are.

---

➤•◄         Describe an important belief of yours that you feel very strongly about. Then explain the reasons or experiences that led you to this belief.

Describe a point of view that is *different* from your belief. Identify some of the reasons why someone might hold this belief.

*Example:*

I feel that a person has the right to die in peace and with dignity.

Up until four months ago, I would have thought differently. My uncle had a stroke and then had another, which put him in a coma. The doctors told my aunt that he had a 75% chance of recovery. They put him on life-supporting apparatus. There was nothing that he was doing by himself. The machines breathed for him, pumped his heart, and fed him. The doctors kept telling my aunt, let's keep him on these one more week. This went on for two months. Finally, they took him off the machines, and two days later he died. You hate to see someone die, but at least you feel there is no more pain.

The doctors seem to believe that you should keep a person alive by using whatever means you can.

1.  Doctors feel that, if there is no brain damage in the case of a coma, there is always a chance of recovery.

2.  Some people feel that, even if there is brain damage and no hope of recovery, we do not have the right to let someone die if we can keep him or her alive.

Working to see different perspectives is crucial for helping us get a more complete understanding of the situations we are involved in. It is also useful in helping us understand other people.

In Chapter One (pp. 25–30), you composed brief personality sketches of people you know—a friend, a teacher, yourself. Select one of these people and then locate two other people who know the person you identified. Ask each of them to give a brief personality sketch of this same person from their perspective. Summarize their viewpoints below.

*Person selected:*_____

*Person A's view of that individual:*_____

_____

_____

_____

_____

*Person B's view of that individual:*_____

_____

_____

_____

_____

1. What are the *similarities* among the three views of the person you selected?

   _____

   _____

   _____

   _____

2. What are the *differences* among the three views of the person you selected?

   _____

   _____

   _____

   _____

3. Did you find that getting additional views of this person helped you develop a fuller understanding of the individual? If so, why do you think this is the case? If not, why do you think this is the case?

   _____

   _____

   _____

   _____

***Being flexible enough to change and modify ideas*** Being open to new ideas and different viewpoints means being *flexible* enough to change or modify our ideas in the light of new information or better insight. Each of us has a tendency to cling to the beliefs we have been brought up with and the conclusions we have arrived at. However, if we are going to continue to grow and develop as thinkers, we have to be willing to change or modify our beliefs when evidence suggests that we should. For example, imagine that you have been brought up with certain views concerning an ethnic group—black, white, Spanish, Oriental, or any other. As you mature and your experience increases, you may find that the evidence of your experience conflicts with the views you have been raised with. As critical thinkers, we have to be *open* to receiving this new evidence and *flexible* enough to change and modify our ideas on the basis of it.

➤•◀        Think about the reasons behind the following viewpoints.

1.    When John F. Kennedy was running for president, there were many people who were afraid that, if a Catholic were elected president, the pope would rule the White House. Did the fears of these people turn out to be well founded? Explain why or why not.

_____

_____

_____

_____

2.    Some people are against the possibility of a woman being elected president.

a.    What do you think might be the reasons for their opposition?

_____

_____

_____

_____

b.    Do you think that their reasons make sense? Explain why or why not.

_____

_____

_____

_____

3.  Some people are against the possibility of a member of a minority group
    (black, Oriental, Hispanic, etc.) being elected president.

    a.  What do you think are the reasons for their opposition?

    _____

    _____

    _____

    _____

    b.  Do you think that their reasons make sense? Explain why or why not.

    _____

    _____

    _____

    _____

In contrast to open and flexible thinking, _uncritical thinking tends to be
one-sided and close-minded._ People who think this way are convinced that they
alone see things as they really are and that everyone who disagrees with them is
wrong. The words we use to describe this type of attitude include "dogmatic,"
"subjective," and "egocentric." It is very difficult for such people to step outside their own viewpoint in order to see things the way others do.

---

When I was in high school, one of the most feared and disliked teachers was a mechanical drawing instructor named Mr. Poindexter. As each of
us completed our drawing that we had been working weeks on, we would
take it up to Poindexter at the front of the room, trying to keep our knees
from shaking while murmuring silent prayers for mercy. Poindexter
would never say a word—if he detected an error or something he disliked,
he would simply take a soft, thick black pencil and ruin our drawing. We
would then return to our desk to begin again, never having had the opportunity to ask a question or give an explanation.

Describe a teacher you had who was the _opposite_ of Poindexter—that is,
someone who encouraged you to be open to other viewpoints and flexible

enough to change or modify your ideas in the light of new information or better insight. Give at least one example to illustrate why you selected this person.

### Thinking critically involves supporting our views with reasons and evidence

When we are thinking critically, what we think makes sense, and we can give good reasons to back up our ideas. As we have seen throughout this book, it is not enough simply to take a position on an issue or make a claim; we have to *back our views up* with other information that we feel supports our position. In other words, there is an important distinction and relationship between *what* we believe and *why* we believe it.

If someone questions *why* we see an issue the way we do, we usually respond by giving reasons or arguments that we feel support our belief. For example, take the question of whether to attend college. In support of your decision to enroll in school, you might give the following reasons:

1. It will qualify me for a more satisfying career.
2. It will enable me to earn a higher salary.
3. It will give me the opportunity to meet people with similar goals.
4. It will help me grow and mature.
5. It will make my parents happy.
6. It will broaden my knowledge and understanding of the world and the people in it.
7. It will sharpen my ability to think clearly, solve problems, and make intelligent decisions.

Fill in three additional reasons that you can think of.

8. _____

9. _____

10. _____

*Seeing all sides of an issue*   Although all these considerations may be reasons that support your decision, some are obviously more important than others to you. In any case, even though going to college may be the right thing for you to do, this decision does not mean that it is the right thing for everyone to do. In order for us really to appreciate this fact, to see both sides of the issue, we have to put ourselves in the position of others and try to see things from their point of view. What might be some of the reasons or arguments someone might give for *not* attending school?

1. _____

2. _____

3. _____

4. _____

    The responses you just gave demonstrate that, if we are interested in seeing all sides of an issue, we have to be able to give supporting reasons and evidence not just for *our* views, but for the views of *others* as well. Seeing all sides of an issue thus combines these two critical thinking abilities:

    Being open to new ideas and different viewpoints

    Supporting our views with reasons and evidence

Combining these two abilities enables us not only to understand other views about an issue, but also to understand *why* these views are held. Consider the issue of whether marijuana should be legalized. As we try to make sense of this issue, we should attempt to identify not just the reasons that support our views, but also the reasons that support other views. Listed below are reasons that support each view of this issue.

*Issue*

| Marijuana should not be legalized | Marijuana should be legalized |
|---|---|
| *Supporting Reasons* | *Supporting Reasons* |
| 1. Marijuana is a dangerous drug. | 1. Marijuana is less harmful than alcohol, which is legal. |
| 2. We don't yet know all of the possible health risks of smoking marijuana. | 2. This is a free country, and people should be allowed to take health risks, as they do when they smoke cigarettes. |

Now see if you can identify additional supporting reasons for each of these views on legalizing marijuana.

3. _____    3. _____

   _____      _____

4. _____    4. _____

   _____      _____

➤•◄        For each of the following issues, identify reasons that support each side of
the issue.

*Issue*

Student's grades should be based
not only on how much they learn,
but also on how hard they try.

Students' grades should be based
only on how much they learn.

*Supporting Reasons*

1. This policy will encourage students who learn slowly.

2. _____

   _____

3. _____

   _____

*Supporting Reasons*

1. Teachers don't always know
   how hard a student is trying.

2. _____

   _____

3. _____

   _____

*Issue*

Multiple-choice and true/false
exams should be given in college
courses

Multiple-choice and true/false
exams should not be given in
college-level courses.

*Supporting Reasons*

1. Grading these exams is objective
   and does not involve the
   teacher's personal feelings.

2. _____

   _____

3. _____

   _____

*Supporting Reasons*

1. These questions are sometimes
   tricky or confusing.

2. _____

   _____

3. _____

   _____

*Issue*

Living in the country has more
advantages than living in the city.

Living in the city has more advantages than living in the country.

*Supporting Reasons*

1. _____

   _____

*Supporting Reasons*

1. _____

   _____

2. _____      2. _____

   _____         _____

3. _____      3. _____

   _____         _____

*Issue*

It's better to live in a democracy,     It's better to live in a society in
where the citizens elect their           which the leaders are not elected by
leaders.                                 the citizens.

   *Supporting Reasons*                     *Supporting Reasons*

1. _____      1. _____

   _____         _____

2. _____      2. _____

   _____         _____

3. _____      3. _____

   _____         _____

*Issue*

The best way to deal with crime is       Long prison sentences will not re-
to give long prison sentences.           duce crime.

   *Supporting Reasons*                     *Supporting Reasons*

1. _____      1. _____

   _____         _____

2. _____      2. _____

   _____         _____

3. _____      3. _____

   _____         _____

*Issue*

When a couple divorces, neither          When a couple divorces, there are
partner should receive alimony.          times when one partner should re-
                                         ceive alimony from the other.

   *Supporting Reasons*                     *Supporting Reasons*

1. _____      1. _____

   _____         _____

2. _____        2. _____
   _____           _____
3. _____        3. _____
   _____           _____

**Examining information**   In Chapter One we examined how our thinking abilities give us the means to make sense of information. Let us apply our
critical thinking skills to some of the passages we explored. At that time we
identified the main idea of the passage and the reasons that supported the main
point. Now let us examine the *other sides* of these issues and the reasons that
support these other viewpoints.

A.   Reread the passage about soap operas (Chapter One, p. 19).

1.   *Main Point:* Soap operas create an unrealistic fantasy world that does
     not represent real life.

2.   *Other View:* Soap operas do show real life situations.
     *Supporting Reasons*
     a.   The issues that soap operas deal with—such as love, infidelity, or
          illness—are drawn from real life.

     b.   _____
          _____
          _____

     c.   _____
          _____
          _____

B.   Reread the passage about violence (Chapter One, p. 21).

1.   *Main Point:* Americans have become callous toward violence in our so-
     ciety because of all the violence we have been exposed to in the movies
     and on television.

2.   *Other View:* Americans are not that callous toward violence in our soci-
     ety, and violence on the screen does not necessarily affect our attitude
     toward it in real life.
     *Supporting Reasons*
     a.   Examples of callousness toward violence—like the case of Kitty
          Genovese—are given a lot of attention in the media whereas ex-

amples that show our concern about violence are ignored because they are not as interesting.

b. _____

_____

_____

c. _____

_____

_____

➤•◄

For each of the following passages,

1.  identify the main point of the passage.
2.  identify the reasons that support the main point.
3.  identify another view of the main issue.
4.  identify the reasons that support the other view.

William Edward Burghardt Du Bois became the main spokesman for blacks opposed to the policies of Booker T. Washington. Both men wanted full equality for blacks, but they proposed different means to reach that goal. Washington's mild approach stressed opportunities rather than grievances, jobs rather than rights, and self-improvement rather than demands for better conditions. Du Bois's approach was the militant one of Frederick Douglass. He insisted that real economic gain for blacks would not be possible without political rights, full access to public accommodations, and equality in funds spent for education. Although challenged by Du Bois, Washington remained the dominant figure in the black movement from his Atlanta Compromise speech until his death in 1915. Even so, Du Bois's militancy became the inspiration and basis for the civil rights movement throughout the twentieth century.[1]

A.  *Main Point:* _____

_____

_____

[1] Edgar A. Toppin, *The Black American in United States History* (Newton, Mass.: Allyn and Bacon, Inc., 1973), p. 192.

*Supporting Reasons*

1. _____

_____

2. _____

_____

3. _____

_____

B.  *Other View:* _____

_____

_____

*Supporting Reasons*

1. _____

_____

2. _____

_____

3. _____

_____

    With the sixties, America said goodbye to the puritan morality that made the 1953 movie *The Moon is Blue* shocking because it used words like *virgin* and *mistress.* Although few mourn the passing of such rigid moral standards, many fear the flood of pornography that has resulted from its loss. If Americans refused to mention pornographic movies in polite society in the fifties, just the reverse is true today. Movies like *The Devil in Miss Jones* and *Deep Throat* are considered pornographic classics, are praised for their humorous approach to success, and still, after a decade, command large audiences. As little as twenty years ago, *Playboy* was considered a rather shocking addition to suburban newsstands, but at the present time, it is being crowded out of the market by a host of competitors, less reluctant to place explicit sex scenes on the covers of their magazines. When the 1981 movie *Body Heat* appeared on the screen, it was praised for introducing ''hard-core'' sex into a film that was otherwise not pornographic. If the fifties were too rigidly opposed to sex, the sixties and seventies appear to have loosened the floodgates, and the eighties may just have to pay for it.

A.   *Main Point:* _____

_____

_____

*Supporting Reasons*

   1.  _____

       _____

   2.  _____

       _____

   3.  _____

       _____

B.   *Other View:* _____

_____

_____

*Supporting Reasons*

   1.  _____

       _____

   2.  _____

       _____

   3.  _____

       _____

   Below are two articles that explore the issue of the draft. Read each article  carefully and then answer the questions that follow.

## We Must Reinstate the Draft
*by Cynthia A. Roberts*

   STANFORD, Calif.—The proposed $258 billion defense budget, up 15 percent from fiscal 1982's total, will not by itself redress the deteriorating military balance. To offset the Soviet Union's military buildup and meet the defense challenges of the rest of this century, we must reinstate the draft.

The Soviet Union leads the United States more than 2 to 1 in most conventional weapons because it spends twice as much on arms, not because its defense budget is larger. Judging from the latest generation of Soviet equipment, Moscow is not even sacrificing sophistication in weapons for numerical superiority. Its advantage stems from allocating roughly 25 percent of its defense budget to manpower. By comparison, we spend more than 50 percent of ours on manpower. As long as this proportion remains constant, the Russians will outproduce us in military equipment despite our large increases in total outlays for defense.

The argument for the draft hinges on this imbalance more than any other factor. Not only must the Pentagon procure more hardware but also it must attract and train people to man it. President Reagan's defense program forecasts a 600-ship Navy, new tactical air squadrons, and additional Army combat divisions. The question of how best to allocate money for procurement of weapons put aside, the principal problem involved in expanding our forces is manpower. Already, the military services want to exceed the ceilings on active-duty personnel by up to 1.5 percent. As new arms enter service, our forces will require increases of about 200,000 people. Considering the high cost of manpower, future defense budgets are likely to skyrocket beyond current estimates.

Conscription is not a panacea for all the manpower problems confronting the armed forces, but it will enable us to spend money more effectively. By paying conscripts meager wages and cutting funds for recruitment, the Pentagon could afford to divert more resources to retention of midcareer people and to the reserves. In 1981, the Pentagon programmed more than $1 billion for recruitment, one feature being $5,000 enlistment bonuses. Since 30 percent of new recruits do not complete their first term of enlistment, such an inducement is wasteful. We would be better served by reformulating the G.I. Bill, dropped in 1976, and increasing funds for in-service education that provides practical skills for military and civilian jobs. If educational and training inducements were expanded and linked to re-enlistment, it is likely that more people would opt for longer, better-paid, voluntary service than for a two-year draft term.

The need to retain skilled personnel and noncommissioned officers is urgent. The Navy, which expects to gain 150 new ships, is already short 20,000 petty officers. Mid-career N.C.O.'s are leaving in droves, frustrated by low-quality recruits and compensation not commensurate with their status. By boosting pay scales, improving living conditions, and offering educational incentives, the Pentagon hopes to stem the tide. But not only are such initiatives costly, some also aggravate rather than alleviate the main problem. Across-the-board pay increases granted for fiscal 1981 and 1982 will not redress inequitably narrow pay differentials between sergeants and new enlistees.

Since the draft ended in 1973, the Pentagon has waged a costly, largely unsuccessful battle to attract sufficient numbers for the All Volunteer Force. Whatever the significance of the Pentagon's assertion this week that test scores show new recruits are "a cut above the average," the result of that battle has been a worrisome decline in the quality and performance standards of recruits. Embarrassingly low standards prompted Congress in 1980 to limit the proportion of enlistees with below-average mental aptitudes to 25 percent in each service. To make matters worse, both the Selected Reserve (which provides a major proportion of our combat power and support forces) and the Individual Ready Reserve (a pool of trained personnel subject to recall) are seriously short of meeting mobilization needs.

The three "R's"—recruitment, retention, reserves—also face adverse demographic trends: The pool of men and women of military age is expected to drop sharply in this decade.

Foes of the draft argue that politically it is too controversial and risks widespread student demonstrations like those of the 60's. But attitudes are changing. Young people are more serious about their studies, more concerned about career opportunities, and more responsive to the idea of strengthening our defenses.

If conscription was offered as a part of a system of universal national service, opposition might dwindle. Enjoying the advantages of a free, prosperous democracy, young Americans should be encouraged to serve one way or another—if not in the military, then perhaps in the Peace Corps, in inner-city projects, or in other programs. An imaginative initiative sponsored by Mr. Reagan and Congress would do much to restore America's strength and credibility.

# A Draft Isn't Needed
*by Doug Bandow*

WASHINGTON—The All-Volunteer Force was created in 1973, but the issue of how to man our military has not died. Despite the success of the All-Volunteer Force, there are still many people calling for a draft to strengthen our national defense.

A draft, however, would do nothing of the kind. Coercing people to serve would increase costs, decrease retention of military personnel, fail to improve both the quality of the armed forces and the degree to which they represent a cross-section of our society, create national disunity, and destroy fundamental values that make America worth defending.

Conscripting labor doesn't reduce costs; it increases and shifts them. Instead of paying a volunteer, say, $15,000—enough to convince him to forego or delay other career opportunities—the Pentagon would pay a draftee, say, $7,500. That means that the draftee in effect is taxed $7,500. Indeed, a defense cost supposedly too great to be borne by the entire society would instead be borne by 18- to 26-year-old males. Such economic expediency is unworthy of a free society.

A draft would not even significantly reduce budgetary costs. Though more than half of the military budget goes to personnel—$80 billion out of $156.1 billion in fiscal 1981—most of that is for career servicemen, civilians, and retirees. Only $6.6 billion was used to pay first-term active-duty servicemen—those who would be drafted.

Thus, if draftees' pay were slashed 50 percent, the savings would be only $3.3 billion. Cuts in recruiting costs might save a half billion dollars more. But there would be added costs of registration, classification, induction, and enforcement of the draft, as well as higher training costs caused by the inevitable decline in retention of first-termers.

A draft would also exacerbate the military's severest personnel problem: retaining skilled noncommissioned officers. The draft cannot directly increase the number of skilled career noncoms because it brings in only untrained 18-year-olds. Also, it hikes the cost of retaining a career force of a set size because of higher turnover among first-termers. This is so because draftees, resentful, re-enlist in smaller numbers than volunteers.

Reinstituting the draft would not increase the quality of armed forces personnel. The proportion of 1981 enlistees scoring highest in intelligence tests is as high today as it was during the draft in the 1960's and 1970's. In 1981, 81 percent of the people entering the armed forces were high school graduates.

Since the military already is nearly a cross-section of our society, conscription would be unlikely to increase that representativeness. For example, the overall educational attainment of military personnel is higher than that of their civilian counterparts: 69 percent as against 36 percent are high school graduates, and 14 percent as against 16 percent are college graduates.

Moreover, the parents of young servicemen are only slightly more blue-collar and less-educated than parents of the servicemen's civilian contemporaries, according to an Ohio State University poll. The educational aspirations of the young servicemen exceed those of their civilian counterparts, it shows.

Finally, though blacks are overrepresented in the military—while 12 percent of the population is black, 19 percent of the overall military and 30 percent of the army is black—the proportion of those serving edged downward in 1981. Indeed, because qualified blacks volunteer and re-enlist in greater numbers than whites, a draft would significantly affect the military's composition only if virtually no volunteers were accepted and if blacks were actively discouraged from re-enlisting.

As for coercion, with the history of violence and controversy it has engendered, it would seriously divide America again. To face the possible challenges in years ahead, we need to forge a consensus on foreign and defense policy. Reinstituting conscription would make acquiescence, let alone consensus, unattainable.

Most important, a draft is inimical to the fundamental principles that constitute the foundation of our country. We have manned our forces with volunteers for most of our history, and for good reason: Requiring involuntary service violates fundamental individual rights.

Indeed, even if free citizens in a free society owe service to the state, why should only the young be liable? National defense benefits everyone; therefore, everyone should be liable. A volunteer military financed by universal taxation, and not the draft, spreads the burden.

A draft will not enhance our national security. Indeed, if America has lost the moral authority to persuade its people to voluntarily defend their freedom, then it has lost something that no amount of coercion will restore.

1.  Identify one view of the draft that is being discussed.

    _____

    _____

2.  Identify the reasons that support this view of the draft.

    a.  _____

        _____

    b.  _____

        _____

    c.  _____

        _____

3.  Identify the other view of the draft being discussed.

    _____

    _____

4.  Identify the reasons that support this view of the draft.

    a.  _____

        _____

b. _____

_____

c. _____

_____

### Thinking critically involves being able to discuss our ideas in an organized way

As we have just seen, exploring different sides of situations and issues helps us come to a clearer understanding of what is taking place. This is how our thinking develops. In order to promote such development, we have to be open to the viewpoints of others and willing to listen and exchange ideas with them. This process of give-and-take, of advancing our views and considering those of others, is known as *discussion*. When we participate in a discussion, we are not simply talking; we are exchanging and exploring our ideas in an organized way. Let us look at an example of this process.

*Person A:*   I have a friend who just found out that she is pregnant and is trying to decide whether she should have an abortion or have the baby. What do you think?

*Person B:*   Well, I think that having an abortion is murder. Your friend doesn't want to be a murderer, does she?

*Person A:*   Of course she doesn't want to be a murderer! But why do you believe that having an abortion is the same thing as murder?

*Person B:*   Because murder is when we kill another human being, and when you have an abortion, you are killing another human being.

*Person A:*   But is a fetus a human being yet? It certainly is when it is born. But what about before it's born, while it's still in the mother's womb? Is it a person then?

*Person B:*   I think it is. Simply because the fetus hasn't been born doesn't mean that it isn't a person. Remember, sometimes babies are born prematurely, in their eighth or even seventh month of development. And they go on to have happy and useful lives.

*Person A:*   I can see why you think that a fetus in the *last stages* of development—the seventh, eighth, or ninth, month—is a person. After all, it can survive outside the womb with special help at the hospital. But what about at the *beginning* of development? Human life begins when an egg is fertilized by a sperm. Do you believe that the fertilized egg is a person?

*Person B:*   Let me think about that for a minute. No, I don't think that a fertilized egg is a person, although many people do. I think that a fertilized egg has the *potential* to become a person—but it isn't a person yet.

*Person A:*   Then at what point in its development do you think a fetus *does* become a person?

*Person B:*   That's a good question, one that I haven't really thought about. I guess you could say that a fetus becomes a person when it begins to look like a person, with a head, hands, feet, and so on. Or you might say that a fetus becomes a person when all of its organs are formed—liver, kidneys, lungs, and so on. Or you might say that it becomes a person when its heart begins to start beating, or when its brain is fully developed. Or you might say that its life begins when it can survive outside the mother. I guess determining when the fetus becomes a person all depends on the *standard* that you use.

*Person A:*   I see what you're saying! Since the development of human life is a continuous process that begins with a fertilized egg and ends with a baby, deciding when the fetus becomes a person depends on at what point in the process of development you decide to draw the line. But *how* do you decide where to draw the line?

*Person B:*   That's a good place to begin another discussion. But right now I have to leave for class. See you later.

Naturally our discussions in life are not always quite this organized and direct. Nevertheless, this dialogue does provide a good model for what actually does take place in our everyday lives when we carefully explore an issue or a situation with someone else. Let us take a closer look at this discussion process.

**When we discuss, we have to listen to each other**   As you review the preceding dialogue, notice how each person in the discussion *listens* to what the other person is saying and then tries to comment directly on what has just been said. A dialogue is in this sense like a game of tennis—you hit the ball to me, and then I return the ball back to you, and then you return my return, and so on. The "ball" that the people keep hitting back and forth is the subject that is gradually being analyzed and explored.

When we have trouble discussing a subject with others, it is often because one or more of the people involved are not really listening. When this happens to us, we are so concerned about expressing our ideas and convincing others that our ideas are right that we do not make much of an effort to understand what they are trying to say. In this case, the discussion goes nowhere. Consider the following exchange:

*Person A:*   I have a friend who just found out that she is pregnant and is trying to decide whether she should have an abortion or have the baby. What do you think?

*Person B:*   Well, I think that having an abortion is murder. Your friend doesn't want to be a murderer, does she?

*Person A:*   How can you call her a murderer? An abortion is a medical operation.

*Person B:*   Abortion *is* murder. It's killing another human being, and your friend doesn't have the right to do that.

*Person A:*   Well, you don't have the right to tell her what to do—it's her body and her decision. Nobody should be forced to have a child that is not wanted.

*Person B:*   Nobody has the right to commit murder—that's the law.

*Person A:*   But abortion isn't murder.

*Person B:*   Yes it is.

*Person A:*   No it isn't.

*Person B:*   Good-by! I can't talk to anyone who defends murderers.

*Person A:*   And I can't talk to anyone who tries to tell other people how to run their lives.

If we contrast this dialogue with the first dialogue, we can see that, unlike the first dialogue, the people here are not really listening to each other; they are not really trying to understand what the other person is saying. They are simply *expressing* their views, not *discussing* them. When we are working hard at listening to others, we are trying to understand the point they are making and the reasons for it. This enables us to imagine ourselves in their position and see things as they see them. Listening in this way often suggests to us new ideas and different ways of viewing the situation that might never have occurred to us.

**When we discuss, we keep asking—and trying to answer—important questions about the subject**   In Chapter One we noted how asking questions and trying to answer them is one of the keys to developing our thinking. We can now see that asking questions is one of the driving forces in our discussions with others. This is how we explore a subject—by raising important questions and then trying to answer them together. This questioning process gradually reveals the various reasons and evidence that support each of the different viewpoints involved.

---

Reread the first dialogue (pp. 84–85) and list the important questions raised    ➤•◀
in it.

1.    Why do you believe that abortion is the same thing as murder?

2.    _____

3.    _____

4.    _____

5.    _____

***When we discuss, our main purpose is to develop a further understanding of the subject we are discussing, not to prove that we are right and the other person wrong***   When we discuss subjects with others, we often begin by disagreeing with them. In fact, this is one of the chief reasons that we have discussions. However, in an effective discussion, our main purpose should be to develop our understanding—not to prove ourselves right at any cost. If we are determined to prove ourselves right at any cost, then we are likely not to be open to the ideas of others and to viewpoints that differ from our own.

Look again at the second dialogue (p. 86). The two people involved are mainly concerned with proving themselves right, not with developing a fuller understanding of what they are discussing. In contrast, the people in the first dialogue are less concerned with proving themselves right than they are with increasing their understanding. By the end of the discussion, they still may not agree, but they have both developed a fuller and deeper understanding of the subject that they are exploring.

---

Reread the first dialogue (pp. 84–85) and describe the main point that each    ➤•◀
person ends up agreeing to.

_____

_____

_____

Such exchange of ideas is crucial to creating an active and critical mind and to keeping such a mind finely tuned. Effective discussions also have the additional benefit of developing our relationships with others and fostering the interpersonal skills we will need throughout our lives.

 Select one of the following topics and create a dialogue similar to the first dialogue you read above (pp. 84–85).

Capital punishment

Mercy killing

Premarital sex

As you write your dialogue, keep in mind the qualities of effective discussions:

1.  Listening carefully to each other and trying to comment directly on what has been said.

2.  Asking and trying to answer important questions about the subject.

3.  Trying to develop a fuller understanding of the subject and not simply proving ourselves right.

 Using subjects suggested by your teacher or class members, practice having discussions in small groups and with the class as a whole.

## Thinking critically about education

Each of us spends a significant portion of our lives being "educated." During this process, we experience different teachers, different schools, and different approaches to education. Some approaches view the main purpose of education as *transferring information* to us, which we can then reproduce when needed. This perspective on education tends to see students as containers into which information is poured. Once we have been "filled" to a certain point, we have become "educated."

Other approaches contend that, although education has the undeniable function of increasing our store of information, it has not accomplished its purpose unless it has done much more than this. In addition to transferring information, this view holds that education should teach us how to *make sense* of that information—how to examine it, explore it, think critically about it, and relate it to our experience. According to this approach, meaningful education is not the unreflective learning of information. Instead, meaningful education involves developing our critical thinking abilities, which in turn give us the tools to develop our own carefully thought-out perspective on the world.

The following reading presents one approach to education. It is written in the form of a *satire*, which means that the view it seems to be expressing is actually intended to lead us to a quite different view. Read the passage carefully and then critically evaluate its ideas by answering the questions that follow.

## The Year the Schools Began Teaching the Telephone Directory
*by Merrill Harmin and Sidney B. Simon*

No one quite knew what had been the motivating factor. It seemed unlikely that the Council for Basic Education was behind it. Sputnik itself seemed a long way off. Some harsh critics, seeking a scapegoat, suspected the Telephone Company, but upon closer examination it was clear that they might have had as much to lose as they would to gain.

No, it was the superintendent's decision, and no apparent pressure group seemed to have motivated it. The memorandum went out on March 18th. It was simple and to the point.

> Beginning with the Fall term, all 7th grade classes will be held responsible for learning the contents of our local telephone directory. Each teacher, working in cooperation with his or her immediate supervisor, will evolve the methods and procedures necessary to effect an efficient and appropriate achievement of the above-stated goal.

. . .

Labor Day with its sad, fond farewell to the summer came and went. School was off and roaring. Most of the teachers weren't settled enough to give the students the telephone directories until the second day of class, but out they came and then it began, usually with some motivation such as this:

"Boys and girls. We are going to have an exciting new unit this term. As a way of studying our city, we're going through this amazing collection of information which tells us about the melting pot our city has been."

One teacher said, "There will be an examination on this material in February, so you'd better learn it."

Another approached it with, "You wouldn't want to hurt my feelings by not memorizing these few names and numbers, would you, children?"

Students dutifully received their directories, wrote their names on the labels, and tactfully checked off the condition, "new." Feeling deeply his professional responsibilities, almost every teacher reminded his class that the books would be rechecked in February to see that no pages had been written upon or in any other way disfigured.

Miss Clark, a not atypical telephone directory teacher, was heard to say: "Now boys and girls, let us look over our new textbooks. You will notice that it has a logical organization. It is arranged by the alphabet, as it were, and that's why they don't have a table of contents or an index. Although there are no illustrations in the part of the book we will be concerned with, you can always turn to the yellow pages for a picture or two. I've always enjoyed the listings for exterminators and moving vans. How about you?"

The students were quickly caught up in the enthusiasm the teachers projected and they pounced fiercely upon the new textbooks. Many looked at their teachers with new respect and admiration, for indeed the textbooks *were* arranged by the alphabet. Ah, to have education and wisdom. It was then that Miss Clark wrote on the board, in clear, Palmer-method letters: "Tonight's assignment. Read and memorize the A's."

Most of the students dragged home the telephone directories and after a short scrap with mothers about the TV-watching policy of the new term, they sat down to the evening's work. Read and memorize the A's. It was hard going, but this is not an easy world. Teachers, parents, and students agreed that school needed to be more rigorous. Nothing comes easily, the students had been told, year after year. So they read and they memorized.

Morning came and the 7th graders filed into their respective classes. "Good morning, boys and girls," greeted our typical telephone directory teacher. "Did you do your homework last night?" (Not wishing to dampen the ardor of learning, she decided against a surprise quiz on this, the first morning of the unit. After all, an understanding of early adolescent behavior had been part of her background.)

"All right, students, let's begin. What is Gregory Arnold's phone number?" A hush fell over the room, but almost instantly, three hands shot up.

"Eloise," the teacher said.

Eloise answered, her voice more questioning than answering, "Tr 8-9754."

"Very good, Eloise," the teacher said, "but, please, class, let's use the full name of the exchange. Digital dialing is not completely with us yet. Let's say, *Triumph* 8-9754. Next, class, tell us who lives at 174 N. Maple Street?"

Almost all of the hands went up. The teacher smiled benevolently. She had asked them an easy one, thrown out to give everyone a little feeling of success. It was the address of Mr. Appleby, the principal, and almost everyone knew about the old mansion he lived in. The teacher, always striving to provide for individual differences, called on the slowest learner in the class and he gave the right answer. Everyone felt warm and good.

"Now boys and girls, we'll take up a little more difficult topic. Whose number is Wentworth 4-7312?" Panic spread through the class. No one seemed to know. Could she have slipped in a number from the B's? Finally, after the silence seemed unbearable, one hand, timidly, climbed towards the ceiling.

"Yes, Henry?" the teacher asked.

"I'm not sure, Miss Clark, but is it Frank Abelard?"

"Now, Henry, *I'm* asking the questions. Do you know or don't you? Do you wish us to count 'Frank Abelard' as your answer?"

Was she supporting now, giving a hint that Frank Abelard was, indeed, the correct answer? Henry wasn't sure. It was difficult to figure Miss Clark sometimes.

"Well," he said, "I guess I'm not sure."

"But Henry" she said, "you were right! It was Frank Abelard. You must have more confidence in yourself. Confidence is the substance of maturity. Right? Now, the next question. What is the name of the home appliance repair company on Front Street?" One hand went up instantly and the teacher was taken a bit aback. "Yes, Gloria, do you know the answer?"

"I certainly do. That's my father, Miss Clark."

"That's all very nice, Gloria, but we're here to find out if you did the assignment or not, so I think I had better give you another question. What is the phone number of the American Bar Association?"

A wave of laughter quickly spread through the group. Most of them knew, but Miss Clark didn't, that very often Gloria's father was not available to fix a reluctant washing machine because he just happened to be in a bar, albeit usually not the American one. Gloria didn't answer, she just blushed, and Miss Clark said, "Now, Gloria, you'll just have to do your work more conscientiously. This is a difficult unit and I want our class to do well on the finals. You're just going to have to work harder, Gloria, and that goes for the rest of you as well."

The hand of a boy named Edward went up from the back row. "Miss Clark, can I ask you a question?"

"Now, now, Edward," Miss Clark said, "Time is running out and we have all of those A's to cover this period. Please save your question. Later, perhaps, in February, we can take it up. Back to our work, class. Which big industrial company in our town has two phone numbers?"

And so it went. Through the B's and through the C's. The students (many of them) studied and the teachers (all of them) cross-examined. After the D's there was increasing anxiety in the air as teachers began to have quizzes. But everyone seemed to know that it was the big marking-period test which was to count the most. That was the time for nerves! Miss Clark was one teacher who did place equal emphasis upon quizzes and tests, and so, of course, anxiety in her room was at a more constant level.

Many questions were raised in the school and in the community about this new seventh-grade curriculum. It wasn't long, however, before a united front of teachers, principals, and the superintendent worked out, in more or less trial-and-error fashion, a set of answers that became quite standard. Soon no one bothered to ask the questions any longer, for the answers had become predictable. For the historically-minded, here is a sample of the more pesky questions.

Q.  *Why learn the telephone book?*

A.  *It develops good study habits which will be necessary in college and it trains the student to concentrate and apply himself, qualities which are useful in adult life. Among other things, disciplined adults are what we want.*

Q.  *Won't they just forget the information after the tests?*

A.  *The less bright student will most likely forget a lot. However, we intend to have regular reviews in later grades and consequently the retention curve will hold fairly satisfactorily.*

Q.  *Why work so hard learning the telephone book when the directories are so handy when you actually need one?*

A.  *After all, this could be said about any subject we teach. If we want our people to look up information when they need it, why teach anything? Furthermore, life is hard and the sooner our students learn this the better off they will be.*

There were, of course, some students who did not concentrate enough to learn the phone book. It is not easy to run a school. There are slow learners in every community. These students were identified and plans were made to place them in special remedial classes the following term, classes which would work mainly on the yellow pages. The color, illustrations, greater interest value, and reduced amount of material were expected to result in success for all but the fundamentally bad or lazy. Some children, it was readily acknowledged, just wouldn't learn no matter what a school did.

Back in the classrooms it was letter after letter until the word was out that there would be a system-wide mid-term examination on A through M. Oh, the cram sessions which were organized by eager mothers, the withheld allowances which were used as bludgeons, the diligent studying which went on! Never before did so many telephone numbers, addresses, and names get committed to so many memories.

Some boy students in the group spent their hours making small strips of answers which they taped to their shins and which were read later by slowly lifting their trouser legs. Some girls wrote their answers upon flat throat lozenges. A few did nothing; they were non-motivated and didn't seem to care to become other than non-motivated. The only numbers they could get even a little excited about were the ones they phoned regularly themselves.

On the day of the test there were the usual amount of absences due to nervous stomachs. The teachers grudgingly set aside time for make-up exams, vowing to make them harder than the regular exams, "otherwise, everyone will want to wait for the make-up test." So the test was given, the papers marked, the grades carefully recorded in the appropriate grade books, and the teaching routine resumed.

But Miss Clark became increasingly uneasy. She was getting weary of asking, "Who lives at so-and-so? Whose number is such-and-such?" Dull days. Slowly, the rich memories of her undergraduate days in education courses came back. She sifted through the jargon and searched for ideas. . . .

The next Monday it was a new Miss Clark. The change rippled through the rows with electrifying results. Miss Clark had gone "progressive." For one thing, she organized a field trip. She and her class went off on a long walk to look up some of the houses in the "N's." It was difficult to plan, but Miss Clark felt that at least she was doing something worthwhile. Then she came up with the idea of inviting a guest speaker to come to class to talk about the P's. She obtained a film strip on the R's, but it turned out to be about the "Three R's" and she couldn't use it. She attempted to organize committee work on the T's but the committee could find nothing to do, so she had to scrap that idea. Miss Clark programmed the U's and this helped some. They had a bulletin board display on the V's—"Victory Lunch" and "Veteran's Taxi Cab Service." She did role playing on the W's, had a discussion-debate on the X's, and then, with that handsome Mr. Brown in room 107, she did team teaching on the Y's.

By the time the Z's were reached, she was worrying about transfer of training. Would they really know how to use their knowledge? And, then, she had had no "correlated motor behavior training," as they sometimes called it in college. So Miss Clark's class spent two whole days, courtesy of the public relations department of the phone company, practicing dialing the numbers that they had learned (on eighteen telephones of various colors and shapes). It was noisy, and difficult to supervise, even though the students were carefully grouped, sociometrically, but Miss Clark was willing to risk a little to be a good teacher.

Finally, this too had to end. The final exam was a mere six weeks away. So, in Miss Clark's class, as well as in all the others, thirty days were spent in review for the "Big Test."

Review was no fun for anyone. The first week of June came with the sweetness of summer air. The girls in their barearmed summer dresses flitted in and out of the classrooms while the boys seemed slower than ever. Finally, the test was taken, the papers marked, and the term was over. A sense of heavy relief settled upon Miss Clark and all the others. The teachers gathered in the telephone directories, properly disciplined those who had written in their books, and stacked the directories in piles of eager readiness. September was not far away.

Miss Clark felt strangely tired. It wasn't that she had really worked harder this term. The feeling of being drained came from something else. Exactly what she wasn't sure and as she walked to her mailbox she was pondering this problem. There was a blue slip of paper in her mailbox among the more routine notices. It was a memo from the superintendent.

> The success of the telephone directory project initiated by this office has earned the well-deserved respect and admiration of the entire community. The rigorous efforts you and your students have made have not gone unnoticed. Certain thoughtful groups of concerned citizens within our district have urged this office to give this project the nation-wide publicity it deserves and also to move the content down further into the elementary school. We agree with those critics who say that we are long overdue in our efforts to reform the softness of the elementary curriculum.
>
> Consequently, we are assigning to the 5th grade the community's telephone directory. Out of appreciation to those faculty members among our 7th grades who gave so much to our pioneer effort in this content area, we are assigning 7th grade teachers the exciting task of teaching the telephone directory of our State Capitol. The 6th grades, to make the study complete, will combine their study of French with at least one unit on various sections of the Paris, France, telephone directory. This is dependent upon whether or not we can obtain government or foundation assistance to purchase the suitable directories, however. You will hear more in September. Have a most pleasant summer.

The blue sheet slipped from Miss Clark's hand and floated to the floor, but she seemed not to notice.

1.  Explain the "new" approach to education described in the passage.
2.  Describe how the students were tested and graded under this program.
3.  Do you think that this approach represents an "information-transfer" view of education or a "critical thinking" view of education? Explain the reasons why.

4.  Do you feel that any of your education has been like studying the tele-
    phone directory? Describe an example to illustrate your answer.
5.  Do you think the approach to education described in this passage is an ef-
    fective way of teaching and learning? Explain the reasons for your re-
    sponse.

---

After reading "The Year the Schools Began Teaching the Telephone
Directory" (pp. 89–94), describe as specifically as possible a previous educational experience that you think was effective. Using the critical thinking skills
we have been developing, analyze this experience by explaining the reasons
why you think that it was effective. Then contrast (describe the differences
between) the approach of this experience with the approach described in the
reading.

# Chapter Four
# Solving Problems

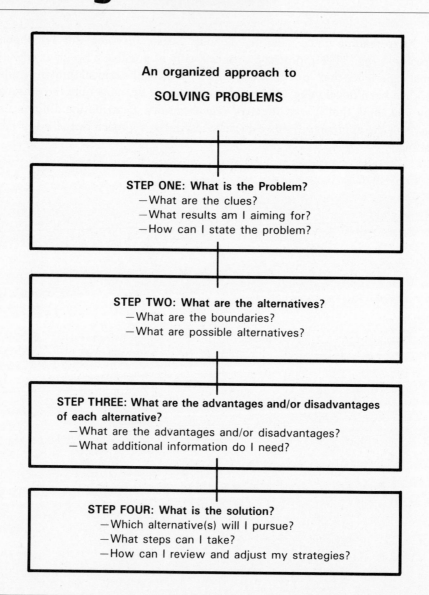

An organized approach to

**SOLVING PROBLEMS**

**STEP ONE: What is the Problem?**
—What are the clues?
—What results am I aiming for?
—How can I state the problem?

**STEP TWO: What are the alternatives?**
—What are the boundaries?
—What are possible alternatives?

**STEP THREE: What are the advantages and/or disadvantages of each alternative?**
—What are the advantages and/or disadvantages?
—What additional information do I need?

**STEP FOUR: What is the solution?**
—Which alternative(s) will I pursue?
—What steps can I take?
—How can I review and adjust my strategies?

IMAGINE YOURSELF in the following situation. What would your next move be and your reasons for it?

>   You're a single parent with one four-year-old child. You have a job as a check-out cashier at a local supermarket. The job just barely pays the bills for you and your child, and you find the job tedious and boring. You have just completed your first semester of school, which you enjoyed immensely. You're hoping that a college education will lead to a career that is financially secure and personally satisfying. Although you're enjoying school, you're physically exhausted and depressed. There just doesn't seem to be enough time in a day for school, your job, and your child. What do you do?

Throughout our life, we are continually solving problems. Every day each one of us has to solve the relatively minor problem of what to wear. In order to make a decision, we have to gather certain information—what clothes are clean and available, what is the weather report, what activities do we have planned. Putting all these factors together, we make our choice.

Simple problems like choosing what to wear do not require a systematic or complex analysis. We can solve them with just a little effort and concentration. But the difficult and complicated problems in our life are a different story.

When we first approach a difficult problem, it very often seems a confused tangle of information, feelings, alternatives, opinions, considerations, and risks. The problem of the single parent described above is a complicated situation in which there does not seem to be just one solution. Without the benefit of a systematic approach, our thoughts might wander through the tangle of issues like this:

>   I want to stay in school. . . but I can't afford to lose my job. . . and I'm not spending enough time with my child—will she stop loving me?. . . but if I don't stay in school, what kind of future do I have?. . . I've got to earn enough to pay the bills, that's most important. . . but if I don't get an education, I'll never get out of the rut I'm in.

Very often when we are faced with difficult problems like this, we simply do not know where to begin in trying to solve them. Every issue is connected to many others. Frustrated by not knowing where to take the first step, we often give up trying to understand the problem. Instead, we may

1.  *act impulsively*, without thought or consideration (e.g., "I'll just quit school—it's too much work").

2.  *do what someone else suggests* without seriously evaluating the suggestion (e.g., "Tell me what I should do—I'm tired of thinking about this").

3.  *do nothing* as we wait for events to make the decision for us (e.g., "I'll just wait and see what happens before doing anything").

Unfortunately, none of these approaches is likely to succeed in the long run, and they can gradually reduce our confidence in dealing with complex problems.

## Solving problems and critical thinking

An alternative to the reactions above is to subject the problem to a careful, organized examination. In the first chapter, "Thinking," we saw that solving problems is one of the important ways our thinking process helps us make sense of the world. In Chapter Two, "Thinking About Thinking," we discovered that by carefully exploring our thinking process we could identify the key steps in solving problems, and then we followed these steps in solving our student council project.

1.   What is the *problem*?
2.   What are the *alternatives*?
3.   What are the *advantages* and/or *disadvantages* of each alternative?
4.   What is the solution?

In the last chapter, "Thinking Critically," we found that, if we carefully examine our thinking and the thinking of others, we can clarify and improve our understanding of the world. This is the purpose of critical thinking, and in this chapter we will be thinking critically about the way we solve problems. As we gradually increase our understanding of the thinking involved in solving problems, we will at the same time be developing our ability to solve effectively the complex problems in our lives, such as the problem of the single parent we considered before.

Of course, we can only solve problems effectively if we are truly interested in making sense of them. This means that we must accept responsibility for the problem, actively work toward a solution, and then commit ourselves to action. If we are unwilling to think critically by taking an active role in figuring things out, then many of the problems in our lives will simply remain unsolved.

## An organized approach to solving problems

The four steps to solving problems that we identified in the first two chapters will form the core of our approach. By integrating the critical thinking abilities we explored in the last chapter, we will further develop this basic approach to thinking through problems. The result of our efforts will be an organized method of analyzing problems that will enable us to work through the complexities of problem situations and help us arrive at thoughtful conclusions. Here is an outline of the method we will be using:

1.  Step One: What is the problem?
    a.  What are the clues to the problem?
    b.  What are the results I am aiming for in this situation?
    c.  How can I state the problem clearly and specifically?
2.  Step Two: What are the alternatives?
    a.  What are the boundaries of the problem situation?
    b.  What are the alternatives that are possible within these boundaries?
3.  Step Three: What are the advantages and/or disadvantages of each alternative?
    a.  What are the advantages and/or disadvantages of each alternative?
    b.  What additional information do I need to evaluate each alternative?
4.  Step Four: What is the solution?
    a.  Which alternative(s) will I pursue?
    b.  What steps can I take to act on the alternatives(s) chosen?
    c.  How can I review how well my strategies are working out and make whatever adjustments are necessary?

Now let's see how this method works when applied to an actual problem such as the one we considered at the beginnning of the chapter.

### Step One: What is the problem?

The first step in solving problems is to be clear on exactly what the central issues of the problem are. If we are not clear at the outset regarding what is really the problem, then our chances of solving it are considerably reduced. We may spend our time trying to solve the wrong problem. For example, consider the different formulations of the following problems. How might these different formulations lead us in different directions in trying to solve the problem?

"I'm too short."      vs.   "I feel short."

"School is boring."   vs.   "I feel bored in school."

"I'm a failure."      vs.   "I just failed an exam."

Let us return to the problem we began considering at the start of this chapter and see if we can answer the question "What is the problem?"

You're a single parent with one four-year-old child. You have a job as a check-out cashier at a local supermarket. The job just barely pays the bills for you and your child, and you find the job tedious and boring. You have just completed your first semester of school, which you enjoyed immensely. You're hoping that a college education will lead to a career that is financially secure and personally satisfying. Although you're enjoying school, you're physically exhausted and depressed. There just doesn't seem to be enough time in a day for school, your job, and your child. What do you do?

***What are the clues to the problem?***   The best place to begin investigating what is really the problem is to examine the *clues* in our experience that are a part of the problem situation. Just as a detective first identifies the key parts of the mystery that he or she is investigating, so it is helpful for us to identify the clues that inform us that we have a problem. There are two types of clues: factual clues and feeling clues.

*Factual clues* are the aspects of the situation that tell us there is a problem. For example, in the problem above, factual clues might include the following:

1.  There doesn't seem to be enough *time* for me to work full-time, go to school, and be a parent, and I want to do all three.

2.  Another part of the problem is *money*. I want to spend time with my child, and I don't want to quit school. But I need enough money to pay the bills.

---

➤•◄         Can you think of an additional aspect of this situation that tells us we have a problem?

3.  _____

    _____

    _____

*Feeling clues* are our feelings about the situation that inform us that there is a problem. Feeling clues might include the following:

*Pressures:*  The pressures of doing well in school, being competent on the job, and providing a good home and solid relationship for my child.

*Fears:*  Fears of failing—as a student, as a worker, as a parent

*Anger:*  Anger directed toward myself for being in this predicament, anger toward my child

*Guilt:*  Feelings of guilt over not being a competent student, a conscientious worker, or a loving parent.

*Confusion:*  Confusion regarding how my time and energy should be spent with respect to the major areas in my life—school, work, parenting.

*Conflicts:*  Conflicts between the competing needs and desires in my life. In other words, should I concentrate simply on my immediate problems—earning enough money to survive—or should I give up some of the present in order to plan for a better future by attending school, so that I will be qualified eventually for a more fulfilling and higher-paying job?

---

Can you identify any additional feelings that might act as clues to the problem? (Some typical feelings experienced in problem situations might be frustration, worry, doubt, anxiety, insecurity, disappointment, and depression).

_____:  _____

_____:  _____

**What are the results I am aiming for in this situation?**  The next part of this first question "What is the problem?" consists in identifying the specific *results* or objectives we are trying to achieve. The results are those aims that will eliminate the problem if we are able to attain them. For instance, in our sample problem, some of the results or objectives might be

1.  gaining an education.
2.  having a meaningful relationship with my child.
3.  paying the bills.

---

Can you think of additional results we might be trying to achieve in this situation?

4.  _____

5.  _____

**How can I state the problem clearly and specifically?**  The final part of answering the question "What is the problem?" consists in stating the problem as clearly and as specifically as possible, based on our examination of the problem's clues and objectives. This sort of clear and specific description of the problem is a crucial step in solving it. For if we state the problem in very *general* terms, we won't have a clear idea of how best to proceed in dealing with it. But if we can describe our problem in more *specific* terms, then our description will begin to suggest actions we can take to solve the problem. For example, examine the differences between the statements of the following problem:

*General:* "My problem is money."

*Specific:* "My problem is budgeting my money so that I won't always run out near the end of the month."

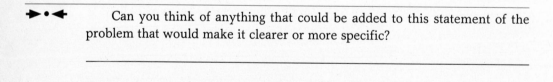

Write more specific statements of the following problems:

*General:* "My problem is homework."

*Specific:* _____

_____

*General:* "My problem is my boss."

*Specific:* _____

_____

In our sample problem, we might begin a clear and specific description of the problem as follows:

I think that my real problem lies in the conflicts between my role as a parent, my dreams for the future, and the reality of paying the bills in order to survive in the present. The question is, how can I fit these three different parts of my life together?

Can you think of anything that could be added to this statement of the problem that would make it clearer or more specific?

_____

_____

_____

### Step Two: What are the alternatives?

Once we have identified our problem clearly and specifically, our next move is to examine each of the possible actions that might help us solve the problem. Before we list the alternatives, however, it makes sense for us to determine which actions are possible and which are impossible. We can do this by exploring the *boundaries* of the problem situation.

*What are the boundaries of the problem situation?* Boundaries are the limitations in the problem situation that we simply cannot change. They are a part of the problem, and they must be accepted and dealt with. Our sample problem might have the following boundaries:

*Time limitations:* A schedule would determine exactly how much time is needed for work, school, child, travel, and sleep.

*Money limitations:* A budget would reveal exactly how much money is needed for living expenses, school, and other expenditures. We should also try to anticipate how much money we will need in the future.

*Skill/education limitations:* What vocational qualifications do we have to earn money at the present time?

*Personal limitations:* What personal obligations do we have to family, friends, or any other people?

---

Can you think of additional boundaries that might be a part of this situation? ➤•◀

_____: _____

_____: _____

*What are the alternatives that are possible within these boundaries?* After we have established a general idea of the boundaries of the problem situation, we can then proceed to identify the possible courses of action that can take place within these boundaries. Of course, identifying all the possible alternatives is not always easy; in fact, it may be part of our problem. Often we do not see a way out of a problem because our thinking is set in certain ruts, fixed in certain perspectives. We are blind to other approaches either because we reject them before seriously considering them ("I'd never consider doing that!") or because they simply do not occur to us. Two techniques designed to help us overcome these difficulties and give serious consideration to *all* the possible alternatives are to

1. *list every possible solution* (or partial solution) to the problem without censoring or evaluating the alternatives in advance.
2. *discuss the problem with other people* who may be able to suggest alternatives that might not have occurred to us.

Discussing possible alternatives with others uses a number of the aspects of critical thinking which we explored in the last chapter. As we saw then, thinking critically involves being open to seeing situations from different viewpoints and exchanging our ideas with others in an organized way. Both these abilities are important in solving problems. As critical thinkers we live—and solve problems—in a community, not simply by ourselves.

In the case of our sample problem, the alternatives might include

1.   quitting school for good.
2.   taking fewer courses.
3.   taking a leave of absence from school and then working hard to save enough money to return to school full-time.
4.   having relatives or friends take care of my child until I finish school.
5.   finding additional sources of income.

---

➤•◄   Can you think of additional alternatives that might help solve this problem?

6.   _____

      _____

7.   _____

      _____

8.   _____

      _____

**Step Three: What are the advantages and/or disadvantages of each alternative?**

Once we have identified the various alternatives, our next step is to *evaluate* them. Each possible course of action has certain advantages in the sense that if we select that alternative there will be some positive results. At the same time, each of the possible courses of action has disadvantages as well, in the sense that if we select that alternative there may be a cost involved or a risk of some negative results. It is important to examine the potential advantages and/or disadvantages in order to determine how helpful each course of action would be in solving the problem. As we saw in Chapter Three, thinking critically means not simply having a viewpoint, but understanding the reasons that support this viewpoint and other viewpoints.

*Back-up*

**What are the advantages and/or disadvantages of each alternative?** The alternatives we have just listed for the sample problem might include the following advantages and disadvantages:

| Alternatives | Advantages and Disadvantages |
|---|---|
| 1. Quitting school for good | *Advantages:* This will immediately end some of the conflicts that are causing the problem, giving me more time for my child, job, and personal life. |
| | *Disadvantages:* I will become frustrated and unhappy if I work at an unfulfilling job. My income will become increasingly inadequate as expenses increase faster than my salary. |
| 2. Taking fewer courses | *Advantages:* This will remove some of the immediate time pressures I am experiencing, while still allowing me to prepare for the future. |
| | *Disadvantages:* I might lose interest or motivation and drop out before completing school because the process is taking so long. |
| 3. Taking a leave of absence from school—returning after saving enough money | *Advantages:* This will permit me to concentrate on one thing at a time, instead of being so divided. |
| | *Disadvantages:* I may get wrapped up in my job and the people there and not return to school (such consequences are known as "job socialization"). |
| 4. Having relatives or friends take care of my child until I finish school | *Advantages:* This will allow me to concentrate fully on school and work while knowing that my child is being well taken care of. |
| | *Disadvantages:* This might threaten my relationship with my child. My child might be adversely affected. I will probably feel guilty about the situation. |
| 5. Finding additional sources of income | *Advantages:* This would permit me to work part-time, go to school part-time, and spend more time with my child. |
| | *Disadvantages:* It will be time-consuming to investigate. If I borrow money, I would have to pay it back in the future. |

---

Identify the advantages and/or disadvantages for each of the alternatives ➤•◄ that you identified on page 104.

| Alternatives | Advantages and Disadvantages |
|---|---|
| 6. _____ | Advantages: _____ |
| _____ | _____ |
| _____ | _____ |
| _____ | Disadvantages: _____ |
|  | _____ |
|  | _____ |
| 7. _____ | Advantages: _____ |
| _____ | _____ |
| _____ | _____ |
| _____ | Disadvantages: _____ |
|  | _____ |
|  | _____ |
| 8. _____ | Advantages: _____ |
| _____ | _____ |
| _____ | _____ |
| _____ | Disadvantages: _____ |
|  | _____ |
|  | _____ |

***What additional information do I need to evaluate each alternative?*** The next part of Step Three consists in determining what *information* we need in order to best evaluate and compare the alternatives. For each alternative there are questions that must be answered if we are to establish which alternatives make sense and which do not. In addition, we need to figure out where best to get this information ("sources of information").

One useful way to identify the information we need is to ask ourselves the question, *"What if* I select this alternative?" For instance, one alternative in our sample problem was "Quitting school for good." When we ask ourselves the question, *"What if* I quit school for good?" we are trying to predict what will occur if we select this course of action. To make these predictions, we must answer certain questions and need information to answer them.

Will I be unhappy if I don't improve my career?

Will I be able to earn enough money to get the things in life that I want?

The information—and the sources for it—that must be located for each of the alternatives in our sample problem might include the following:

| *Alternatives* | *Information Needed and Sources* |
| --- | --- |
| 1. Quitting school for good | *Information:* Will I be unhappy if I don't improve my career? Will I be able to earn enough money to get the things in life that I want? |
| | *Sources:* myself, friends, career counselors. |
| 2. Taking fewer courses | *Information:* How long can I continue in school without losing interest and dropping out? |
| | *Sources:* myself, other part-time students, school counselors. |
| 3. Taking a leave of absence from school—returning after saving enough money | *Information:* Will I be able to save enough money? How much money do I need to complete my education? Will I have the determination to return to school once I leave? |
| | *Sources:* myself, school counselors, other students that took time off and then either returned or did not. |
| 4. Having relatives or friends take care of my child until I finish school | *Information:* Are there any family or friends able and willing to take my child? Are they responsible and trustworthy? What effect will this have on my child and my relationship with him or her? |
| | *Sources:* family, friends, my child, other parents in similar situations, family counselors. |
| 5. Finding additional sources of income | *Information:* What different sources of income are available? Where can I find out more about these possible income sources? If I have to borrow money, will I be hurting my future when I have to pay it back? |
| | *Sources:* family, friends, financial aid office, banks, other parent of child. |

---

Identify the information needed and the sources of this information for each of the alternatives that you identified on page 104.    ➤•◄

| Alternatives | Information Needed and Sources |
|---|---|
| 6. _____ | Information: _____ |
| _____ | _____ |
| _____ | _____ |
|  | Sources: _____ |
|  | _____ |
| 7. _____ | Information: _____ |
| _____ | _____ |
| _____ | _____ |
|  | Sources: _____ |
|  | _____ |
| 8. _____ | Information: _____ |
| _____ | _____ |
| _____ | _____ |
|  | Sources: _____ |
|  | _____ |

**Step Four: What is the solution?**

The purpose of Steps One, Two, and Three is to analyze our problem in a systematic and detailed fashion—to work through the problem in order to become thoroughly familiar with it and the possible solutions to it. After breaking down the problem in this way, our final step should be to try to put the pieces back together: to decide on a thoughtful course of action based on our increased understanding. Even though this sort of problem analysis does not guarantee finding a specific solution to the problem, it should *deepen our understanding* of exactly what the problem is about. And in locating and evaluating our alternatives, it should give us some very good ideas about the general direction we should move in and the immediate steps we should take.

*What alternative(s) will I pursue?*   There is no simple formula or recipe to tell us which alternatives to select. As we work through the different courses of action that are possible, we may find that we can immediately rule some out. For example, we may know with certainty that we do not want friends or relatives to take care of our child until we finish school (alternative 4). However, it may not be so simple to select which of the other alternatives we wish to pursue. How do we decide?

The decisions we make usually depend on what we believe to be most important to us. These beliefs regarding what is most important to us are known as *values*. Our values are the starting points of our actions and strongly influence our decisions. For example, if we value staying alive (as most of us do), then we will make many decisions each day that express this value—not walking in front of moving traffic, eating proper meals, and so on.

Our values help us set the *priorities* in our life—that is, decide what aspects of our life are most important to us. We might decide that for the present going to school is more important than having an active social life. In this case, going to school is a higher priority than having an active social life. Unfortunately, our values are not always consistent with each other—we may have to choose *either* to go to school *or* to have an active social life. Both activities may be important to us; they are simply not compatible with each other. Very often the *conflicts* between our values constitute the problem.

In the sample problem we have been considering, the person involved may feel that he or she values creating a future in order to reach his or her full potential as an individual, as well as being a loving parent. This could lead to the selection of alternative 5.

*Alternative 5:*   Finding additional sources of income that will enable me to work part-time, go to school part-time, and spend more time with my child.

---

Select another alternative that you believe might make sense in solving this   ➤•◄ problem.

*Alternative* ____:  _____

_____

_____

*What steps can I take to act on the alternative(s) chosen?*   Once we have decided which alternative(s) to pursue, our next move is to plan the steps we will have to take in order to act. This is the same process of working toward our goals that we explored in Chapters One and Two. Planning the specfic steps we will take is extremely important. Although thinking carefully about our problem is necessary, it is not enough if we hope to solve the problem. We have to *take action,* and planning our specific steps is where we begin. The specific steps that we will take to move toward solving the problem might include the following:

1. Contact the financial aid office at the school to see what aid is available and what I have to do to apply for it.

2. Contact some of the local banks to see what sort of student loans are available.

3. Talk to my parents about the problem to determine what assistance they might be willing and able to offer.

4. Contact the other parent of my child to see if he or she is willing to contribute to the child's support. (If not, consider whether legal action makes sense.)

5. Talk to other students who are attending part-time, to share their experiences.

---

➤•◄        Identify the steps you would have to take in pursuing the alternative(s) you identified on page 104.

1. _____

_____

2. _____

_____

3. _____

_____

4. _____

_____

5. _____

_____

**How can I review how well my strategies are working out and make whatever adjustments are necessary?**   As we work toward reaching a reasonable and informed conclusion, we should not fall into the trap of thinking that there is only one "right" decision and that all is lost if we do not figure out what it is and carry it out. We should remind ourselves that any analysis of problem situations, no matter how careful and systematic, is ultimately limited. We simply can not anticipate or predict everything that is going to happen in the future. As a result, every decision we make is provisional, in the sense that our ongoing experience will inform us if our decisions are working out, or if they need to be changed and modified. As we saw in Chapter Three, this is precisely the attitude of the critical thinker—someone who is *open* to new ideas and experiences and *flexible* enough to change or modify beliefs based on new information. Critical thinking is not a compulsion to find the "right" answer or make the "correct" decision; it is instead an ongoing process of exploration and discovery.

For example, in our sample problem, we may find that it is impossible for us to find additional sources of income so that we can work part-time instead of full-time. In that case, we simply have to go back and review the other alternatives that we explored, in order to discover another possible course of action.

---

Work through the problems on the following pages by using the method     ➤•◄
developed in this chapter to guide your analysis. Make use of the same strategies and approaches we explored and refer to our discussions as you work through each problem.

## Problem 1

### *Background Information*

An important problem in my life at present is not knowing how to organize my time and divide it among school, work, and friends. It seems like there is not enough time during my week to meet my responsibilities.

It started my first term here at college. When I made my schedule, I had four courses. I came to school every day except Wednesday. I thought that was great because this way I could spend the entire free day doing my schoolwork. This way I would never be behind. I had no idea how much work each teacher gave. I now realize how easy high school actually was. One of my main problems is just not knowing *how* to study.

I also just recently started a new job as a unit clerk at St. Mary's Hospital. I work on weekends, Saturday and Sunday from 7:30 A.M. to 3:30 P.M. The job is very trying and it takes a lot out of me mentally and physically. It's so much more than I expected. I usually don't leave before 4:30 P.M. All during the day I am constantly moving. When I get home I only have time to eat and then go to bed. But this pattern is no good because on Saturday and Sunday I have to force myself to stay up and do schoolwork. I just can't understand where my time is going.

My schooling and my job are also conflicting with my social life. I try to see my boyfriend and my other friends as much as possible, but this isn't very much.

In addition, I joined an exercise spa during the summer. I wish I hadn't because I don't have time to go anymore. When I do have time, I'm usually too tired to exercise because of all the things I had to accomplish a day.

A.  Step One: What is the problem?

1.  What are the clues to the problem?

   a.  Factual clues

      (1)  There doesn't seem to be enough time to accomplish all my activities.

      (2)  _____

      _____

      (3)  _____

      _____

   b.  Feeling clues

      (1)  *Fears:* Hoping that I don't lose friends because I don't spend much time with them anymore.

      If I quit my job to relieve some tension, I will have to borrow money. I hate to be in debt.

      The fear of not having enough time to study, which can make my grades go down even though I have the ability to do well.

      (2)  *Anger:* Not having free time to myself so that I can do what I want. Wishing I had some time for recreation.

      (3)  *Confusions:* I enjoy school, I like my job, I love my friends. I don't know how to work it out so that I have some free time to relax.

      (4)  *Pressures:* Lately it seems that I've been having more pressures than ever before, mostly because of school. I know that I have to do well. It seems that even when I'm with my friends I'm thinking about what homework is due for the next day or what exam is coming up.

      (5)  *Guilt:* I feel guilty if I'm out with my friends and I didn't get a chance to complete a homework assignment.

      I feel bad that I haven't been spending much time with my boyfriend.

(6) _____

_____

(7) _____

_____

2. What are the results I am aiming for in this situation?

   a. I need much more time to study in order to do well in school.

   b. _____

      _____

   c. _____

      _____

3. How can I state the problem clearly and specifically?

_____

_____

_____

_____

B. Step Two: What are the alternatives?

  1. What are the boundaries of the problem situation?

    a. Time limitations: there are only twenty-four hours in a day.

    b. _____

       _____

    c. _____

       _____

  2. What are the alternatives that are possible within these boundaries?

    a. Explain to my friends that I'd like to go out with them, but I don't have the time.

    b. _____

       _____

    c. _____

       _____

    d. _____

       _____

C. Step Three: What are the advantages and/or disadvantages of each alternative?

   1. What are the advantages and/or disadvantages of each alternative?

      a. Explain to my friends that I'd like to go out with them, but I don't have the time.

        *Advantages:* They will understand that I can't spend time with them right now because I have to concentrate on my school and work.

        *Disadvantages:* We may drift apart.

      b. _____

        _____

        *Advantages:* _____

        _____

        _____

        *Disadvantages:* _____

        _____

        _____

      c. _____

        _____

        *Advantages:* _____

        _____

        _____

        *Disadvantages:* _____

        _____

        _____

      d. _____

        _____

        *Advantages:* _____

        _____

        _____

*Disadvantages:* _____

_____

_____

2.  What additional information do I need to evaluate each alternative?

a.  Explain to my friends that I'd like to go out with them, but I don't have the tme.

*Information needed:*   Will my friends understand? Will we still be able to maintain our friendships even though we aren't seeing as much of each other?

*Sources:*   My friends.

b. _____

_____

*Information needed:* _____

_____

_____

*Sources:* _____

c. _____

_____

*Information needed:* _____

_____

_____

*Sources:* _____

d. _____

_____

*Information needed:* _____

_____

_____

*Sources:* _____

D.  Step Four:  What is the solution?

1.  Which alternative(s) will I pursue?

Alternative _____: _____

_____

2. What steps can I take to act on the alternative(s) chosen?

a. _____

_____

b. _____

_____

c. _____

_____

d. _____

_____

e. _____

_____

3. How can I review how well my strategies are working out and make whatever adjustments are necessary?

_____

_____

_____

_____

## Problem 2

### Background Information

My problem is being overweight. All my life I've been fighting the big bulge. I think the only time I fitted into a normal size was when I was 6 pounds 4 ounces, and 22 inches long.

I've tried numerous ways to lose weight, such as eating only one meal a day, using diet pills, and using all kinds of fad diets. Most of these ways worked for a while, but when I went off them, the weight shot back on. A few months ago I tried losing weight the Richard Simmons way. His method of losing weight was great and it helped, but now the weight is back on and maybe a little more.

I try to watch what I eat but it's hard when your family's diet consists of starchy foods. I am hoping that in the near future I'll find some way of conquering the big bulge and keeping it off.

A. Step One: What is the problem?

1. What are the clues to the problem?

a. Factual clues

   (1)  I weigh more than I would like to and I always have.

   (2)  _____

b. Feeling clues

   (1)  *Fears:* I'm afraid of getting fatter and not being accepted by others for who I am.

   (2)  *Anger:* Sometimes I get angry because there are a lot of styles that I can't wear because I'm overweight. Sometimes I get angry because there are many people my height who look great in the clothes they wear because they are thin.

   (3)  *Confusions:* I'm confused about whether being overweight is my choice or a genetic problem. Most of my family is overweight, except my father and brother.

   (4)  *Pressures:* Some pressures that I face in being overweight are not being able to be thin like everyone else and not being able to fit in perfectly in a crowd of thin people whether they are friends or people I just met.

   (5)  *Guilt:* Sometimes I feel guilty because I constantly say that I want to be thin, but as I say this I am shoveling fat food down my throat.

   (6)  _____

       _____

   (7)  _____

       _____

2. What are the results I am aiming for in this situation?

   a.  Once I'm thin, I'd like to stay that way for the rest of my life. If I could reach my ideal waistline, then my weight would no longer be a problem when I went to a store.

   b.  _____

      _____

   c.  _____

      _____

3. How can I state the problem clearly and specifically?

   _____

   _____

_____

_____

B.  Step Two: What are the alternatives?
    1.  What are the boundaries of the problem situation?
        a.  I find it very difficult to change my eating habits because my
            family's diet consists of starchy foods. I cannot afford the price of
            special foods and neither can my parents.

        b.  _____

            _____

        c.  _____

            _____

    2.  What are the alternatives that are possible within these boundaries?
        a.  Decide to quit trying to lose weight.

        b.  _____

            _____

        c.  _____

            _____

        d.  _____

            _____

C.  Step Three: What are the advantages and/or disadvantages of each alter-
    native?
    1.  What are the advantages and/or disadvantages of each alternative?
        a.  Decide to quit trying to lose weight.
            *Advantages:*   I can stop spending so much time and energy fighting
                the battle of the bulge and just eat the way I want to.
            *Disadvantages:*   If I decide to quit trying to lose weight, I'll be un-
                happy and as fat as the Goodyear blimp. I can't afford to get any
                bigger than I am now because I pay extra for my clothes now. I
                can't imagine the price if I get any bigger.

        b.  _____

            _____

            *Advantages:*  _____

            _____

            _____

*Disadvantages:* _____

_____

_____

c. _____

_____

*Advantages:* _____

_____

*Disadvantages:* _____

_____

_____

d. _____

_____

*Advantages:* _____

_____

_____

*Disadvantages:* _____

_____

_____

2. What additional information do I need to evaluate each alternative?

   a. Decide to quit trying to lose weight.

     *Information needed:*   If I decide to quit trying to lose weight, will I be happy with my ever expanding waistline? Will I be happy as an individual of a weight conscious society? Will I be able to afford the bills that go along with expanding?

     *Sources:*   Myself, other people with weight problems.

   b. _____

_____

     *Information needed:* _____

_____

_____

     *Sources:* _____

c. _____

_____

*Information needed:* _____

_____

_____

*Sources:* _____

d. _____

_____

*Information needed:* _____

_____

_____

*Sources:* _____

D. Step Four: What is the solution?
   1. Which alternative(s) will I pursue?
      *Alternative _____:* _____

      _____

   2. What steps can I take to act on the alternative(s) chosen?

      a. _____

      _____

      b. _____

      _____

      c. _____

      _____

      d. _____

      _____

      e. _____

      _____

   3. How can I review how well my strategies are working out and make
      whatever adjustments are necessary?

      _____

      _____

      _____

## Problem 3

*Background Information*

The most important unsolved problem that exists for me is the inability to make that crucial decision of what to major in. I want to be secure with respect to both money and happiness when I make a career for myself, and I don't want to make a mistake in choosing a field of study.

I want to make this decision before beginning the next semester so that I can start immediately in my career. I've been thinking about managerial studies. However, I often wonder if I have the capacity to make executive decisions when I can't even decide on what I want to do with my life.

A. Step One: What is the problem?

    1. What are the clues to the problem?

       a. Factual clues

          (1) _____

          _____

          (2) _____

          _____

       b. Feeling clues

          (1) *Fears:* I fear that I'll make the wrong decision.

          (2) *Frustration:* I'm frustrated because I can't make a decision.

          (3) *Conflicts:* Conflicts arise when I make a decision, think about it, and change my mind again.

          (4) *Confusions:* Why is it taking so long? Is there something wrong with me?

          (5) *Pressures:* Time is a definite pressure in my case because it keeps running out and I'm not getting anywhere.

          (6) _____

          _____

          (7) _____

          _____

    2. What are the results I am aiming for in this situation?

       a. To be successful at whatever career I make for myself.

       b. _____

       _____

       c. _____

       _____

3. How can I state the problem clearly and specifically?

_____

_____

_____

_____

B. Step Two: What are the alternatives?
1. What are the boundaries of the problem situation?
   a. My insecurities and fears that keep me from climbing.

   b. _____

   _____

   c. _____

   _____

2. What are the alternatives that are possible within these boundaries?
   a. I can meet with different store managers and ask questions regarding their duties.

   b. _____

   _____

   c. _____

   _____

   d. _____

   _____

C. Step Three: What are the advantages and/or disadvantages of each alternative?
1. What are the advantages and/or disadvantages of each alternative?
   a. Meet with different store managers and ask questions regarding their duties.

      *Advantages:* I can get a more specific and concrete idea of what this field is like, which will help me decide if I want to choose it for a career.

      *Disadvantages:* I may get confused with all the different responses. It will be time-consuming.

   b. _____

   _____

*Advantages:* _____

_____

_____

*Disadvantages:* _____

_____

_____

c. _____

_____

*Advantages:* _____

_____

_____

*Disadvantages:* _____

_____

_____

d. _____

_____

*Advantages:* _____

_____

_____

*Disadvantages:* _____

_____

_____

2. What additional information do I need to evaluate each alternative?

a. Meet with different store managers and ask questions regarding their duties.

*Information needed:* Which store managers should I meet with? What should I ask them? Will their responses help me make my decision?

*Sources:* Career counselor, store managers.

b. _____

_____

*Information needed:* _____

_____

_____

*Sources:* _____

c. _____

_____

*Information needed:* _____

_____

_____

*Sources:* _____

d. _____

_____

*Information needed:* _____

_____

_____

*Sources:* _____

D.  Step Four: What is the solution?
  1.  Which alternative(s) will I pursue?
      Alternative ____: _____

      _____

  2.  What steps can I take to act on the alternative(s) chosen?

      a. _____

      _____

      b. _____

      _____

      c. _____

      _____

      d. _____

      _____

      e. _____

      _____

3. How can I review how well my strategies are working out and make whatever adjustments are necessary?

_____

_____

_____

_____

## Problem 4

### Background Information

One of my problems is my difficulty in taking tests. It's not that I don't study. What happens is that when I get the test I become nervous and my mind goes blank. For example, in my social science class, the teacher told the class on Tuesday that there would be a test on Thursday. That afternoon I went home and began studying for the test. By Thursday I knew most of the work, but when the test was handed out, I got nervous and my mind went blank. For a long time I just stared at the test, and I ended up failing it.

A. Step One: What is the problem?

1. What are the clues to the problem?

   a. Factual clues

      (1) _____

      _____

      (2) _____

      _____

   b. Feeling clues

      (1) *Fears:* I'm afraid of not passing the class.

      (2) *Anger:* I become angry at myself for doubting my abilities and because I put myself through such mental pain.

      (3) *Conflicts:* I have conflicts with my feelings. One part of me says you studied for the test, so what's the problem? But another part of me asks, are you sure that's what you learned in class? Is that the correct answer?

      (4) *Guilt:* I feel guilty when I do poorly and I know that I could have done better. I just don't have enough confidence in myself and my abilities.

(5) *Confusion:* Sometimes I wonder if college is for me.

(6) _____

_____

(7) _____

_____

2. What are the results I am aiming for in this situation?

   a. I want my confidence in myself to be so strong that I won't doubt my answer when I know it's the right answer to the question.

   b. _____

   _____

   c. _____

   _____

3. How can I state the problem clearly and specifically?

   _____

   _____

   _____

   _____

B. Step Two: What are the alternatives?

   1. What are the boundaries of the problem situation?

      a. I tend to be a nervous person in pressure situations.

      b. _____

      _____

      c. _____

      _____

   2. What are the alternatives that are possible within these boundaries?

      a. Have a family member or friend quiz me and time my answers.

      b. _____

      _____

      c. _____

      _____

d. _____

_____

C. Step Three: What are the advantages and/or disadvantages of each alternative?

  1. What are the advantages and/or disadvantages of each alternative?

    a. Have a family member or friend quiz me and time my answers.

      *Advantages:* This sort of practice will help me get used to test like
situations so that I won't be as nervous when I get in a real test
situation.

      *Disadvantages:* The family member or friend may laugh or make
fun of me if I get an answer wrong. I would become very angry
and upset.

    b. _____

_____

      *Advantages:* _____

_____

_____

      *Disadvantages:* _____

_____

_____

    c. _____

_____

      *Advantages:* _____

_____

_____

      *Disadvantages:* _____

_____

_____

    d. _____

_____

*Advantages:* _____

_____

_____

*Disadvantages:* _____

_____

_____

2. What additional information do I need to evaluate each alternative?
   a. *Information needed:* Who do I know who would be willing to quiz me? Would it really be helpful? How do I know that I won't just freeze up again when I take the test?
   *Sources:* Other students, my teachers, counselors.

   b. _____

   _____

   *Information needed:* _____

   _____

   _____

   *Sources:* _____

   c. _____

   _____

   *Information needed:* _____

   _____

   _____

   *Sources:* _____

   d. _____

   _____

   *Information needed:* _____

   _____

   _____

   *Sources:* _____

D.  Step Four: What is the solution?

   1.  Which alternative(s) will I pursue?

       Alternative _____: _____

       _____

   2.  What steps can I take to act on the alternative(s) chosen?

       a.  _____

           _____

       b.  _____

           _____

       c.  _____

           _____

       d.  _____

           _____

       e.  _____

           _____

   3.  How can I review how well my strategies are working out and make
       whatever adjustments are necessary?

       _____

       _____

       _____

       _____

---

   Select a problem from your own life. It should be one that you are currently    ►•◄
grappling with and have not yet been able to solve.

   After selecting the problem you want to work on, use the format in the preceding exercise (pp. 111–129) to guide your analysis.

---

   Our problems are not only of a personal nature. We also face problems as    ►•◄
members of a community, society, and world. We need to approach these problems in an organized and thoughtful way in order to explore the issues, develop
a clear understanding, and decide on a plan of action.

Select a current problem in your school or community—such as lack of funding for a popular student program or neighborhood crime or vandalism. Use the format in the preceding exercises to guide your analysis.

---

➤•◄     As a nation, we face many domestic and international problems: acid rain, unemployment, the threat of nuclear war, controversial foreign policies (to name but a few). Select a national problem that you are particularly concerned about. Use the format in the preceding exercises to guide your analysis.

# Chapter Five
# Perceiving

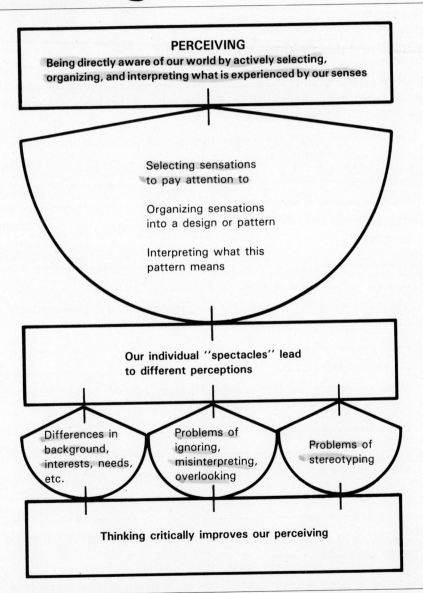

**PERCEIVING**
Being directly aware of our world by actively selecting,
organizing, and interpreting what is experienced by our senses

Selecting sensations
to pay attention to

Organizing sensations
into a design or pattern

Interpreting what this
pattern means

**Our individual "spectacles" lead
to different perceptions**

Differences in
background,
interests, needs,
etc.

Problems of
ignoring,
misinterpreting,
overlooking

Problems of
stereotyping

**Thinking critically improves our perceiving**

THINKING IS THE WAY we make sense of the world. By thinking in an active, purposeful and organized way, we are able to understand what is happening in our experience—to solve problems, work toward our goals, make sense of information, and understand other people. Our experience of the world is presented to us by means of our *senses:* sight, hearing, smell, touch, and taste. These senses are our bridges to the world, making us aware of what occurs outside us.

## Senses are our bridges to the world

Take turns concentrating on each sense you possess. Try to focus on sensations that you were not aware of before concentrating on that particular sense and then describe these sensations.

1. What can you *see?* (For example, the shape of the letters on the page, the design of the clothing on your arm.)

   _____

   _____

2. What can you *hear?* (For example, the hum of the air circulator, the rustling of a page.)

   _____

   _____

3. What can you *feel?* (For example, the pressure of the clothes against your skin, the texture of the page on your fingers.)

   _____

   _____

4. What can you *smell?* (For example, the perfume or cologne someone is wearing, the odor of stale cigarette smoke.)

   _____

   _____

5. What can you *taste?* (for example, the aftereffects of your last meal.)

   _____

   _____

The activity of using our senses to experience and make sense of our world is known as *perceiving.*

**Perceiving** • Being directly aware of our world based on what is experienced through our senses.

## Perceiving is an active process

It is tempting to think that our senses simply record what is happening out in the world, as if we were human cameras or tape recorders. However, we are not simply passive receivers of information, "containers" into which sense experience is poured. Instead we are *active participants* who are always trying to understand the sensations we are encountering. As we perceive our world, our experience is the result of combining the sensations we are having with the way we understand these sensations. For example, examine the collection of markings below. What do you see?

If you all see is a collection of black spots, try looking at the group sideways. After a while, you will probably perceive a very familiar animal.

From this example we can see that when we perceive the world we are doing more than simply recording what our senses experience. In addition to experiencing sensations, we are also actively making sense of these sensations. That is why this collection of black spots suddenly became man's best friend—because we were able actively to organize these spots into a pattern we recognized. Or think about the times you were able to look up at the white, billowy clouds in the sky and see different figures and designs. The figures you were perceiving were not actually in the clouds but the result of your giving a meaningful form to the shapes and colors you were experiencing.

The same is true for virtually everything we experience. Our perceptions of the world result from combining the information provided by our senses with the way we actively make sense of this information. And since making sense of information is what we are doing when we are thinking, we can see that perceiving our world involves using our minds in an active way. Of course we are usually not aware that we are using our minds to interpret the sensations we are experiencing. We simply see the dog or the figures in the clouds as if they were really there.

When we actively perceive the sensations we are experiencing, we are usually doing three different things:

1.   We are actively *selecting* certain sensations to pay attention to.
2.   We are actively *organizing* these sensations into a design or pattern.
3.   We are actively *interpreting* what this design or pattern means to us.

In the case of the figure on page 133 we were able to perceive a dog because we

1.   *selected* certain of the markings to concentrate on.
2.   *organized* these markings into a pattern.
3.   *interpreted* this pattern as representing a familiar animal.

Of course, when we perceive, these three operations of selecting, organizing, and interpreting are usually performed quickly, automatically, and often at the same time. We are normally unaware that we are performing these operations; they are so rapid and automatic, like choosing a flavor of ice cream from a spread of forty varieties. In this chapter we are trying to slow down this normally automatic process of perceiving so that we can understand how the process works.

Let us explore another example that illustrates how we actively select, organize, and interpret our perceptions of the world. Carefully examine the figure pictured on page 134. Do you see both the young woman and the old woman? If you do, try switching back and forth between the two images. As you switch back and forth between the two images, notice how for each image you are:

*selecting* certain lines, shapes, and shadings to focus your attention on

*organizing* these lines, shapes and shadings into different patterns

*interpreting* these patterns as representing things that you are able to recognize— a hat, a nose, a chin.

Another way for us to become aware of our active participation in perceiving our world is to consider how we see objects. Examine the illustration below. Do you perceive different-sized people, or the same-sized people at different distances?

When we see someone who is far away, we usually do not perceive a tiny person. Instead, we perceive a normal-sized person who is far away from us. Our experience in the world has enabled us to discover that the farther things are from us, the smaller they look. The moon in the night sky appears about the size of a quarter, yet we perceive it as being considerably larger. As we look down a long stretch of railroad tracks or gaze up at a tall building, the boundary lines seem to come together. However, even though these images are what our eyes "see," we do not usually perceive the tracks meeting or the building coming to a point. Instead, our minds actively organize and interpret a world composed of constant shapes and sizes, even though the images we actually see usually vary, depending on how far we are from them and the angle from which we are looking at them.

Examine the four different images pictured on page 136. Do you see four different-shaped objects, or one rectangular door? Can you explain why?

➤•◄    Examine carefully the engraving pictured below, entitled "Satire on False Perspective," completed by William Hogarth in 1754. In this engraving, the artist has changed many of the clues we use to perceive a world of constant shapes and sizes, thus creating some unusual effects.

Whoever makes a DESIGN, without the Knowledge of PERSPECTIVE, will be liable to such Absurdities as are shewn in this Frontispiece.

1.  Identify which elements of the picture are different from the way we nor-
    mally perceive things in the world.

    a.  The fishing pole held by the man in the foreground is too large.

    b.  _____

    _____

    c.  _____

    _____

    d.  _____

    _____

2.  For each "mistake" you have identified, explain how the artist created a
    perception that is different from the way our minds usually organize and
    interpret the world.

    a.  The fishing pole seems to extend into the background of the picture be-
        cause the artist did not reduce its size.

    b.  _____

    _____

    c.  _____

    _____

    d.  _____

    _____

## People often perceive the same experience differently

So far, we have been exploring how our mind actively participates in the way
we perceive the world. By combining the sensations we are receiving with the
way our mind selects, organizes, and interprets these sensations, we perceive a
world of things that is stable and familiar, a world that usually makes sense to
us. Of course, in addition to all the *things* in our world, we also perceive and try
to make sense of the *people* in our world as well. And although people have
physical bodies that we perceive, they also express nonphysical qualities:
thoughts, feelings, intentions, motives, and actions. Just as we discovered that
we are active participants in the way we perceive the physical world, we find
that we are also active participants in the way we perceive and try to make
sense of the non-physical aspects of our world as well.

►•◄   Examine carefully the following picture. What do you think is occurring?

1.   Describe as specifically as possible what you perceive is taking place in the picture.

_____

_____

_____

_____

2.   Now describe what you think will take place next.

_____

_____

_____

_____

3.   Compare your perceptions to the perceptions of other students in the class. List perceptions that differ from yours.

   a. _____

   b. _____

   c. _____

In most cases, people in a group will have a variety of perceptions about what is taking place in the picture. Some will see the boy as frustrated because the music is too difficult. Others will see him concentrating on what has to be done. Still others may see him as annoyed because he is being forced to do something he does not want to do. In each case, what the person perceives depends on how the person is actively using his or her mind to organize and interpret what is taking place. Since the situation pictured is by its nature somewhat puzzling, different people perceive it in different ways.

---

Examine closely the photograph pictured below.

1.   Describe as specifically as possible what you think is taking place in the photograph.

   _____

   _____

_____

_____

2.  Now describe what you think will take place next.

    _____

    _____

    _____

    _____

3.  Compare your perceptions to the perceptions of the other students in the class. List the perceptions that differ from yours.

    a. _____

    b. _____

    c. _____

The fact that we actively participate in perceiving our world is something we are not usually aware of. We normally assume that what we are perceiving is what is actually taking place. Only when we find that our perception of the same event differs from the perceptions of others are we forced to examine the manner in which we are selecting, organizing, and interpreting the events in our world.

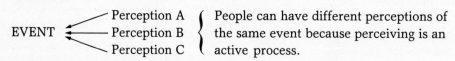

EVENT ← Perception A / Perception B / Perception C — People can have different perceptions of the same event because perceiving is an active process.

At the beginning of the chapter we defined perceiving as "being directly aware of our world based on what is experienced through our senses." Based on what we have discovered so far, we can now make this definition somewhat more specific:

**Perceiving** • Being directly aware of our world by actively selecting, organizing, and interpreting what is experienced by our senses.

Let us examine another situation in which a number of different people had somewhat different perceptions about an event they were describing. In the first chapter of this book, we read a passage by Malcolm X (pp. 12–15), written when he was just beginning his life's work. A few years later, this work came to a tragic end with his assassination at a meeting in Harlem. Included below are four different accounts of what took place on that day. As you read through the various accounts, pay particular attention to the different perceptions each one presents of this event. After you have completed reading the accounts, describe some of the differences in these perceptions.

1.  *The New York Times*
2.  *Life* magazine
3.  *The New York Post*
4.  *Associated Press*

### The New York Times

Malcolm X, the 39-year-old leader of a militant Black Nationalist movement, was shot to death yesterday afternoon at a rally of his followers in a ballroom in Washington Heights. The bearded Negro extremist had said only a few words of greeting when a fusillade rang out. The bullets knocked him over backwards.

A 22-year-old Negro, Thomas Hagan, was charged with the killing. The police rescued him from the ballroom crowd after he had been shot and beaten.

Pandemonium broke out among the 400 Negroes in the Audubon Ballroom at 160th street and Broadway. As men, women and children ducked under tables and flattened themselves on the floor, more shots were fired. The police said seven bullets struck Malcolm. Three other Negroes were shot. Witnesses reported that as many as 30 shots had been fired. About two hours later the police said the shooting had apparently been a result of a feud between followers of Malcolm and members of the extremist group he broke with last year, the Black Muslims. . . .

### Life

His life oozing out through a half dozen or more gunshot wounds in his chest, Malcolm X, once the shrillest voice of black supremacy, lay dying on the stage of a Manhattan auditorium. Moments before, he had stepped up to the lectern and 400 of the faithful had settled down expectantly to hear the sort of speech for which he was famous—flaying the hated white man. Then a scuffle broke out in the hall and Malcolm's bodyguards bolted from his side to break it up—only to discover that they had been faked out. At least two men with pistols rose from the audience and pumped bullets into the speaker, while a third cut loose at close range with both barrels of a sawed-off shotgun. In the confusion the pistol man got away. The shotgunner lunged through the crowd and out the door, but not before the guards came to their wits and shot him in the leg. Outside he was swiftly overtaken by other supporters of Malcolm and very likely would have been stomped to death if the police hadn't saved him. Most shocking of all to the residents of Harlem was the fact that Malcolm had been killed not by "whitey" but by members of his own race.

### The New York Post

They came early to the Audubon Ballroom, perhaps drawn by the expectation that Malcolm X would name the men who firebombed his home last Sunday...I sat at the left in the 12th row and, as we waited, the man next to me spoke of Malcolm and his followers: "Malcolm is our only hope... You can depend on him to tell it like it is and to give Whitey hell."...

There was a prolonged ovation as Malcolm walked to the rostrum... Malcolm looked up and said "A salaam aleikum (Peace be unto you)" and the audience replied "We aleikum salaam (And unto you, peace)."

Bespeckled and dapper in a dark suit, sandy hair glinting in the light, Malcolm said: "Brothers and sisters..." He was interrupted by two men in the center of the ballroom,...who rose and, arguing with each other, moved forward. Then there was a scuffle at the back of the room...I heard Malcolm X say his last words: "Now, brothers, break it up," he said softly. "Be cool, be calm."

Then all hell broke loose. There was a muffled sound of shots and Malcolm, blood on his face and chest, fell limply back over the chairs behind him. The two men who had approached him ran to the exit on my side of the room, shooting wildly behind them as they ran....I heard people screaming. "Don't let them kill him." "Kill those bastards."...At an exit I saw some of Malcolm's men beating with all their strength on two men....I saw a half a dozen of Malcolm's followers bending over his inert body on the stage. Their clothes stained with their leader's blood....

Four policemen took the stretcher and carried Malcolm through the crowd and some of the women came out of their shock ... and one said: "...I hope he doesn't die, but I don't think he's going to make it."...

### Associated Press

A week after being bombed out of his Queens home, Black Nationalist leader Malcolm X was shot to death shortly after 3 p.m. yesterday at a Washington Heights rally of 400 of his devoted followers. Early today, police brass ordered a homicide charge placed against a 22-year-old man they rescued from a savage beating by Malcolm X supporters after the shooting. The suspect, Thomas Hagan, had been shot in the left leg by one of Malcolm's bodyguards as, police said, Hagan and another assassin fled when pandemonium erupted. Two other men were wounded in the wild burst of firing from at least three weapons. The firearms were a .38, a .45 automatic and a sawed-off shotgun. Hagan allegedly shot Malcolm X with the shot-gun, a double barrelled sawed-off weapon on which the stock also had been shortened, possibly to facilitate concealment. Cops charged

Reuben Frances, of 871 E. 179th. St., Bronx, with felonious assault in the shooting of Hagan, and with Sullivan Law violation—possession of the .45. Police recovered the shotgun and the .45.

### We view the world through "spectacles"

We have just examined three situations in which a number of people were exposed to the same basic events:

a boy looking at a musical instrument (p. 138)
a photograph of a social scene (p. 139)
the assassination of Malcolm X (pp. 141–143)

In each of these cases, we have found that people do not always agree about what they are perceiving, even though they are viewing the same situation. The reason why people can perceive the same event differently is clear: perceiving is an active process, and we are active participants in this process. What we perceive depends on

the details that we *select* to focus on
how we *organize* these various details
how we *interpret* what is taking place

A diagram of this process might look as follows:

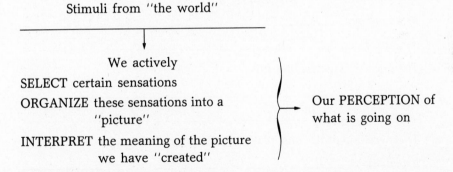

Stimuli from "the world"

We actively
SELECT certain sensations
ORGANIZE these sensations into a
    "picture"                            Our PERCEPTION of
                                         what is going on
INTERPRET the meaning of the picture
    we have "created"

To understand how various people can be exposed to the same stimuli or events and yet have different perceptions, it helps to imagine that each of us views the world through our own individual pair of spectacles (or contact lenses if you prefer). Of course, we are not usually aware of the spectacles we are wearing. Instead, our spectacles act as *filters* that select and shape what we perceive without our realizing it.

This image of "spectacles" helps explain why people can be exposed to the same stimuli or events and yet perceive different things. It is because people are wearing *different spectacles* that influence what they are perceiving. When members of your class had different perceptions of the boy with the instrument and of the photograph of social groups, their different perceptions were the result of the different spectacles through which each views the world. The same is true of the varying accounts of Malcolm X's assassination.

In order to understand the way people perceive the world, we have to understand their individual spectacles, which influence how they actively select, organize, and interpret the events in their experience.

---

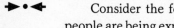     Consider the following pairs of statements. In each of these cases, both people are being exposed to the same basic *stimulus* or *event,* yet each has a totally different *perception* of the experience.

1.  a.  That chili was much too spicy to eat.

    *Explanation:*   This person may have little experience eating spicy food.

    b.  That chili needed more hot peppers and chili powder to spice it up a little.

    *Explanation:*   This person may have a lot of experience eating spicy food and so is used to its taste.

2.  a.  The glass of water is half-empty.

    *Explanation:*  _____

    _____

    b.  The glass of water is half-full.

    *Explanation:*  _____

    _____

3.  a.  That was one of the best-played football games I've ever seen.

    *Explanation:*  _____

    _____

    b.  All I saw was a bunch of men running around and knocking each other down.

    *Explanation:*  _____

    _____

4.  a.  I think that the newest music just sounds like a lot of noise.

    *Explanation:*  _____

    _____

b. I think the newest music is the creative expression of important forces in our culture.

   *Explanation:* _____

   _____

5. a. The man who mugged us was short and thin and had a mustache.

   *Explanation:* _____

   _____

   b. The man who mugged us was of medium height and weight and had a beard.

   *Explanation:* _____

   _____

6. a. What I like about Miller beer is that it's less filling.

   *Explanation:* _____

   _____

   b. What I like about Miller beer is that it tastes great.

   *Explanation:* _____

   _____

7. a. Mr. Brown is a very stimulating and challenging teacher.

   *Explanation:* _____

   _____

   b. Mr. Brown is much too difficult and asks the students to do an unfair amount of work.

   *Explanation:* _____

   _____

➤•◄

For each of the following *stimuli,* create a pair of statements that reflect entirely different *perceptions.* Then give an explanation of how these different perceptions might occur, based on the different spectacles through which the person is experiencing the world.

1.   *Stimuli:* The skin on roast chicken

   a.   *Perception:* _____

   _____

   *Explanation:* _____

   _____

   b.   *Perception:* _____

   _____

   *Explanation:* _____

   _____

2.   *Stimuli:* People who wear lots of make-up and jewelry.

   a.   *Perception:* _____

   _____

   *Explanation:* _____

   _____

   b.   *Perception:* _____

   _____

   *Explanation:* _____

   _____

3.   *Stimuli:* Large, crowded, noisy cities

   a.   *Perception:* _____

   _____

   *Explanation:* _____

   _____

   b.   *Perception:* _____

   _____

   *Explanation:* _____

   _____

4.   *Stimuli:* Camping out in the woods

   a.   *Perception:* _____

   _____

*Explanation:* _____

_____

b.   *Perception:* _____

_____

*Explanation:* _____

_____

As we are beginning to see, each of us experiences the world in our own in-dividual ways, influenced by the particular spectacles we are wearing. These spectacles reflect the way we actively select, organize, and interpret the stimuli we encounter.

**Our "spectacles" influence the way we select, organize, and interpret our perceptions**

*Selecting our perceptions*   At almost every waking moment of our lives, we are being bombarded by a tremendous number of stimuli: images to see, noises to hear, odors to smell, textures to feel, and things to taste. The experience of all these sensations happening at once creates what the nineteenth-century American philosopher William James called "a bloomin' buzzin' confusion." Yet for us, the world usually seems much more orderly and understandable. Why is this so?

In the first place, our sense equipment can receive sensations only within certain limited ranges. For example, there are many sounds and smells that animals can detect but we cannot because their sense organs have broader ranges in these areas than ours do.

A second reason that we can handle this sensory bombardment is that from the stimulation available to us we *select* only a small amount on which to focus our attention. At the beginning of this chapter you took turns concentrating on each of your senses. As you focused on each sense, you probably became aware of many sensations that you were not previously aware of. By practicing this simple exercise, we learn that for every sensation that we focus our attention on there are countless sensations that we are simply ignoring. If we were aware of *everything* that is happening at every moment, we would be completely overwhelmed. By selecting certain sensations, we are able to perceive our world in a relatively orderly way.

---

➤•◄    When we focus our attention, we are able to experience aspects of our environment in a much more specific and detailed way. Have the members of your class list all the sounds they can hear in a three-minute period. Such lists often include forty to fifty distinct sounds, a considerably more detailed experience than we are typically aware of.

We spend much of the time experiencing the world in a very general way, not aware of many of the details of the events that are taking place. Police officers encounter this problem when they ask witnesses for a description of the people involved in a crime. Most witnesses can provide only very general descriptions—"medium height, average weight, dark clothes," etc. In order to communicate to others the specific details of our experience, we have to first develop the habit of becoming aware of these details.

Draw a picture of a telephone dial or the face of a Touch Tone phone, complete with numbers and letters. Then compare your drawing with an actual phone dial. Did you have any difficulty? Why? (Consider all the times you have looked at such a dial.)

We tend to select perceptions regarding subjects that have been called to our attention for some reason. For example, while driving, someone might point out a vanity license plate (HOTSHOT) or an amusing bumper sticker. Suddenly, we start seeing other license plates or bumper stickers because we have had our attention focused on that type of perception. At the age of three, my daughter suddenly became aware of beards. Upon entering a subway car, she would ask in a penetrating voice, "Any beards here?" and then proceed to count them out loud. In doing this, she naturally focused my attention on beards, as well as the attention of many of the other passengers.

As another aspect of our perceiving spectacles, we tend to notice what we need, desire, or find of interest. When we go shopping, we focus on the items we are looking for. Walking down the street, we tend to notice certain kinds of people or events while completely ignoring others. Even watching a movie or reading a book, we tend to concentrate on and remember the elements we find of interest. Another person can perform *exactly* the same actions—shop at the same store, walk down the same street with us, read the same book, or go to the same movie—and yet see and remember entirely different things. In other words, what we see and do not see depends largely upon our interests, needs, and desires.

Consider the following lists of perceptions compiled by two people taking a walk together. What are the different needs and interests reflected in the two lists?

*Person A*

1. Antique store with quilt
2. Fire engine—siren blaring
3. Boutique with cable sweaters and wool plaid skirt
4. Woman charging $3 to analyze handwriting
5. Jewelry store with bracelets on sale
6. Strange man asking for $1 for coffee

*Person B*

1. Three teenage boys taking loudly
2. Hook and ladder on way to fire
3. Woman driving BMW motorcycle
4. Ray's Famous Pizza
5. Elderly man pushing grocery cart
6. Woman at card table offering handwriting analysis

| *Person A* | *Person B* |
|---|---|
| 7. Dance classes in second floor studio | 7. Szechuan restaurant |
| 8. Leather store—belts made while you wait | 8. Young man carrying large radio |
| 9. Five-and-Ten—Halloween costumes in window | 9. Panhandler—unshaven, shabby clothes, bloated stomach |
| 10. Cat sleeping in store window | 10. Mercedes stretch limousine |
| | 11. Messenger on bicycle weaving through traffic |

The way we are feeling—our mood or emotional state—can also affect the perceptions we select. Imagine that you are at home alone or camping out in the woods and you begin to feel uneasy. Suddenly, you may begin to hear suspicious noises that you are certain come from an ax-wielding murderer or a ferocious beast. (The makers of horror films know exactly how to focus our attention on certain details—like a creaking door—in order to frighten us.) Or think back on the times when you have felt cranky, perhaps because you did not get enough sleep or were under pressure, and recall how you behaved. When we are in a bad mood, we often seem ready to focus our attention on every potential insult or criticism by others—and ready to respond the same way.

We also tend to select stimuli that are very familiar or very unfamiliar to us. Imagine that you are in a public place—in a restaurant or at a party—surrounded by the conversations of other people. These conversations are simply "noise" to you until you hear something familiar—your first name perhaps, or a subject that interests you. Suddenly you find yourself tuning in to that particular conversation. The sound of something familiar made you select that conversation from all the others to listen to. The process is something like flipping the radio dial and stopping when you hear a recognizable song. Or consider the following.

How many *F*s can you count in this sentence?

UFO'S HAVE BEEN THE SUBJECTS OF STUDY OF MANY FINE PEOPLE, SOME OF WHOM HAVE FINALLY CONCLUDED THAT THE EYEWITNESS ACCOUNTS OF SIGHTINGS ARE BOTH FALSE AND FARFETCHED.

If you counted fewer than ten *F*s, it is probably because you failed to count the *F*s in the words *OF*. Since the *F* in *OF* is pronounced like a *V*, we are not in the habit of thinking of it as an *F*. And so we simply do not "see" it as an *F*.

Although we tend to focus on what is familiar to us, we are normally not aware that we are doing so. In fact, we often take for granted what is familiar to us—the taste of chili or eggs, the street that we live on, our family or friends—and normally do not think about our perception of it. But when something happens that makes the familiar seem strange and unfamiliar, we become aware of our perceptions and start to evaluate them.

To sum up, we actively select our perceptions from our experience, based on what has been called to our attention, on our needs or interests, our mood or feelings, and on what seems familiar or unfamiliar. The way we select our perceptions is an important part of the spectacles through which we view the world.

Let us think back on the three examples we considered earlier in the chapter and explore how our selecting played a crucial role in what was being perceived.

1. *The boy with the instrument (p. 138).* Review your description of what was taking place and what you thought would take place next.

   a. Identify the details of the picture that led you to your perceptions.

      (1) _____

      (2) _____

      (3) _____

   b. Compare the details that you selected to focus on with the details other members of the class focused on.

      _____

      _____

      _____

      _____

2. *The photograph of a social scene (p. 139).* Review your description of what was taking place.

   a. Identify the details of the photograph which led you to your perceptions.

      (1) _____

      (2) _____

      (3) _____

      (4) _____

b.  Compare the details that you selected to focus on with the details other
    members of the class focused on.

    _____

    _____

    _____

    _____

3.  *The assassination of Malcolm X (pp. 141–143).* Review the various accounts
    of Malcolm X's assassination and identify the details of the event that each
    account focused on.

    a.  *The New York Times*

        (1)  _____

        (2)  _____

        (3)  _____

        (4)  _____

        (5)  _____

        (6)  _____

        (7)  _____

    b.  *Life* magazine

        (1)  _____

        (2)  _____

        (3)  _____

        (4)  _____

        (5)  _____

        (6)  _____

        (7)  _____

    c.  *The New York Post*

        (1)  _____

        (2)  _____

        (3)  _____

(4) _____

(5) _____

(6) _____

(7) _____

   d. *Associated Press*

      (1) _____

      (2) _____

      (3) _____

      (4) _____

      (5) _____

      (6) _____

      (7) _____

***Organizing our perceptions***   Not only do we actively *select* certain perceptions, but we also actively *organize* these perceptions into meaningful relationships and patterns. Consider the series of lines below.

Do you perceive them as individual lines or did you group them into pairs? We seem to naturally try to organize our perceptions to create order and meaning. Consider the items pictured below.

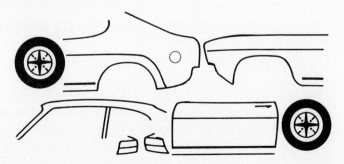

Let us organize the pieces into patterns that are probably more familiar to you. Do the pieces express more meaning than they did before?

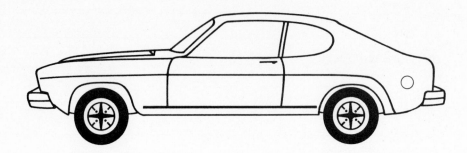

In the case above, the individual pieces of the puzzle look much different by themselves than when they are put together into a whole pattern. As we perceive the world, we naturally try to order and organize what we are experiencing into patterns and relationships that make sense to us. And when we are able to do so, the completed whole means more to us than the sum of the individual parts.

We are continually organizing our world in this way at virtually every waking moment. We do not live in a world of isolated sounds, patches of color, random odors, and individual textures. Instead, we live in a world of objects and people, language and music—a world in which all these individual stimuli are woven together. We are able to perceive this world of complex experiences because we are able to organize the individual stimuli we are receiving into re-lationships that have meaning to us.

The way we organize our experience is an important part of the spectacles through which we perceive the world. Think back on the examples we consid-ered earlier in the chapter. You were able to perceive objects, human expres-sions, and potential human action because of your ability to organize the lines, shapes, and shadings into meaningful patterns.

---

➤•◄    Review the various accounts of Malcolm X's assassination (pp. 141–143), and describe how each account *organizes* the details that have been selected. Remember that newspapers usually present what they consider the most im-portant information first and the least important information last.

1.  *The New York Times:* _____

    _____

    _____

    _____

2.  *Life* magazine: _____

    _____

    _____

    _____

3.  *The New York Post:* _____

    _____

    _____

    _____

4.  *Associated Press:* _____

    _____

    _____

    _____

***Interpreting our perceptions***   In addition to selecting and organizing our perceptions, we also actively *interpret* what we perceive. When we interpret, we are figuring out what something means. For example, imagine that you are a parent of a baby and that you are having a party at your house. Suddenly, through all the sounds of people talking, you hear your baby cry. As you actively *select* this perception to focus your attention on and *organize* the sounds into a recognizable human cry, you also attempt to *interpret* what the crying means. Is your baby startled by the noise of the party? Frightened? Hungry? Wet? Frustrated? Lonely? By trying to interpret your perception, you are attempting to determine exactly what meaning is being expressed by the crying.

One of the elements that influences our interpretations of what we are perceiving is the *context,* or overall situation, within which the perception is occurring. Examine the center figure in the group of figures pictured on page 156. What do you see?

$$12$$
$$A\ 13\ C$$
$$14$$

When most people view the center figure as part of the horizontal line, they perceive the letter *B,* whereas, if they view it as part of the vertical line, they perceive the number *13.* In each case, our interpretation of the figure depends on the context within which it is occurring. The same is true for most of our perceptions; our interpretation of the perception is related to the overall situation within which it is taking place. For example, imagine that you see a person running down the street. Describe some of the various ways we might interpret this situation, and also describe the different contexts that might have led to these interpretations.

*Example:*

*Interpretation:*   The person is running for a bus.

*Context:*   There is a bus stopped at the corner with its doors open.

1.   *Interpretation:*  _____

     *Context:*  _____

2.   *Interpretation:*  _____

     *Context:*  _____

   In living our lives, we are continually trying to figure out interpretations of what we are perceiving, whether it is a design, someone's behavior, or a social situation. Like the example of a baby crying, most of the perceptions we experience can be interpreted in more than one way. When a situation has more than one possible interpretation, we say that the situation is "ambiguous." The more ambiguous a situation is, the greater the number of possible meanings or interpretations it has. This is one of the main reasons why people who are *observing* the same thing may disagree about what they are *perceiving.* When such disagreement occurs, it is often because people are giving the same situation different interpretations.

Let us think again about the pictures we examined earlier—they boy with the musical instrument (p. 138) and the photograph of a social scene (p. 139). In each instance, your description of what was happening—and what was about to happen—was based on your interpretation of the situation. Other members of the class may have given different descriptions of what was occurring because they interpreted the situation differently. Since these two pictures are by their nature puzzling and ambiguous, no one interpretation is necessarily more correct than the other interpretations. Instead, each interpretation simply reveals the spectacles through which this person views the world. Of course, we may feel that some interpretations make more sense than others, based on the details and the relationships that we perceive in the situation. Let's explore some of the ways our interpretations of our perceptions reveal the spectacles through which we are viewing the event.

As we saw in the last section, our interests and desires influence the perceptions we select to focus our attention on. However, our interests and desires can also affect our interpretation of what we are perceiving. Watching our team play baseball, for example, we may really believe that the opposing runner was "out by a mile"—even though the replay may show otherwise. Or imagine that you are giving a speech to the class, and that you are being evaluated by two people—someone who likes you and someone who does not. Do you believe that different perceptions of your performance may result? Describe how each of the following perceptions might be influenced by each person's interests.

1.   Your perception of your performance.

2.   Your friend's perception of your performance.

3.   Perception of your performance by someone who does not like you.

Similarly, the way we are feeling can influence our interpretations of what we are experiencing. When we feel happy and optimistic, the world often seems friendly and the future full of possibilities, and we interpret the problems we encounter as challenges to be overcome. On the other hand, when we are depressed or unhappy, our world may be perceived entirely differently. The future can appear full of problems that are trying to overcome us. In both cases the circumstances in our world may be very similar; it is our interpretation of our world through our spectacles that varies so completely.

Our perceptions of the world are dramatically influenced by our past experiences: the way we were brought up, the relationships we have had, the training and education we have undergone. For example, imagine that an accident between a car and a tractor trailer has just taken place. Notice how the event might be perceived differently based on the interests and the past experience of the individuals involved.

*Policeman:*   Who was coming down the main road with the right of way? Why didn't both of you slow down at the intersection? Didn't you see that the streets were icy? Give me your licenses and registrations.

*Tow-truck Operator:*   These tractor trailers don't have very much control on the ice. If he did stop before the intersection, it still wouldn't give him enough time to make a full stop. The truck has suffered only minor damage, but the car is totally disabled. It will definitely have to be towed.

*Doctor:*   Is anybody seriously hurt? Is anything broken? Are you experiencing any head or neck pains? Why don't you just lie down and relax while I look you over. Help is on the way.

*A Friend of the Victim:*   I thought that he had better sense than to drive on icy roads. I just hope that he's all right. I'd better call his parents to let them know what happened. I know they won't care about the car—just let him be all right.

Or to take another example, the perceptions of a person raised in a small town in the country are likely to be different from those of a person raised in a large city, based on the contrasting experiences they have had. Identify below what some of these different interpretations might be.

| *Perceptions* | *City* | *Country* |
|---|---|---|
| Time | _____ | _____ |
| | _____ | _____ |
| | _____ | _____ |
| | _____ | _____ |
| Sound | _____ | _____ |
| | _____ | _____ |
| | _____ | _____ |
| | _____ | _____ |
| Neighbors | _____ | _____ |
| | _____ | _____ |
| | _____ | _____ |
| | _____ | _____ |

| Perceptions | City | Country |
|---|---|---|
| Nature | _____ | _____ |
| | _____ | _____ |
| | _____ | _____ |
| | _____ | _____ |

What we perceive also depends on our past experience in terms of how "educated" our eyes are. Take the case of two people who are watching a football game. One person, who has very little understanding of football, sees merely a bunch of grown men hitting each other for no apparent reason. The other person, who loves football, sees complex play patterns, daring coaching strategies, effective blocking and tackling techniques, and zone defenses with "seams" that the receivers are trying to "split." Both persons have their eyes glued to the same event, but they are perceiving two entirely different situations. The perceptions differ because each person is actively selecting, organizing, and interpreting the available stimuli in different ways. The same is true of any situation in which we are perceiving an area in which we have special knowledge or expertise, such as

> a builder examining the construction of a new house.
>
> a music lover attending a concert.
>
> a naturalist experiencing the outdoors.
>
> a wine expert tasting various vintages.
>
> a lawyer examining a contract.
>
> an art lover visiting a museum.

Can you list some examples of your own?

_____

_____

_____

_____

In all these cases, the perceptions of the knowledgeable person differ substantially from the perceptions of a person who lacks knowledge of that particular area. Of course we do not have to be an expert to have more fully developed perceptions. It is a matter of degree. In general, the more understanding we have of a particular area, the more detailed and complete our perceptions can be of that area.

➤•◄          Review your interpretations of the boy with the musical instrument (p.
138) and the photograph of a social scene (p. 139). In each of these cases, your
interpretation of what was taking place was influenced by your individual spectacles through which you view the world. For example, how you interpreted
the picture of the boy with the trumpet may have been influenced by your own
experience learning to play an instrument. For each picture, see if you can identify any of the interests, desires, or past experiences that might have influenced
your interpretations.

1.   *Boy with the trumpet:* Factors that influenced my perception

_____

_____

2.   *Photograph:* Factors that influenced my perception

_____

_____

➤•◄          Review once again the accounts of Malcolm X's assassination (pp.
141–143). We have already examined the details that each writer *selected* and
the way each writer *organized* these details. Now let us explore how each writer
*interpreted* this event. For each account, we will ask ourselves the following
questions:

1.   How did the writer perceive Malcolm X?
2.   How did the writer perceive the gunmen?
3.   How did the writer perceive the significance of Malcolm X's assassination?

*The New York Times*

1.   _____

_____

2.   _____

_____

3.   _____

_____

*Life* magazine

1.   _____

_____

2. _____

   _____

3. _____

   _____

*The New York Post*

1. _____

   _____

2. _____

   _____

3. _____

   _____

*Associated Press*

1. _____

   _____

2. _____

   _____

3. _____

   _____

***Summary*** Through our daily experience we develop ways of perceiving our world. These ways of perceiving form the spectacles through which we actively select, organize, and interpret our perceptions of the world—a world we create out of the "bloomin' buzzin' confusion" of stimuli that we are exposed to. Although our spectacles are in many ways similar to the spectacles of others—after all, we do often agree with others regarding what we are perceiving—there are also important differences between each of our spectacles. These differences help account for the fact that we often select, organize, and interpret the same stimuli in different ways from other people.

The following situations are designed to help us explore further the way our individual spectacles influence the way we select, organize, and interpret our perceptions.

1.  When I entered college, one of my first purchases was a Navy style pea jacket, which I was quite proud of. However, after my purchase, I suddenly discovered (to my dismay) that almost everyone seemed to be wearing Navy style pea jackets!

    a.  Think about a situation in which you made a purchase and then started "seeing" more of these items than before your purchase. Describe this particular experience and what you specifically saw.

    b.  Analyze this experience in the light of the various aspects of our perceiving spectacles that we have been exploring.

2.  Describe a situation in which your perception of someone you thought you knew really well changed. In describing this experience, answer the following questions:

    a.  What did you know about this person before this incident?

    b.  What happened to change your perception?

    c.  How did your perception change?

    d.  Was it a change in the person or a change in your perception of the person? How do you know?

    Then analyze this experience in the light of the various aspects of our perceiving spectacles that we have been exploring.

3.  Read carefully the following story by the American poet Carl Sandburg.

    > Drove up a newcomer in a covered wagon: "What kind of folks live around here?" "Well, stranger, what kind of folks was there in the country you come from?" "Well, they was mostly a lowdown, lying, gossiping, backbiting lot of people." "Well, I guess, stranger, that's about the kind of folks you'll find around here." And the dusty grey stranger had just about blended into the dusty grey cottonwoods in a clump on the horizon when another newcomer drove up. "What kind of folks live around here?" "Well, stranger, what kind of folks was there in the country you come from?" "Well, they was mostly a decent, hardworking, law abiding, friendly lot of people." "Well, I guess, stranger, that's about the kind of people you'll find around here." And the second wagon moved off and blended with the dusty grey. . . .

    a.  Describe how you think each of the newcomers will find the people in his or her new hometown.

    b.  Explain *why* you think each newcomer might have different perceptions of the people in his or her new hometown.

    c.  Analyze this story in the light of the various aspects of our perceiving spectacles that we have been exploring.

# Thinking critically about our perceptions

So far, we have been emphasizing the great extent to which we actively participate in what we perceive by selecting, organizing, and interpreting. We have
suggested that each of us views the world through our own unique spectacles.
This means that no two of us perceive the world in exactly the same way.

However, because we actively participate in selecting, organizing, and
interpreting the sensations we are experiencing, our perceptions are often incomplete, inaccurate, or subjective. For example:

1. By *selecting* certain aspects of a situation, we often *ignore* other crucial elements that may also be present. In examining the photograph on page 139,
   we may focus our attention on certain parts of it while completely ignoring
   others. Or a man chasing a hat blown off his head may be unaware of the
   speeding cars approaching him.

2. By *organizing* our perceptions in a certain way, we often *do not see* other
   possible organizations. For instance, a person witnessing an event like
   Malcolm X's assassination may perceive the order of events differently
   from the way they actually took place.

3. By *interpreting* the meaning of our perceptions, we may *overlook* additional
   possible interpretations or we may *mis*interpret what is taking place because we lack sufficient information. For instance, the boy with the trumpet
   may be frustrated by the instrument, *or* he may be a child genius who is in
   the process of composing his own music. The man offering candy to the
   young child may just be trying to be nice, *or* he may be up to no good.

To complicate the situation even more, our own limitations in perceiving
are not the only ones that can cause us problems. Other people often purpose-
fully create perceptions and *mis*perceptions. An advertiser who wants to sell a
product may try to create the impression that our life will be changed if we use
this product. Or a person who wants to discredit someone else may spread un-
true rumors about her, in order to influence others' perceptions of her.

The only way we can correct the mistakes, distortions, and incompleteness
of our perceptions is to *become aware* of this normally unconscious process by
which we perceive and make sense of our world. By becoming aware of this
process, we can think critically about what is going on and then correct our mistakes and distortions. In other words, we can use our critical thinking abilities
to create a clearer and more informed idea of what is taking place. Perception
alone cannot be totally relied on, and if we remain unaware of how it operates

and of our active role in it, then we will be unable to exert any control over it. And in that case, we will be convinced that the way *we see* the world is the way the world *is*, even when our perceptions are mistaken, distorted, or incomplete.

The first step in critically examining our perceptions is to be willing to *ask questions* about what we are perceiving. As long as we believe that the way we see things is the only way to see them, we will be unable to recognize when our perceptions are distorted or inaccurate. For instance, if we are certain that our interpretation of the boy with the instrument or the photograph of a social scene is the only correct one, then we will not be likely to try and see other possible interpretations. However, if we are willing to question our perception ("What are some other possible interpretations?"), then we will open the way to more fully developing our perception of what is taking place.

In addition to asking questions, we have to try to become aware of the personal factors our spectacles bring to our perceptions. As we have seen, each of us brings to every situation a whole collection of expectations, interests, fears, and hopes that can influence what we are perceiving. Consider the following situations:

> You've been fishing all day without a nibble. Suddenly you get a strike! You reel it in, but just as you're about to pull the fish into the boat, it frees itself from the hook and swims away. When you get back home later that night, your friends ask you: "How large was the fish that got away?"

> You're walking through a strange neighborhood, when suddenly some unfriendly people start chasing you. Running for your life, you finally are able to escape and contact the police. They want to know: "How many people were there?" "How large were they?" "Did they have any weapons?"

> The teacher asks you to evaluate the performance of a classmate who is giving a report to the class. You don't like this other student, since he acts as if he's superior to the rest of the students in the class. How do you evaluate his report?

> You are asked to estimate the size of an audience attending an event that your organization has sponsored. How many people are there?

In each of these cases, you can imagine that your perceptions might be influenced by certain hopes, fears, or prejudices that you brought to the situation, causing your observations to become distorted or inaccurate. Although we usually cannot eliminate the personal feelings that are influencing our perceptions, we can become aware of them and try to control them. For instance, if we are asked to evaluate a group of people, one of whom is a good friend, we should try to keep these personal feelings in mind when making our judgment in order to make our perceptions as accurate as possible.

When we explored the different aspects of critical thinking in Chapter Three, we emphasized the importance of seeing things from different perspectives. One of the best ways to do so is by communicating with others and engaging in *dialogue* with them. This means exchanging and critically examining ideas in an open and organized way. Similarly, dialogue is one of the main ways that we check out our perceptions—by asking others what their perceptions are and then comparing and contrasting these with our own. This is exactly what you did when you discussed the different possible interpretations of the boy with the trumpet, the photograph of a social scene, and the assassination of Malcolm X. By exchanging your perceptions with the perceptions of other class members, you developed a more complete sense of how these different events could be viewed.

Of course, in attempting to view things from different perspectives, it is not always possible to discuss our perceptions with others. Sometimes we simply have to use our minds to *imagine* other possible perceptions. For example, imagine that you have just been hired in a new job as an administrative assistant. Things are going well on the job until your boss announces to you that he would like you to get him coffee in the morning and the afternoon. Then the following conversation takes place:

*Boss:*  As part of your job, I would like you to get me coffee in the morning and in the afternoon.

*You:*  But that's not what I was hired for! It's not part of my job.

*Boss:*  Well, it's part of your job as far as I'm concerned. I'm a very busy person, and this is one way you can help me work more productively.

*You:*  Well, I want to work productively too. And getting coffee makes me feel like a waiter or waitress, not an administrative assistant.

*Boss:*  Then why don't you view it as a personal favor to me?

*You:*  _____

_____

*Boss:*  _____

_____

*You:*  _____

_____

*Boss:*  _____

_____

The situation you are being asked to deal with here is difficult and complex. However, your chances of dealing with it effectively depend in part on your ability to try to see the situation from your boss's perspective, to understand his perception of what is going on. Try to imagine yourself as the boss in this situation and to understand the reasons for his request. With that perception in mind, see if you can complete the dialogue so that you keep both your pride and your job.

As this situation illustrates, thinking critically means not just seeing different possible perceptions of a situation, but also understanding the *reasons* for these perceptions. This is probably what occurred when the class discussed various perceptions of the boy with the trumpet, the photograph of a social scene, and other situations. As different people expressed their interpretation of what was taking place, they should have also been giving the reasons or evidence that supported their interpretations. Think back on your interpretations of these pictures—why did *you* arrive at these perceptions? When we understand the reasons that support the various interpretations of a situation, we are bringing our perception of the situation into much sharper focus.

Looking for reasons that support various perceptions also involves trying to discover any independent proof or evidence regarding the perception. When evidence is available in the form of records, photographs, videotapes, or experimental results, this will certainly help us evaluate the accuracy of our perceptions. For example, consider the situation we mentioned before:

> You are asked to estimate the size of an audience attending an event that your organization has sponsored. How many people are there?

What are some of the independent forms of evidence you could look for in trying to verify your perception?

1. _____

2. _____

3. _____

Thinking critically about our perceptions means trying to avoid developing impulsive or superficial perceptions that we are unwilling to change. As we saw in Chapter Three, a critical thinker is *thoughtful* in approaching the world and *open* to modifying his or her views in the light of new information or better insight. Consider the following perceptions:

> Women are very emotional; men are very stubborn.
>
> Politicians are corrupt.
>
> Teen-agers are wild and irresponsible.

Movie stars are self-centered.

People who are good athletes are usually poor students.

These types of general perceptions are known as *stereotypes* because they express a belief about an entire group of people without recognizing the individual differences betweeen members of the group. For instance, it is probably accurate to say that there are *some* politicians who are corrupt, but this is not the same thing as saying that all, or even most, politicians are corrupt. Stereotypes affect our perception of the world because they encourage us to form an inaccurate and superficial idea of a whole group of people (''All cops are brutal''). When we meet someone who falls into this group, we automatically perceive that person as having these stereotyped qualities (''This person is a cop and so he's brutal''). Even if we find that this person does not fit our stereotyped perception (''This cop is not brutal''), this sort of superficial and unthoughtful labeling does not encourage us to change our perception of the group as a whole. Instead, it encourages us to overlook the conflicting information in favor of our stereotyped perception (''All cops are brutal—except for this one''). On the other hand, when we are perceiving in a thoughtful fashion, we try to see what a person is like as an individual, instead of trying to fit him or her into a preexisting category.

Finally, we think critically about our perceptions by examining all the evidence that is available and then considering whether our interpretation of what we are experiencing is consistent with other things we know about the world. For example, we might attend a magic show and see the magician raise —''levitate''—a person off a table with no visible support. Our perception may be supported by the following evidence:

Everyone in the audience agrees about the perception.

The magician repeats the trick over and over.

The magician appeals to different senses (for example, someone from the audience may be asked to pass a hoop over the person).

Yet despite all this support, we still might not believe in the accuracy of what we are perceiving. Why not? Because this perception is *not consistent* with what we know and understand about how the world operates. We believe that our eyes are deceiving us because what we are perceiving contradicts other strongly rooted beliefs about the world.

The greater our knowledge and understanding of the world, the better able we are to evaluate our perceptions and to arrive at informed opinions. A well-developed understanding enables us to closely examine, question, and analyze the context in which the perception is occurring. For example, we know that the role of the magician is to fool us, and so we can concentrate on the question: "What are some alternative explanations for the trick?" In other words, "How did he do it?"

As our minds develop through the experiences we have and our reflection on these experiences, our perceptions of the world should continue to develop as well. By thinking critically about our perceptions, by seeking to view our world from perspectives other than our own and to understand the reasons that support these perspectives, our understanding of the world should become increasingly accurate and complete. We can view our efforts to think critically about what we are perceiving as a problem-solving process, as we attempt to continually arrive at interpretations that enable us to make sense of what we are experiencing. But these interpretations are not permanent. As we learn more about our experience and our own spectacles through which we are actively perceiving this experience, our interpretations should continue to develop in ways that reflect our increased understanding.

---

 Each of the following situations involves critically evaluating perceptions to make sense of what is going on. For each example,

1.  Describe what your immediate perception of the situation might be.
2.  Describe how you could critically examine what you are perceiving in order to insure that your perception is as accurate and complete as possible. As you do this, keep in mind the various ways to critically evaluate our perceptions that we explored.
    a.  Being willing to question our perceptions.
    b.  Becoming aware of the personal factors we bring to our perceptions.
    c.  Seeing other possible perceptions through discussions with others and trying to imagine other viewpoints.
    d.  Identifying the reasons and evidence that supports the various perceptions involved.
    e.  Being thoughtful in examining our perceptions, and willing to change or modify them in light of new information or improved insight.
    f.  Considering whether our perception is consistent with other things we know about the world.

1.  Down the block you see what appears to be your boyfriend or girlfriend getting into a car with an attractive member of the opposite sex.
    a.  What is your immediate perception of what is taking place?
    b.  What methods could you use to examine critically your perception?

2.   Late one night you see what appears to be a flying saucer moving across the sky.

   a.   What is your immediate perception of what is taking place?

   b.   What methods could you use to critically examine your perception?

3.   While attending a religious service, you observe a faith healer apparently miraculously curing a man sitting in a wheelchair.

   a.   What is your immediate perception of what is taking place?

   b.   What methods could you use to critically examine your perception?

4.   You are asked to serve as a judge in a talent show in which your best friend is an entrant. After the performances, you believe that your friend deserves first place.

   a.   What methods could you use to critically examine your perception?

5.   One of your teachers seems to call on you much more than on other members of the class.

   a.   What is your immediate perception of what is taking place?

   b.   What methods could you use to critically examine your perception?

6.   During an interview for a job, you are asked the following questions:

   a.   What is your greatest strength?

   b.   What is your greatest weakness?

   After answering these questions, describe what methods you could use to critically evaluate your perceptions.

7.   A popular commercial on television indicates that if you purchase a certain brand of designer fashions then people will admire you and be attracted to you.

   a.   What is your immediate perception of the situation?

   b.   What methods could you use to critically examine your perception?

8.   Describe how two members of your family perceive you.

   a.   How do these perceptions compare with how you perceive yourself?

   b.   What methods could you use to critically examine each of these perceptions?

As we think critically about our perceptions, we learn more about how we make sense of the world. Our perceptions may be strengthened by this understanding, or they may be changed by this understanding. In the following narrative, Robert Acuna describes changes in his perceptions of his world. This selection is taken from the book *Working: People Talk About What They Do All Day and How They Feel About What They Do* by Studs Terkel. Terkel traveled all around America interviewing people from a wide range of occupations, from farmers and steelworkers to corporate executives and prostitutes. In his narrative, Roberto Acuna describes how he became an organizer for the United Farm Workers of America. Consider the following questions before and during your reading.

1.   What did you know about migrant farm labor before reading this narrative?
2.   What did you learn about migrant farm labor from reading this narrative?
3.   What details does Acuna recount about his childhood?
4.   How does Acuna get out of the fields? Why does he leave?
5.   When did Acuna have a change in his perception? What caused this change? What does he now "see"?
6.   At the beginning of his narrative, Acuna says "The things I saw shaped my life." After reading his story, what do you think this statement means? Did "things" shape Acuna's life? Or, did Acuna shape and reshape the "things I saw" into his life?

## Roberto Acuna

I walked out of the fields two years ago. I saw the need to change the California feudal system, to change the lives of farm workers, to make these huge corporations feel they're not above anybody. I am thirty-four years old and I try to organize for the United Farm Workers of America.

*His hands are calloused and each of his thumbnails is singularly cut. "If you're picking lettuce, the thumbnails fall off 'cause they're banged on the box. Your hands get swollen. You can't slow down because the foreman sees you're so many boxes behind and you'd better get on. But people would help each other. If you're feeling bad that day, somebody who's feeling pretty good would help. Any people that are suffering have to stick together, whether they like it or not, whether they be black, brown, or pink."*

According to Mom, I was born on a cotton sack out in the fields, 'cause she had no money to go to the hospital. When I was a child, we used to migrate from California to Arizona and back and forth. The things I saw shaped my life. I remember when we used to go out and pick carrots and onions, the whole family. We tried to scratch a livin' out of the ground. I saw my parents cry out in despair, even though we had the whole family working. At the time, they were paying sixty-two and a half cents an hour. The average income must have been fifteen hundred dollars, maybe two thousand.*

---

*"Today, because of our struggles, the pay is up to two dollars an hour. Yet we know that is not enough."

This was supplemented by child labor. During those years, the growers used to have a Pick-Your-Harvest Week. They would get all the migrant kids out of school and have 'em out there pickin' the crops at peak harvest time. A child was off that week and when he went back to school, he got a little gold star. They would make it seem like something civic to do.

We'd pick everything: lettuce, carrots, onions, cucumbers, cauliflower, broccoli, tomatoes—all the salads you could make out of vegetables, we picked 'em. Citrus fruits, watermelons—you name it. We'd be in Salinas about four months. From there we'd go down into the Imperial Valley. From there we'd go to picking citrus. It was like a cycle. We'd follow the seasons.

After my dad died, my mom would come home and she'd go into her tent and I would go into ours. We'd roughhouse and everything and then we'd go into the tent where Mom was sleeping and I'd see her crying. When I asked her why she was crying she never gave me an answer. All she said was things would get better. She retired a beaten old lady with a lot of dignity. That day she thought would be better never came for her.

*"One time, my mom was in bad need of money, so she got a part-time evening job in a restaurant. I'd be helping her. All the growers would come in and they'd be laughing, making nasty remarks, and make passes at her. I used to go out there and kick 'em and my mom told me to leave 'em alone, she could handle 'em. But they would embarrass her and she would cry.*

*"My mom was a very proud woman. She brought us up without any help from nobody. She kept the family strong. They say that a family that prays together stays together. I say that a family that works together stays together—because of the suffering. My mom couldn't speak English too good. Or much Spanish, for that matter. She wasn't educated. But she knew some prayers and she used to make us say them. That's another thing: when I see the many things in this world and this country, I could tear the churches apart. I never saw a priest out in the fields trying to help people. Maybe in these later years they're doing it. But it's always the church taking from the people.*

*"We were once asked by the church to bring vegetables to make it a successful bazaar. After we got the stuff there, the only people havin' a good time were the rich people because they were the only ones that were buyin' the stuff. . ."*

I'd go barefoot to school. The bad thing was they used to laugh at us, the Anglo kids. They would laugh because we'd bring tortillas and frijoles to lunch. They would have their nice little compact lunch boxes with cold milk in their thermos and they'd laugh at us because all we had was dried tortillas. Not only would they laugh at us, but the kids would pick fights. My older brother used to do most of the fighting for us and he'd come home with black eyes all the time.

What really hurt is when we had to go on welfare. Nobody knows the erosion of man's dignity. They used to have a label of canned goods that said, "U.S.

Commodities. Not to be sold or exchanged.'' Nobody knows how proud it is to feel when you bought canned goods with your own money.

*"I wanted to be accepted. It must have been in sixth grade. It was just before the Fourth of July. They were trying out students for this patriotic play. I wanted to do Abe Lincoln, so I learned the Gettysburg Address inside and out. I'd be out in the fields pickin' the crops and I'd be memorizin'. I was the only one who didn't have to read the part, 'cause I learned it. The part was given to a girl who was a grower's daughter. She had to read it out of a book, but they said she had better diction. I was very disappointed. I quit about eighth grade.*

*"Any time anybody'd talk to me about politics, about civil rights, I would ignore it. It's a very degrading thing because you can't express yourself. They wanted us to speak English in the school classes. We'd put out a real effort. I would get into a lot of fights because I spoke Spanish and they couldn't understand it. I was punished. I was kept after school for not speaking English."*

We used to have our own tents on the truck. Most migrants would live in the tents that were already there in the fields, put up by the company. We got one for ourselves, secondhand, but it was ours. Anglos used to laugh at us. "Here comes the carnival," they'd say. We couldn't keep our clothes clean, we couldn't keep nothing clean, because we'd go by the dirt roads and the dust. We'd stay outside the town.

I never did want to go to town because it was a very bad thing for me. We used to go to the small stores, even though we got clipped more. If we went to the other stores, they would laugh at us. They would always point at us with a finger. We'd go to town maybe every two weeks to get what we needed. Everybody would walk in a bunch. We were afraid. (Laughs.) We sang to keep our spirits up. We joked about our poverty. This one guy would say, "When I get to be rich, I'm gonna marry an Anglo woman, so I can be accepted into society." The other guy would say, "When I get rich I'm gonna marry a Mexican woman, so I can go to that Anglo society of yours and see them hang you for marrying an Anglo." Our world was around the fields.

I started picking crops when I was eight. I couldn't do much, but every little bit counts. Every time I would get behind on my chores, I would get a carrot thrown at me by my parents. I would daydream: If I were a millionaire, I would buy all these ranches and give them back to the people. I would picture my mom living in one area all the time and being admired by all the people in the community. All of a sudden I'd be rudely awaken by a broken carrot in my back. That would bust your whole dream apart and you'd work for a while and come back to daydreaming.

We used to work early, about four o'clock in the morning. We'd pick the harvest until about six. Then we'd run home and get into our supposedly clean clothes and run all the way to school because we'd be late. By the time we got to school, we'd be all tuckered out. Around maybe eleven o'clock, we'd be dozing off. Our teachers would send notes to the house telling Mom that we were inattentive. The only thing I'd make fairly good grades on was spelling. I couldn't do anything else. Many times we never did our homework, because we were out in the fields. The teachers couldn't understand that. I would get whacked there also.

School would end maybe four o'clock. We'd rush home again, change clothes, go back to work until seven, seven thirty at night. That's not counting the weekends. On Saturday and Sunday, we'd be there from four thirty in the morning until about seven thirty in the evening. This is where we made the money, those two days. We all worked.

I would carry boxes for my mom to pack the carrots in. I would pull the carrots out and she would sort them into different sizes. I would get water for her to drink. When you're picking tomatoes, the boxes are heavy. They weigh about thirty pounds. They're dropped very hard on the trucks so they have to be sturdy.

The hardest work would be thinning and hoeing with a short-handled hoe. The fields would be about a half a mile long. You would be bending and stooping all day. Sometimes you would have hard ground and by the time you got home, your hands would be full of calluses. And you'd have a backache. Sometimes I wouldn't have dinner or anything. I'd just go home and fall asleep and wake up just in time to go out to the fields again.

I remember when we just got into California from Arizona to pick up the carrot harvest. It was very cold and very windy out in the fields. We just had a little old blanket for the four of us kids in the tent. We were freezin' our tail off. So I stole two brand-new blankets that belonged to a grower. When we got under those blankets it was nice and comfortable. Somebody saw me. The next morning the grower told my mom he'd turn us in unless we gave him back his blankets—sterilized. So my mom and I and my kid brother went to the river and cut some wood and made a fire and boiled the water and she scrubbed the blankets. She hung them out to dry, ironed them, and sent them back to the grower. We got a spanking for that.

I remember this labor camp that was run by the city. It was a POW camp for German soldiers. They put families in there and it would have barbed wire all around it. If you were out after ten o'clock at night, you couldn't get back in until the next day at four in the morning. We didn't know the rules. Nobody told us. We went to visit some relatives. We got back at about ten thirty and they wouldn't let us in. So we slept in the pickup outside the gate. In the morning, they let us in, we had a fast breakfast and went back to work in the fields.*

---

*"Since we started organizing, this camp has been destroyed. They started building housing on it."

The grower would keep the families apart, hoping they'd fight against each other. He'd have three or four camps and he'd have the people over here pitted against the people over there. For jobs. He'd give the best crops to the people he thought were the fastest workers. This way he kept us going harder and harder, competing.

When I was sixteen, I had my first taste as a foreman. Handling braceros, aliens, that came from Mexico to work. They'd bring these people to work over here and then send them back to Mexico after the season was over. My job was to make sure they did a good job and pushin' 'em even harder. I was a company man, yes. My parents needed money and I wanted to make sure they were proud of me. A foreman is recognized. I was very naïve. Even though I was pushing the workers, I knew their problems. They didn't know how to write, so I would write letters home for them. I would take 'em to town, buy their clothes, outside of the company stores. They had paid me $1.10 an hour. The farm workers' wage was raised to eighty-two and a half cents. But even the braceros were making more money than me, because they were working piece-work. I asked for more money. The manager said, "If you don't like it you can quit." I quit and joined the Marine Corps.

*"I joined the Marine Corps at seventeen. I was very mixed up. I wanted to become a first-class citizen. I wanted to be accepted and I was very proud of my uniform. My mom didn't want to sign the papers, but she knew I had to better myself and maybe I'd get an education in the services.*

*"I did many jobs. I took a civil service exam and was very proud when I passed. Most of the others were college kids. There were only three Chicanos in the group of sixty. I got a job as a correctional officer in a state prison. I quit after eight months because I couldn't take the misery I saw. They wanted me to use a rubber hose on some of the prisoners—mostly Chicanos and blacks. I couldn't do it. They called me chicken-livered because I didn't want to hit nobody. They constantly harassed me after that. I didn't quit because I was afraid of them but because they were trying to make me into a mean man. I couldn't see it. This was Soledad State Prison."*

I began to see how everything was so wrong. When growers can have an intricate watering system to irrigate their crops but they can't have running water inside the houses of workers. Veterinarians tend to the needs of domestic animals but they can't have medical care for the workers. They can have land subsidies for the growers but they can't have adequate unemployment compensation for the workers. They treat him like a farm implement. In fact, they treat their implements better and their domestic animals better. They have heat and insulated barns for the animals but the workers live in beat-up shacks with no heat at all.

Illness in the fields is 120 percent higher than the average rate for industry. It's mostly back trouble, rheumatism and arthritis, because the damp weather and the cold. Stoop labor is very hard on a person. Tuberculosis is high. And now because of the pesticides, we have many respiratory diseases.

The University of California at Davis has government experiments with pesticides and chemicals. To get a bigger crop each year. They haven't any regard as to what safety precautions are needed. In 1964 or '65, an airplane was spraying these chemicals on the fields. Spraying rigs they're called. Flying low, the wheels got tangled on the fence wire. The pilot got up, dusted himself off, and got a drink of water. He died of convulsions. The ambulance attendants got violently sick because of the pesticides he had on his person. A little girl was playing around a sprayer. She stuck her tongue on it. She died instantly.

These pesticides affect the farm worker through the lungs. He breathes it in. He gets no compensation. All they do is say he's sick. They don't investigate the cause.

There were times when I felt I couldn't take it any more. It was 105 in the shade and I'd see endless rows of lettuce and I felt my back hurting . . . I felt the frustration of not being able to get out of the fields. I was getting ready to jump any foreman who looked at me cross-eyed. But until two years ago, my world was still very small.

I would read all these things in the papers about Cesar Chavez and I would denounce him because I still had that thing about becoming a first-class patriotic citizen. In Mexicali they would pass out leaflets and I would throw 'em away. I never participated. The grape boycott didn't affect me much because I was in lettuce. It wasn't until Chavez came to Salinas, where I was working in the fields, that I saw what a beautiful man he was. I went to this rally, I still intended to stay with the company. But something—I don't know—I was close to the workers. They couldn't speak English and wanted me to be their spokesman in favor of going on strike. I don't know—I just got caught up with it all, the beautiful feeling of solidarity.

You'd see the people on the picket lines at four in the morning, at the camp fires, heating up beans and coffee and tortillas. It gave me a sense of belonging. These were my own people and they wanted change. I knew this is what I was looking for. I just didn't know it before.

My mom had always wanted me to better myself. I wanted to better myself because of her. Now when the strikes started, I told her I was going to join the union and the whole movement. I told her I was going to work without pay. She said she was proud of me. (His eyes glisten. A long, long pause.) See, I told her I wanted to be with my people. If I were a company man, nobody would like me any more. I had to belong to somebody and this was it right here. She said, "I pushed you in your early years to try to better yourself and get a social position. But I see that's not the answer. I know I'll be proud of you."

All kinds of people are farm workers, not just Chicanos. Filipinos started the strike. We have Puerto Ricans and Appalachians too, Arabs, some Japanese, some Chinese. At one time they used us against each other. But now they can't and they're scared, the growers. They can organize conglomerates. Yet when we try organization to better our lives, they are afraid. Suffering people never dreamed it could be different. Cesar Chavez tells them this and they grasp the idea—and this is what scares the growers.

Now the machines are coming in. It takes skill to operate them. But anybody can be taught. We feel migrant workers should be given the chance. They got one for grapes. They got one for lettuce. They have cotton machines that took jobs away from thousands of farm workers. The people wind up in the ghettos of the city, their culture, their families, their unity destroyed.

We're trying to stipulate it in our contract that the company will not use any machinery without the consent of the farm workers. So we can make sure the people being replaced by the machines will know how to operate the machines.

Working in the fields is not in itself a degrading job. It's hard, but if you're given regular hours, better pay, decent housing, unemployment and medical compensation, pension plans—we have a very relaxed way of living. But the growers don't recognize us as persons. That's the worst thing, the way they treat you. Like we have no brains. Now we see they have no brains. They have only a wallet in their head. The more you squeeze it, the more they cry out.

If we had proper compensation we wouldn't have to be working seventeen hours a day and following the crops. We could stay in one area and it would give us roots. Being a migrant, it tears the family apart. You get in debt. You leave the area penniless. The children are the ones hurt the most. They go to school three months in one place and then on to another. No sooner do they make friends, they are uprooted again. Right here, your childhood is taken away. So when they grow up, they're looking for this childhood they have lost.

If people could see—in the winter, ice on the fields. We'd be on our knees all day long. We'd build fires and warm up real fast and go back onto the ice. We'd be picking watermelons in 105 degrees all day long. When people have melons or cucumber or carrots or lettuce, they don't know how they got on their table and the consequences to the people who picked it. If I had enough money, I would take busloads of people out to the fields and into the labor camps. Then they'd know how that fine salad got on their table.

Describe a shaping experience that you have had in your life. Consider ➤•◄ these questions:

What was the experience?

How did it shape my life and the way that I perceive the world?

An example of a shaping experience written by another student is included in Chapter Six (p. 180).

As we have seen in this chapter, much of our knowledge of the world begins in perceiving. But to develop knowledge and understanding, we must make use of our thinking abilities in order to examine this experience critically. Increased understanding of the way the world operates thus improves the accuracy of our perceptions and leads us to informed opinions about what is happening. In the next chapter we will be exploring further how we develop an understanding of the world by combining our perceiving with critical thinking.

# Chapter Six
# Believing & Knowing

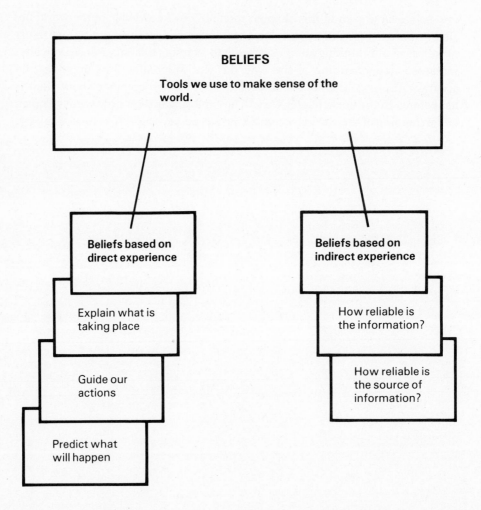

**BELIEFS**

Tools we use to make sense of the world.

**Beliefs based on direct experience**

Explain what is taking place

Guide our actions

Predict what will happen

**Beliefs based on indirect experience**

How reliable is the information?

How reliable is the source of information?

IT SEEMS TO BE a natural human impulse to try to understand the world we live in. This is the overall goal of thinking, which we have defined as the process by which we make sense of the world. As we saw in the last chapter, perceiving is an important part of this process of making sense because it is the way we actively select, organize, and interpret our sense experience. Another crucial part of this process of making sense is the way we form beliefs that help explain how and why the world is the way it is. Consider the following statements:

|  | Yes | No | Not Sure |
|---|---|---|---|

1.  Humans must eat in order to stay alive.
2.  Smoking marijuana is a harmless good time.
3.  Every human life is valuable.
4.  Developing our mind is as important as taking care of our body.
5.  Humans should care about other people, not just themselves.

Our reactions to these statements reflect certain beliefs that we have, and these beliefs help us explain how and why the world is the way it is. In this chapter we will see that beliefs are the main tools we use to make sense of the world and to decide how we ought to behave.

## Why do we form beliefs?

In Chapter Three, "Thinking Critically," we noted that our beliefs about the world are shaped by the experiences we have had and what we have been taught. We are often not aware of our beliefs, although our beliefs are usually reflected in the decisions that we make. Becoming aware of our beliefs starts when we begin to question our experience. In the first chapter we explored the idea that thinking is an activity that enables us to make sense of our world by solving problems, working toward our goals, comprehending information, and understanding others. In each of these cases, the purpose of our thinking is to ask questions that will guide us toward certain beliefs about what is taking place.

What is the solution to this problem?
I *believe* the solution is . . .

How can I work toward my goal?
>   I *believe* I can work toward my goal by . . .

What does this information mean?
>   I *believe* this information means . . .

What is this person like?
>   I *believe* this person is . . .

Once we develop beliefs that inform us of what is taking place (or what we believe *will* take place), we are in a position to decide what we ought to do. This is one of the main functions of beliefs—to guide our actions.

---

➤•◀      Describe how each of your beliefs that you identified on page 179 may have influenced your actions today.

## How do we form beliefs?

As we attempt to make sense of the world, our thinking abilities give us the means to

1.  ask questions about our experience.
2.  work toward forming beliefs that will enable us to answer these questions and make useful decisions.

When we ask questions, it means that we are not simply content to take things for granted. Asking questions encourages us to try and form more accurate beliefs to explain what is taking place. By questioning our experience, we are better able to understand the situation we are in and to take effective control.

Let us explore how these activities of asking questions and forming beliefs enable us to make sense of our world. Read carefully the following passage, in which a student, whom we will call Maria, describes her experiences with the "system."

### A Shaping Experience

A few years ago my oldest son went to a party. On his way home (about 11 p.m.) he was accosted by three individuals who tried to take his belongings. Seeing guns, my son's first reaction was to run away, which he did. While running he was shot. His wounds left him paralyzed from his neck down. As he lay in the intensive care unit of the hospital, I started to receive threatening phone calls telling us that "if we identify them to the police, they will finish the work."

At this time I reported the phone calls to both the police
and the telephone company. I was irritated by the way the police
handled the whole situation. I was told that there was no reason
why the city should pay for having a police officer protect my
son and was asked what he was doing in the streets at this time.
(The time was 11 p.m., and the age of my son at the time was almost eighteen.) Finally I was told there was nothing that could
be done. In my anger, I called the mayor's office, the senator's
office, and the councilman. Also, I immediately wrote a letter to
the police commissioner regarding the whole situation and mailed
it special delivery, registered, for proof in case the matter became worse. In less than a few hours, there was an officer at my
son's bedside making sure that nothing further happened to him.

I learned that, although there are many laws to protect citizens, if citizens don't fight for their rights these laws will
never be exercised. My opinion of the "system" changed after this
experience. I believe that I shouldn't have had to go through so
much red tape in order to have my legal rights. I feel that, if
you don't take a stand, there is no one who will go out of the
way to instruct you or to help out. I was never informed at the
police headquarters about what to do and how to go about doing
it. I was left standing without any hope at all. I feel sorry for
those persons who are ignorant about how you can make the system
work for you.

Throughout this experience, it was Maria's beliefs that shaped her perceptions of what was occurring and influenced her decisions. Before her son got
shot, she had formed certain beliefs about the law, the police, and the legal system as a whole. What were these initial beliefs?

1. Initial beliefs about the situation
   a. What were Maria's initial beliefs about *the law?*
      The law exists to protect the citizens.
   b. What were her initial beliefs about *the police?*

      _____

   c. What were her initial beliefs about *the system?*

      _____

After her son was shot, Maria tried to make sense of the situation in terms
of the beliefs that she brought to the situation and then acted on the basis of
these beliefs. What actions did she take once she received phone calls
threatening to "finish the work" if she identified the culprits to the police?

2. Actions based on her initial beliefs

    a. _____

    _____

    b. _____

    _____

Once she took these actions, Maria began to discover that the beliefs she had initially thought to be true did not seem to be working very well in terms of explaining what was happening. Her experiences with the police department forced her to have doubts and ask questions about her beliefs concerning the law, the police, and the system. What were the police's reactions to Maria's request that her son be protected from further harm?

3. Experiences that raised doubts and questions about her initial beliefs

    a. _____

    _____

    b. _____

    _____

    c. _____

    _____

As Maria came to doubt the accuracy of her initial beliefs, she began to form new beliefs to explain what was happening in this situation. What were the new beliefs she formed about the law, the police, and the system?

4. Revised beliefs that she formed about the situation

    a. What were Maria's revised beliefs about *the law?*

    _____

    _____

    b. What were her revised beliefs about *the police?*

    _____

    _____

    c. What were her revised beliefs about *the system?*

    _____

    _____

As Maria took actions based on her revised beliefs, she was naturally anxious to discover whether these actions would lead to more satisfactory results than those produced by her initial beliefs. What responses did she receive to these actions?

5.  Responses to actions based on her revised beliefs

    a. _____

       _____

    b. _____

       _____

The responses that Maria received seemed to support the revised beliefs that she had formed about the law, the police, and the system. These revised beliefs helped her to understand and control the situation in a way that her initial beliefs had not, leading her to the conclusion that

> I learned that, although there are many laws to protect citizens, if citizens don't fight for their rights these laws will never be exercised.

After reflecting critically on her experiences, Maria was convinced that the revised beliefs that she had formed to explain her situation and guide her actions were more accurate than her initial beliefs. As a result, she advises us that, when we find ourselves in similiar circumstances, we should "take a stand" and "make the system work" for us. In giving us this advice, Maria is using her newly formed beliefs to predict what will happen in similar encounters with the system.

Maria's story illustrates the process by which we form and re-form our beliefs, a process that often follows this sequence of steps:

1.  We *form* beliefs to explain what is taking place.
2.  We *test* these beliefs by acting on the basis of them.
3.  We *revise* (or re-form) these beliefs if our actions do not result in our desired goals.
4.  We *retest* these revised beliefs by acting on the basis of them.

As we actively participate in this ongoing process of forming and reforming beliefs, we are using our critical thinking abilities to identify our beliefs and to examine them critically by asking the following questions:

> How effectively do our beliefs *explain* what is taking place?
>
> How effectively do our beliefs *guide our actions* so that we can reach our desired goals?

How effectively do our beliefs help us *predict* what will happen in similiar situations that occur in the future?

This process of critical exploration enables us to develop a greater understanding of various situations in our experience, as well as giving us the means to exert more effective control in these situations. Let us examine another example illustrating this belief-forming process at work.

In Chapter Five, we read a narrative by Roberto Acuna, a migrant worker who became a union organizer for the United Farm Workers of America. His story also illustrates the way we form and re-form beliefs as an ongoing process. Like Maria's story, we find in Roberto's description of his life how his beliefs changed and reshaped his perceptions of what he had experienced and was experiencing and then influenced his decisions.

Reread the narrative by Roberto Acuna (pp. 170–176). What were Roberto's initial beliefs regarding his situation?

1. Initial beliefs about his situation

   a. What were Roberto's initial beliefs about being a *migrant worker?*

      He felt that this was a miserable and demeaning life from which he wanted to escape.

   b. What were his initial beliefs about his *future goals?*

      _____

      _____

   c. What were his initial beliefs about *the growers?*

      _____

      _____

   d. What were his initial beliefs about his *fellow migrant workers?*

      _____

      _____

In Maria's essay, she reveals her initial beliefs about the law, the police, and the system, but she does not have an opportunity to explain how she formed these beliefs. In contrast, Roberto states that "The things I saw shaped my life." What were the experiences that shaped his initial beliefs?

2. Experiences that shaped his initial beliefs

   a. What experiences shaped his initial beliefs about being a *migrant worker?*

      _____

      _____

b. What experiences shaped his initial beliefs about *the growers?*

_____

_____

c. What experiences shaped his initial beliefs about his *future goals?*

_____

_____

Just like Maria, Roberto tried to make sense of his situation in terms of the beliefs that he brought to the situation and then acted on the basis of these beliefs. What actions did Roberto take based on the beliefs that he had formed about the world?

3. Actions taken based on his initial beliefs

a. Roberto became a foreman, working for the growers.

b. _____

c. _____

After taking these actions, Roberto began to find out that the beliefs about his life and his goals that he had initially thought to be true did not seem to be working effectively in explaining his experience. He states that "I began to see how everything was so wrong." Explain how the following experiences influenced him to raise doubts and ask questions about his initial beliefs.

4. Experiences that raised doubts and questions about his initial beliefs

a. How did *becoming a foreman* raise doubts about his initial beliefs?

_____

_____

b. How did *becoming a prison guard* raise doubts about his initial beliefs?

_____

_____

c. How did *meeting Cesar Chavez* raise doubts about his initial beliefs?

_____

_____

As Roberto questioned the accuracy of his initial beliefs, he began to form revised beliefs to make sense of his life and who he wanted to become. Describe the new beliefs that he formed as a result of having these experiences and thinking critically about them.

5. Revised beliefs that he formed about the situation

    a. What were Roberto's revised beliefs about being a *migrant worker?*
"Working in the fields is not in itself a degrading job. It's hard, but if you're given regular hours, better pay, decent housing, unemployment and medical compensation, pension plans—we have a very relaxed way of living."

    b. What were Roberto's revised beliefs about his *future goals?*

_____

_____

_____

_____

    c. What were Roberto's revised beliefs about *the growers?*

_____

_____

_____

_____

    d. What were Roberto's revised beliefs about his relationship toward his *fellow migrant workers?*

_____

_____

_____

_____

After reflecting critically on his experiences, Roberto changed the course of his life and became a union organizer for the United Farm Workers of America. As we saw with Maria, this process of forming and re-forming beliefs based on his experiences resulted in a new and clearer understanding of his life. In the case of Maria, she began with an unexamined faith in the system and how it operates and ended with a much more realistic view of how you have to make the system work for you.

For Roberto, the process of coming to a new awareness based on a critical examination of his beliefs was more complex. As a migrant worker, he was an oppressed member of a system that dominated and exploited him. He tried to escape from this domination while staying within the system by becoming a foreman, a Marine, and a prison guard. His goal was to become socially accepted, "a first-class citizen." However, his experiences conflicted with this belief in social acceptability. As a foreman, he found that "My job was to make sure they did a good job and pushin' 'em even harder. I was a company man, yes." While he was working as a prison guard, he explains, "I quit after eight months because I couldn't take the misery I saw. They wanted me to use a rubber hose on some of the prisoners—mostly Chicanos and blacks."

These experiences and his reflection on them brought him to the awareness that he was becoming a part of the system of oppression that he himself had suffered under and that he despised for its inhuman treatment of people. His encounter with Cesar Chavez led him to the deeper understanding that, instead of trying to become part of the system, he should try to change it. While acting as a spokesperson for striking workers, he says, "I don't know—I just got caught up with it all, the beautiful feeling of solidarity. . . . It gave me a sense of belonging. These were my own people and they wanted change. I knew this is what I was looking for. I just didn't know it before."

Both Maria's and Roberto's stories illustrate the main purpose of our ongoing attempts to form and re-form beliefs about ourselves and our experience. By engaging in this process, we are continually trying to develop a clearer understanding of what is taking place so that we can make the most effective decisions in our lives.

---

Let's explore an example of the way we form and re-form beliefs by ►•◄ analyzing the essay that you wrote at the end of Chapter Five (p. 177) in which you described a shaping experience in your life. Think through your essay by answering the following questions.

1. *Your initial beliefs about the situation:* As you began the experience described in your essay, you brought into the situation certain beliefs about the experience and the people involved. Identify the most important beliefs you began with.

   a. _____

   b. _____

   c. _____

2. *Experiences that shaped your initial beliefs:* The beliefs that you brought to the situation were probably shaped by previous experiences you had undergone. Can you identify some of the influences that helped shape these beliefs?

a. _____

b. _____

c. _____

3. *Actions based on your initial beliefs:* The beliefs that you just identified formed the basis for the initial actions you decided to take (or planned to take). Describe the actions based on your initial beliefs that you either took or thought about taking.

a. _____

b. _____

c. _____

4. *Experiences that raised doubts and questions* about your initial beliefs: As you became involved in the situation that you described, it is likely that something occurred to raise doubts concerning the accuracy or completeness of your beliefs about the situation. Describe what elements in the situation influenced you to begin thinking about the experience in a different way.

a. _____

_____

b. _____

_____

c. _____

5. *Revised beliefs that you formed about the situation:* The experiences that raised doubts about your initial understanding of the experience probably started you thinking about new ways to view the situation that would better explain what was taking place. Identify these revised beliefs that you began to form about the experience.

a. _____

b. _____

c. _____

6. *Actions based on your revised beliefs:* As your revised beliefs about what was occurring began to take shape, this new understanding quite likely suggested decisions and courses of action that were different from those you planned at the beginning of the situation. Describe what steps you decided to take based on your re-formed beliefs.

a. _____

_____

b. _____
_____

c. _____
_____

7. *Responses to actions based on your revised beliefs:* After making these decisions and taking these actions, you probably examined carefully your experience to see whether these revised beliefs would be able to explain the situation in a more satisfactory way. Describe the results of your revised decisions.

_____

_____

_____

_____

Did these results lead you to predict what would happen in future situations that might be similar to this one? Explain why or why not.

_____

_____

_____

_____

8. *Critical reflection on this experience:* Describe how your critical reflection on this shaping experience developed your awareness of yourself and your world.

_____

_____

_____

_____

## Believing and perceiving

The experiences described by Maria, Roberto Acuna, and yourself underscore the fact that much of our understanding about the world begins with our perceptions. Roberto states that "The things I saw shaped my life," and by this he means that the things he saw and experienced growing up shaped his initial beliefs about the world. What he perceived, in other words, influenced what he came to believe.

However, although our perceptions influence our beliefs, they do not by themselves cause us to believe. What we come to believe results from the combination of what we are perceiving with how we *think* about what we are perceiving. Roberto experienced a great deal of hardship growing up, but it was his thinking that influenced him to form the belief that he was being treated as a second-class citizen and to seek to escape from the system. These beliefs formed part of the spectacles through which he perceived the world. As we saw in Chapter Five, perceiving is an active process, and Roberto's beliefs influenced the way he actively selected, organized, and interpreted his perceptions of the world.

Yet our beliefs do not stand still, as Maria's and Roberto's experiences remind us. We continue to form and re-form our beliefs, based in part on what we are experiencing and how we think about what we are experiencing. When Roberto was working as a foreman and later as a prison guard, his experiences influenced him to *change* the way he was actively perceiving his world. He states, "I began to see how everything was so wrong," and instead of simply trying to escape from the system, he begins to think about trying to change it.

When he began working with the striking workers, his beliefs—and his perceptions—continued to develop. Before this experience, he had seen himself as an individual seeking to escape from the oppression of the system. However, working with the strikers stimulated a different perception of himself—a perception of himself as a member of a community working for common purposes. He explains this shift of perspective: "You'd see the people on the picket lines at four in the morning, at the campfires, heating up beans and coffee and tortillas. It gave me a sense of belonging. These were my own people and they wanted change. I knew this is what I was looking for. I just didn't know it before."

What this situation suggests is that perceiving and believing are two aspects of the way we make sense of the world that continually influence each other.

What we believe influences what we perceive.

What we perceive influences what we believe.

---

➤•◄      Let us examine how this mutual relation between perceiving and believing was at work in the shaping experience that you described (p. 177).

1. Describe how you initially perceived the situation, based on the beliefs that you brought to the situation.

2.  Describe what experiences influenced you to change these beliefs.

3.  Describe how changing these beliefs resulted in you perceiving the situation in a different way.

The process of forming and re-forming beliefs for the purpose of explaining our experience in increasingly effective ways enables us to exert more control over what we actively perceive. And by increasing our understanding and awareness, we are able to become more active shapers of our lives, both in terms of the beliefs we form about the world and the way we actively perceive our world as a result of these beliefs.

## Believing and knowing

We have been seeing that beliefs are a main tool we have to explain how and why the world is the way it is and to guide us in making effective decisions. As we form and re-form our beliefs, based on our experiences and our thinking about these experiences, we are usually trying to develop beliefs that are as accurate as possible. As we found in exploring the experiences of Maria and Roberto Acuna, the more accurate our beliefs are, the better able we are to understand what is taking place and to predict what will occur in the future.

The beliefs we form vary tremendously in terms of their accuracy. For example, how accurate do you think the following beliefs are?

1.  I believe that there is a very large man who lives on the moon.

2.  I believe that there is life on other planets.

3.  I believe that a college education will lead me to a satisfying and well-paying job.

4.  I believe that there is life on this planet.

In considering these beliefs, you probably came to the conclusion that

belief 1 was not accurate at all.

belief 2 was possible but far from being certain.

belief 3 was likely but not guaranteed to be accurate.

belief 4 was definitely accurate.

The idea of *knowing* is one of the ways that humans have developed to distinguish beliefs that are supported by strong reasons or evidence (such as belief 4) from beliefs for which there is less support (such as beliefs 2 and 3) or from beliefs disproved by reasons or evidence to the contrary (such as belief 1). In the statements above, let us try replacing the word *believe* with the word *know*.

1. I *know* that there is a very large man who lives on the moon.
2. I *know* that there is life on other planets.
3. I *know* that a college education will lead me to a satisfying and well-paying job.
4. I *know* that there is life on this planet.

The only statement in which it seems to make sense to use the word *know* is the fourth one because we have conclusive evidence that this belief is accurate. In the case of sentence 1, we would say that this person is seriously mistaken. In the case of sentence 2, we might say that, although life on other planets is a possibility, there is no conclusive evidence (at present) that supports this view. In the case of sentence 3, we might say that, although for many people a college education leads to a satisfying and well-paying job, this is not always the case. As a result, we can not say that we *know* that this belief (or belief 2) is accurate. Another way of expressing the difference between "believing" and "knowing" is by means of the following saying:

You can *believe* what isn't so, but you can't *know* what isn't so.

---

➤ • ◄       For each of the following beliefs, state whether you think that the belief is

1. *completely accurate* (so that you would say, "I know this is the case").
2. *generally accurate,* but not completely accurate (so that you would say, "This is often, but not always, the case").
3. *generally not accurate,* but sometimes accurate (so that you would say, "This is usually *not* the case, but is sometimes true").
4. *definitely not accurate* (so that you would say, "I know that this is *not* the case").

After determining the *degree of accuracy* in this way, explain *why* you have selected your answer.

>   *Example:*  I believe that if you study hard that you will achieve good grades.

>   *Degree of accuracy:*  Generally, but not completely, accurate.

>   *Explanation:*  Although many people who study hard achieve good grades, this is not always true. Sometimes people have difficulty understanding the work, no matter how hard they study. And sometimes they just don't know *how* to study effectively.

1.  I believe that essay exams are more difficult than multiple-choice exams.

    *Degree of accuracy:* _____

    *Explanation:* _____

    _____

    _____

    _____

2.  I believe that longer prison sentences will discourage people from commit-
    ting crimes.

    *Degree of accuracy:* _____

    *Explanation:* _____

    _____

    _____

    _____

3.  I believe that there are more people on the earth today than there were one
    hundred years ago.

    *Degree of accuracy:* _____

    *Explanation:* _____

    _____

    _____

    _____

4.  I believe that if people had been meant to fly, we would have been born
    with little propellers on our heads.

    *Degree of accuracy:* _____

    *Explanation:* _____

    _____

    _____

    _____

5.  I believe that you will never get rich by playing the lottery.

    *Degree of accuracy:* _____

    *Explanation:* _____

_____

_____

6. *Your example of a belief:* _____

_____

*Degree of accuracy:* _____

*Explanation:* _____

_____

_____

_____

7. *Your example of a belief:* _____

_____

*Degree of accuracy:* _____

*Explanation:* _____

_____

_____

_____

When someone indicates that he or she thinks a belief is completely accurate by saying, *"I know,"* our response is often *"How* do you know?" If the person cannot give us a satisfactory answer to this question, we are likely to say something like "If you can't explain how you know it, then you don't *really* know it—you're just saying it." Consider the following exchange:

I know that the teachers here don't really care about the students.
How do you know that?
I can't explain how I know it, I just do.
Then you don't really know it—you're just saying it.

In other words, when we say that "we know" something, we mean at least two different things.

1. I think this belief is completely accurate.
2. I can explain to you the reasons or evidence that supports this belief.

If either of these standards is not met, we would usually say that the person does not really "know." Think back on the exercise that you just completed (pp. 192–194). For each of the beliefs you identified as "completely accurate," were you able to give satisfactory reasons or evidence that supports this belief?

---

Review the essay written by Maria on page 180. Identify a belief that you think Maria would say that she knows to be accurate. Then describe what reasons or evidence she would support this belief with.

1. *Belief Maria knows to be accurate:* _____

   _____

   *Reasons or evidence that supports this belief:* _____

   _____

---

Review the essay written by Roberto Acuna on page 170. Identify two beliefs that you think he would say that he knows to be accurate. Then describe what reasons or evidence he would support these beliefs with.

1. *Belief Roberto Acuna knows to be accurate:* _____

   _____

   *Reasons or evidence that supports this belief:* _____

   _____

2. *Belief Roberto Acuna knows to be accurate:* _____

   _____

   *Reasons or evidence that supports this belief:* _____

   _____

---

Review the "shaping" essay that you wrote on page 177. Identify two beliefs described in the essay that you would say you know to be accurate. Then describe the reasons or evidence that you think supports these beliefs.

1. *Belief from "shaping" essay that you know to be accurate:* _____

   _____

*Reasons or evidence that supports this belief:* _____

_____

2. *Belief from "shaping" essay that you know to be accurate:* _____

_____

*Reasons or evidence that supports this belief:* _____

_____

From these explorations we can see that one way of examining our beliefs is to try to determine how accurate they are. We work at evaluating the accuracy of our beliefs by examining the reasons or evidence that supports them (known as the *justification* for the beliefs). Looked at in this way, our beliefs form a *range* as pictured below.

| Beliefs that we *know* are | Beliefs that we are *not sure* are | Beliefs that we *know* are |
|---|---|---|
| Inaccurate | Accurate | Accurate |
| Unjustified | Justified | Justified |

Just as temperature is a scale that varies from cold to hot, with many degrees in between, so our beliefs can be thought of as forming a rough scale based on their accuracy and justification. As we learn more about the world and ourselves, we try to form beliefs that are increasingly accurate and justified. As critical thinkers, we should experience an ongoing development of the beliefs in our lives as we try to make sense of the world in increasingly effective ways.

Of course, determining the accuracy and justification of our beliefs is a very challenging project. As we attempt to do so, we generally use a number of different questions to explore and evaluate our beliefs, including the following:

How well do our beliefs *explain* what is taking place?

How do these beliefs *relate to other beliefs* we have about the world?

How well do these beliefs enable us to *predict* what will happen in the future?

How well do the *reasons or evidence* support our beliefs?

How *reliable is the information* on which our beliefs are based?

We have already dealt with some of these questions, and we will explore others in the chapters ahead. The key point is that as critical thinkers we should continually try to form and re-form our beliefs to enable us to make sense of the world in increasingly effective ways. Even when we find that we are maintaining certain beliefs over a long period of time, we should discover that our explorations result in a deeper and fuller understanding of these beliefs.

# The limits of direct experience

Until now, we have been exploring the way we form and revise beliefs based on our direct experiences. Yet no matter how much we have experienced in our life, the fact is that no one person's direct experiences are enough to establish an adequate set of accurate beliefs. Each of us is only one person. We can only be in one place at one time—and with a limited amount of time at that. As a result, we depend on the direct experience of *other people* to provide us with beliefs and also to act as foundations for those beliefs. For example, does China exist? How do you know? Have you ever been there? Have you seen it with your own eyes, walked it with your own feet? Probably not, although in all likelihood you still believe in the existence of China and its 800 million inhabitants. Or consider the following questions. How would you go about explaining the reasons or evidence for your beliefs?

1. Were you really born on the day that you have been told you were?
2. Do germs really exist?
3. Do you have a brain in your head?
4. Are those really stars in the sky, or very large lightbulbs?

In all probability, your responses to these questions reveal beliefs that are based on reasons or evidence that goes beyond your direct experience. Of all the beliefs that each one of us has, very few are actually based on our direct experience. Instead, virtually *all* are founded on the experiences of others, who then communicated to us these beliefs and the evidence for them in some shape or form.

Of course, there are some people who claim that they do not really believe anything unless they have personally experienced it. They say "Seeing is believing," "The proof is in the pudding," or "Show me" (the famous slogan of the state of Missouri). However, a little critical reflection should convince us that these people are simply being unrealistic and unreasonable. It would be impossible for us to make most of the choices or decisions that we do without depending on beliefs based on the experiences and knowledge of others. For instance, if I step out into moving traffic, will I really get hurt? Do guns really kill? Do I really have to eat to survive?

As we reach beyond our personal experience to form and revise beliefs, we find that the information provided by other people is available in two basic forms:

The writings of others

The spoken testimony of others

Of course, we should not accept the beliefs of others without question. It is crucial that we use all our critical thinking abilities to examine what others suggest we believe. In critically examining the beliefs of others, we are pursuing the same goals of accuracy and completeness that we seek when examining beliefs based on our personal experience. As a result, we are interested in the reasons or evidence that supports the information others are presenting. When we ask directions from others, we try to evaluate how accurate the information is by examining the reasons or evidence that seems to support the information being given.

However, when we depend on information provided by others, there is a further question to be asked: how *reliable* is the person providing the information? For instance, what sort of people do you look for if you need to ask directions? Explain *why* you look for these particular types of people. In most cases, when we need to ask directions, we try to locate someone who we think will be reliable—in other words, a person who, we believe, will give us information that is accurate.

During the remainder of this chapter, we will be exploring the various ways we depend on others to form and revise our beliefs. In each case we will be trying to evaluate the information that is being presented by asking the following questions:

1. How reliable is the *information?*
2. How reliable is the *source* of the information?

### Forming beliefs based on written sources of information

In Chapter One we found that one of the main goals of our thinking is to make sense of information. At that time we analyzed a number of passages, including a Nissan Stanza advertisement. Let us take a closer look at the information presented in this ad by answering the questions that follow it:

> This is the new Nissan Stanza GL. A family car that seats 5 with room to spare. Room that includes luxuries like 6-speaker stereo with cassette, power windows and door locks, and plush upholstery. Now you're talking major value.
>
> And when a family sedan has Nissan technology going for it, you get even more than room and luxuries. You also get performance. Performance from a hemi-combustion engine with two spark plugs per cylinder, fed by electronic fuel-injection. Go ahead, step on it, and feel your Stanza come to life.
>
> Another nice thing about owning a Nissan Stanza, you don't have to feel guilty every time you step on the gas. Because Stanza's highly developed Nissan engine is as gas efficient as it is responsive.

So before you buy your family's next car, compare its specs to that of a new Stanza. Stanza thrives on comparison. After all, Stanza has Nissan technology behind it. And that takes it way beyond transportation; all the way to Major Motion.

1. How reliable is the information?

   a. Is the information accurate? Is there anything you believe to be false? Is there anything that you believe has been left out?

   _____

   _____

   b. What are the reasons or evidence that supports the information being offered?

   _____

   _____

2. How reliable is the source of the information?

   a. Who is the source of the information?

   _____

   b. What are the interests or purposes of the source of this information?

   _____

   c. How have the interests and purposes of the source of the information influenced

   the information selected for inclusion?

   _____

   _____

   the way this information is presented?

   _____

   _____

In trying to answer this last question, it's helpful to recall one of the key lessons we learned in Chapter Five, "Perceiving": each of us views the world through our own unique "spectacles," which influence the way we select, organize, and interpret our perceptions. When we examined the different accounts of the assassination of Malcolm X (pp. 141–143), we saw that the various reports reflected the different interests and purposes of those reporting the event. As a result, if we are to evaluate effectively the accuracy and completeness of information, we have to try to understand the "spectacles" of the people who are presenting the information. These spectacles, and the individual needs and interests that they represent, influence the information that the source has decided to include as well as the manner in which this information is presented.

Another insight we discovered in examining the various accounts of Malcom X's assassination was that our evaluation of the accuracy of the information and the reliability of each source was aided by comparing the different accounts. Since each account reflects the individual spectacles of the source, comparing different accounts helps us to identify the different interests and purposes involved. For example, examine carefully this description of the Nissan Stanza GL from *Consumer Reports*, a magazine that tests various consumer products and then reports its findings.

> *On the road*. The 2-liter Four started quickly and ran well. The 5-speed manual transmission shifted easily. This front-wheel-drive model handled very well. Excellent brakes.
>
> *Comfort and convenience*. Very comfortable individual front seats. Short on driver leg room. Comfortable rear seat for two, fairly comfortable for three. Moderate noise level. Choppy ride on poor roads, satisfactory on expressways. Excellent climate-control system, controls, displays.
>
> *Major options*. Automatic transmission, $350. Air-conditioner, $650.
>
> *Fuel economy*. Mpg with 5-speed manual transmission: city, 23; expressway, 45. Gallons used in 15,000 miles, 465. Cruising range, 485 miles.
>
> *Predicted reliability*. Much better than average.

Analyze the information being presented here by answering the following questions:

1. How reliable is the information?
   a. Is the information accurate? Is there anything you believe to be false? Is there anything that you believe has been left out?

   _____

   _____

   b. What are the reasons or evidence that supports the information being offered?

   _____

   _____

2. How reliable is the source of the information?
   a. Who is the source of the information?

   _____

   _____

b.  What are the interests or purposes of the source of this information?

_____

_____

c.  How have the interests and purposes of the source of the information influenced

the information selected for inclusion?

_____

_____

the way this information is presented?

_____

_____

Another passage that we examined in the first chapter dealt with the preservation of wildlife and natural resources. Let us review this information and then analyze it by answering the questions we have been considering:

A growing number of scientists are worried about the destruction of wildlife. The most outspoken among them seem to be the zoologists (people who study animals) who warn that continued hunting and slaughtering of wildlife will endanger humanity. Zoologists claim that people can learn much about their own lives by studying other species and that useful knowledge is lost when animals are carelessly destroyed. Perhaps even more dangerous, according to the scientists, is the way the careless destruction of wildlife disturbs the balance of nature.

1.  How reliable is the information?
    a.  Is the information accurate? Is there anything you believe to be false? Is there anything that you believe has been left out?

    _____

    _____

    b.  What are the reasons or evidence that support the information being offered?

    _____

    _____

2.  How reliable is the source of the information?
    a.  Who is the source of the information?

    _____

    _____

b. What are the interests or purposes of the source of this information?

_____

_____

c. How have the interests and purposes of the source of the information influenced

the information selected for inclusion?

_____

_____

the way this information is presented?

_____

_____

Now review the following passage, which provides a different perspective on the issue of the preservation of wildlife and natural resources. After reading the passage, analyze the information by answering the questions which follow.

People who are committed to protecting the environment often ignore economic realities. The lifestyles that people in our society—including environmentalists—have become accustomed to depend on making use of our natural resources. And if we prevent the natural growth of communities, then we will be undercutting the construction trades and depriving people of the dream of owning their own home. Finally, if we handcuff industry with restrictive environmental controls, businesses will be threatened and consumer prices will rise. Environmentalists should become more aware of the economic effects of their policies.

1. How reliable is the information?
   a. Is the information accurate?

_____

_____

   b. What are the reasons or evidence that support the information being offered?

_____

_____

2. How reliable is the source of the information?
   a. Who is the source of the information?

_____

_____

b.  What are the interests or purposes of the source of this information?

_____

_____

c.  How have the interests and purposes of the source of the information influenced

the information selected for inclusion?

_____

_____

the way this information is presented?

_____

_____

Locate two different passages for each of the following topics and then analyze each passage using the questions we have developed:

1.  Two different reviews about a movie, a play, a book, an art exhibition, or a concert.
2.  Two different passages analyzing a current event (for example, nuclear power, American foreign policy, etc.)

The information that we have reviewed and analyzed so far is the type of information that is usually presented in the general media—newspapers, magazines, television, or radio. Another important source of information is the textbooks that we read as part of our education. Since textbooks are usually written in a very authoritative style, we often forget that we should critically question and evaluate the information they are providing in the same way we examine media sources. After all, textbooks are written by human beings wearing their own individual spectacles, which shape the way they view the world. These spectacles also influence the way they present information to others.

The following passages are from two psychology textbooks. We might assume that the view of personality development that each presents is accurate. But is it? Read these two passages, and analyze each according to the questions we have developed in this chapter.

The basic assumption of Freud's theory is that much of our behavior stems from processes that are unconscious. By *unconscious processes* Freud meant thoughts, fears, and wishes a person is unaware of but which never-theless influence behavior. He believed that many of the impulses that are forbidden or punished by parents and society during childhood are derived from *innate instincts.* Because each of us is born with these impulses, they exert a pervasive influence that must be dealt with in some manner. Forbidding them merely drives them out of awareness into the unconscious, where they remain to affect behavior. According to Freud, unconscious impulses find expression in dreams, slips of speech, mannerisms, and symptoms of mental illness as well as through such socially approved behavior as artistic or literary behavior.[1]

Personality development is the name given to the gradual transformation from biological organism to biosocial person. Each child, through continual interaction with other human beings in a human environment, comes in time to feel, to think and to act fundamentally as others feel and think and act. He builds for himself a stable external world of space and time, containing persons, things and causal relations, a world that eventually corresponds to the one that the adults in his culture experience. In short, the sweeping changes in outward appearance and behavior, which continue throughout a child's growth and maturing, are paralleled by sweeping perceptual and cognitive changes within him. Every human being builds within him a stable mental organization, one that continually adapts to the external world and absorbs it, while at the same time it keeps shifting the balance of its internal forces to cope with the internal shifting needs which continually arise and to find means of satisfying them.[2]

In each of these textbook passages, the information is presented in a way that seems authoritative and factual, and it would be natural for us to conclude that the information is accurate. However, when we compare the two accounts side by side, we can see that each description of personality development is influenced by the interests and purposes of the sources of the information. Of course, it is not just psychology textbooks that demand our critical examination. We should approach *any* textbook with the same critical attitude.

 As college students, you use textbooks in many of your courses—sociology, psychology, political science, biology, composition, etc. Select a passage from one of your textbooks, one that deals with an idea key to the study of that subject. Analyze it, using the questions we have developed in this chapter. Then, in a competing textbook, find a passage that deals with the same idea; analyze it. You may find it valuable to coordinate and discuss your comparative analyses with other members of your class.

---

[1]Ernest R. Hilgard, Richard C. Atkinson, and Rita L. Atkinson, *Introduction to Psychology,* 8th ed. (Orlando, Florida: Harcourt Brace Jovanovich, 1983), p. 9.

---

[2]Norman Cameron, *Personality Development and Psychopathology* (Boston: Houghton Mifflin Co., 1963), p. 29.

## Forming beliefs based on spoken sources of information

In addition to relying on the written information of others to form our beliefs, we also make use of their spoken testimony. In order to determine the accuracy of this spoken information, we have to ask the same questions we do when we examine written information:

1. How reliable is the information?
   a. Is the information accurate?
   b. What are the reasons or evidence that support the information being offered?
2. How reliable is the source of the information?
   a. Who is the source of the information?
   b. What are the interests or purposes of the source of this information?
   c. How have the interests and purposes of the source of the information influenced

      the information selected for inclusion?

      the way this information is presented?

Consider again the example of asking a stranger for directions. In order to evaluate how accurate the information is, we have to answer the first set of questions. By asking these questions, we are trying to determine whether the *information* we are receiving makes sense and fits in with what we already believe or know to be the case. For instance, if someone sends us off in a direction we know to be wrong, we naturally question the information being offered.

However, in addition to trying to evaluate the accuracy of the information, we try to determine how reliable the *source* of the information is. If we have confidence in the source, we are more likely to trust the accuracy of the information. On the other hand, if we are suspicious of the source, then our suspicion carries over to the information that source is providing. For example, would you judge the accuracy of directions provided by a policeman differently from the information given by a five-year-old child? Why? Our critical evaluation of the sources of information is so important that it even influences who we select to ask for information. For instance, when you stop a stranger to ask directions, what qualities do you look for? (Profession, age, dress, etc.) *Why* do you look for these qualities?

As your responses to these questions suggest, we usually employ a variety of standards or criteria in evaluating the reliability of the person or persons who are giving us information. Let us examine some of the most frequently used criteria for evaluating the reliability of sources. Of course, these criteria apply to written, as well as spoken, testimony.

1. Was the source of the information able to make accurate observations?
2. What do we know about the past reliability of the source of the information?
3. How knowledgeable or experienced is the source of the information?

Let us explore these different criteria in more detail.

**Was the source of the information able to make accurate observations?**  Imagine that you are serving as a juror at a trial in which two youths are accused of mugging and stealing the social security check of an elderly person. During the trial the victim gives the following account of the experience:

> I was walking into the lobby of my building at about 6 o'clock. It was beginning to get dark. Suddenly these two young men rushed in behind me and tried to grab my pocketbook. However, my bag was wrapped around my arm, and I just didn't want to let go of it. They pushed me around, yelling at me to let go of the bag. They finally pulled the bag loose and went running out of the building. I saw them pretty well while we were fighting, and I'm sure that the two boys sitting over there are the ones who robbed me.

In trying to evaluate how accurate this information is, we have to try to determine how reliable the source of the information is. In doing this, we might ask ourselves whether the person attacked was in a good position to make accurate observations. In the case of this person's testimony, what questions could you ask in order to evaluate the accuracy of the testimony?

1. How sharp is the person's eyesight? (Does she or he wear glasses? Were the glasses knocked off in the struggle?)
2. _____

   _____
3. _____

   _____
4. _____

   _____
5. _____

   _____

When trying to determine the accuracy of testimony, we should try to use the same standards we would apply to ourselves if we were in a similar situation. Was there enough light to see clearly? Did the excitement of the situation influence my perceptions? Were my senses operating at full capacity? And so on.

Very often the questions we ask regarding someone's initial testimony lead us to locate additional information. Imagine that you were the police detective assigned to the case just described. Identify some of the ways you mght look for additional information to supplement the victim's testimony.

1. Interview other witnesses who might have seen the robbers.

2. _____

3. _____

4. _____

5. _____

As we work toward evaluating the reliability of the source of the information, it is helpful to locate whatever additional sources of information are available. For instance, if we can locate others who can identify the muggers or if we find stolen items in their possession, this will serve as evidence to support the testimony given by the witness.

Finally, just as we saw in Chapter Five, "Perceiving," accurate observations depend not just on how well our senses are functioning. Accurate observations also depend on how well we understand the personal factors (our "spectacles") we or someone else brings to a situation. These personal feelings, expectations, and interests often influence what we are perceiving without our being aware of it. Once we become aware of these influencing factors, we can attempt to make allowances for them in order to get a more accurate view of what is taking place.

Imagine that your child comes home and tells you that her teacher made  fun of her in front of the rest of the class.

1. Describe how you would go about determining how reliable this information is by speaking to the source (your child). For instance, what questions could you ask to help clarify the situation?

   a. What exactly did the teacher say or do to make fun of you?

   b. _____

   c. _____

2. Describe how you could go about locating additional information to supplement this initial information.

   a. _____

   b. _____

   c. _____

---

➤•◄     Your friends have sponsored an antinuclear rally on your college campus. The campus police estimate the crowd to be 250, while your friends who organized the rally claim it was over 500.

1. Describe how you would go about determining the reliability of your friends' information by speaking to them. What questions could you ask them to help clarify the situation?

   a. _____

   b. _____

   c. _____

2. Describe how you could go about locating additional information to gain a more accurate understanding of the situation.

   a. _____

   b. _____

   c. _____

***What do we know about the past reliability of the source of the information?*** As we work at evaluating the reliability of our information sources, it is useful for us to consider how accurate and reliable their information has been in the past. If someone we know has consistently given us sound information over a period of time, we gradually develop confidence in the accuracy of that person's reports. Such is the case with people like police officers and newspaper reporters, who are continually evaluating the reliability of information sources. People in these professions tend to establish gradually information sources they can trust, who have consistently provided reliable information. For instance, according to *The Washington Post* reporters Bob Woodward and Carl Bernstein, much of the Watergate investigation was based on the information provided by one key source, whom they named "Deep Throat."

Of course this works the other way as well. When people consistently give us *in*accurate or *in*complete information, we gradually lose confidence in their reliability and the reliability of their information. In the comic strip *Peanuts,* created by Charles Schulz, Charlie Brown and his sister, Lucy, illustrate this type of relationship very effectively. Each fall, as Charlie Brown is practicing place-kicking his football, Lucy offers to hold the ball and promises not to yank it away at the last minute, as she has always done in the past. Charlie Brown always ends up trusting her and always ends up on his back as Lucy once again yanks the ball away.

However, we should not make the mistake of judging others' testimony solely on the basis of their past actions. For one thing, people may be very reliable in one type of situation and less reliable in others (or vice versa). A police informant may provide completely accurate information to the police but may be totally unreliable with other people in his life. Or, if we were to take a closer look at Lucy, we might find that her information is more trustworthy when given to people other than her brother.

Additionally, few people are either completely reliable or completely unreliable in the information they offer. Our reliability tends to vary, depending on the situation, the type of information we are providing, and the person we are giving the information to. In trying to evaluate the information offered by others, we have to explore each of these different factors before arriving at a provisional conclusion, which may then be revised in the light of additional information.

---

A friend of yours who has been caught shoplifting several times asks you to lend him $20. He assures you that he will pay you back after his next paycheck.

1. Describe how you would go about determining the reliability of your friend's information by speaking to him. What questions could you ask him to help clarify the situation?

   a. _____

   b. _____

   c. _____

2. Describe how you could go about locating additional information to gain a more accurate understanding of this situation.

   a. _____

   b. _____

   c. _____

➤•◀        The teacher of one of your courses assures you that the final exam questions will be based only on material that was covered in the readings or class.

1. Describe how you would go about determining the reliability of your teacher's information by speaking to her. What questions could you ask her to help clarify the situation?

   a. _____

   b. _____

   c. _____

2. Describe how you could go about locating additional information to gain a more accurate understanding of this situation.

   a. _____

   b. _____

   c. _____

➤•◀        A local politician comes to your school to campaign for votes. He assures you that he fully supports higher education.

1. Describe how you would go about determining the reliability of the politician's information by speaking to him. What questions could you ask him to help clarify the situation?

   a. _____

   b. _____

   c. _____

2. Describe how you could go about locating additional information to gain a more accurate understanding of this situation.

   a. _____

   b. _____

   c. _____

*How knowledgeable or experienced is the source of the information?* When we evaluate information from other sources, we usually try to determine how knowledgeable or experienced the person is in that particular area. When we seek information from others, we try to locate people who, we believe, will have a special understanding of the area in which we are interested. When asking directions, we look for a policeman, a cab driver, or a resident. When seeking information in school, we try to find a school employee or another student who may be experienced in that area. When our car begins making strange noises, we search for someone who has knowledge of car engines. In each case, we try to identify a source of information who has special experience or understanding of a particular area because we believe that this person will be more reliable in giving us information that is accurate.

Of course, there is no guarantee that, even when we carefully select knowledgeable sources, the information will be accurate. Cab drivers do sometimes give the wrong directions; school personnel do occasionally dispense the wrong information; and people experienced with cars cannot always figure out the problem the first time. However, by seeking people who are experienced or knowledgeable rather than those who are not, we increase our chances of gaining accurate information.

But the fact that someone has experience working in a particular area for a period of time does not necessarily mean that this person is extremely knowledgeable. When we say that people learn from experience, we usually mean that people learn by *critically examining* their experiences on an ongoing basis in order to increase their understanding.

---

Suppose you are interested in finding out more information about the career you are planning to go into. Identify some of the people you would select to gain further information and explain why you have selected them.

1. *Source of information:* _____

   *Reasons for selection:* _____

   _____

2. *Source of information:* _____

   *Reasons for selection:* _____

   _____

3. *Source of information:* _____

   *Reasons for selection:* _____

   _____

In seeking information from others whom we believe to be experienced or knowledgeable, it is important to distinguish between the opinions of "average" sources, such as ourselves, and the opinions of experts. Experts are people who have specialized knowledge in a particular area, based on special training and experience. If you are experiencing chest pains and your friend (who is not a doctor or nurse) tells you, "Don't worry, I've had a lot of experience with this sort of thing—it's probably just gas," you may decide to seek the opinion of an expert to confirm your friend's diagnosis. (After all, you don't want to find out the hard way that your friend was mistaken.)

Who qualifies as an expert? Someone with professional expertise as certified by the appropriate standards qualifies as an expert. For instance, we do not want someone working on our teeth just because he or she has always enjoyed playing with drills or inflicting pain on other people. Instead, we insist on someone who has graduated from dental college and been professionally certified.

It is also useful to find out how up-to-date the expert's credentials are. Much knowledge has changed in medicine, dentistry, and automobile mechanics in the last twenty years. If practitioners have not been keeping abreast of these changes, they would have gradually lost their expertise, even though they may have an appropriate diploma. When I was much younger, I was the patient of a very kindly dentist, who never once took x rays of my teeth. (He did not even have an x ray machine in his office.) He also left decay rotting my teeth away under the fillings he put in. This kindly man ended up costing me years of suffering and financial expense because his expertise had expired.

---

►•◄     Identify two experts whose information and services you rely on. Then explain how you could go about discovering how up-to-date and effective their expertise is.

1. *Expert:* _____

   *Explanation:* _____

   _____

2. *Expert:* _____

   *Explanation:* _____

   _____

---

We should also make sure that the experts are giving us information and opinions in their field of expertise. It is certainly all right for someone like Muhammed Ali to give his views on roach sprays, but we should remember that he is speaking as another human being, not as a scientific expert. This is exactly the type of mistaken perception encouraged by advertisers to sell their products. Muhammed Ali is an undeniable expert on boxing, but what specialized knowledge does he have of the roach spray he is advertising?

---

Identify two "experts" in television or magazine advertising who are giving testimony *outside* of their field of expertise.

1. _____

2. _____

Explain why you think each was chosen for the particular product he or she is endorsing and whether you trust such expertise in evaluating this product.

_____

_____

_____

_____

Finally, we should not accept expert opinion without question or critical examination, even if the experts meet all the criteria that we have been exploring. Just because a mechanic assures us that we need a new transmission for $900 does not mean that we should accept her opinion at face value. Or simply because one doctor assures us that surgery is required for our ailment does not mean that we should not investigate further. In both cases, seeking a second (or even third) expert opinion makes a lot of sense. A number of years ago, when I was experiencing some back problems, I spoke with a renowned surgeon, who urged back surgery. I also consulted with an orthopedist, who suggested a program of back exercises. The surgeon was looking at my case with "spectacles" for surgical correction whereas the orthopedist was also using "spectacles" for exercise. We must be sure to examine which spectacles we wish to accept. In my case, the exercises worked perfectly, without spilling a drop of blood.

## Thinking critically about our beliefs

In this chapter we have explored the way we form and revise our beliefs. The purpose of this ongoing process of forming and revising beliefs is to develop a clear understanding of what is taking place so that we can make the most effective decisions in our lives. Our ability to think critically about our beliefs guides us in asking the questions necessary to explore, evaluate, and develop our beliefs. The standards that we use in critically evaluating our beliefs include the following:

How effectively do our beliefs *explain* what is taking place?

How effectively do our beliefs *guide our actions* so that we can reach our desired goals?

How effectively do our beliefs help us *predict* what will happen in similar situations that occur in the future?

In addition to our direct experience, we also depend on information provided by other people to form beliefs about the world. In order to evaluate critically these outside sources of information (both written and spoken), we have to ask the following questions:

How reliable is the *information*? (How accurate and justified?)

How reliable is the *source* of the information?

By thinking critically about the process by which we form and revise our beliefs about the world, we are able to develop our understanding insightfully and creatively.

---

 Using the strategies and insights we have explored in this chapter, complete the following project.

1. Select a topic from a list provided by your teacher or generated by your class.

2. Explain what you believe and know about this topic.

3. Locate and research two articles that analyze this topic.

4. Interview two people who you think are knowledgeable about or experienced in this topic.

5. Using the information provided by the articles and the interviews, write a paper presenting your position on the topic. Be sure to explain carefully the reasons why you have arrived at your conclusion.

6. Analyze how the articles and interviews may have changed or developed your initial beliefs and knowledge about this topic.

# Chapter Seven
# Language

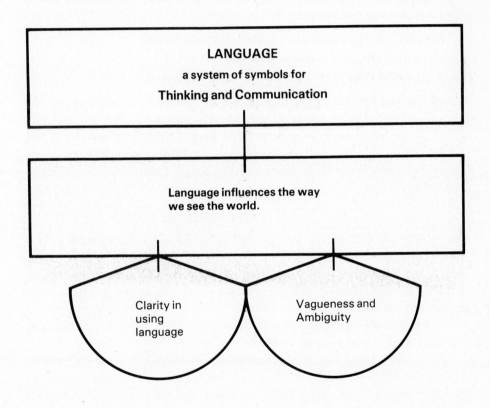

**LANGUAGE**
a system of symbols for
**Thinking and Communication**

**Language influences the way
we see the world.**

Clarity in
using
language

Vagueness and
Ambiguity

UP TO THIS POINT in the book, we have been exploring the various ways we use our thinking abilities to make sense of the world: solving problems, working toward our goals, understanding information, making sense of people, perceiving, forming beliefs, and gaining knowledge. In all these cases, we have found that by *thinking critically* about the different ways in which we are trying to make sense of the world ("thinking about our thinking") we can sharpen and improve our thinking abilities. Through the process of critically examining the way we solve problems, work toward our goals, understand information, perceive, and form beliefs, we learn to perform these activities more effectively.

Throughout this process, language is the tool we have been using to understand and develop our thinking. We have been

learning about the thinking of others through *reading*.

expressing our own thinking through *writing*.

exchanging ideas with others by *speaking* and *listening*.

We could not be developing our thinking without the ability to use language. As we will see in the pages ahead, if we lacked the ability to use language, we would not be able even to *think* in any meaningful sense. The purpose of this chapter is to focus our attention on language. As we develop our skill in using language, we will at the same time be improving our ability to think and make sense of the world.

## Language is the way we communicate with others

Imagine a world without language. Imagine that you suddenly lost your ability to speak, to write, to read. Imagine that your only means of expression were grunts, shrieks, and gestures. And finally, imagine that you soon discovered that *everyone* in the world had also lost their ability to use language. What do you think such a world would be like?

As this exercise of our imagination illustrates, language forms the bedrock of our relations with others. It is the means we have to communicate our thoughts, feelings, and experiences to others, and they to us. This mutual sharing draws us together and leads to our forming relationships. Consider the social groups in your school, your neighborhood, or your community. Notice how language plays a central role in bringing people together into groups and in maintaining these groups.

A loss of language would both limit the complexity of our individual relationships with others and drastically affect the entire way we live in society.

Virtually all the achievements of our civilization are based on our ability to communicate with each other. Without communication, the social cooperation necessary for our culture would break down, and our society would soon become very primitive indeed.

---

Read the following story of the Tower of Babel, from the biblical book of Genesis, chapter 11. Then answer the questions after the passage.

## The Tower of Babel

Hitherto, the world had only one way of speech, only one language. And now, as men travelled westwards, they found a plain in the land of Sennaar, and made themselves a home there; Here we can make bricks, they said to one another, baked with fire; and they built, not in stone, but in brick, with pitch for their mortar. It would be well, they said, to build ourselves a city, and a tower in it with a top that reaches to heaven; we will make ourselves a great people, instead of scattering over the wide face of earth. But now God came down to look at the city, with its tower, which Adam's children were building; and he said, Here is a people all one, with a tongue common to all; this is but the beginning of their undertakings, and what is to prevent them carrying out all they design? It would be well to go down and throw confusion into the speech they use there, so that they will not be able to understand each other. Thus God broke up their common home, and scattered them over the earth, and the building of the city came to an end. That is why it was called Babel, Confusion, because it was there that God confused the whole world's speech, and scattered them far away, over the wide face of earth.

1. Explain why you think that the people in the story decided to stop work on the city and the tower they were building.

   _____

   _____

   _____

   _____

2. Imagine that you were the head builder of this project. Describe what steps you could take to enable work to continue, and explain why you would take each step.

a.  *Step:* _____

    *Explanation:* _____

b.  *Step:* _____

    *Explanation:* _____

Language is the framework that makes all of our social activities and relationships possible. Let us explore how language can accomplish this task.

## Language and symbols

As human beings, we are able to share our thoughts and feelings with each other because of our ability to *symbolize*. When we symbolize, we are letting one thing represent something else. For example, the word "sailboat" represents a type of water-going vessel with sails that is propelled by the wind.

 *Sailboat*

When we speak or write the symbol "sailboat," we are able to communicate the sort of thing we are thinking about. Of course, if other people are to understand what we are referring to when we use this symbol, they must first agree that this symbol ("sailboat") does in fact represent that wind-propelled vessel that floats on the water. If others do not agree with us on what this symbol represents, then we will not be able to communicate what we would like to. Naturally, we could always take others to the object we have in mind and point it out to them, but using a symbol instead is much easier.

Language symbols can take two different forms; they can be written markings or spoken sounds. The symbol "sailboat" can be either written down or spoken aloud. Either way it will communicate the sort of thing we are referring to, providing that others share our understanding of what the symbol means.

Since using language is so natural to us, we rarely stop to realize that our language is really a system of written markings and spoken sounds that we use to represent various aspects of our experience. These markings and sounds enable us to communicate our thoughts and feelings to others, based on a shared understanding of what the markings and sounds symbolize. Consider the following list of markings. What do you think they symbolize?

*segelboot*

*velero*

*bateau à voiles*

*barco de vela*

These markings are actually the symbols used by other languages to represent the same type of thing we have referred to with the symbol "sailboat." To understand what these other symbols mean, we would first have to develop an understanding of what each symbol represents in that particular language.

From this we can see that, in most cases, there is no real link between the symbol and what the symbol represents. For instance, we could use any symbol to represent those types of wind-propelled, water-going vessels, provided that others share our understanding. In most languages there are some words that are clearly related to what they represent—such as "bang bang" or "quack quack"—but these words are relatively few compared with all the other language symbols that are unrelated to what they represent.

*sailboat*
*segelboot*     have no necessary link to               .
*velero*

---

Identify two things in your experience and then locate the words used in
different languages for each.

1. _____

   a. _____

   b. _____

   c. _____

2. _____

   a. _____

   b. _____

   c. _____

Learning a new language is a process of learning how its system of symbols represents our world of experience. For example, consider the following statement:

President Reagan was the actor who starred in the movie *Bedtime for Bonzo,* the story of an adorable chimpanzee.

This collection of words communicates information that some other people can make sense of because they understand what aspects of our experience the words we have chosen represent:

President Reagan

actor

movie

story

adorable

chimpanzee

The words also represent the relationships between the things being symbolized:

was the actor

who starred in

If this statement was expressed in symbols that we did not understand—such as a foreign language we were not familiar with—then the statement would not be a very effective way for us to learn information about the world. Consider the following example:

President Reagan war der Schauspieler der in dem Film, *Bedtime for Bonzo,* spielte, die Geschichte eines drolligen Affens.

This collection of symbols will only make sense to us if we understand the German language. Thus the possibility of communicating experiences to others depends on our having a shared understanding of what exactly the symbols we are using will represent.

### The symbolic structure of language

In certain respects, language is like a set of symbolic building blocks. The basic blocks are letters, which symbolize various sounds.

Letters—A T C Q Y N—symbolize sounds

The sounds of letters form the phonetic foundation of a language, and this explains why different languages have such distinctly different "sounds" to them. Try having various members of the class recite the alphabets of different languages and then speak a few sentences in the language. Listen to how the sound of each language differs from the others. When humans are infants, they are able to make all the sounds of all the alphabets. As they are continually exposed to the particular group of sounds of their society's language, they gradually concentrate on making only those sounds while discarding or never developing others.

Letters combine to form larger sets of blocks called words. Words are used to represent the various aspects of our world of experience, including "shoes and ships and sealing wax, and cabbages and kings."

$$\text{Words—} \textit{love students learning} \text{—symbolize} \begin{cases} \text{objects} \\ \text{thoughts} \\ \text{feelings} \end{cases}$$

The rules of a language tell us how to spell and pronounce the words of the language (for example, "Use *i* before *e*, except after *c*, or when sounded as *a* as in *neighbor* and *weigh*").

The rules of a language also tell us how to organize words together into various combinations called sentences. Sentences can be used to represent relationships between different aspects of our experience. ("The cat is on the mat." "I feel like a million dollars.")

Sentences—*students love learning*—Symbolize the relationships between objects, thoughts, and feelings in our experience

Once formed, sentences can then be combined into a variety of larger groups: paragraphs, essays, books. These larger and more complex combinations of language symbols can be used to represent and express many of the aspects of our experience. Of course, words are often not able to communicate our complete thought or feeling, nor is a description of an experience a substitute for actually having the experience. Nevertheless, language is capable of communicating in powerful and effective ways.

The ability to communicate clearly what is being symbolized is a key measure of using language effectively. However, although describing aspects of our experience is an important function of language (and the function we will be focusing most of our intention on in this chapter), it is by no means the only role that language plays in our lives. Consider the following uses of language:

"I love you."

"Get up and close the door."

"God bless you."

"I now pronounce you man and wife."

Each of these statements uses language in ways other than describing experience. Saying "I love you" expresses our feelings towards someone, usually with the hope that we will evoke similar feelings in them for us. When we tell someone to "Get up and close the door," we are using language to direct someone else's behavior. The statement "God bless you" represents a social ritual said after someone sneezes—the meaning of the words is less important than the fact that we said them. And when the proper authority states "I now pronounce you man and wife" in the appropriate circumstances, the saying of the words performs the meaning that the words are expressing.

Language has a variety of important functions in our lives, including describing and communicating information. Language is involved in virtually every aspect of our thinking, feeling, and acting. As a result, in order for us to understand the meaning of a word or group of words, we have to explore the manner and the circumstances in which language is being used.

---

►•◄      The following passages are from a book entitled *Blue Highways*, written by a young man of Indian heritage named William Least Heat Moon. After losing his teaching job at a university and separating from his wife, he decided to explore America. He outfitted his van (named "Ghost Dancing") and followed a route that took him around the country using only the backroads (represented on the maps by blue lines) rather than the super-highways. In the course of his travels, he saw fascinating sights, met intriguing people, and developed some significant insights about himself.

Read carefully the following passages, which use language to communicate aspects of the writer's experience. As you read each passage, write down your responses to the following questions:

1. How effectively does the passage share the thoughts, feelings, or experiences of the author?
2. If the passage is effective, how has the author's use of language made this communication possible?

## A Place

Two Steller's jaybirds stirred an argy-bargy in the ponderosa. They shook their big beaks, squawked and hopped and swept down the sunlight toward Ghost Dancing and swooshed back into the pines. They didn't shut up until I left some orts from breakfast; then they dropped from the branches like ripe fruit, nabbed a gobful, and took off for the tops of the hundred-foot trees. The chipmunks got in on it too, letting loose a high peal of rodent chatter, picking up their share, spinning the bread like pinwheels, chewing fast.

It was May Day, and the warm air filled with the scent of pine and blooming manzanita. To the west I heard water over rock as Hat Creek came down from the snows of Lassen. I took towel and soap and walked through a field of volcanic ejections and broken chunks of lava to the stream bouncing off boulders and slicing over bedrock; below one cascade, a pool the color of glacier ice circled the effervescence. On the bank at an upright stone with a basin-shaped concavity filled with rainwater, I bent to drink, then washed my face. Why not bathe from head to toe? I wet down with rainwater and lathered up.

## An Experience

Now, I am not unacquainted with mountain streams; a plunge into Hat Creek would be an experiment in deep-cold thermodynamics. I knew that, so I jumped in with bravado. It didn't help. Light violently flashed in my head. The water was worse than I thought possible. I came out, eyes the size of biscuits, metabolism running amuck and setting fire to the icy flesh. I buffed dry.

Then I began to feel good, the way the old Navajos must have felt after a traditional sweat bath and roll in the snow. I dressed and sat down to watch Hat Creek. A pair of dippers flew in and began feeding. Robin-like birds with stub tails and large, astonished eyes, dippers feed in a way best described as insane. With two or three deep kneebends (hence their name) as if working up nerve, they hopped into the water and walked upstream, completely immersed, strolling and pecking along the bottom. Then they broke from the water, dark eyes gasping. I liked Hat Creek. It was reward enough for last night.

## Another Person

Back at Ghost Dancing, I saw a camper had pulled up. On the rear end, by the strapped-on aluminum chairs, was something like ''The Wandering Watkins.'' Time to go. I kneeled to check a tire. A smally furry white thing darted from behind the wheel, and I flinched. Because of it, the journey would change.

''Harmless as a stuffed toy.'' The voice came from the other end of the leash the dog was on. ''He's nearly blind and can't hear much better. Down just to the nose now.'' The man, with polished cowboy boots and a part measured out in the white hair, had a face so gullied even the Soil Conservation Commission couldn't have reclaimed it. But his eyes seemed lighted from within.

''Are you Mr. Watkins?'' I said.

"What's left of him. The pup's what's left of Bill. He's a Pekingese. Chinese dog. In dog years, he's even older than I am, and I respect him for that. We're two old men. What's your name?"

"Same as the dog's."

"I wanted to give him a Chinese name, but old what's-her-face over there in the camper wouldn't have it. Claimed she couldn't pronounce Chinese names. I says, 'You can't say Lee?' She says, 'You going to name a dog Lee?' 'No,' I says, 'but what do you think about White Fong?' Now, she's not a reader unless it's a beauty parlor magazine with a Kennedy or Hepburn woman on the cover, so she never understood the name. You've read your Jack London, I hope. She says, 'When I was a girl we had a horse called William, but that name's too big for that itty-bitty dog. Just call him Bill.' That was that. She's a woman of German descent and a decided person. But when old Bill and I are out on our own, I call him White Fong."

Watkins had worked in a sawmill for thirty years, then retired to Redding; now he spent time in his camper, sometimes in the company of Mrs. Watkins.

"I'd stay on the road, but what's-her-face won't have it."

As we talked, Mrs. What's-her-face periodically thrust her head from the camper to call instructions to Watkins or White Fong. A finger-wagging woman, full of injunctions for man and beast. Whenever she called, I watched her, Watkins watched me, and the dog watched him. Each time he would say, "Well, boys, there you have it. Straight from the back of the horse."

"You mind if I swear?" I said I didn't. "The old biddy's in there with her Morning Special—sugar doughnut, boysenberry jam, and a shot of Canadian Club in her coffee. In this beauty she sits inside with her letters."

"What kind of work you in?" he asked.

That question again. "I'm out of work," I said to simplify.

"A man's never out of work if he's worth a damn. It's just sometimes he doesn't get paid. I've gone unpaid my share and I've pulled my share of pay. But that's got nothing to do with working. A man's work is doing what he's sup-posed to do, and that's why he needs a catastrophe now and again to show him a bad turn isn't the end, because a bad stroke never stops a good man's work. Let me show you my philosophy of life." From his pressed Levi's he took a billfold and handed me a limp business card. "Easy. It's very old."

The card advertised a cafe in Merced when telephone numbers were four digits. In quotation marks was a motto: "Good Home Cooked Meals."

" 'Good Home Cooked Meals' is your philosophy?"

"Turn it over, peckerwood."

Imprinted on the back in tiny, faded letters was this:

I've been bawled out, balled up, held up, held down, hung up, bulldozed, blackjacked, walked on, cheated, squeezed and mooched; stuck for war tax, excess profits tax, sales tax, dog tax, and syntax, Liberty Bonds, baby bonds, and the bonds of matrimony, Red Cross, Blue Cross, and the double cross; I've worked like hell, worked others like hell, have got drunk and got others drunk, lost all I had, and now because I won't spend or lend what little I earn, beg, borrow or steal, I've been cussed, discussed, boycotted, talked to, talked about, lied to, lied about, worked over, pushed under, robbed, and damned near ruined. The only reason I'm sticking around now is to see

WHAT THE HELL IS NEXT.

"I like it," I said.

"Any man's true work is to get his boots on each morning. Curiosity gets it done about as well as anything else."

---

After rereading the passages from *Blue Highways* (pp. 222–225), create your  own descriptions of

1. a *place* you are familiar with.
2. an important *experience* you have had.
3. a *person* whom you know.

As you write your passages, try to use language to communicate as effectively as possible the thoughts, feelings, and experiences you are trying to share. Included below are passages written by other students.

### My House

It's a three-level house constructed of beige-colored stone. There are three balconies painted white and in front of the house a big tree. The front garden consists of a few patches of grass, two bushes, and a cement driveway. Inside the house there are three separate apartments. The first floor is decorated in a very old-fashioned way. In this apartment lives the eldest of the family, who is the owner of the house. The apartment has tiled floors and a musty smell mixed with the constant brewing of coffee. The second floor is decorated with fashionable furniture.

There are hardwood floors, sounds of children laughing, and pots and pans clanging in the kitchen. The in-laws live here, taking care of the family's younger members. The top floor has brightly painted walls, shiny hardwood floors, and modern furniture. There is a skylight in the hall where bright light pours in. There is a comfortable feeling and a relaxed atmosphere in this space. The apartment smells of fresh paint and furniture polish. Music is almost always playing. The youngest married couple lives here with their children. This house invites people to feel welcome and provides different atmospheres for people of different ages.

### An Experience

The most important experience that I've ever had was leaving home to go live in a group home.

I was nine years old on the day I was leaving. I knew why I was going, but I still didn't really understand what good my leaving home was going to do.

It was 12:00 p.m. and there was a knock at the door. I looked through the peephole, and I saw a tall, Caucasion woman. My heart started to race; I knew she was here to take me away from everything I had ever known and loved. I looked at my mother and she said, "What are you waiting for? Open the door." When I opened the door, Miss Gold smiled at me and said, "Good morning." She and my mother spoke for a while while I got my suitcases from my room. I came out of the room, and asked her if she was ready. I didn't want to spend too much time saying goodbye, because I knew that after more than 3 minutes of this I'd break down in tears. I was supposed to be strong and brave and leave with a smile; so I did.

I got into the car and I said nothing to Miss Gold during the ride to the Bronx.

It felt as though I was starting a new life all over again. I was to live in a place where I had never lived before. I was to live with girls I had never met in my life. I was to be taken care of by people whom I didn't know and, worst of all, by people who didn't know me. In a way, I had to forget the lifestyle I was living and start a new one, but I was never going to forget the fact that I had to be strong and brave and always with a smile.

I lived there for 3 years. I learned a lot from this experience. I learned how to deal with strangers. I learned to appreci-

ate a family, family life, and all the things that go along with
it. Most of all I learned a lot about myself and how to deal with
certain feelings that I had. Ever since then I've been the kind
of person who keeps a lot of thoughts to myself. I've learned to
deal with a lot of problems myself.

All in all, I feel it was a good experience for me. I've
matured much faster than I would have if I didn't experience
this, and this helps me with a lot of people and things I deal
with now. When I look back at this experience, I say to myself,
"If you made it through that, Kathy, you can make it through almost anything."

### Another Person

He was old; his face contained highways of experience. He
could barely see the world anymore, but it didn't seem to bother
him. His time of death was nearing, so he held my hand with a
softness that was incomparable. I looked down at this elderly man
who waited for death. Grandfather, I said, please don't die. I
never got to have long walks or go to buy ice cream with you. His
face turned to sadness as he watched me plead. He knew that his
existence would soon cease.

His eyes softly closed; his hands grasped tightly onto mine
as if wishing to stay alive a little longer. I rested my head on
his chest; his heart pounded weakly saying goodbye to me. It was
the end. I looked at the highways on his face, and I tried to
find myself on them. I did, but the highway soon faded away.
Grandfather must have taken it with him wherever he had gone.

## Symbolizing experience

If we are to improve our ability to represent effectively our thoughts, feelings,
and experiences, then we have to continue to develop our mastery over the process of symbolizing. The first step in this process is to become familiar with the
details of the experience we are trying to represent. This means that we must be
*open and sensitive* to what we are experiencing. For example, if we fall asleep at
a baseball game or don't pay attention at a concert we are attending, then our
symbolic representations of these experiences will be of little use.

Next, as we saw in Chapter Five, "Perceiving," symbolizing our experiences effectively involves *understanding* what we are experiencing. If we lack

knowledge of the elements and the context of the experience—whether it is wine, art, or hockey—then our symbolic description will be much less effective than it might have been if we had this understanding.

For instance, how adequate do you think the following descriptions are?

1. The wine was red and tasted kind of sweet.
2. There were a lot of paintings with big blotches of color on them.
3. There were a bunch of guys skating after a black disc, who took time out to fight with each other every now and then.

In each case, what is missing from the descriptions that are being shared?

Finally, representing our experiences effectively also requires *facility with the language symbols* that we are using to describe our experiences. We need a large enough vocabulary, as well as knowledge of how to put these words together, in order to describe all of the various details and aspects of the experience. If we are to symbolize our experiences effectively, so that others can share them, we must

1. be *open and sensitive* to what we are experiencing.
2. have an *understanding* of what we are experiencing.
3. possess a *facility with language* in order to represent what we are experiencing.

### Naming and describing

Representing our thoughts, feelings, and experiences begins with trying to identify these thoughts, feelings, and experiences by giving them names. Our thinking abilities develop as we learn to symbolize our world in increasingly precise and distinct ways. When a baby cries ''mama'' or ''dada,'' that one word is being used to represent one of a number of experiences: ''I'm hungry,'' ''I'm wet,'' ''I'm lonely,'' etc. As children develop, their ability to use more specific symbols for their experience also develops as they learn to distinguish each of these experiences by giving them different names. Our ability to symbolize thoughts, feelings, and objects in our experience by giving them descriptive names thus enables us to

*identify* the various things in our experience.

*distinguish* these things from one another.

*describe* these things to others who share an understanding of our symbols.

Imagine that you have in front of you a large bowl containing a wide variety of different fruits. You are able to identify the various fruits (plum, apple, orange, cherry, banana, etc.) because you have given them names. Identifying these different fruits means that you can distinguish these fruits from one an-other and that you can recognize various types of fruits if you see them again. Finally, if a friend asks, ''What are you eating?'' you are able to describe what you are eating by giving the name that symbolizes it (''I'm eating a kumquat'').

Naming is therefore the thinking activity that enables us to organize our world. If we could not give various things in our experience different names, our world would be very chaotic, for we would not be able to identify or distin-guish the various aspects of it. A vivid illustration of the power of naming can be found in the life of Helen Keller, a woman who was unable to see or hear from birth. In the following passage, written by her teacher, Anne Sullivan, we can see how learning to name things in her experience becomes the key that transforms her world from one of confusion to one of order and intelligibility.

## Learning to Name

I must write you a line this morning because something very important has happened. Helen has taken the second great step in her education. She has learned that everything has a name, and that the manual alphabet is the key to everything she wants to know.

In a previous letter I think I wrote that ''mug'' and ''milk'' had given Helen more trouble than all the rest. She confused the nouns with the verb ''drink.'' She didn't know the word for ''drink'' but went through the pantomime of drinking whenever she spelled ''mug'' or ''milk.'' This morning, while she was washing, she wanted to know the name for ''water.'' When she wants to know the name of anything, she points to it and pats my hand. I spelled ''w-a-t-e-r'' and thought no more about it until after breakfast. Then it occurred to me that with the help of this new word I might succeed in straightening out the ''mug-milk'' difficulty. We went out to the pump-house and I made Helen hold her mug under the spout while I pumped. As the cold water gushed forth, filling the mug I spelled ''w-a-t-e-r'' in Helen's free hand. The word coming so close upon the sensation of cold water rushing over her hand seemed to startle her. She dropped the mug and stood as one transfixed. A new light came into her face. She spelled ''water'' several times. Then she dropped on the ground and asked for its name and pointed to the pump and the trellis, and suddenly turning round she asked for my name. I spelled ''Teacher.'' Just then the nurse brought Helen's little sister into the pump-house, and Helen spelled ''baby'' and point-ed to the nurse. All the way back to the house she was highly excited, and learned the name of every object she touched, so that in a few hours she had added thirty new words to her vocabulary. Here are some of them: Door, open, shut, give, go, come, and a great many more.

P.S.—I didn't finish my letter in time to get it posted last night; so I shall add a line. Helen got up this morning like a radiant fairy. She has flitted from object to object, asking the name of everything and kissing me for very gladness. Last night when I got in bed, she stole into my arms of her own accord and kissed me for the first time, and I thought my heart would burst, so full was it of joy.

As this passage explains, Helen was unable to distinguish "mug," "milk", and "drink" as different aspects of her experience because she had not yet developed the idea that "everything has a name, and that the manual alphabet is the key to everything she wants to know." Helen comes to this critical insight when she realizes that the substance she was washing with in the morning ("water") is the same substance coming out of the pump ("water") and that she can identify both of these substances, now and in the future, by *giving them a name* ("water").

### Clarity and precision in naming

Naming is the way that we identify things in the world, make distinctions between them, and describe them to others. Additionally, as we will see in the chapters ahead, naming is also the way that we *relate* things together. For example, using the name "apple" enables us to recognize and group together all the various kinds of apples in the world. At the same time, our more precise names for apples (such as MacIntosh, Delicious, Northern Spy, etc.) give us the means to distinguish the various kinds of apples contained in this larger group of "apples."

---

▶•◀     In the space below, list all the different types of ice and snow that you can think of.

1. _____   4. _____   7. _____

2. _____   5. _____   8. _____

3. _____   6. _____   9. _____

Your ability to give descriptive names for ice and snow probably depends on what part of the country you live in (people in southern climates don't see a lot of ice and snow) and what your outdoor interests are (do you enjoy skiing?). Each different kind of ice and snow you are able to identify represents a distinction you are able to make in the world. Even people who live in northern climates will probably only be able to identify nine or ten different kinds of ice and snow.

One of the most striking examples of the power of naming in helping us identify and distinguish things in the world was discovered by the anthropologist Benjamin Lee Whorf. While studying the language of the Eskimos, he found that it had seventy-six different names for ice and snow. Each name described a distinct kind of ice and snow condition. Why do you think that the Eskimo language has so many more names for ice and snow than we do?

If you examine the names for ice and snow that you listed on page 230, you will find that each of the words you identifed represents a distinction you make in describing and understanding the world. "Slush" is much different from hard, or "glare," ice. Making these distinctions is necessary in order for us to understand what is going on in the world (Is it snowing or sleeting?), as well as making intelligent decisions based on this understanding. If we are driving a car, knowing whether we are driving on slush or glare ice will dramatically affect the decisions we make—how fast to drive, how much time to allow for braking, or whether we should be driving at all.

Thus the names we have for ice and snow represent our understanding or this area of experience. Although these names are probably adequate for our needs and purposes, the knowledge that they represent is very general compared to the very detailed understanding that the Eskimos have. For the Eskimos, almost every aspect of life (housing, travel, hunting, and fishing) depends on understanding the *exact* nature of ice and snow. Their detailed knowledge of this area of experience is created by using names to symbolize all the distinctions being made.

In most cases, our ability to develop a detailed understanding of an area of experience depends on our needs and interests. As we saw when exploring the perceiving process, the precision of our perceptions is based on our knowledge of the territory we are experiencing. For example, a person with musical expertise is able to make many more distinctions regarding the music he or she is listening to because of his or her interest in this particular area of experience.

---

Select an area of experience in which you have a special interest and knowledge—plants, cars, music, sewing, food, sports, etc.

Express your understanding of this particular area of experience by naming some of the important distinctions that are a part of this experience. For example:

*Woodworking Joints*

1. Butt
2. Miter
3. Lap
4. Dado

5. Rabbet
6. Mortise and tenon
7. Dovetail
8. Halved-together

9. Edge
10. Tongue and groove
11. Finger
12. Lock

Using the names you have identified, write a passage that describes this particular area of experience. A passage based on some of the various woodworking joints is included below.

After completing your descriptive passage, share it with other members of your class so that they can experience your detailed understanding of this particular area of experience.


## Woodworking Joints

At the heart of woodworking is the question: How do you join two pieces of wood together? In fact, this is the reason why cabinetmaking was traditionally known as the art of "joinery."

The simplest way to attach two pieces of wood is simply to nail or screw the edge of one board to another. This is known as a *butt joint,* from the word "abut." Though this is a simple joint, it is not a very strong joint because it depends entirely on the nail or screw to hold the two pieces together.

The *miter joint*, used in most picture frames, is like a butt joint except that the two edges which are to be joined are cut at an angle (usually 45 degrees) which together form a 90 degree corner.

Although it sounds like a cartoon character, the *dado joint* is in reality a strong, effective joint found in many bookshelves. It is formed by cutting a channel across one of the pieces to be joined into which the other board fits snugly.

To understand the *tongue and groove joint,* imagine sticking your tongue into a small opening—and then having it glued in place! Because of its unusual strength, this joint is used extensively in the construction of furniture (particularly chairs), which will receive a lot of active use over their lifetime.

The *dovetail joint*, cut in the shape of a dove's tail, is formed by fitting together two interlocking sets of "tails" in the same way that you interlock your fingers together. It is one of the strongest edge joints, and for this reason is used in making desk and bureau drawers because of the constant pulling and pushing these joints will receive.

In summary, joining two pieces of wood is not simply a matter of nailing them together—it is an art which has been developed over the last seven thousand years. In each case, the particular wood joint selected should reflect the specific purposes for which the joint will be used.

### Vagueness

Although our ability to name and identify gives us the power to describe the world in a precise way, we often do not use words that are precise. Instead, many of our descriptions of the world involve words that are very *imprecise* and general. Such general and nonspecific words are known as *vague* words. Consider the following sentences:

I had a *nice* time yesterday.

That is an *interesting* book.

She is an *old* person.

In each of these cases, the italicized word is vague because it does not give a precise description of the thought, feeling, or experience that the writer or speaker is trying to communicate. A word (or group of words) is vague if its meaning is not clear and distinct. Or seen a different way, vagueness occurs when a word is used to represent an area of experience in such a way that the area is not clearly defined.

Let us examine the last sentence in the list above: "She is an old person." At what age do you think that a person becomes "old"? The word "old" is considered to be vague because it does not seem to have one clear meaning. If you compare your idea of an old person with the other members of your class, you will probably find considerable variation. For instance, when we are children, the age of twenty-one seems old, and we can hardly wait to get there. People who are twenty-one traditionally do not trust those over thirty years old because of their advanced age and possible senility. When we become thirty, forty-five then seems old, and when we turn forty-five, then sixty becomes old, and so on. When my grandmother was seventy-nine years old, my father accidently referred to her as being "old." "I'm not old!" she said angrily and stormed out of the room. If we were anthropologists, our idea of an "old" person might be one who lived 10,000 years ago. The problem with the word "old" is simply that its meaning is not clear and distinct.

**A Vague Word** • A word that lacks a clear and distinct meaning.

The problem of vagueness is natural to most words of general measurement—short, tall, big, small, heavy, light, etc. In each case, the exact meaning of the word depends on the specific situation in which it is being used and on the particular perspective of the person using it.

➤•◀ Give specific definitions for the following words. Then compare your responses to those of other members of the class. Can you account for the differences in meaning?

1. *middle-aged:* A *middle-aged* person is one who is _____ years old.
2. *tall:* A *tall* person is one who is _____ feet _____ inches tall.
3. *cold:* It's *cold* outside when the temperature is _____ degrees.
4. *wealthy:* A person is *wealthy* when _____

_____.

However, another type of vagueness is considerably more widespread than the natural vagueness associated with forms of measuring. This second type of vagueness is the major threat to clear expression—and to clear thinking.

➤•◀ Answer the following question: What was the name of a movie that you saw recently? Then describe as specifically as possible what you thought of the movie.

Now examine the following response to the same question. As you read through the passage, circle all the vague, general words that do not express a clear meaning.

> *Purple Rain* is a terrific movie about the Detroit superstar Prince. It's got lots of energy, dynamite music, and an interesting plot. Prince's woman in the picture—Apollonia—is sexy and soulful. This movie is exciting and I liked it a lot.

The vague language illustrated in this passage expresses only a very general approval or disapproval—it does not explain in any exact or precise terms what the experience was like. And since sloppy language does such a poor job of describing the thoughts and feelings we are trying to communicate, other people cannot share our recollection of the experience in any direct or complete way. Strong writers have the gift of symbolizing their experiences so clearly that we can actually relive those experiences with them. We can identify with them, sharing the same thoughts, feelings, and perceptions that they had when they underwent (or imagined) the experience. Consider how effectively the passages we explored on pages 222–227 communicate the thoughts, feelings, and experiences of the authors.

One strategy that is often useful for clarifying vague language is to ask and try to answer the following questions: *Who? What? Where? When? How? Why?* Let us see how this strategy applies to the movie vaguely described above.

*Who* were the people involved in the movie? (Actors, director, producer, characters portrayed, etc.)

*What* took place in the movie? (Setting, events, plot development, etc.)

*Where* does the movie take place? (Physical location, cultural setting, etc.)

*When* do the events in the movie take place? (Historical situation)

*How* does the film portray its events? (How do the actors create their characters? How does the director use film techniques to accomplish his or her goals?)

*Why* do I have this opinion of the film? (What are the reasons that I formed that particular opinion?)

Now let us examine a review of this same film by a professional movie reviewer. As you read through the review, notice how well the writer is able to communicate his thoughts and feelings about the film by answering the questions that we just examined.

# Dr. Feelgood

*by David Denby*

It's easy enough to make fun of Prince, the whirling rock star who dominates *Purple Rain*—easy, that is, when he's not performing. The tiny fop hero of Minneapolis wears black breeches, white silk shirts with ruffles, and white stock ties hanging to his belly; he has long black curly hair, a thin, libidinous mustache over wet lips, and plenty of liner around the eyes. He looks, perhaps, like one of the minor characters from an M-G-M period picture of the thirties—a disreputable musketeer, or a tiny, decadent minion in the court of a mad king played by Robert Morley. He isn't greasy, but he's certainly liquid—tearful and petulant in repose and all lathered up when he performs without his ruffled shirt (in the movie, at least, he keeps his pants on). No one this short trying this hard to be sexy should be able to get away with it. But Prince does—when he sings.

Vincent Canby has called *Purple Rain* "the flashiest album cover ever to be released as a movie," which would be witty if it were true. But *Purple Rain* is a real movie. Some of it isn't very good, but it's juicy and high-powered work—perhaps the first rock movie in years that will stir people up. Written by Albert Magnoli and William Blinn, who worked closely with Prince, and directed by Magnoli (his first feature), *Purple Rain* is a rock star's mixed-up confession and self-glorifying fantasy. Prince plays a character called the Kid, the leader of a struggling band that performs at the First Avenue Club & 7th Street Entry in Minneapolis (indeed, it is Prince's own band, the Revolution). The Kid comes from a tragic home in which his black father, a failed musician, regularly beats his white mother, leaving the Kid traumatized, loveless, and ungiving. He can let loose only in performance, and when Appollonia (Apollonia Kotero), a new girl in town, sees him perform, she is transfixed. But he treats her badly and loses her to the giggly scoundrel Morris Day (in real life the leader of the Time, a group that appears in the movie). *Purple Rain* is about the Kid's learning to love, learning to be generous to women, "growing," and all that.

Banal? Yeah, sure, but that's not all there is to say about it. The frenetic off-stage scenes are not intended to stand up as fully worked-out dramatic material. Magnoli gives us very short scenes, fragments almost, in which a few powerful generalized moods are developed—the Kid's anguish at home, say—and are then extended and transformed in the numbers onstage. In other words, even though *Purple Rain* has lots of music performed in front of an audience, it's not a concert film. The numbers crystallize the emotions suggested by the sketchy, rather lurid rock-soap-opera story. Onstage Prince comes out of his brooding sulk; he becomes a performer, and by performing he gets involved with people in the audience, which sends the story hurtling forward. So the plot may be banal, but the movie is all of a piece, and the music wipes the banality away. At the climactic moments, *Purple Rain* says that rock gives you the power to transcend the pain and mess of your life; it speaks of revolution—personal, not social—with a fervor not heard since the early days of the Stones.

Along the way, *Purple Rain* offers entertaining gimpses of a rock scene that some of us (me, for instance) know nothing about—the racially and sexually mixed bands of Minneapolis, which now, thanks to the patronage of Prince, have gone national. The faces, the moves, are fresh. The leader of the Time, Morris Day, dresses in double-breasted suits and cream coats—sort of the zoot-pimp look. Day satirizes generations of swank black dudes who have made a style out of supreme confidence and outrageous flirtatiousness. "Your lips would make a lollipop happy," he tells Apollonia, before setting her up in her own all-girl band. But Day is only a pseudo-stud. He has a goony streak—a high, shrieking laugh and a jaw that sneaks away from confrontation like a cowardly dog. Day and Jerome Benton, who is both his chauffeur-sidekick and a member of his band, demonstrate nifty timing in their slick comedy routines together, including a manic misunderstanding about a password that plays at a faster, hipper tempo than Abbott and Costello's "Who's on First?" classic.

When a woman who's been stood up confronts Morris Day on the street, he and Jerome Benton toss her into a dumpster. This is supposed to be a big laugh, and so is the scene in which Prince tricks the beautiful Apollonia into stripping off and dunking herself in a lake, while he sits watching, fully clothed, on the shore. The scene has a teasing rhythm to it that women may experience as an insult. Later, Prince whomps Apollonia across the face a couple of times, and we realize the movie is stumbling around something serious; the misery of the Kid's mother and father suggests what the habit of slamming women can lead to. *Purple Rain* catches black popular culture at a moment of near-schizophrenia. For comedy, the motive casually relies on the misogyny that is endemic in the rock world and in pimp attitudes; for tragedy, the movie says that woman-whomping is hell even for men. The conflict is resolved when Prince sings "Purple Rain", a song written by two female members of the band that he had earlier scoffed at. The number, a long, solemnly ecstatic supplication with a healing gospel sound to it, is both an apology to women and a promise of erotic good times.

But most of Prince's contradictions remain unresolved: He is both black and white, straight and gay, narcissist and mesmerist, withdrawn and commanding. He jumps and whirls around the stage making love to himself and the audience, mixing sexual mastery and masturbatory self-pity, and sometimes he gets so wound up he falls down in a heap. But the music has some giddy, high-powered moments. Prince is either shrewd enough or exploitive enough (I can't tell which) to gather up the fragments of our culture and send them whirling back at an audience hungry for self-confirmation. He could make an awful lot of people feel good.

---

Analyze the preceding movie review by answering the following questions. According to the movie reviewer,

1. *Who* were the people involved with the movie?
2. *What* took place in the movie?
3. *Where* does the movie take place?
4. *When* do the events in the movie take place?
5. *How* does the film portray its events?
6. *Why* did the reviewer form this particular opinion about the film?

▶•◀        Return to your review of the film that you saw recently (p. 234). Using these six questions as a guide, create a more precise description of your thoughts and feelings about the film.

▶•◀        Examine the following response to the question: "Describe what you think about the school you are attending." Circle the vague words.

> I really like it a lot. It's a very good school. The people are nice and the teachers are interesting. There are a lot of different things to do, and students have a good time doing them. Some of the courses are pretty hard, but if you study enough, you should do all right.

As you consider this passage, notice the difference between saying something like "The people are nice" and giving concrete and specific descriptions of *why* you think the people are nice. For example,

"Everyone says hello."

"The students introduced themselves to me in class."

"I always feel welcome in the student lounge."

"The teachers take a special interest in each student."

▶•◀        Using the following six questions as a guide, describe as specifically as possible your thoughts and feelings about the school you attend.

Who?

What?

Where?

When?

Why?

How?

▶•◀        Review the passages that you created on page 225, where you described

a *place* you are familiar with.

an important *experience* you have had.

a *person* you know.

Identify any vague words or phrases and underline them. Then see if you can improve the precision of your passages by using more specific descriptions.

As we have just seen, creating verbal descriptions that are precise and effective involves both

an awareness and understanding of the experiences that we are describing *and*

a knowledge and command of the language that we are using to symbolize and communicate these experiences.

These abilities can always be improved, but they do not develop automatically. First, we have to *want* to develop our capacity for using language clearly. This requires an extra effort on our part, because the easiest thing to do is to give vague, general descriptions. In the second place, using language effectively requires constant *practice*. It was the great orchestra conductor Toscanini who pointed out: "You don't do anything in a performance that you haven't rehearsed a thousand times." Being able to give precise descriptions of our experience is not a switch that we can turn on and off; it requires continual development. We need to be like athletes preparing for an event; They will not magically excel if they have not spent many hours and great effort slowly developing their expertise. In the case of our language ability, we cannot spend our days and nights expressing ourselves in vague, general terms, and then suddenly expect to be able to communicate our experiences in words that are clear and specific. Much of the time that we are speaking—or writing—we should be striving to express ourselves in the clearest terms possible.

In pursuing this goal, it certainly helps to be talking to people who share the same interest in clear and precise expression. When we are with people who are content with vague and general expression, we, too, will tend to be satisfied with it. For example, if we report, "That was a terrific movie," and we are not asked to clarify this statement, then we will probably leave it at this imprecise level. But, if the people we are with ask us *why* we thought the movie was terrific, to specify the *reasons why* we had this reaction, then we will be encouraged and stimulated to think in more critical and articulate ways.

Virtually all of us use vague language extensively in our day-to-day conversations. In many cases, it is natural that our immediate reaction to an experience would be fairly general ("That's nice," "She's interesting," etc.). However, if we are truly concerned with sharp thinking and meaningful communication, we should follow up these initial general reactions with a more precise clarification of what we really mean.

I think that she is a nice person *because*...

I think that he is a good teacher *because*...

I think that this is an interesting class *because*...

This type of attitude will encourage the clearest thinking and communication that we are capable of.

### Ambiguity

In addition to vagueness, *ambiguity* is another obstacle that can interfere with clear expression of our thoughts and feelings. We have noted that words are used to represent various areas of experience. We sometimes make the mistake of thinking that each word stands for one distinct area of experience—an object, thought, or feeling. In fact, a word may represent various areas of experience and so have a number of different meanings. When a word has more than one distinct meaning and we are not sure which meaning is being intended, then we say that the word is *ambiguous*. For example, the word *rich* can mean having lots of money (like a millionaire), *or* it can mean having lots of sugar and calories (like chocolate cream pie). Thus *rich* is a potentially ambiguous word.

**Ambiguous Word** • A word with more than one meaning that is open to different interpretations.

How do we know which of its multiple meanings an ambiguous word is referring to? Usually we can tell by *how* the word is used—the situation, or context, in which it is employed. When someone asks you if you are "rich," you can be pretty certain that that person is *not* asking if you are full of sugar and calories.

---

➤•◄         Give at least two meanings for the following potentially ambiguous words.

1. *Exercise:* _____

   _____

2. *Bad:* _____

   _____

3. *Major:* _____

   _____

4. *Firm:* _____

   _____

5. *Fast:* _____

_____

6. *Free:* _____

_____

7. *Bar:* _____

_____

8. *Battery:* _____

_____

9. *Heavy:* _____

_____

10. *Cool:* _____

_____

List two additional words that are potentially ambiguous and give the various meanings.

11. _____

_____

12. _____

_____

---

I remember that, when I was much younger, my mother used to ask for ➤•◀ "hose" for Christmas each year. Since we had plenty of garden hose, I was puzzled over why she should keep asking for additional sections each year. (If she had told me that she wanted to wear the hose on her legs, I really would have been confused!)

Describe an incident in your life in which the misinterpretation of an ambiguous word resulted in confusion for you.

Not only individual words but groups of words, too, can be ambiguous. Someone might say to you: "I hope you get what you deserve!" Unless the context of the remark makes clear the speaker's intention, we may not be sure if he or she is wishing us well or ill.

In addition to words, actions and situations can be ambiguous as well. An action or situation is considered to be ambiguous if it can be given more than one possible interpretation. For example,

Someone you know slaps you on the back—*hard!*

A casual friend gives you a passionate good-night kiss.

In each of these situations, we may be unclear as to exactly what is being expressed, and so we are not sure how to interpret the meaning of the action or the situation. This is the same circumstance that we discussed in Chapter Six, when we examined how we develop our beliefs about the world based on how we interpret our perceptions. (e.g., Is the man offering the child candy to be commended—or arrested?)

In all cases of ambiguous human behavior, whether verbal or nonverbal, the same principle applies: We have to carefully examine all the relevant aspects of the situation in order to arrive at the most accurate and complete interpretation.

 Describe an ambiguous experience from your own life, in which you were not initially sure of the "correct" interpretation of what was taking place. How did you figure out which of the several possible interpretations was the most accurate explanation?

## Language and thinking

Throughout this book, we have found that thinking is the organized and purposeful way we make sense of the world. In this chapter we have been discovering that the process of making sense of the world effectively depends on our ability to represent our thoughts, feelings, and experiences with language. In using language, we are able to

*identify* (or name) our experiences.

*distinguish* these experiences from one another.

*relate* these experiences (an aspect we will be examining more fully in the chapters ahead).

*describe* these experiences to others who share an understanding of our language.

The more we examine language and thinking, the clearer it becomes that these two human activities are so closely related that it is difficult to separate them. Reread the passages that you wrote on page 238. You were not simply putting words together but instead using language to express your thinking. The same is true when we use language to speak. We are not simply making sounds; we are conveying ideas, expressing feelings, and describing experiences.

Working together, thinking and language enable us to identify, represent, and give form to our thoughts, feelings, and experiences. Once these experiences are represented, we can share them with others who have the same language system.

---

Can you describe what the following language is expressing?                    ➤•◄

### Thi Tartli end thi Rebbot

Unci apun e tomi, thiri wes e tartli end e rebbot. Thi rebbot asid tu meki fan uf thi tartli, seyong thongs loki: "Yua eri thi sluwist thong un fuar ligs." Thos rodocali asid tu hart thi tartli's fiilongs, dispoti hos herd shill end thock skon. Uni dey hi gut fid ap end seod tu thi errugent rebbot: "Lit's hevi e reci, yua mosirebli, huppong hutshut!"

Now translate this language into a different language by substituting letters according to the following formula:

e = a, i = e, o = i, a = u, u = o

Can you now describe the thoughts and feelings that are being expressed? Write down your translation:

_____

_____

_____

_____

_____

_____

_____

---

Reflecting on this experience, you probably found initially that the group of markings above had little or no meaning for you. For, although English letters were being used, the groups of letters were not part of a language system you understood. However, once you "cracked the code" by substituting the appropriate letters, these markings should have expressed a fairly definite meaning to you. After these markings were translated into a shared system of language symbols, this language could then communicate the thoughts and feelings the writer was trying to express.

►•◄     Create your own message of approximately forty words by using a coded language. Then see if the other members of your class can make any sense of the thinking you are trying to communicate.

Even when we are not trying to communicate our thinking and feelings to others, language is a crucial part of our thinking process. Take a minute out and think about what you are going to be doing tonight. Now reflect on the thinking process in which you just engaged. In all likelihood, as you thought about your plans for tonight, you were using language to think about your plans. In fact, much of the thinking that we do involves using language, as we often seem to be carrying on a conversation with ourselves.

Of course, there is an advantage to expressing our thinking out loud in writing or speaking. Once our thoughts are actually expressed in language, we and others can examine and evaluate them, that is, "think about our thinking." This process of critically reflecting on our thinking serves continually to sharpen and develop our thinking and is also a crucial step in the process of writing. In fact, it is what we are doing when we write a draft of something and then revise this draft in order to clarify and improve the thinking it is expressing (the same way you revised your passages on page 238).

### Clarity in language and thinking

Since language and thinking are so closely related, how well we do with one is directly related to how well we do with the other. In most cases, when we are thinking clearly, we are able to express our ideas clearly in language. For instance, reflect on when you were writing the four passages earlier in the chapter. You probably found that you were able to express yourself clearly in language as you developed a clear idea of what you wanted to say.

On the other hand, if we are *not* able to develop a clear and precise idea of what we are thinking about, then we have great difficulty in expressing our thinking in language. When this happens, we usually say something like this:

"I know what I want to say, but I just can't find the right words."

Of course, when this happens, we usually don't "know" exactly what we want to say. When we have unclear thoughts, it is usually because we lack a clear understanding of the situation *or* we do not know the right language to give form to these thoughts. When our thoughts are truly clear and precise, this means that we know the words to give form to these thoughts and so are able to express them in language. One of the benefits of critically examining our writing, as you did when you revised your passages, is that we are able to develop the language that more clearly expresses our thinking.

## Language influences thinking

Not only does unclear thinking contribute to unclear language expression; unclear language contributes to unclear thinking. For example, read the following passage from William Shakespeare's *As You Like It,* Act 5, scene i. Language is being used in a confusing way for the purpose of confusing our thinking. Examine the passage carefully and then describe as clearly as you can the thinking that the author is trying to express:

> Therefore, you clown, abandon—which is in the vulgar, leave—the society—which in the boorish is company, of this female—which in the common is woman; which together is, abandon the society of this female, or clown, thou perishest; or, to thy better understanding, diest; or, to wit, I kill thee, make thee away, translate thy life into death.

Write your translation:

_____

_____

_____

_____

_____

_____

_____

_____

Reread the passages you revised on page 238. Are there any points at which your meaning is not clear? Rethink what you want to say. Revise your writing as needed.

The relationship between language and thinking is like a circle. When our use of language is sloppy—that is, vague, general, indistinct, imprecise, foolish, inaccurate, and so on—it leads to thinking of the same sort:

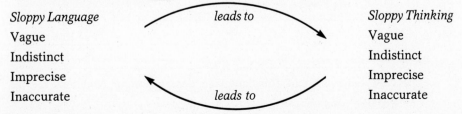

| Sloppy Language | *leads to* | Sloppy Thinking |
|---|---|---|
| Vague | | Vague |
| Indistinct | | Indistinct |
| Imprecise | | Imprecise |
| Inaccurate | *leads to* | Inaccurate |

Of course, the reverse is also true. Language use that is clear and precise leads to clear and precise thinking:

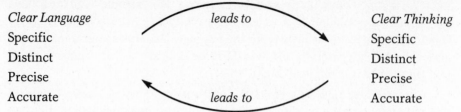

| Clear Language | leads to | Clear Thinking |
|---|---|---|
| Specific | | Specific |
| Distinct | | Distinct |
| Precise | | Precise |
| Accurate | leads to | Accurate |

If we are really interested in developing our ability to think clearly, then we will have to pay a great deal of attention to developing our command of language.

### Language shapes the way we see the world

Language gives form to our thoughts and feelings and enables us to express them. As we have also seen in this chapter, our thinking affects our language and vise versa. That is, when we work at thinking in a clear and precise way, this contributes to a clear and precise use of language. And when we use language in a clear and precise way, this contributes to clear and precise thinking.

Language plays a significant role in our lives, for it affects

our perceptions of the world.

the beliefs and knowledge we develop.

our decisions on how to act.

---

 Reread the accounts of Malcolm X's assassination from *Life* magazine and *The New York Post* (pp. 141–142). In each of these cases, the language that the author has selected to portray Malcolm X expresses a way of seeing him, reflects certain beliefs about him, and suggests a way of acting toward him.

After reading each passage carefully, respond to the following questions.

A.  *Life* magazine

    1.  Identify the key words or phrases in this passage that describe Malcolm X.

        a. _____

        b. _____

        c. _____

    2.  *If* you believed that this language description of Malcolm X was accurate,

     a.  how would you *perceive* him? _____

               _____

     b.  what *beliefs* might you have formed about him? _____

               _____

     c.  how would you be inclined to *act* toward him? _____

               _____

B.  *The New York Post*

   1.  Identify the key words or phrases in this passage that describe Malcolm X.

     a.  _____

     b.  _____

     c.  _____

   2.  *If* you believed that this language description of Malcolm X was accurate,

     a.  how would you *perceive* him? _____

               _____

     b.  what *beliefs* might you have formed about him? _____

               _____

     c.  how would you be inclined to *act* toward him? _____

               _____

As this exercise suggests, the language we use influences the way we make sense of the world. A change in language suggests different ways of seeing and understanding the world. For example, review the narrative by Roberto Acuna (pp. 170–176). Acuna originally characterizes himself with the words "migrant worker," a description that influenced him to make sense of the world in a certain way. In thinking of himself as a "migrant worker,"

   1.  how did Acuna *perceive* himself? _____

        _____

   2.  what *beliefs* did he form regarding his situation and his future? _____

        _____

3. what *actions* did he take based on this view of himself and his situation? ___

_____

_____

As Acuna evolved from thinking of himself as a "migrant worker" to conceiving of himself as a "union organizer," this change in language reflected and influenced a change in the way he was making sense of the world. In describing himself as a "union organizer,"

1. how did Acuna *perceive* himself? _____

_____

2. what *beliefs* did he form regarding his situation and his future? _____

_____

3. what *actions* did he take based on this view of himself and his situation? ___

_____

_____

Of course, from the standpoint of the produce growers, Acuna evolved from being an obedient worker ("I was a company man, yes") to being a trouble-maker and a nuisance. *If* you adopted the perspective of the growers that Acuna was a trouble-maker,

1. how would you *perceive* Acuna? _____

_____

2. what *beliefs* might you form regarding him? _____

_____

_____

3. what *actions* might you be inclined to take toward him? _____

_____

_____

Review the shaping essay by Maria (p. 180). At the beginning of her experience, Maria might have described herself as "a law-abiding citizen" with faith in the criminal justice system. By the end of the experience, she might have characterized herself as "a less naive citizen" with a more realistic view of the manner in which the system operates. Each of these descriptions of herself reflect and influence Maria's way of making sense of the world.

Now reread the shaping essay that you wrote (p. 177) and analyze it by ➤•◄
answering the following questions:

1. What language would you use to describe yourself at the *beginning* of the experience?

   _____

   _____

2. Explain how this description of yourself reflected and influenced the way you made sense of the world.

   a. How did you *perceive* yourself and the situation?

      _____

      _____

   b. What *beliefs* did you form regarding yourself and the situation?

      _____

      _____

      _____

   c. What *actions* did you take based on this conception of yourself?

      _____

      _____

      _____

3. What language would you use to describe yourself at the *end* of this experience?

   _____

   _____

4. Explain how this description of yourself influenced the way you now made sense of the world.

   a. How did you *perceive* yourself and the situation?

      _____

      _____

   b. What *beliefs* did you form regarding yourself and the situation?

      _____

      _____

c.  What *actions* did you take based on this conception of yourself?

   During every day of our lives, we are presented with descriptions of things and events that are designed to influence the way we think.

Select an important national or world event or issue that is currently in the news. Identify and describe at least two different descriptions of this event or issue. For each description, analyze the event by answering the following questions:

1.  How does the language influence my *perception* of the event or issue?
2.  How does the language influence the *beliefs* I will form about the event or issue?
3.  How does this description influence the *actions* I might be inclined to take regarding the event or issue?

# Chapter Eight
# Symbolizing & Map-Making

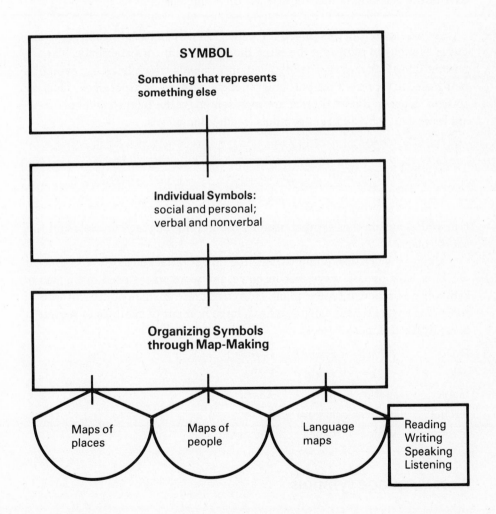

**SYMBOL**

**Something that represents something else**

**Individual Symbols:**
social and personal;
verbal and nonverbal

**Organizing Symbols through Map-Making**

Maps of places

Maps of people

Language maps

Reading
Writing
Speaking
Listening

OUR LANGUAGE is the most powerful thinking tool that we have. This power of language is based on the way in which it is able to give form to our thoughts, feelings, and experiences by representing them. The process of using one thing, such as our language, to represent something else is known as *symbolizing*. For example, when we use the word *tree* to represent a particular sort of plant in the world the word *tree* is acting as a symbol.

**Symbol** • Something that represents something else.

As we saw in Chapter Seven, "Language," we can use any number of language symbols to represent the same thought, feeling, or experience. The important thing is that everyone involved understands which language symbol is being used to represent the particular thought, feeling, or experience. Thus the sorts of things in the world that are represented by the English symbol "tree" are represented by different symbols in other languages.

*Das Baum* (German)

Can you name another symbol used by a different language to represent this sort of plant?

Chapter Seven also demonstrated the power of language to represent our world in very precise ways. For instance, the word *tree* is used in English to symbolize a particular type of plant. However, there are many different sorts of trees in the world. Each language has a large number of symbols to represent these different kinds of trees:

| *English* | *French* | *Spanish* | *German* |
|-----------|----------|-----------|----------|
| oak | chêne | roble | Eiche |
| maple | érable | arce | Ahorn |
| birch | bouleau | abedul | Birke |
| mahogany | acajou | caoba | Mahagoni |

## Non-language symbols

Although language is the most comprehensive and precise way we have for symbolizing our thoughts, feelings, and experiences, it is by no means the only way. Consider the following figures. In each case, describe what the figure represents to you.

In reviewing these figures, you probably found that virtually all of them were meaningful because they represented some thought, feeling, or experience to you. If they did represent something to you, then the figures were acting as *symbols* for you. And just like language symbols, non-language symbols such as these figures can be used to communicate with others.

It is possible for us to use symbols to share our experiences with each other because people are able to agree on what the symbols are going to represent. When the meaning of a symbol is established by shared agreement (e.g., $ represents money), these symbols are termed conventional, since they reflect the shared conventions of a group of people. The only reason that we can all drive our cars, trucks, and motorcycles together in groups is because we all recognize—and accept—symbols like stop signs, yield signs, and stoplights. Without these conventional symbols, our roads would resemble a giant game of bumper cars.

However, even in the case of conventional symbols, which have a shared social meaning, we sometimes find that the symbols do not represent exactly the same things to each one of us. To illustrate this, compare your descriptions of the symbols above with the descriptions written by other members of the class. In doing so, focus your attention on the *differences* in meaning that the symbols have for various class members. You will probably find that even though a symbol may have the same general meaning for various individuals, there are often some differences in exactly what the symbol represents.

Draw pictures of two symbols in your life that have a special meaning for you. Then describe what thoughts or feelings these symbols represent in your experience.

### Social and personal meaning

The descriptions that you have just written are explanations of what these symbols mean to you, what they represent in your experience. The meaning these symbols have for you may be shared by other people, or they may have a special, personal meaning for you that other people are unaware of. Or the symbols may have *both* social and personal meanings.

Select one of the symbols that you drew on page 253 and show it to another class member or the class as a whole. Have them describe in their own words what the symbol means to them.

Compare this description of the meaning of the symbol with your own description. How close did they come to expressing the thoughts or feelings that the symbol represents for you? Describe the shared social meaning.

*Shared social meaning:* _____

_____

_____

Now describe the personal meaning the symbol has for you that was not shared by others.

*Personal meaning:* _____

_____

_____

This exercise illustrates how the same symbol can represent a variety of different thoughts or feelings at the same time. It can embody certain socially agreed-upon meanings. But these socially shared meanings of symbols may be different if we change the social and political situation in which they occur. For instance, in recent Western culture, the swastika has represented the National Socialist (Nazi) party of Germany. However, in India, the same design is a symbol that means "Good luck!"

     Describe what you think is the socially shared meaning of the following symbol.

Now imagine that you are a Soviet citizen living in Russia. Describe what you think is the socially shared meaning of this same symbol in these different circumstances.

In addition to socially shared meanings, the analysis of your symbol above illustrates that symbols can also be surrounded by a network of personal meanings that are not shared by others. Consider the following figure, which depicts a New York City subway token:

The social meaning of this symbol is clear and is shared by everyone who is familiar with its use—it is a "token" of our paid fare to ride the subway. However, the personal meaning of this symbol for the student who chose it as an example was *not* shared by everyone, as he explains in the following statement:

> Two years ago I had an opportunity to work for the MTA selling tokens. The job paid well and was secure. Instead of taking the job, I decided to return to school, because I wanted a more fulfilling job than selling tokens. Every morning when I put my token in the turnstile on my way to school, I realize that the token is putting me on board a train taking me to a different life with new opportunities.

The process of symbolizing—of letting certain things represent other things—is a natural human activity. In fact, we are continually creating symbols, expressing ourselves with symbols, and interpreting the symbols of others. Virtually anything in our experience can become a symbol *if* we chose to let it represent some thought or feeling. For example, the length and style of a person's hair has symbolized (and continues to symbolize) a variety of different things at various times in our culture. Can you describe some of the things that "hair" has represented (or represents)?

| *Length and Style of Hair* | *What the Hair Represented* |
|---|---|
| 1. Men wearing shoulder-length hair in the 1960s | Rebellion against "the establishment"; having a different set of values |
| 2. _____ | _____ |
| _____ | _____ |
| 3. _____ | _____ |
| _____ | _____ |

►•◄        Select items from the following list and explain how they can serve as symbols, representing thoughts and feelings. Be specific.

a ring        home address        accent in speech
a beard       brand of cigarette   style of clothes
a college     or type of drink     type of car
education      music preference

*Symbol*                          *What the Symbol Represents*

1. _____        1. _____

   _____

2. _____        2. _____

   _____

3. _____        3. _____

   _____

Now identify two additional symbols in our culture and explain what the symbols represent to you and to those who share your understanding.

4. _____        4. _____

   _____

5. _____        5. _____

   _____

    Since symbols have socially accepted meanings, they can be used as extremely effective tools for influencing our thinking and feelings. When we see someone wearing a uniform, it carries a clear and often influential meaning for us, depending on the type of uniform. For each of the following categories, identify two symbols and describe what the symbols represent.

*Symbols of Authority*            *What the Symbol Represents*

1. _____        1. _____

   _____

2. _____        2. _____

   _____

*Symbols of Success*                    *What the Symbol Represents*

1. _____              1. _____

                                          _____

2. _____              2. _____

                                          _____


*Masculine Symbols*                     *What the Symbol Represents*

1. _____              1. _____

                                          _____

2. _____              2. _____

                                          _____


*Feminine Symbols*                      *What the Symbol Represents*

1. _____              1. _____

                                          _____

2. _____              2. _____

                                          _____


*Religious Symbols*                     *What the Symbol Represents*

1. _____              1. _____

                                          _____

2. _____              2. _____

                                          _____

---

    Locate an advertisement from a magazine that contains a variety of social symbols. Analyze the advertisement by identifying each of the symbols and explaining what the symbol represents.

    Then locate, from a time in the past (e.g., 1960s, 1950s, etc.), an advertisement that contains a variety of social symbols. Analyze the advertisement by identifying each of the symbols and explaining what you think the symbol represents.

    Write a short passage explaining the differences between these two different examples of symbol use.

## Organizing symbols

Symbols do not usually exist in isolation. Instead, we tend to cluster them together in groups, relating them to one another. Suppose someone handed you a pencil and a piece of paper with the request: Please draw me a detailed map that shows how to get to where you live from where we are now. Draw that map.

Maps, like the one you just drew, are often the simplest and clearest way to give directions to another person. Of course you could have shown the other person the way to where you live by actually taking the person there. However, using various symbols to construct a map is a much faster and more convenient way to accomplish the same purpose.

Maps are really groups of symbols that are organized in a particular way. Your map may have contained lines to represent streets; figures to represent lights, stop signs, buildings, etc.; as well as some numbers, letters, or words. All of these various items that you used to explain the way to where you live are symbols because they are being used to represent other things in the world. Identify the individual symbols that went into the making of your map and describe what they are symbols for. If it would be useful to add any other symbols to your map, then do so.

Of course, as we saw in the last chapter, even the words that you just used to explain what your visual symbols represent are symbols themselves (and so are the words you are now reading). Both the words "stop light" and the visual symbol are symbols representing the type of metal box with the red, yellow, and green lenses in it that hangs at a particular street corner.

In analyzing our maps, we can see that each of our individual symbols has a meaning because it represents an aspect of our experience. However, what makes our maps meaningful is not just the individual symbols, but the way these symbols are put together into a whole picture that makes sense to us. The entire map is a symbol that represents an area of our experience—the route to our home. And this larger symbol is composed of a number of individual symbols that stand in certain relationships to each other.

This is the way most of our symbols function, whether they are language symbols or non-language symbols. They are woven together like threads in a fabric, each symbol connecting to other symbols in many different ways.

### Verbal maps

Our ability to symbolize gives us the capacity to translate our thinking from one system of symbols into another system of symbols. For example, here is a translation of the *visual* map found on page 259 into a *verbal* map. Both maps express the same thinking by using different symbol systems.

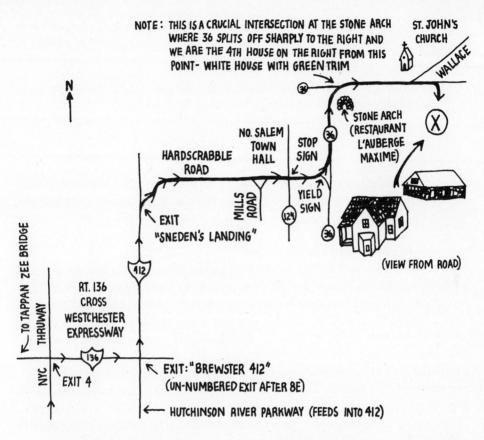

NOTE: THIS IS A CRUCIAL INTERSECTION AT THE STONE ARCH WHERE 36 SPLITS OFF SHARPLY TO THE RIGHT AND WE ARE THE 4TH HOUSE ON THE RIGHT FROM THIS POINT- WHITE HOUSE WITH GREEN TRIM

ST. JOHN'S CHURCH

WALLACE

STONE ARCH (RESTAURANT L'AUBERGE MAXIME)

N

HARDSCRABBLE ROAD

NO. SALEM TOWN HALL

STOP SIGN

36

MILLS ROAD

YIELD SIGN

124

36

(VIEW FROM ROAD)

EXIT "SNEDEN'S LANDING"

412

RT. 136 CROSS WESTCHESTER EXPRESSWAY

TO TAPPAN ZEE BRIDGE THRUWAY

136

NYC

EXIT 4

EXIT: "BREWSTER 412" (UN-NUMBERED EXIT AFTER 8E)

HUTCHINSON RIVER PARKWAY (FEEDS INTO 412)

Travel north on the New York State Thruway until you reach Exit 4. Take Exit 4 (be careful of the ramp—it's a sharp bend) and travel east on route 136 for about 12 miles. Take the exit marked Route 412 North, which is the next exit after Exit 8E (it doesn't have a number). Travel north on Route 412 to Exit 9 (Sneden's Landing), where you pick up Hardscrabble Road (east). Follow this around the north side of the Titicus Reservoir (look for the family of swans!) for about 8 miles until you reach a stop sign. Just before the stop sign, you'll pass the Town Hall on the left (built in 1767), and when you reach the intersection, you'll see the St. James Episcopal Church across the road.

Continue past the church until you reach a yield sign, which marks the intersection of Route 36. Take Route 36 north for about 3 miles. You'll pass through the center of town, which includes several old mills and churches that have been restored as houses. Take note of the huge boulder balanced on three smaller rocks ("The Balanced Rock"), supposedly left by the last glacier to cover this continent. Just beyond, look for the large 3-story building that used to serve as the post office, general store, and opera house, all rolled into one. After 3 miles, Hardscrabble Road bears off to the right from Route 36. Take this turnoff. The intersection is marked by a large fieldstone arch, which was built by an eccentric resident as a decoration for his front yard. Continue past the Catholic chapel on the left nestled alongside Artemis Horse Farm. The fourth house on the right is the one you are looking for. It's a small Victorian farmhouse—white clapboard with green trim—with a stone barn in the back. You're there.

➤•◄     Now translate the visual map you drew on page 258 into a verbal map. Remember to give a precise description of the information that you want to communicate.

### Making maps and making sense

We have seen in this chapter that the purpose of symbols is to represent (re-present) various aspects of the world in which we live. (Remember that "the world" includes not just the *physical* world, but also our *psychological/personal* and *social* worlds as well.) Symbols—whether visual or verbal—are the tools we use to make sense of the world. We cannot directly experience everything. In fact, our world of direct experiences is extremely limited, for we can only be in one place at one time. However, using symbols gives us the means to represent our personal experiences, enabling us to share our experiences with others and have them share their experiences with us. This is exactly what would happen if you showed the maps you just created to others. The symbols they contain would enable them to benefit from your personal knowledge of how to reach your home by showing them how to do so themselves.

In addition to profiting from the experiences of others, we can go beyond our world of direct experience by organizing symbols into a limitless number of different patterns. In fact, this is precisely what you were doing when you constructed your maps. In creating your visual map and your verbal map, you were trying to both represent *and* organize various aspects of your experience into a pattern that made sense for yourself and others. As you constructed your maps, you probably traveled the route home "in your mind," trying to recall the correct turns, street names, buildings, and so on. You then symbolized these experiences and organized the symbols into a meaningful pattern: your map.

We stated at the beginning of this section on organizing symbols that symbols do not usually exist in isolation. Instead, we tend to cluster them together into groups and relate them to one another. We can now see that the activity of making maps draws on both of the skills needed for making sense of our world:

1. Representing our experience with symbols
2. Organizing and relating these symbols into various patterns in order to gain an increased understanding of our experience

These two abilities—symbolizing and organizing—provide the foundation of our efforts to make sense of the world. We saw this in Chapters One and Two when we defined thinking as our ongoing attempts to make sense of the world in active, organized, and purposeful ways. In Chapter Four we found that we can solve many problems by identifying the key aspects of the problem situation and then organizing these parts in a systematic way. The activity of perceiving, we discovered in Chapter Five, involves our actively identifying, organizing, and interpreting our sensations. In Chapter Six we explored the way in which we use verbal and nonverbal symbols to construct our beliefs about the world in order to understand and anticipate what is going on in our experience. Additionally, we saw that our beliefs form a system or network that constitutes our "map" of the world. And in Chapter Seven we examined how language—our most articulate form of symbolizing—gives us the means to represent and organize our experience into patterns that we can think about and share with others.

If we could not represent our experience with symbols, we would not be able to organize and relate it in order to make sense of our world. This whole process of creating, organizing, and relating symbols in order to make sense of things is central to our thinking process, and it is going on all the time in an active mind.

### Creating accurate and precise maps

Creating maps is thus the way that we represent and organize our experience so that we can make sense of it. For example, if the visual and verbal maps that you constructed are accurate and if the people you show them to understand what your symbols represent, then they will be able to figure out

where they are.

where they are going.

the best way to get where they are going.

As we live our lives, we are usually interested in creating the most accurate and precise maps that we are able to. If our maps of the world are in fact relatively accurate, we will be able to do a pretty good job of making sense of things by

explaining what has happened.

understanding what is going on now and why it is occurring.

predicting what will take place in the future.

If we are effective in making sense of the world in this way, we will be in a good position to make intelligent decisions based on our understanding and predictions. This in turn will give us the means to reach our goals and increase our awareness of our world, ourselves, and others.

Our map of the world, formed by the system of beliefs that we develop, should *not* remain unchanged once we have created it. Instead, we should be continually modifying and developing it on the basis of new experiences and our critical examination of these experiences. As our knowledge and understanding increase, our developing insight should be reflected in an increasing accuracy and precision of our maps.

 Revise the map that you created on page 260, making it more precise and accurate. Here are some suggestions in working toward this goal:

Use orienting words—east, west, north, south

Establish distances—100 yards, three stop lights

Add more details—additional buildings, signs, landmarks

Use more specific descriptions—e.g., The Baptist church—white clapboard, red doors, lots of gingerbread trim, and a large steeple with a clock in it

**Nonphysical maps**

When we think of maps, we tend to think of symbolizing aspects of our *physical* world. However, we use the same mapping techniques to make sense of other, *non*physical aspects of our experience as well. For example, when someone introduces herself as Charlie's sister-in-law, we often create a mental diagram or map to make sense of this information.

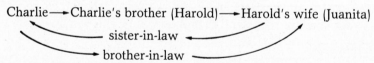

Suppose someone introduces himself as Charlie's cousin Alfred. How could you map this relationship? Suppose someone introduces herself to you as Charlie's great-niece, Felicia. How could you map this relationship?

Although, in order to make sense of the information that we encounter, we often create maps, we are usually not aware that we are doing so. To become more aware of this activity, construct maps that express the relationships indicated in the following information:

1. Paul is two inches taller than Arlene and twice the height of Ana Maria but is slightly shorter than Tom.

2. On a scale of one to ten, I would rate that movie a six and a half, which is four points higher than the one I saw last week—"I Ate the Mummy's Brain."

3. Affirmed won by a nose over Have-A-Heart, with Bell Dancer two lengths back and Satisfaction a distant fourth.

4. Oklahoma is located north of Texas, west of Arkansas, south of Kansas and east of Colorado.

### Creating maps of other people

In addition to using maps to understand the relationships expressed in much of the information we receive, we also create maps of a different sort to understand other people. For instance, select a person whom you think you know pretty well. Ask yourself the question: If you were to call this person up and ask to borrow $50, how do you think he or she would respond? Identify the reasons why you think that he or she would respond in this way.

Your prediction and analysis of how this person would respond is based on your experience of this person—your understanding of "who" he or she is. Your beliefs about this person may act as a map, in your mind, of what he or she is like. This map gives you a basis for predicting and anticipating how this person is likely to respond in various situations—like the one above.

The fact is that all human personalities display a certain *pattern* or *organization,* and our beliefs about people can be thought of as a "map" of their personality. If our map is reasonably accurate, then we will be able, with some degree of confidence, to

understand the things they have done and said in the past.

make sense of the things they are doing and saying in the present (and *why* they are doing and saying them).

predict the things they will do and say in the future.

For example, one way of expressing a friend's willingness or unwillingness to lend you $50 might be like the map on page 264.

---

Now think about the person you identified above. Construct a map similar  to the one on page 264 that expresses your thinking about your friend's willingness or unwillingness to lend you $50.

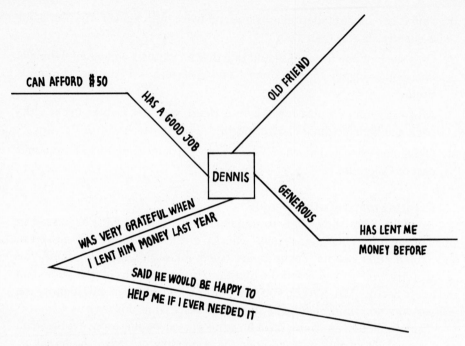

### Creating maps of ourselves

Not only do we continually construct maps of other people, we also construct maps of ourselves as well. The map we construct of ourselves is sometimes called our "self-concept," and it refers to the pattern or organization of our personality as we see it.

List ten words that you believe best describe you.

1. _____        6. _____

2. _____        7. _____

3. _____        8. _____

4. _____        9. _____

5. _____       10. _____

Relying on these words as points of reference, construct a map that expresses certain aspects of yourself, using the same form as we used above. The map on page 265 shows how one student completed this exercise.

HUMOROUS                    ENJOY NEW EXPERIENCES
INTELLIGENT                 LIKE TO MEET PEOPLE
CARING                      ATHLETIC
STRONG                      OPEN-MINDED
DEPENDABLE

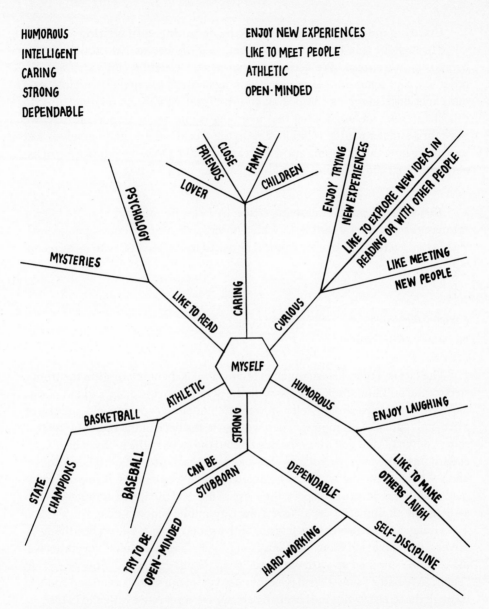

Just like our maps of other people, the map we create of ourselves may be relatively accurate *or* it may be relatively *in*accurate. When our maps are reasonably accurate, we say that we have a fairly realistic understanding of who we are. However, if our map is inaccurate, then we will have a distorted and unrealistic idea of who we are, what we want, and why we do the things we do.

**Creating maps for reading, speaking, listening, and writing**

Throughout this book, we have seen that we are active participants in composing our world. We actively organize and interpret our experience in order to make sense of it. Using our thinking abilities to organize and interpret our experience involves composing and interpreting various relationships. In this chapter we are suggesting that mapping is one of the important tools we have for representing the relationships in the world, others, and ourselves. Let us explore how this mapping approach can be applied to some other areas of experience, including reading, speaking, listening, and writing.

*Reading*    Read the following article by Peter Rondinone, entitled ''Open Admissions and the Inward 'I,' '' which describes his experiences going to college. After reading the article, you will be asked to outline the main ideas it contains.

## Open Admissions and the Inward 'I'
*by Peter J. Rondinone*

The fact is, I didn't learn much in high school. I spent my time on the front steps of the building smoking grass with the dudes from the dean's squad. For kicks we'd grab a freshman, tell him we were undercover cops, handcuff him to a banister, and take his money. Then we'd go to the back of the building, cop some ''downs,'' and nod away the day behind the steps in the lobby. The classrooms were overcrowded anyhow, and the teachers knew it. They also knew where to find me when they wanted to make weird deals: If I agreed to read a book and do an oral report, they'd pass me. So I did it and graduated with a ''general'' diploma. I was a New York City public school kid.

I hung out on a Bronx streetcorner with a group of guys who called themselves ''The Davidson Boys'' and sang songs like ''Daddy-lo-lo.'' Everything we did could be summed up with the word ''snap.'' That's a ''snap.'' She's a ''snap.'' We had a ''snap.'' Friday nights we'd paint ourselves green and run through the streets swinging baseball bats. Or we'd get into a little rap in the park. It was all very perilous. Even though I'd seen a friend stabbed for wearing the wrong colors and another blown away with a shotgun for ''messin' '' with some dude's woman, I was too young to realize that my life too might be headed toward a violent end.

Then one night I swallowed a dozen Tuminols and downed two quarts of beer at a bar in Manhattan. I passed out in the gutter. I puked and rolled under a parked car. Two girlfriends found me and carried me home. My overprotective brother answered the door. When he saw me—eyes rolling toward the back of my skull like rubber—he pushed me down a flight of stairs. My skull hit the edge of a marble step with a thud. The girls screamed. My parents came to the door and there I was: a high school graduate, a failure, curled in a ball in a pool of blood.

The next day I woke up with dried blood on my face. I had no idea what had happened. My sister told me. I couldn't believe it. Crying, my mother confirmed the story. I had almost died! That scared hell out of me. I knew I had to do something. I didn't know what. But pills and violence didn't promise much of a future.

I went back to a high school counselor for advice. He suggested I go to college.

I wasn't aware of it, but it seems that in May 1969 a group of dissident students from the black and Puerto Rican communities took over the south campus of the City College of New York (CCNY). They demanded that the Board of Higher Education and the City of New York adopt an open-admission policy that would make it possible for anybody to go to CCNY without the existing requirements: SATs and a high school average of 85. This demand was justified on the premise that college had always been for the privileged few and excluded minorities. As it turned out, in the fall of 1970 the City University's 18 campuses admitted massive numbers of students—15,000—with high school averages below 85. By 1972, I was one of them.

On the day I received my letter of acceptance, I waited until dinner to tell my folks. I was proud.

"Check out where I'm going," I said. I passed the letter to my father. He looked at it.

"You jerk!" he said. "You wanna sell ties?" My mother grabbed the letter.

"God," she said. "Why don't you go to work already? Like other people."

"Later for that," I said. "You should be proud."

At the time, of course, I didn't understand where my parents were coming from. They were immigrants. They believed college was for rich kids, not the ones who dropped downs and sang songs on streetcorners.

My mother had emigrated from Russia after World War II. She came to the United States with a bundle of clothes, her mother and father, a few dollars, and a baby from a failed marriage. Her first job was on an assembly line in a pen factory where she met my father, the production manager.

My father, a second-generation Italian, was brought up on the Lower East Side of Manhattan. He never completed high school. And when he wasn't working in a factory, he peddled Christmas lights door to door or sold frankfurters in Times Square.

My family grew up in the south Bronx. There were six children, and we slept in one room on cots. We ate spaghetti three times a week and were on welfare because for a number of years my father was sick, in and out of the hospital.

Anyhow, I wasn't about to listen to my parents and go to work; for a dude like me, this was a big deal. So I left the dinner table and went to tell my friends about my decision.

The Davidson Boys hung out in a rented storefront. They were sitting around the pool table on milk boxes and broken pinball machines, spare tires and dead batteries. I made my announcement. They stood up and circled me like I was the star of a cockfight. Sucio stepped to the table with a can of beer in one hand and a pool stick in the other.

''Wha' you think you gonna get out of college?'' he said.

''I don't know, but I bet it beats this,'' I said. I shoved one of the pool balls across the table. That was a mistake. The others banged their sticks on the wood floor and chanted, ''Oooh-ooh—snap, snap.'' Sucio put his beer on the table.

''Bull!'' he yelled. ''I wash dishes with college dudes. You're like us—nuttin', man.'' He pointed the stick at my nose.

Silence.

I couldn't respond. If I let the crowd know I thought their gig was uncool, that I wanted out of the club, they would have taken it personally. And they would have taken me outside and kicked my ass. So I lowered my head. ''Aw, hell, gimme a hit of beer,'' I said, as if it were all a joke. But I left the corner and didn't go back.

I spent that summer alone, reading books like *How to Succeed in College* and *30 Days to a More Powerful Vocabulary*. My vocabulary was limited to a few choice phrases like, ''Move over, Rover, and let Petey take over.'' When my friends did call for me I hid behind the curtains. I knew that if I was going to make it, I'd have to push these guys out of my consciousness as if I were doing the breaststroke in a sea of logs. I had work to do, and people were time consuming. As it happened, all my heavy preparations didn't amount to much.

On the day of the placement exams I went paranoid. Somehow I got the idea that my admission to college was some ugly practical joke that I wasn't prepared for. So I copped some downs and took the test nodding. The words floated on the page like flies on a crock of cream.

That made freshman year difficult. The administration had placed me in all three remedial programs: basic writing, college skills, and math. I was shocked. I had always thought of myself as smart. I was the only one in the neighborhood who read books. So I gave up the pills and pushed aside another log.

The night before the first day of school, my brother walked into my room and threw a briefcase on my desk. "Good luck, Joe College," he said. He smacked me in the back of the head. Surprised, I went to bed early.

I arrived on campus ahead of time with a map in my pocket. I wanted enough time, in case I got lost, to get to my first class. But after wandering around the corridors of one building for what seemed like a long time and hearing the sounds of classes in session, the scrape of chalk and muted discussions, I suddenly wondered if I was in the right place. So I stopped a student and pointed to a dot on my map.

"Look." He pointed to the dot. "Now look." He pointed to an inscription on the front of the building. I was in the right place. "Can't you read?" he said. Then he joined some friends. As he walked off I heard someone say, "What do you expect from open admissions?"

I had no idea that there were a lot of students who resented people like me, who felt I was jeopardizing standards, destroying their institution. I had no idea. I just wanted to go to class.

In Basic Writing I the instructor, Regina Sackmary, chalked her name in bold letters on the blackboard. I sat in the front row and reviewed my *How to Succeed* lessons: Sit in front/don't let eyes wander to cracks on ceilings/take notes on a legal pad/make note of all unfamiliar words and books/listen for key phrases like "remember this," they are a professor's signals. The other students held pens over pads in anticipation. Like me, they didn't know what to expect. We were public school kids from lousy neighborhoods and we knew that some of us didn't have a chance; but we were ready to work hard.

Before class we had rapped about our reasons for going to college. Some said they wanted to be the first in the history of their families to have a college education—they said their parents never went to college because they couldn't afford it, or because their parents' parents were too poor—and they said open admissions and free tuition ($65 per semester) was a chance to change that history. Others said they wanted to be educated so they could return to their neighborhoods to help "the people"; they were the idealists. Some foreigners said they wanted to return to their own countries and start schools. And I said I wanted to escape the boredom and the pain I had known as a kid on the streets. But none of them said they expected a job. Or if they did they were reminded that there were no jobs.

Ms. Sackmary told us that Basic Writing I was part of a three-part program. Part one would instruct us in the fundamentals of composition: sentence structure, grammar, and paragraphing; part two, the outline and essay; and part three, the term paper. She also explained that we weren't in basic writing because there was something wrong with us—we just needed to learn the basics, she said. Somehow I didn't believe her. After class I went to her office. She gave me a quick test. I couldn't write a coherent sentence or construct a paragraph. So we made an agreement: I'd write an essay a day in addition to my regular classwork. Also, I'd do a few term papers. She had this idea that learning to write was like learning to play a musical instrument—it takes practice, everyday practice.

In math I was in this remedial program for algebra, geometry, and trigonometry. But unlike high school math, which I thought was devised to boggle the mind for the sake of boggling, in this course I found I could make a connection between different mathematical principles and my life. For instance, there were certain basics I had to learn—call them 1, 2, and 3— and unless they added up to 6 I'd probably be a failure. I also got a sense of how math related to the world at large: Unless the sum of the parts of a society equaled the whole there would be chaos. And these insights jammed my head and made me feel like a kid on a ferris wheel looking at the world for the first time. Everything amazed me!

Like biology. In high school I associated this science with stabbing pins in the hearts of frogs for fun. Or getting high snorting small doses of the chloroform used for experiments on fruit flies. But in college biology I began to learn and appreciate not only how my own life processes functioned but how there were thousands of other life processes I'd never known existed. And this gave me a sense of power, because I could deal with questions like, Why do plants grow? not as I had before, with a simple spill of words: " 'Cause of the sun, man.'' I could actually explain that there was a plant cycle and cycles within the plant cycle. You know how the saying goes—a little knowledge is dangerous. Well, the more I learned the more I ran my mouth off, especially with people who didn't know as much as I did.

I remember the day Ms. Sackmary tossed Sartre's *No Exit* in my lap and said, ''Find the existential motif.'' I didn't know what to look for . What was she talking about? I never studied philosophy. I turned to the table of contents, but there was nothing under E. So I went to the library and after much research I discovered the notion of the absurd. I couldn't believe it. I told as many people as I could. I told them they were absurd, their lives were absurd, everything was absurd. I became obsessed with existentialism. I read Kafka, Camus,

Dostoevski, and others in my spare time. Then one day I found a line in a book that I believed summed up my unusual admittance to the college and my determination to work hard. I pasted it to the headboard of my bed. It said: "Everything is possible."

To deal with the heavy workload from all my classes, I needed a study schedule, so I referred to my *How to Succeed* book. I gave myself an hour for lunch and reserved the rest of the time between classes and evenings for homework and research. All this left me very little time for friendships. But I stuck to my schedule and by the middle of that first year I was getting straight A's. Nothing else mattered. Not even my family.

One night my sister pulled me from my desk by the collar. She sat me on the edge of the bed. "Mom and Dad bust their ass to keep you in school. They feed you. Give you a roof. And this is how you pay them back?" She was referring to my habit of locking myself in my room.

"What am I supposed to do?" I said.

"Little things. Like take down the garbage."

"Come on. Mom and Dad need me for that?"

"You know Dad has arthritis. His feet hurt. You want *him* to take it down?" My sister can be melodramatic.

"Let Mom do it," I said. "Or do her feet hurt too?"

"You bastard," she said. "You selfish bastard. The only thing you care about is your books."

She was right. I *was* selfish. But she couldn't understand that in many ways college had become a substitute for my family because what I needed I couldn't get at home. Nobody's fault. She cried.

When I entered my second year my family began to ask, "What do you want to do?" And I got one of those cards from the registrar that has to be filled out in a week or you're dropped from classes. It asked me to declare my major. I had to make a quick decision. So I checked off BS degree, dentistry, though I didn't enroll in a single science course.

One course I did take that semester was The Writer and the City. The professor, Ross Alexander, asked the class to keep a daily journal. He said it should be as creative as possible and reflect some aspect of city life. So I wrote about different experiences I had with my friends. For example, I wrote "Miracle on 183rd Street" about the night "Raunchy" Rick jumped a guy in the park and took his portable radio. When the guy tried to fight back Rick slapped him in the face with the radio; then, using the batteries that spilled out, he pounded this guy in the head until the blood began to puddle on the ground. Those of us on the sidelines dragged Rick away. Ross attached notes to my papers that said things like: "You really have a great hit of talent and ought to take courses in creative writing and sharpen your craft! Hang on to it all for dear life."

In my junior year I forgot dentistry and registered as a creative writing major. I also joined a college newspaper, *The Campus.* Though I knew nothing about journalism, I was advised that writing news was a good way to learn the business. And as Ross once pointed out to me, "As a writer you will need an audience."

I was given my first assignment. I collected piles of quotes and facts and scattered the mess on a desk. I remember typing the story under deadline pressure with one finger while the editors watched me struggle, probably thinking back to their own first stories. When I finished, they passed the copy around. The editor-in-chief looked at it last and said, "This isn't even English." Yet, they turned it over to a rewrite man and the story appeared with my by-line. Seeing my name in print was like seeing it in lights—flashbulbs popped in my head and I walked into the school cafeteria that day expecting to be recognized by everyone. My mother informed the relatives: "My son is a writer!"

Six months later I quit *The Campus.* A course in New Journalism had made me realize that reporting can be creative. For the first time I read writers like Tom Wolfe and Hunter S. Thompson, and my own news stories began to turn into first-person accounts that read like short stories. *The Campus* refused to publish my stuff, so I joined *The Observation Post,* the only paper on campus that printed first-person material. I wanted to get published.

My first *Post* feature article (a first-person news story on a proposed beer hall at CCNY) was published on the front page. The staff was impressed enough to elect me assistant features editor. However, what they didn't know was that the article had been completely rewritten by the features editor. And the features editor had faith in me, so he never told. He did my share of the work and I kept the title. As he put it: "You'll learn by hanging around and watching. You show talent. You might even get published professionally in 25 years!" Another thing they didn't know—I still hadn't passed my basic English proficiency exam.

Get into this: When people hear me tell this story about how I struggled without friends and closed myself off from most things, they often wonder: "Well, what did you do for . . .uh, you know, GIRLS!" And so I tell them: The only girlfriend I had, in my junior year, left me after 10 months. She got tired of watching television every weekend while I occupied myself with reading and studying; and she got tired of my pulling English usage books from under the pillow after we'd made love. But I did pass the English proficiency exam at the end of my junior year.

During my four years at CCNY I have learned something else—that an awful lot of people were put off by open-admission students. And some of them were City College professors. Take a book I reviewed a few months ago in *The Observation Post*—*The End of Education* by Geoffrey Wagner, a CCNY English professor. Wagner refers repeatedly to open-admission students as "Joe Blows," "dunces," and "sleeping beauties." And he also clearly detests blacks ("Leroi" he calls them) and others who wear afros, whom he describes in a cruel and absurd fashion: "I would find myself telling some charming child whose only visible sign of imminent anarchy was an afro so wide she had difficulty navigating my door, 'See, you've used "imperialist" four times.' "

Shortly after my review appeared, protesting that the book "is so full of inaccuracies that people at the college are calling it a great work of fiction," I received a copy of a letter attached to another, favorable review of *The End of Education* by Wagner's colleague Robert K. Morris. The letter said:

> Perhaps you would be so kind as to pass this one on to the ineffable (& unlovely) RONDINONE, with my compliments—*if* he can read!
>
> Best, Geoffrey

Though Wagner questions my ability to read (me, this open-admission "dummy"), he should in fact remember that I was once a student in his Writing for Humanities course—and he gave me an A!

Not all the detractors of open admissions were insiders. I once watched a network television crew interview a campus newspaper staff for a documentary on open admissions. An interviewer from "60 Minutes," notebook on his lap, sat like he had a box of Cracker Jacks, opposite three campus editors who looked as if they were waiting for the prize. I stood in a corner. He passed a remark: "I was down at the Writing Center today. Those kids are animals. They can't write." The editors, who were a conservative bunch, shook their heads as if they understood this to be their terrible legacy. I wanted to spit.

"Hey you!" I said. "Do I look like an animal?"

He closed his notebook and looked down his long nose at me. I felt like an ant at the mercy of an aardvark. The editors got puffy. "Who is this kid?" they mumbled. "Who do you think you are?" I yelled back. "Those kids you are talking about are not only willing to learn, but they are learning. They've written some beautiful essays and stories. You stupid jerk!"

God, those early days were painful. Professors would tear up my papers the day they were due and tell me to start over again, with a piece of advice—"Try to say what you really mean," Papers I had spent weeks writing. And I knew I lacked the basic college skills; I was a man reporting to work without his tools. So I smiled when I didn't understand. But sometimes it showed and I paid the price: A professor once told me the only reason I'd pass his course was that I had a nice smile. Yes, those were painful days.

And there were nights I was alone with piles of notebooks and textbooks. I wanted to throw the whole mess out the window; I wanted to give up. Nights the sounds of my friends singing on the corner drifted into my room like a fog over a graveyard and I was afraid I would be swept away. And nights I was filled with questions but the answers were like moon shadows on my curtains: I could see them but I could not grasp them.

Yet I had learned a vital lesson from these countless hours of work in isolation: My whole experience from the day I received my letter of acceptance enabled me to understand how in high school my sense of self-importance came from being one of the boys, a member of the pack, while in college the opposite was true. In order to survive, I had to curb my herd instinct.

Nobody, nobody could give me what I needed to overcome my sense of inadequacy. That was a struggle I had to work at on my own. It could never be a group project. In the end, though people could point out what I had to learn and where to learn it, I was always the one who did the work; and what I learned I earned. And that made me feel as good as being one of the boys. In short, college taught me to appreciate the importance of being alone. I found it was the only way I could get any serious work done.

But those days of trial and uncertainty are over, and the open-admission policy has been eliminated. Anybody who enters the City University's senior colleges must now have an 80 percent high school average. And I am one of those fortunate individuals who in a unique period of American education was given a chance to attend college. But I wonder what will happen to those people who can learn but whose potential doesn't show in their high school average; who might get into street crime if not given a chance to do something constructive? I wonder, because if it weren't for open admissions, the likelihood is I would still be swinging baseball bats on the streets on Friday nights.

---

➤•◄         Reread the article by Peter Rodinone (pp. 266–274). Create an outline of what you consider the most important ideas in the reading.

After writing your outline, describe any problems you had in writing it.

As you worked on the project of outlining this reading, your efforts probably took the form of a listing of ideas or of a traditional outline that organizes information using the following format:

A.   First most important idea
　　1.   Ideas related to A
　　　　a.   Ideas related to 1

        (1) Ideas related to a

B.   Next most important idea

In trying to express your ideas in this sort of sequential order, you may have experienced some of the following difficulties:

1. Which are the most important points? What order should they come in? Where do I begin and end?
2. What are the subpoints and the sub-subpoints? How many of each should I try to identify?
3. How can I add to or revise the outline without redoing the whole thing?

These common difficulties highlight a number of problems with using a list or a traditional outline format to describe ideas and their relationships to each other. For instance, one important drawback of the listing or outline format is that it forces us to organize the entire subject before all of the information has been thought through. You may have found that part way through your outline you wanted to make some changes because the overall organization of the article suddenly looked different. Unfortunately, the outline format does not permit easy revision. To add new ideas or reorganize the ideas already included in the outline means that we often have to cross out what we have done and begin again.

    A second drawback to this sort of format is that we can only express a limited number of relationships between the ideas we are describing.

    Most important

     Less important

      Least important

In addition, once an idea has been identified, it tends to be left alone and forgotten, even though it may have important relationships to other ideas in the article.

    Let us try the mapping approach to organizing information that we have been exploring and see if it avoids any of these problems associated with the traditional outline format. In using this mapping approach, we will be following these guidelines:

1. Begin with what you consider to be the most important idea as the "center" of the map and then branch out from it to related ideas.
2. Your ideas should be written on lines that are connected to other lines, in order to express clearly the relationship between the various ideas.
3. Print the ideas in capital letters so that they can be easily read and referred to.

As we try to outline the Rondinone article, a number of ideas might be considered as central or important. We will be focusing on the following ones:

Rondinone's experience in high school

Rondinone's experience in college

A partially completed map of the first of these ideas—Rondinone's experience in high school—is pictured below. Reread the first part of the article and then add to the map any ideas that you think are appropriate.

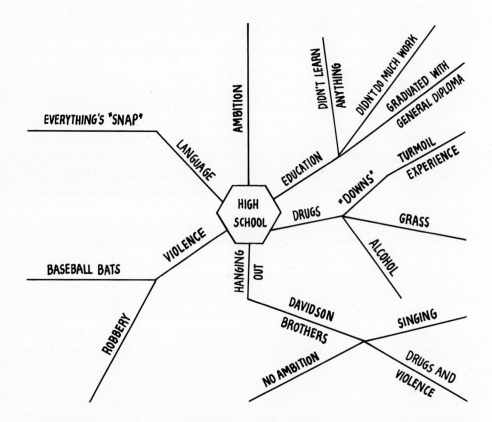

There are a number of advantages to using this sort of mapping strategy to express ideas and their relationships. First, the organization grows naturally, reflecting the way our mind naturally makes associations and organizes information. Second, the organization can be easily revised on the basis of new information and our developing understanding of how this information should be organized. Third, we can express a variety of relationships among the various ideas. And instead of being identified once and then forgotten, each idea remains an active part of the overall pattern, suggesting new possible relationships. Fourth, we do not have to decide initially on a beginning, subpoints, subsubpoints, etc. This can be done after our pattern is complete, saving us time and frustration.

---

Using this mapping approach, let us explore the second of the ideas we identified in this essay: Rondinone's experiences at college. You might want to quickly reread the second part of the essay, which deals with this. Then, starting with the central ideas of his experience at college, map out the various ideas contained in the article.

---

Reread the passages written by Malcolm X (p. 12) and Roberto Acuna (p. 170). Construct maps exploring the relationships among ideas in each of these articles.

---

Read carefully the following passage, which deals with the two different sides of our brain. Then construct a map that explores the relationships among ideas in this reading.

## Our Two-Sided Brain

One of the most intriguing areas of scientific and educational exploration concerns the manner in which our brain processes information. It has been known for a long time that the brain is divided into two seemingly identical halves, usually termed the left hemisphere and the right hemisphere. Until recently, it was assumed that these two hemispheres were similar in the way that they operated. However, a variety of current research has shown conclusively that each hemisphere has a distinct "personality," processing information in its own unique way.

The left hemisphere exhibits those qualities that we normally associate with higher intellectual activities. For example, the left hemisphere functions analytically, tending to break things and processes down into component parts, like taking apart an automobile engine in order to diagnose the problem. The left hemisphere is also the seat of most of our verbal activity, decoding and encoding the bulk of our language, mathematical symbols, and musical notations. Finally, the left hemisphere tends to process information in a linear, sequential way, one step at a time. This is consistent with the verbal capacities which it exhibits, since language is spoken/heard/read one word at a time, and the meaning of the words depends in large measure on the order in which the words are placed. In short, the left hemisphere is similar to a modern, digitable computer in that its individual operations unfold in an orderly, logical sequence.

The right hemisphere operates in a much different fashion. Instead of analyzing things and processes into component parts, it seeks to synthesize by organizing parts into patterns and wholes—like arranging individual flowers into a floral arrangement. The right hemisphere normally has much less to do with verbal activity. Instead, it is much more visually oriented, focusing on shapes, arrangements, and images. It also processes information based on what we personally experience with all of our senses (including touch). So, for example, while the left hemisphere might enable us to remember someone by their name, the right hemisphere might enable us to recognize them by their face or the feel of their handshake. Finally, rather than processing information in a linear, sequential fashion, the right hemisphere tends to organize information into patterns and relationships which are experienced as a whole. For instance, in listening to music, the right hemisphere focuses on the overall melody rather than the individual notes, or on the pattern of play on the chessboard rather than the individual pieces. While we compared the linear functioning of the left hemisphere to a digital computer, we might compare the functioning of the right hemisphere to a kaleidoscope, as it continually works to organize information into meaningful shapes and patterns.

The modern research into how our brain functions has significant implications for human learning. Much of our education is structured for left hemisphere thinking—analytical, verbal, logical, and sequential. Yet much of our understanding about the world is based on the activities of the right hemisphere—synthesizing, visual, experiential, and pattern-seeking. If education is to become as effective as it can be, it must introduce teaching methods that address the right hemisphere as well as the left hemisphere.

***Speaking and listening*** In addition to the written information encountered in reading, a mapping approach can also help us organize and interpret the information spoken by others. Although people read and hear words in a sequence, one at a time, we normally try to make sense of the *entire* meaning that these words are expressing. Reflect on the last two sentences you have just read: did you try to understand them one word at a time, or did you try to make sense of the complete ideas being expressed? In all likelihood you were trying to interpret the overall meaning being expressed, including the relations between the various ideas.

The same is true when we speak. Although we pronounce the words in sequence, one at a time, they form part of an entire meaning and network of relations we are trying to express. Again, examine your thinking process as you attempt to explain an idea to someone. Are you thinking one word at at time, or do you find there is a complex process of examining, sorting, and relating the various words in order to express the meaning you are trying to communicate? Probably the latter.

Based on these considerations, we can see that a mapping approach offers some clear advantages in organizing the information being spoken by others. For instance, when you as students take notes of what a teacher is speaking about, you usually try to copy down sentences and quotes of what the teacher has said. When you return to study these notes, you often find that the notes are not adequate because they do not include the various relationships between the ideas that were expressed. Using a mapping approach to note taking will help provide you with the means for identifying the key ideas and their relationships.

---

During your next lecture class, make a special effort to use the mapping approach to aid in your note taking. Following the class, compare these notes with previous notes taken in the same class. What results do you find?

Mapping is also an effective aid in preparing for oral presentations. By organizing the information we want to present in this way, we have all the key ideas and their relations in a single whole. Probably the greatest fear of people making oral presentations is that they will "get stuck" or lose their train of thought. If you have a clear map of the main ideas and their relationships either in your mind or in notes, the chances of this sort of "freeze-up" become considerably reduced.

One of the advantages to using maps is that once they are constructed you can place the ideas in whatever order you may need by simply numbering them or circling them in different colors. As a result, a map not only represents all the key ideas and their relationships simultaneously, but it can also be used to construct more traditional outlines or speaking notes.

---

Select a topic about which you would like to make a five- to-ten-minute oral presentation.

Explore the topic by creating a map that represents the ideas that you want to communicate.

Identify the order in which you plan to present the various central ideas and indicate how you plan to relate them.

In addition to note taking and oral presentations, discussing ideas with others is another area in which mapping can help us organize the information being presented.

The maps we create reflect our understanding of what we are trying to describe. If we do not know people very well, the maps we have of them may be inaccurate. We may have seen only one aspect of their personality in limited circumstances, and so there may be vast areas of uncharted territory in their personality that we are unaware of. The only way to correct this distorted picture is to find out more about them, giving us the means to create a more accurate map of them.

---

 Identify a student in the class whom you do not know very well, and then work through the following exercise

1. Make a list of ten words that you think best describe this person, in the same way that you listed words to identify yourself on page 264.

2. Using this list of words as a guide, create a map of this person similar to the maps you constructed of yourself (p. 264) and of Peter Rondinone (p. 277).

3. After completing your initial map of the student in your class, gather more information about this person by

   a. interviewing the person.

   b. interviewing two other classmates.

   In discussing this person with others, be sure to find out not only the "facts" about him or her (age, major, history, etc.) but also his or her ideas, feelings, attitudes, goals, personality characteristics, and so on). After each discussion, construct a map of that particular person's view of the individual in question.

4. Based on these experiences, create a revised map of the person you have been exploring.

5. Compare this revised map to your initial map and identify the similarities and the differences between them.

**Writing**

Along with reading, listening, and speaking, mapping is useful for writing. For example, consider the following writing assignment:

Describe an experience that turned out to be much different from the way you thought it was going to be. Include the following information:

1. Your original idea of what the experience was going to be like
2. Aspects of the experience that changed this original idea
3. Your revised idea of this experience

Traditional approaches to a writing assignment like this are usually in the form of a list or an outline of ideas. However, there are significant advantages to using a mapping approach as a way of generating ideas and organizing information. Mapping enables us to represent a wider range of relationships between the ideas we are exploring and encourages us to develop new ideas and form different relationships among them. For this particular writing assignment, we are really dealing with two maps:

Our original ideas of what the experience was going to be like

Our revised ideas of what the experience was actually like

On page 282 are two maps created by a student in response to this writing assignment.

---

Describe an experience that turned out to be much different from the way you thought it was going to be. Include the following information:

1. Your original idea of what the experience was going to be like
2. Aspects of the experience that changed this original idea
3. Your revised idea of this experience

By creating two maps, explore your two different ideas of this particular experience (before and after). In working on your maps, try to relax your mind as much as possible, letting the ideas and associations flow freely. As you complete your maps, look for possible connections between different branches. This strategy often suggests relationships you might not have thought of before.

Once your maps are more or less complete, you have laid the foundation for your writing assignment. Review your maps and decide which ideas and relationships you want to include and how you want to organize this information. Once you have accomplished this, you can begin to express your ideas using full sentences and paragraphs. Using your maps as a guide, write a two- to three-page description of your experience.

On page 283 is the paper that grew out of the student's maps on page 282.

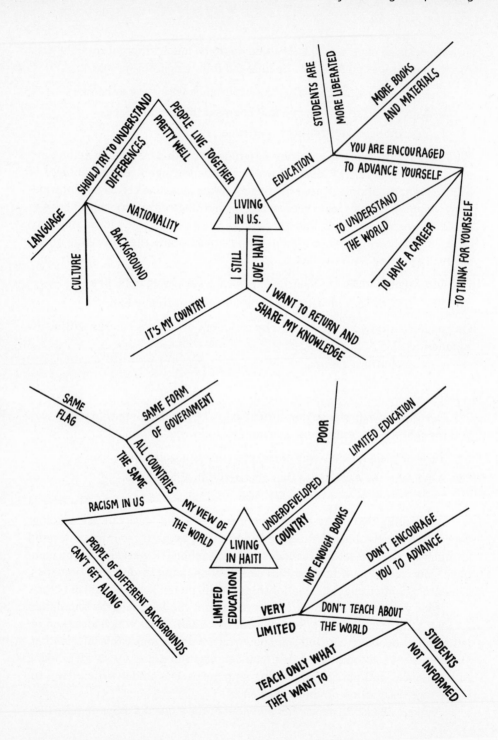

Living in the U.S.

The maps I would like to write about concern my ideas about
living in the United States. My original map of the United States
was very limited. This is because I am from an underdeveloped
West Indian island called Haiti. While I lived in Haiti, I always
thought that all of the other countries were the same, except
that the people spoke different languages. For instance, I
thought that all countries shared the same flag and had the same
form of government. In addition, I always had the idea that in
the United States people from other nationalities couldn't live
in peace because of racism.

Finally, I came to the United States and I was able to see
things from a different perspective. This led me to develop a new
map about living in the United States. All of my false perceptions of the world were changed when I started attending school
here. I noticed that the students were different. They were very
liberated compared to the students that I knew in Haiti. I also
found that people from different nationalities get along pretty
well together. I really think that being friendly and understanding makes people better because everybody is different in so many
ways.

As I attended school in the United States, I started to realize the reasons why my original map of the world was wrong. I became aware that in Haiti education was very limited. The schools
taught only what they felt was necessary for the students to
learn. Their main concern was to teach people how to survive and
remain in Haiti. The schools also didn't have enough documents
and books. As a result, the students were not properly informed
and were not able to advance themselves.

I feel happy in this country because I have found a lot of
opportunities to develop and make my life successful. I have had
the chance to learn a new language and work for a career that
will change my life. Attending school in the United States has
provided me with all the knowledge I couldn't get in Haiti and
has helped satisfy the curiosity I have always had. However, I
still remember that there are others still living in Haiti that
need to develop their thinking about the world. It would pain me
very deeply if my people remained primitive and underprivileged
because of the lack of education. In the future, when I have be-

come well prepared, I will make it my concern to nurture my people with the knowledge that they have been deprived of for so
long.

Using the mapping strategies we have explored in this chapter, complete
the following assignment.

1. Select a subject that you are interested in or one suggested by your teacher
   or by other class members.
2. Research the subject by locating at least two written sources that deal with
   the subject. Use maps to represent and organize the information from these
   sources.
3. Interview at least one person who is knowledgeable about the subject. Use
   a map to represent and organize the information from your discussion.
4. Using the maps from your research as a resource, create a map that represents and organizes the ideas about your subject.
5. Review your map and identify which ideas and relationships you want to
   include and how you want to organize them.
6. Using your map as a guide, translate your ideas into a two- to-three-page
   paper.
7. Construct a map of the key ideas in this passage and their various relationships, to be used as reference for a five-minute oral presentation to the
   class.
8. Give your oral presentation to the class, using the map you created as a
   guide.

# Chapter Nine
# Forming Concepts

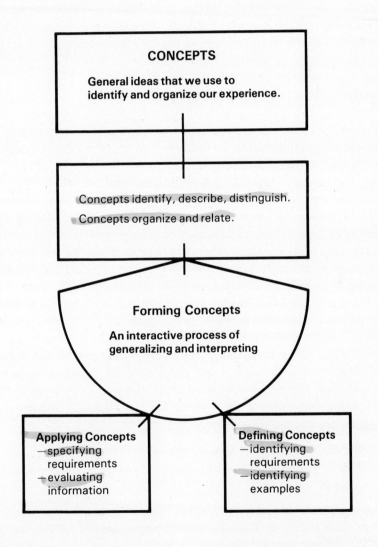

AS WE MAKE SENSE of the world, we are both *identifying* aspects of our experience with symbols and *organizing* what we have identified into various relationships. The maps we made in the last chapter involved both of these thinking activities. Each map we constructed represented the relationships between various thoughts, feelings, or objects that we had identified in our experience. Our abilities to identify and organize into relationships are made possible by our capacity to form concepts. *Concepts* are general ideas that we use to identify and organize our experience so that we can make sense of what is taking place. In this chapter we will be exploring concepts: what they are, the way we form and apply them, and the strategies we can use for improving our skill with them.

## Concepts describe and distinguish

Each of us lives in a world populated with concepts. A large number of the words and other symbols that we use to represent our experience express concepts we have formed, including the following: "sailboat," "person," "education," "computer," "sport," "elated," "thinking," and so on. For example, consider the sorts of things that most people in our culture wear on their feet. The word we use to identify and describe these sorts of things—"shoes" —expresses a general idea we have formed. This general idea represents *all* the different types of shoes that people actually wear, including the specific things we are wearing on our feet. In this respect, concepts are different from names that refer to a specific individual, such as "Alexandria." The name "Alexandria" is not a general idea. Instead, it represents a specific person. Concepts, on the other hand, describe a general type of thing—such as "shoes"—that may represent many individual items.

In Chapter Seven, on language, we found that we are able to symbolize objects, thoughts, and feelings in our experience by giving them descriptive names. We can now see that, in most cases, these descriptive names express general ideas—concepts—we have formed. These concepts enable us to

*identify* the various things in our experience as "kinds" of things.

*distinguish* these kinds of things from other kinds of things.

*describe* these kinds of things to others who share an understanding of our
symbols.

For instance, let us consider the concept "shoes." When we see people on the street or in our company, we are able to recognize and *identify* the types of things they are wearing on their feet. At the same time, the concepts we have formed enable us to *distinguish* these things from other types of things they might be wearing on their feet, such as slippers, cowboy boots, sneakers, overshoes, or sandals. Each of these names identifies other types of footwear, which express other concepts we have formed. Concepts also enable us to *describe* what people are wearing on their feet by listing the features that make up the concept.

---

Study the diagram below, which identifies and shows the relationships between various types of footwear. Replace the question marks with concepts that you think are appropriate. Now select three of the different types of footwear identified in the diagram (including two that you identified), and describe them in a way that distinguishes them from each other.

*Example*:  Snowshoes—Large footwear strapped to boots or shoes, used for walking in soft snow to prevent sinking. They are usually made with wooden frames bent into a horseshoe shape and strung with leather webbing.

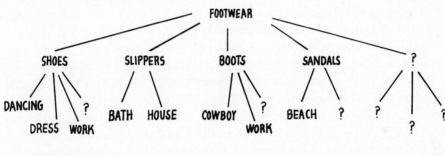

1. *Footwear:* _____

   *Description:* _____

   _____

   _____

2. *Footwear:* _____

   *Description:* _____

   _____

   _____

3. *Footwear:* _____

   *Description:* _____

   _____

   _____

## Concepts organize and relate

If we examine the diagram on page 287, we can see that, in addition to describing and distinguishing, concepts enable us to create relationships. "Footwear" is the most general concept and includes other concepts, such as "shoes," "slippers," "boots," and "sandals." And each of these concepts includes other concepts, such as "cowboy boots," "work boots," and so on. These various concepts can thus be organized in a way that identifies the different types of footwear and represents their relationships to each other.

The way we form concepts also leads to discovering and creating many other kinds of relationships. For example, imagine that we are physicians and that one of our patients comes to us complaining of shortness of breath and occasional pain in his left arm. After he describes his symptoms, we would ask a number of questions, examine him, and perhaps administer some tests. Our ability to identify the underlying problem depends on our knowledge of various human diseases. Each disease is identified and described by a different concept. Identifying these various diseases means that we can distinguish different concepts and that we know in what situations to apply a given concept correctly. In addition, when our patient asks, "What's wrong with me, doctor?" we are able to describe the concept and explain how it is related to his symptoms.

As our thinking abilities develop, we gradually form concepts that enable us to symbolize our world in increasingly precise ways. Fortunately for us, modern medicine has developed (and is continuing to develop) remarkably precise concepts to describe and explain the diseases that afflict us. In the case of the patient above, we may conclude that the problem is heart disease. Of course, there are many different kinds of heart disease, represented by different concepts, and success in treating our patient will depend on our figuring out exactly which type of disease is involved.

Thus we can see that forming concepts enables us to identify and distinguish various aspects of our experience, such as different kinds of heart disease. In addition, forming these concepts gives us the means to shape and discover how these concepts relate to each other. For example, exploring the general concept "heart disease" enables us to recognize and group together all the different types of heart disease, which are represented by other concepts.

In addition to these groupings, the concept "heart disease" suggests other relationships as well. For example, identify some of the common symptoms of heart disease.

1. Shortness of breath

2. _____

3. _____

4. _____

5. _____

   Another type of relationship suggested by the concept "heart disease" is the things we do (or fail to do) that contribute to the development of heart disease.

1. Smoking

2. _____

3. _____

4. _____

5. _____

   In short, our ability to form concepts gives us the means to both identify and relate the objects, thoughts, and feelings that make up our world. And by organizing the concepts that represent our experience into various relationships, we are able to make sense of what is going on in our world.

---

   Develop further the map below. Some of the basic concepts associated  with the subject of heart disease are provided to suggest directions your map may take.

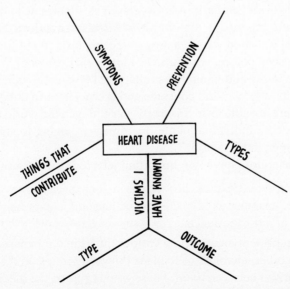

### Concepts group items based on their similarities

Concepts are general ideas that we use to identify, distinguish, and relate the various aspects of our experience. As a result, we are able to organize our world into patterns that make sense to us. This is the process by which we discover and create meaning in our lives.

In their role as organizers of experience, concepts act to group aspects of our experience based on their similarity to one another. Consider the thing that you usually write with: a pen. The concept "pen" represents a type of object that we use for writing. But look around the classroom at all the other instruments people are using to write. We use the concept "pen" to identify these things as well, even though they may look very different from the one you are using.

Thus the concept "pen" not only helps us to make distinctions in our experience by indicating how pens differ from pencils, crayons, or magic markers, but it also helps us determine which items are similar enough to each other to be called pens. When we put items into a group with a single description—like "pen"—we are focusing on the *similarities* between the items:

They use ink

They are used for writing

They are held with a hand

But we are ignoring the *differences* among them:

Their color, size, brand, etc.

This ability to see similarities between things enables us to *recognize* various things in our experience (the word "re-cognize" means to "re-know" or "know again"). So, when we see a new, ink-using instrument for writing that we have never seen before, we can say "I know that is a pen."

Being able to see and name the similarities between certain things in our experience is the way we form concepts and is crucial for making sense of our world. If we were not able to do this, then everything in the world would be different, with its own individual name. Just imagine having to give a different name to every pen in the world.

Concepts therefore have two important jobs to fulfill for us:

1. Concepts represent/express how things in our experience are *different* from each other, enabling us to make distinctions and create increasingly precise maps of our experience.

2. Concepts represent/express how various things in our experience are *similar* to each other, enabling us to place things in groups on the basis of certain similarities between them. These groups give us the means to identify each thing as a kind of thing—"That's a kind of pen."

For each of the following concepts, describe the similar characteristics that ➤•◄
form that concept.

1. Crayon

   a. _____

   b. _____

   c. _____

   d. _____

2. Pencil

   a. _____

   b. _____

   c. _____

   d. _____

3. Magic marker

   a. _____

   b. _____

   c. _____

   d. _____

4. _____

   a. _____

   b. _____

   c. _____

   d. _____

5. _____

   a. _____

   b. _____

   c. _____

   d. _____

## Concepts classify

The process by which concepts place things into various groups based on
their similarities is known as *classifying*. Classifying is a natural human activity
that is going on all of the time. And the way that we classify things in the world

is the way we form concepts. For example, there are hundreds of different automobiles in existence, in a wide variety of makes, models, and colors. When we talk about "automobiles" in general, however, we place all of these individual cars into the general category of "automobile." It is not necessary for us to have a *specific* automobile in mind when we talk or think about automobiles *in general*. The concept "automobile" is a general idea that refers to all members of this classification.

How do we decide which things this general idea or concept will refer to? The same way that we classify: by focusing on certain similarities between a collection of things that distinguish this classification from others in the world. For example, imagine that you have just landed from another planet, making your first visit to earth. As you stand on the street, you begin noticing these strange contraptions going by, making noise, belching smoke, and carrying human creatures. Although each looks different from the others in color, size, and shape, you gradually begin to classify them into a single group. And you form this classification by focusing on certain similarities among these objects that distinguish the things in this classification from other things in the world. What are some of these common features that you identify?

1. _____

2. _____

3. _____

4. _____

5. _____

As you gradually create this classification, you decide to give it a name: _____. This name represents a concept you have just formed, which is being used by you to stand for all the individual things contained in this classification. The way we classify is thus the way we form concepts: by focusing on certain common features that distinguish this classification from others in the world.

When we classify something, we can do it consciously by saying things like

X belongs to this class or group (e.g., He is a member of our Critical Thinking class.)

X is this kind of thing (e.g., That looks like a kind of jumbo jet.)

In most cases, however, we are not conscious that we are classifying something in a particular sort of way; it is done automatically. This process of classifying is one of the main ways that we order, organize, and make sense of our world. And since no two things or experiences are exactly alike, our ability to classify things into various groups is what enables us to recognize things in our experience. When we perceive an "automobile" or a "human being," we recognize it as a *kind of thing* we have seen before. Even though we may not have seen this particular automobile or human being, we recognize that it belongs to a group of things that we are familiar with.

---

For each of the following concepts, identify the common features shared ►•◄ by the members of the classification.

1. *table*

   a. _____

   b. _____

   c. _____

2. *dance*

   a. _____

   b. _____

   c. _____

3. *human being*

   a. _____

   b. _____

   c. _____

Identify two concepts from your experience and describe the common features shared by the members of the classification.

4. _____

   a. _____

   b. _____

   c. _____

5. _____

   a. _____

   b. _____

   c. _____

**We discover and create classifications** Concepts are general ideas that are formed by classifying aspects of our experience based on certain common features. The individual things or experiences belong to no particular class until we classify them. In fact, the same things can often be classified in many different ways. For example, imagine that someone handed you a tomato and asked: "Which class does this tomato belong in, fruit or vegetable?" How would you respond? The fact is, a tomato can be classified as *both* a fruit and a vegetable, depending on our purposes. Interestingly enough, the government tried at one point to have tomato catsup classified as a vegetable for the school lunch program so that it would not have to provide a regular vegetable as part of a balanced meal.

Let us take another example. Imagine that you are walking on some undeveloped land with some other people when you come across an area of soggy ground with long grass and rotting trees. One person in your group surveys the parcel and announces: "That's a smelly marsh. All it does is breed mosquitoes. It ought to be covered with landfill and built on, so that we can use it productively." Another member of your group disagrees with the classification "smelly marsh," stating: "This is a wetland of great ecological value. There are many plants and animals that need this area and other areas like it in order to survive. Wetland areas also help prevent the rivers from flooding by absorbing excess water during heavy rains." Which person is right? Should the wet area be classified as a "smelly marsh" or a "valuable wetland"? Actually, the wet area can be classified both ways. The particular classification that we select depends on our needs and our interests. Someone who is active in construction and land development may tend to view the parcel through spectacles that reflect his or her interests and experience and classify it accordingly. On the other hand, someone who is involved in preserving our natural resources will tend to view the same parcel through different perceiving spectacles and place it in a different category.

This example illustrates that the way we classify reflects and influences the way we see the world, the way we think about the world, and the way we behave in the world. This is true for virtually all the classifications we make. Consider the race horse Secretariat, who won the Triple Crown in 1973. Which classification should Secretariat be placed into?

A magnificent thoroughbred

A substantial investment

An animal ill equipped for farming

A large horse (seventeen hands high)

A descendant of Bold Ruler

A valuable stud horse

A candidate for the glue factory

As with the wet area above, the specific classification in which we place Secretariat depends on our interests and experience, reflecting (and influencing) the way we see and think about the world.

---

Identify the classification in which you think the following items should be placed and explain the reasons why.

1. *Marijuana:*   a. a dangerous drug
                  b. a harmless good time

   *Classification:* _____

   *Explanation:* _____

   _____

2. *Large cars:*   a. gas guzzlers
                   b. safer vehicles to drive

   *Classification:* _____

   *Explanation:* _____

   _____

3. *New Wave music:*   a. noise
                       b. a creative expression

   *Classification:* _____

   *Explanation:* _____

   _____

4. *Welfare:*   a. a necessary social support
                b. a haven for freeloaders

   *Classification:* _____

   *Explanation:* _____

   _____

5. *Capital punishment:*   a. a useful deterrent
                           b. murder

   *Classification:* _____

   *Explanation:* _____

   _____

6. *Draft*:   a. an essential part of our national defense

b. an infringement on individual freedom

*Classification*: _____

*Explanation*: _____

_____

In addition to the subjects we have been considering, we also place people into various classifications. In Chapter Seven, "Language," we noted that we could place Roberto Acuna into each of the following categories:

Migrant worker

Labor organizer

Troublemaker

The specific classification we select depends on who we are and how we see the world. Similarly, each of us is placed into a variety of classifications by different people. For example, here are some of the classifications that certain people place me into:

| *Classification* | *People Who Classify Me* |
|---|---|
| first-born son | my parents |
| taxpayer | Internal Revenue Service |
| tickler | my daughter |
| egg on a toasted roll | cook at the restaurant where I pick up my breakfast every morning |

►•◄     List some of the different ways that you can be classified, and identify the people who would classify you that way.

| *Classification* | *People Who Classify You* |
|---|---|
| 1. _____ | _____ |
| 2. _____ | _____ |
| 3. _____ | _____ |
| 4. _____ | _____ |
| 5. _____ | _____ |

Not only do we continually classify things and people into various groups based on the common features that we choose to focus on, but we also classify ideas, feelings, actions, and experiences. For instance, identify below how the killing of another person might be classified in different ways, depending on different circumstances.

| Classification | Circumstances | Example |
|---|---|---|
| 1. Manslaughter | killing someone accidentally | while driving intoxicated |
| 2. Self-defense | _____ | _____ |
| | _____ | _____ |
| 3. _____ | _____ | _____ |
| | _____ | _____ |
| 4. _____ | _____ | _____ |
| | _____ | _____ |
| 5. _____ | _____ | _____ |
| | _____ | _____ |

Finally, in addition to classifying the same thing or event in a variety of different ways, we can classify most *collections* of things in various ways. For example, consider the different ways the members of your class can be classified. You could group them according to their majors, their ages, their food preferences, and so on. The specific categories you would use depend on the purposes of your classification. If you were trying to organize career counseling, then classifying according to majors would make sense. On the other hand, if you were trying to plan the menu for a class party, then food preferences would be the natural category for classification.

---

Develop a list of five different ways of classifying your class (already a classification), and in each case describe a purpose for which that way of classifying could be used.

---

Construct a list containing ten different items (for example, a shopping list, a list of the ten bestselling books or records). After constructing the list, develop five different ways of classifying the items on the list, and in each case describe a purpose for which that way of classifying could be used.

***Drawing the line***   One of the frustrating things about classifications is that they often seem fuzzy around the edges. For example, take the grade classifications: A, B, C, D, F. There may be a clear difference between the work of a student receiving an A and the work of a student receiving a B, but what about those borderline cases—between an A – and a B +, for instance? Is the line between these classifications really that sharp? Often it is not. Nevertheless, a line must be drawn somewhere. If we are the person receiving the B + instead of an A –, we may feel that the line has been drawn incorrectly. Unfortunately, this type of reaction is unavoidable in any situation where a line must be drawn. And perhaps the only thing worse than drawing a line incorrectly is drawing no line at all. This is particularly true in the case of law, as the famous jurist Oliver Wendell Holmes explains in the following passage:

> When a legal distinction is determined . . . between night and day, childhood and maturity, or any other extremes, a point has to be fixed or a line has to be drawn, or gradually picked out by successive decisions, to mark where the change takes place. Looked at by itself without regard to the necessity behind it, the line or point seems arbitrary. It might as well be a little more to the one side or the other. But when it is seen that a line or point there must be, and that there is no mathematical or logical way of fixing it precisely, the decision of the legislature must be accepted unless we can say that it is very wide of any reasonable mark.

▶ • ◀   Examine the following legal "lines" that have been drawn. Select two items for analysis and explain the justification for the "line" that has been drawn. Then describe an alternative way for drawing the line and explain the reasons that support this choice.

1. A child born on December 31 will enter school one year earlier than a child born on January 1.
2. Beer, wine, or liquor cannot be sold to anyone under eighteen years of age.
3. You must be eighteen years of age in order to vote.
4. You must register for the draft when you turn eighteen years old.
5. People must retire when they turn sixty-five years old.
6. A person under sixteen years of age who commits a serious crime, such as murder, must be tried as a juvenile offender and cannot receive a sentence that exceeds two years.

***Forming concepts by classifying***   We have noted that the process of forming concepts usually involves the process of classifying aspects of our experience into groups, based on the common features they share. This process is going on all the time as we work to organize and make sense of our world. In the following selection from the bestselling book *Passages,* Gail Sheehy suggests concepts that classify the development of our lives into six stages. Read the selection carefully and then use the questions that follow it to explore the major points of the reading.

## from *Passages*
*by Gail Sheehy*

. . . A person's life at any given time incorporates both external and internal aspects. The external system is composed of our memberships in the culture: our job, social class, family and social roles, how we present ourselves to and participate in the world. The interior realm concerns the meanings this participation has for each of us. In what ways are our values, goals, and aspirations being invigorated or violated by our present life system? How many parts of our personality can we live out, and what parts are we suppressing? How do we *feel* about our way of living in the world at any given time?

The inner realm is where the crucial shifts in bedrock begin to throw a person off balance, signaling the necessity to change and move on to a new footing in the next stage of development. These crucial shifts occur throughout life, yet people consistently refuse to recognize that they possess an internal life system. Ask anyone who seems down, "Why are you feeling low?" Most will displace the inner message onto a marker event: "I've been down since we moved, since I changed jobs, since my wife went back to graduate school and turned into a damn social worker in sackcloth," and so on. Probably less than ten percent would say: "There is some unknown disturbance within me, and even though it's painful, I feel I have to stay with it and ride it out." Even fewer people would be able to explain that the turbulence they feel may have no external cause. And yet it may not resolve itself for *several years*.

During each of these passages, how we feel about our way of living will undergo subtle changes in four areas of perception. One is the interior sense of self in relation to others. A second is the proportion of safeness to danger we feel in our lives. A third is our perception of time—do we have plenty of it, or are we beginning to feel that time is running out? Last, there will be some shift at the gut level in our sense of aliveness or stagnation. These are the hazy sensations that compose the background tone of living and shape the decisions on which we take action.

The work of adult life is not easy. As in childhood, each step presents not only new tasks of development but requires a letting go of the techniques that worked before. With each passage some magic must be given up, some cherished illusion of safety and comfortably familiar sense of self must be cast off, to allow for the greater expansion of our own distinctiveness. . . .

### Pulling Up Roots

Before 18, the motto is loud and clear: "I have to get away from my parents." But the words are seldom connected to action. Generally still safely part of our families, even if away at school, we feel our autonomy to be subject to erosion from moment to moment.

After 18, we begin Pulling Up Roots in earnest. College, military service, and short-term travels are all customary vehicles our society provides for the first round trips between family and a base of one's own. In the attempt to separate our view of the world from our family's view, despite vigorous protestations to the contrary—"I know exactly what I want!"—we cast about for any beliefs we can call our own. And in the process of testing those beliefs we are often drawn to fads, preferably those most mysterious and inaccessible to our parents.

Whatever tentative memberships we try out in the world, the fear haunts us that we are really kids who cannot take care of ourselves. We cover that fear with acts of defiance and mimicked confidence. For allies to replace our parents, we turn to our contemporaries. They become conspirators. So long as their perspective meshes with our own, they are able to substitute for the sanctuary of the family. But that doesn't last very long. And the instant they diverge from the shaky ideals of "our group," they are seen as betrayers. Rebounds to the family are common between the ages of 18 and 22.

The tasks of this passage are to locate ourselves in a peer group role, a sex role, an anticipated occupation, an ideology or world view. As a result, we gather the impetus to leave home physically and the identity to *begin* leaving home emotionally.

Even as one part of us seeks to be an individual, another part longs to restore the safety and comfort of merging with another. Thus one of the most popular myths of this passage is: We can piggyback our development by attaching to a Stronger One. But people who marry during this time often prolong financial and emotional ties to the family and relatives that impede them from becoming self-sufficient.

A stormy passage through the Pulling Up Roots years will probably facilitate the normal progression of the adult life cycle. If one doesn't have an identity crisis at this point, it will erupt during a later transition, when the penalties may be harder to bear.

## The Trying Twenties

The Trying Twenties confront us with the question of how to take hold in the adult world. Our focus shifts from the interior turmoils of late adolescence—"Who am I?" "What is truth?"—and we become almost totally preoccupied with working out the externals. "How do I put my aspirations into effect?" "What is the best way to start?" "Where do I go?" "Who can help me?" "How did *you* do it?"

In this period, which is longer and more stable compared with the passage that leads to it, the tasks are as enormous as they are exhilarating: To shape a Dream, that vision of ourselves which will generate energy, aliveness, and hope. To prepare for a lifework. To find a mentor if possible. And to form the capacity for intimacy, without losing in the process whatever consistency of self we have thus far mustered. The first test structure must be erected around the life we choose to try.

Doing what we "should" is the most pervasive theme of the twenties. The "shoulds" are largely defined by family models, the press of the culture, or the prejudices of our peers. If the prevailing cultural instructions are that one should get married and settle down behind one's own door, a nuclear family is born. If instead the peers insist that one should do one's own thing, the 25-year-old is likely to harness himself onto a Harley-Davidson and burn up Route 66 in the commitment to have no commitments.

One of the terrifying aspects of the twenties is the inner conviction that the choices we make are irrevocable. It is largely a false fear. Change is quite possible, and some alteration of our original choices is probably inevitable.

Two impulses, as always, are at work. One is to build a firm, safe structure for the future by making strong commitments, to "be set." Yet people who slip into a ready-made form without much self-examination are likely to find themselves *locked in.*

The other urge is to explore and experiment, keeping any structure tentative and therefore easily reversible. Taken to the extreme, these are people who skip from one trial job and one limited personal encounter to another, spending their twenties in the *transient* state.

Although the choices of our twenties are not irrevocable, they do set in motion a Life Pattern. Some of us follow the locked-in pattern, others the transient pattern, the wunderkind pattern, the caregiver pattern, and there are a number of others. Such patterns strongly influence the particular questions raised for each person during each passage, and so the most common patterns will also be traced throughout the book.

Buoyed by powerful illusions and belief in the power of the will, we commonly insist in our twenties that what we have chosen to do is the one true course in life. Our backs go up at the merest hint that we are like our parents, that two decades of parental training might be reflected in our current actions and attitudes.

"Not me," is the motto, "I'm different."

## Catch-30

Impatient with devoting ourselves to the "shoulds," a new vitality springs from within as we approach 30. Men and women alike speak of feeling too narrow and restricted. They blame all sorts of things, but what the restrictions boil down to are the outgrowth of career and personal choices of the twenties. They may have been choices perfectly suited to that stage. But now the fit feels different. Some inner aspect that was left out is striving to be taken into account. Important new choices must be made, and commitments altered or deepened. The work involves great change, turmoil, and often crisis—a simultaneous feeling of rock bottom and the urge to bust out.

One common response is the tearing up of the life we spent most of our twenties putting together. It may mean striking out on a secondary road toward a new vision or converting a dream of "running for president" into a more realistic goal. The single person feels a push to find a partner. The woman who was previously content at home with children chafes to venture into the world. The childless couple reconsiders children. And almost everyone who is married, especially those married for seven years, feels a discontent.

If the discontent doesn't lead to a divorce, it will, or should, call for a serious review of the marriage and of each partner's aspirations in their Catch-30 condition. The gist of that condition was expressed by a 29-year-old associate with a Wall Street law firm:

"I'm considering leaving the firm. I've been there four years now; I'm getting good feedback, but I have no clients of my own. I feel weak. If I wait much longer, it will be too late, too close to that fateful time of decision on whether or not to become a partner. I'm success-oriented. But the concept of being 55 years old and stuck in a monotonous job drives me wild. It drives me crazy now, just a litte bit. I'd say that 85 percent of the time I thoroughly enjoy my work. But when I get a screwball case, I come away from court saying, 'What am I doing here?' It's a *visceral* reaction that I'm wasting my time. I'm trying to find some way to make a social contribution or a slot in city government. I keep saying, 'There's something more.' "

Besides the push to broaden himself professionally, there is a wish to expand his personal life. He wants two or three more children. "The concept of a home has become very meaningful to me, a place to get away from troubles and relax. I love my son in a way I could not have anticipated. I never could live alone."

Consumed with the work of making his own critical life-steering decisions, he demonstrates the essential shift at this age: an absolute requirement to be more self-concerned. The self has new value now that his competency has been proved.

His wife is struggling with her own age-30 priorities. She wants to go to law school, but he wants more children. If she is going to stay home, she wants him to make more time for the family instead of taking on even wider professional commitments. His view of the bind, of what he would most like from his wife, is this:

I'd like not to be bothered. It sounds cruel, but I'd like not to have to worry about what she's going to do next week. Which is why I've told her several times that I think she should do something. Go back to school and get a degree in social work or geography or whatever. Hopefully that would fulfill her, and then I wouldn't have to worry about her line of problems. I want her to be decisive about herself."

The trouble with his advice to his wife is that it comes out of concern with *his* convenience, rather than with *her* development. She quickly picks up on this lack of goodwill: He is trying to dispose of her. At the same time, he refuses her the same latitude to be "selfish" in making an independent decision to broaden her own horizons. Both perceive a lack of mutuality. And that is what Catch-30 is all about for the couple.

### Rooting and Extending

Life becomes less provisional, more rational and orderly in the early thirties. We begin to settle down in the full sense. Most of us begin putting down roots and sending out new shoots. People buy houses and become very earnest about climbing career ladders. Men in particular concern themselves with "making it." Satisfaction with marriage generally goes downhill in the thirties (for those who have remained together) compared with the highly valued, vision-supporting marriage of the twenties. This coincides with the couple's reduced social life outside the family and the in-turned focus on raising their children.

### The Deadline Decade

In the middle of the thirties we come upon a crossroads. We have reached the halfway mark. Yet even as we are reaching our prime, we begin to see there is a place where it finishes. Time starts to squeeze.

The loss of youth, the faltering of physical powers we have always taken for granted, the fading purpose of stereotyped roles by which we have thus far identified ourselves, the spiritual dilemma of having no absolute answers—any or all of these shocks can give this passage the character of crisis. Such thoughts usher in a decade between 35 and 45 that can be called the Deadline Decade. It is a time of both danger and opportunity. All of us have the chance to rework the narrow identity by which we defined ourselves in the first half of life. And those of us who make the most of the opportunity will have a full-out authenticity crisis.

To come through this authenticity crisis, we must reexamine our purposes and reevaluate how to spend our resources from now on. "Why am I doing all this? What do I really believe in?" No matter what we have been doing, there will be parts of ourselves that have been suppressed and now need to find expression. "Bad" feelings will demand acknowledgment along with the good.

It is frightening to step off onto the treacherous footbridge leading to the second half of life. We can't take everything with us on this journey through uncertainty. Along the way, we discover that we are alone. We no longer have to ask permission because we are the providers of our own safety. We must learn to give ourselves permission. We stumble upon feminine or masculine aspects of our natures that up to this time have usually been masked. There is grieving to be done because an old self is dying. By taking in our suppressed and even our unwanted parts, we prepare at the gut level for the reintegration of an identity that is ours and ours alone—not some artificial form put together to please the culture or our mates. It is a dark passage at the beginning. But by disassembling ourselves, we can glimpse the light and gather our parts into a renewal.

Women sense this inner crossroads earlier than men do. The time pinch often prompts a woman to stop and take an all-points survey at age 35. Whatever options she has already played out, she feels a "my last chance" urgency to review those options she has set aside and those that aging and biology will close off in the *now foreseeable* future. For all her qualms and confusion about where to start looking for a new future, she usually enjoys an exhilaration of release. Assertiveness begins rising. There are so many firsts ahead.

Men, too, feel the time push in the mid-thirties. Most men respond by pressing down harder on the career accelerator. It's "my last chance" to pull away from the pack. It is no longer enough to be the loyal junior executive, the promising young novelist, the lawyer who does a little *pro bono* work on the side. He wants now to become part of top management, to be recognized as an established writer, or an active politician with his own legislative program. With some chagrin, he discovers that he has been too anxious to please and too vulnerable to criticism. He wants to put together his own ship.

During this period of intense concentration on external advancement, it is common for men to be unaware of the more difficult, gut issues that are propelling them forward. The survey that was neglected at 35 becomes a crucible at

40. Whatever rung of achievement he has reached, the man of 40 usually feels stale, restless, burdened, and unappreciated. He worries about his health. He wonders, ''Is this all there is?'' He may make a series of departures from well-established lifelong base lines, including marriage. More and more men are seeking second careers in midlife. Some become self-destructive. And many men in their forties experience a major shift of emphasis away from pouring all their energies into their own advancement. A more tender, feeling side comes into play. They become interested in developing an ethical self.

### Renewal or Resignation

Somewhere in the mid-forties, equilibrium is regained. A new stability is achieved, which may be more or less satisfying.

If one has refused to budge through the midlife transition, the sense of staleness will calcify into resignation. One by one, the safety and supports will be withdrawn from the person who is standing still. Parents will become children; children will become strangers; a mate will grow away or go away; the career will become just a job—and each of these events will be felt as an abandonment. The crisis will probably emerge again around 50. And although its wallop will be greater, the jolt may be just what is needed to prod the resigned middle-ager toward seeking revitalization.

On the other hand . . .

If we have confronted ourselves in the middle passage and found a renewal of purpose around which we are eager to build a more authentic life structure, these may well be the best years. Personal happiness takes a sharp turn upward for partners who can now accept the fact: ''I cannot expect *anyone* to fully understand me.'' Parents can be forgiven for the burdens of our childhood. Children can be let go without leaving us in collapsed silence. At 50, there is a new warmth and mellowing. Friends become more important than ever, but so does privacy. Since it is so often proclaimed by people past midlife, the motto of this stage might be ''No more bullshit.''

1. *We form and use concepts to identify, describe, and distinguish aspects of our world so that we can make sense of what is going on.* Identify and describe the six main concepts that the author uses to understand the development of our lives.

    a. _____ : _____

    _____

    b. _____ : _____

    _____

c. _____ : _____
_____

d. _____ : _____
_____

e. _____ : _____
_____

f. _____ : _____
_____

2. *Concepts classify by grouping items based on the common features that they share.* For each of the six concepts that you identified above, list the common features characterizing that stage of life.

a. _____ : _____
_____
_____

b. _____ : _____
_____
_____

c. _____ : _____
_____
_____

d. _____ : _____
_____
_____

e. _____ : _____
_____
_____

f. _____ : _____
_____
_____

3. *Concepts give us the means to organize the world by discovering and creating relationships.* Using these six concepts as a starting point, create a

map that represents the various relationships expressed by the concepts. Include other concepts and relationships that go beyond those found in the article.

4. *We discover and create classifications. The same things can be classified in different ways, depending on our interests and purposes.* The author has used one set of concepts to classify and make sense of the development of our lives. Identify and describe another set of concepts that you could use to classify and make sense of the development of our lives.

a. _____ : _____
_____
_____

b. _____ : _____
_____
_____

c. _____ : _____
_____
_____

d. _____ : _____
_____
_____

e. _____ : _____
_____
_____

f. _____ : _____
_____
_____

5. *The way we classify reflects and influences the way we perceive and think about the world.* The concepts that Sheehy uses to classify reflect and influence the way she sees the experience of living. Using the concepts for classifying life's development that you created above, write a passage demonstrating how your concepts express a way of perceiving and thinking about the world. (You may want to create a map to identify your main ideas and represent their relationships to help organize your thoughts for the passage).

### Concepts generalize

In most cases, the concepts we form through the process of classifying are *generalizations* based on experiences we have had. We generalize by focusing on certain similarities that characterize all things in that category, and this collection of similarities then goes to make up the concept. When we think of a car, we think of something with more than two wheels that is used to transport human beings (motorcycles and bicycles transport humans as well, but do not have enough wheels to be classified as automobiles). An automobile usually has doors, a motor, and a windshield. These qualities, along with perhaps other essential qualities, combine to make up the general concept of "automobile."

Other qualities that many cars have are *not* part of the concept because there are many cars that do not have these qualities. For instance, many cars are painted red, have a radio, and sport a pair of baby shoes dangling from the rear-view mirror. These qualities are *not* usually considered to be an essential part of the concept of "automobile" since these things are not necessary for qualifying as a member of the class "automobile."

Just like cars, people come in all shapes and sizes, and like snowflakes, no two are exactly alike. Forming a concept of "human being" is accomplished the same way that we formed a concept of "automobile"—by focusing on certain common features that people share. Like automobiles, each person exhibits many qualities that are not essential to the concept of human being—for example, size of ears, ability to do crossword puzzles, favorite food, and so on. Most of us formed the concepts of "automobile" and "human being" by generalizing from our experience the essential qualities that make up these concepts.

---

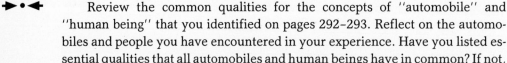  Review the common qualities for the concepts of "automobile" and "human being" that you identified on pages 292–293. Reflect on the automobiles and people you have encountered in your experience. Have you listed essential qualities that all automobiles and human beings have in common? If not, then cross out the nonessential qualities. Are there additional essential qualities that you omitted? If so, then add them to your list.

---

 Return to the concepts you formed to explain the different stages of human development on pages 307. Describe the experiences you have had that led you to form these concepts, and then identify and describe the common qualities that make up each of your concepts (as you did with Gail Sheehy's concepts on page 305.)

## Applying concepts

We do not simply *form* concepts by focusing on the similarities between various experiences. As the concepts are formed, we are also interested in *applying* these concepts to our experience. Applying concepts is one of the main ways that we make sense of our experience because concepts help us figure out what is going on. Imagine that you are standing on a street corner when you see a vehicle approaching. It has four wheels, an engine, and someone is driving it. Is it a car? You notice that the rear wheels are much larger than the front wheels, and that there are no doors or frame surrounding the driver—he is just sitting perched on a metal seat. You decide that the concept "automobile" does not apply to the vehicle. Instead, you settle on the concept "tractor." This concept seems to fit, and as a result this concept helps you understand—make sense of—what you are experiencing. Identify the general qualities that make up the concept "tractor" and enable you to distinguish this concept from that of "automobile."

1. _____

2. _____

3. _____

4. _____

To take another example, think back to the first day of classes. For most students, this is a time to evaluate their courses by trying to determine which concepts apply.

Will this course be interesting? Useful? A lot of work?

Is the teacher stimulating? Demanding? Entertaining?

Are the other students friendly? Intelligent? Conscientious?

Each of these words or phrases represents a concept we are attempting to apply so that we can understand what is occurring at the moment and also anticipate what the course will be like in the future.

The activities of forming concepts and applying concepts are closely related and work together. When we *form* concepts, we are trying to determine the common features or general qualities that make up the concept. When we *apply* concepts, we are trying to identify examples of the concept. For instance, Gail Sheehy in *Passages* has formed the concept "The Deadline Decade" to explain one of the periods in human development. In applying this concept, she offers the following qualities:

We notice faltering physical powers.

We re-examine and re-evaluate our basic purposes.

We discover that we are alone.

Once we understand the general qualities that make up her concept of "The Deadline Decade," we can look for examples to which we can apply the concept.

---

►•◄         Select which one of Gail Sheehy's developmental stages (pp. 299–305) you consider yourself currently in and describe an experience you have had to which the concept could be applied.

---

►•◄         Now review the concepts that you formed to classify the development of our lives (p. 307). Select one of these concepts and then

a. describe an experience from which you generalized to form the concept.
b. describe a recent example either in your life or in someone else's to which you could apply the concept.

Let us explore further the way that these two different activities—forming and applying concepts—work together. Explain what you mean when you apply the concept "city" (or more simply: "What is a city?")

_____

_____

_____

_____

Now consider the following sample conversation between two people trying to form and clarify the concept "city."

*A:*   What is your idea of a "city?"

*B:*   Well, I guess that it's a place where different people live together—like Chicago.

*A:*   Is our neighborhood a city? After all, it's a place where different people live together.

*B:*   No. A neighborhood may be *part* of a city, but a city usually has many different neighborhoods in it, like Miami.

*A:*  What about North Salem—is that a city? After all, it contains different neighborhoods in which different people live together.

*B:*  I don't think North Salem is a city; it's too small. I think that North Salem is only a town or maybe only a village. A city needs to have *a lot* of people living there—like New York.

*A:*  Then what about Monroe County—is *that* a city? It's got neighborhoods and lots of different people living together.

*B:*  I'm afraid not. A county is usually much larger than a city. In fact, some counties contain more than one city. I think that a city needs to be concentrated in a smaller area. And I think that it needs a lot of rather large buildings, businesses, sidewalks, traffic and so on—like Los Angeles.

*A:*  What about Boston? Is that a city? I believe that it has all the qualities that you mentioned.

*B:*  *Now* you've got it!

As we review this dialogue, we can see that *forming* the concept "city" works hand in hand with *applying* the concept to different examples. When two or more things work together in this way, we say that they interact. In this case, there are two parts of this interactive process.

1. We form concepts by *generalizing,* by focusing on the similarities between different things. In the dialogue above, the things from which generalizations are being made are the cities—Chicago, Miami, New York, and Los Angeles. By focusing on the similarities between these cities, the two people in the dialogue develop a list of common elements that the cities share, including
   a.  different people living together.
   b.  many different neighborhoods.
   c.  a lot of people residing there.
   d.  being larger than a town.
   e.  being concentrated in a limited area.
   f.  containing a lot of buildings, sidewalks, businesses, traffic, etc.

   These common elements act as the *requirements* that something must meet in order to be considered a city.

2. We apply concepts by *interpreting,* by looking for different examples of the concept and seeing if they meet the requirements of the concept that we are developing. In the conversation above, one of the participants attempts to apply the concept "city" to the following examples:

a. North Salem

b. A neighborhood

c. Monroe County

d. Boston

Each of the proposed examples suggests the development of new requirements for the concept, which helps to clarify how the concept can be applied. Applying a concept to different possible examples thus becomes the way that we develop and gradually sharpen our idea of the concept.

The process of developing concepts involves a constant back-and-forth movement between these two activities:

**Generalizing** • Focusing on certain basic similarities between things in order to develop the requirements for the concept

**Interpreting** • Looking for different things to apply the concept to, in order to determine if they ''meet the requirements'' of the concept which we are developing.

As the back-and-forth movement progresses, we gradually develop a specific list of requirements that something must have in order to be considered an example of the concept. As we develop a more specific list of requirements, we are at the same time giving ourselves a clearer idea of how it is defined. We are also developing a collection of examples that embody the qualities of the concept and demonstrate in what situations the concept applies.

Select a type of music that you are familiar with (e.g., pop music) and write a dialogue similar to the one above. In the course of the dialogue, be sure to include

1. examples that you are generalizing from (e.g., soul, rock).
2. general similarities between types of pop music (e.g., its main audience is younger people).
3. examples to which you are trying to apply the developing concept (e.g., is ''salsa'' or ''reggae'' pop music?).

Analyze the dialogue that you created above the way we analyzed the earlier one, by answering the following questions:

1. What examples of pop music did you use to generalize from?
2. What are the common features or requirements of the music style that you selected?
3. What are some of the examples that you tried to apply the concept to? Did the concept apply? Why or why not?

Now focus on the list of features shared by all examples of the music style you selected. This list constitutes the *requirements* for applying the concept that must be met in order for something to qualify as an example of the concept. Are there other common features/requirements that you can think of? Compare your list with the lists of other classmates. Add to your list any requirements that you may have overlooked.

The process of forming concepts therefore involves moving back and forth at the same time between the requirements and examples of the concept:

1. We can move from individual objects, experiences, and activities to the general concept of which they are examples, based on certain similarities they have in common. This is called *generalizing*.
2. We can move from the general concept we have developed by applying this concept to specific examples in order to determine if the example meets the requirements of the concept. This is called *interpreting*.

Forming clear concepts with specific requirements involves moving in *both* directions, as we saw in the dialogue regarding "city." Developing concepts is thus an ongoing process of generalizing and interpreting.

As we move back and forth between the general concept that we are developing and the specific examples of it, our idea of the concept gradually becomes sharper and more detailed. This ongoing, back-and-forth movement (generalizing and interpreting) gradually refines and clarifies our concept, while also generating and developing examples of it. As we indicated, this back and forth process is an *interactive* process.

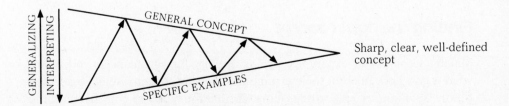

Forming concepts involves performing both of these operations together, because

1. You cannot form a concept unless you know how it might apply. If you have absolutely *no idea* what "pop music" or "city" might be examples of, then you cannot begin to form the concept, even in vague or general terms.

2. You cannot gather up examples of the concept unless you know what they might be examples of. Until you begin to develop some idea of what the concepts "city" or "pop music" might be (based on certain similarities between various things), you will not know where to look for examples of the concept (or how to evaluate them).

This interactive process is the way that we usually form all concepts, particularly the complicated ones. In school, much of your education is focused on carefully forming and exploring key concepts such as "democracy," "dynamic equilibrium," "personality," and so on. This book has also focused on certain key concepts, such as

thinking critically

solving problems

perceiving

believing

knowing

language

mapping

In each case, we have carefully explored these concepts through the interactive process of *generalizing* the requirements of the concept and *interpreting* the concept by examining examples to which the concept applies.

---

     Review the concepts listed above and in each case

1. identify the requirements and boundaries of the concept.
2. identify an example to which the concept applies.

---

## Finding the right concept

Making sense of our experience means finding the right concept to explain what is going on. In order to determine whether the concept we have selected fits the situation, we have to determine whether the requirements that form the concept are being met. For example, the original television series "Superman" used to begin with the words:

"Look—up in the sky! It's a bird! It's a plane! No! It's *Superman!*"

In order to figure out which concept applies to the situation (so that we can figure out what is going on), we have to

1.  be aware of the requirements that form the boundaries of the concept.
2.  determine whether the experience meets those requirements, for only if it does, can we apply the concept to it.

In the example above, what are some of the requirements for using the concepts being identified?

1.  *Bird:*

    a.  _____

    b.  _____

    c.  _____

2.  *Plane:*

    a.  _____

    b.  _____

    c.  _____

3.  *Superman:*

    a.  _____

    b.  _____

    c.  _____

If we have the requirements of the concept clearly in mind, we can proceed to figure out which of these requirements are met by the experience—whether it is a bird, a plane, or the "man of steel" himself. This is the way that we apply concepts, which is one of the most important ways that we figure out what is going on in our experience.

In determining exactly what the requirements of the concept are, we can ask ourselves the question:

"Would something still be an example of this concept, if it did not meet this requirement?"

If the answer to this question is "no"—that is, something would *not* be an example of this concept if it did not meet this requirement—then we can say that the requirement is a necessary part of the concept.

Consider the concept "dog." Which of the following descriptions are requirements of the concept that must be met in order to say that something is an example of the concept "dog"?

1. Is an animal
2. Normally has four legs and a tail
3. Barks
4. Bites the postman

It is clear that (1) and (2) are necessary requirements that must be met in order to apply the concept "dog," because if we apply our "test" question,

> "Would something be an example of this concept, if it did not meet this requirement?"

we can say that something would not be an example of the concept "dog" if it did not fit the first two descriptions: if it was not an animal and did not normally have four legs and a tail.

However, this does not seem to be the case with descriptions 3 and 4. If we ask ourselves the same test question, we can see that something might still be an example of the concept "dog" *even if* it did not bark or bite the postman. This is because even though *many* dogs *do* in fact bark and bite, these are *not* necessary requirements for being a dog.

Of course, there may be other things that meet these requirements but are not dogs. For example, a cat (1) is an animal that (2) normally has four legs and a tail. What this means is that the requirements of a concept only tell us what something *must* have in order to be an example of the concept. As a result, we often have to identify additional requirements that will define the concept more sharply. This point is clearly illustrated as children form concepts. Not identifying a sufficient number of the concept's requirements leads to such misconceptions as "All four-legged animals are doggies," or "All yellow-colored metal is gold."

This is why it is so important for us to have a very clear idea of the greatest possible number of specific requirements of each concept. These requirements determine when the concept can be applied and indicate which things qualify as examples of it. When we are able to identify *all* of the requirements of the concept, we say that these requirements are both necessary *and* sufficient for applying the concept.

What are some additional requirements of the concept "dog" that would ➤•◄ help us differentiate it from the concept "cat"?

a. _____

b. _____

Each concept below is followed by several possible descriptions of it. Indi- ➤•◄ cate for each description whether it is a necessary requirement for the concept. If the description is *not* a necessary requirement, explain why it is not. For example:

*Child:*  a. is young

b. has a biological mother and father

c. likes to play games

*Explanation:*  (c) is not a necessary requirement; although most children like to play games, someone would still be a child even if he or she did not enjoy playing games.

1. *Policeman*

   a.  wears a uniform

   b.  is suposed to enforce the law

   c.  has a badge and a gun

   *Explanation:* _____

   _____

   _____

   _____

2. *School*

   a.  has students

   b.  has teachers

   c.  learning takes place

   *Explanation:* _____

   _____

   _____

   _____

3. *Religion*
    a.  has a set of spiritual beliefs
    b.  people worship God
    c.  members gather in a church

    *Explanation:* _____

    _____

    _____

    _____

4. *Music*
    a.  has a rhythm and melody
    b.  is created by various instruments
    c.  people can sing and dance to it

    *Explanation:* _____

    _____

    _____

    _____

5. *Work*
    a.  is done to earn money
    b.  is not creative or enjoyable
    c.  is something everyone has to do

    *Explanation:* _____

    _____

    _____

    _____

➤•◄      For each concept below, give at least three descriptions that are necessary
requirements for the concept to apply to a situation. Then share your responses
with the other members of your class and see if they agree with the requirements you have identified. If they do not agree, ask them to explain why the
requirement is not an essential part of the concept.

1. *Game*

    a. _____

    b. _____

    c. _____

2. *Learn*

    a. _____

    b. _____

    c. _____

3. *Successful*

    a. _____

    b. _____

    c. _____

4. *Successful teacher*

    a. _____

    b. _____

    c. _____

5. *Friend*

    a. _____

    b. _____

    c. _____

6. _____

    a. _____

    b. _____

    c. _____

### Evaluating information

We have just seen that finding the right concept to best explain what is taking place in a situation involves both

1. being aware of the requirements that determine when the concept can be applied.

2. determining whether the experience meets those requirements, for if it does, we can then apply the concept to it.

As a result, information plays a central role in the way that we develop, select, and apply concepts to our experience. In fact, our lives are a continual process of receiving and evaluating information to determine whether it *supports* or *conflicts* with the concepts we have adopted to understand a situation.

For example, as we try to size up a course on the first day of class, we form our initial concepts based on information we have already received.

What have I heard about the course?

What is the reputation of the instructor?

What do I know about the other students?

As the course progresses, we gather further information from our actual experiences in the class. This information may support our initial concepts, or it may conflict with these initial concepts. If the information we receive supports these concepts, we tend to maintain them ("Yes, I can see that this is going to be a difficult course"). On the other hand, when the information we receive conflicts with these concepts, we tend to find new concepts to explain the situation ("No, I can see that I was wrong—this course isn't going to be as difficult as I thought at first"). A diagram of this process might look something like this:

*Experience:* Attending the first day of class

leads to

*Applying a concept to explain the situation:* This course will be very difficult and I might not do very well.

leads to

Looking for information to support or conflict with our concept.

| *Supporting Information* | *Conflicting Information* |
|---|---|
| The teacher is very demanding. | I find that I am able to keep up with the work. |
| There are lots of writing assignments. | leads to |
| The reading is challenging. | Forming a new concept to explain the situation: This course is difficult, but I will be able to handle the work and do well. |
|  | action |

We see in this example that, if we get new information that does not fit into the picture we had of what was going on, we may change the picture based on that new information. We look for a different concept to understand what has happened. Using the new concept, we look for more information to find out whether the new concept applies. On the other hand, when things go smoothly, the new information we are getting fits into our picture of the situation formed by the concepts we have adopted. This encourages us to keep these concepts until new conflicting information suggests they are not giving us an accurate or adequate explanation of the situation.

---

Identify an initial concept you had about one of your courses that changed ➤ • ◄ as a result of your experiences in the class. The concept can involve the course, the teacher, or the students. After identifying your initial concept, describe the experiences that led you to change or modify the concept and then explain the new concept that you formed to explain the situation.

1. Initial concept
2. New information provided by additional experiences in the class
3. New concept formed to explain the situation

Our lives are a continual process of conceptual clarification as we seek to evaluate our present situation and our future needs by forming and applying the most appropriate concepts. Those who can develop this conceptual facility will best be able to make sense of their experience, to meet the challenges and solve the problems that they encounter, to understand themselves, and to exert meaningful control over their lives. Another important aspect of developing our conceptual skills is learning how to define and express the concepts we are forming.

## Defining concepts

Our language is founded on definitions and without them communication would be impossible. We rely on commonly accepted definitions of concepts in order to understand one another. By learning how to define concepts accurately, we know exactly when the concept can be used. Clear and precise definitions are thus a giant step toward clearing up misunderstandings and communicating what we are thinking and feeling. In addition, learning how to define concepts clearly and precisely helps sharpen our own thinking, giving us a much clearer idea of what is going on and aiding us in making the best decisions possible based on that understanding.

In order to understand how we define, we have to understand how we form and apply concepts. As we have seen in this chapter, concepts are general ideas that we use to organize our experience. We form concepts by the interactive process of *generalizing* (focusing on the common qualities shared by a group of things) and *interpreting* (finding examples of the concept). The common qualities form the necessary requirements that must be met in order to apply the concept to our experience.

### Definitions: identifying the necessary requirements

When we define a concept, we usually identify the necessary requirements that determine when the concept can be applied. In fact, the word "definition" is derived from the Latin word meaning "boundary" because that is exactly what a definition does: it gives the boundaries of the territory in our experience that can be described by the concept. For example, a definition of the concept "horse" might include the following requirements:

1. Large strong animal
2. Four legs with solid hoofs
3. Flowing mane and tail
4. Domesticated long ago for drawing or carrying loads, carrying riders, etc.
5. _____

By understanding the requirements of the concept "horse," we understand what conditions must be met in order for something to qualify as an example of the concept. This lets us know in what situations we can apply the concept: to the animals running around the race track, the animals pulling wagons and carriages, the animals being ridden on the range, and so on. In addition, understanding the requirements lets us know to which things the concept can be applied. No matter how much a "zebra" looks like a horse, we won't apply the concept "horse" to it if we really understand the definition of the concept involved. Even if we take the drastic step of erasing the zebra's stripes, we still would not apply the concept "horse" to it, because it still does not meet the necessary requirements of the concept.

---

 As a class, generate a list of concepts that you are learning in other courses. Define these concepts by listing the requirements that form the boundaries of each concept.

### Definitions: identifying examples

Providing an effective definition means listing the general qualities of a concept, the requirements that indicate the situations in which it can be used.

Definitions also often make strategic use of *examples* of the concept being defined. Consider the following definition by Ambrose Bierce.

> *An edible:* Good to eat and wholesome to digest, as a worm to a toad, a toad to a snake, a snake to a pig, a pig to a man, and a man to a worm.

Contrast this definition with the one illustrated in the following passage from Charles Dickens's *Hard Times:*

> "Bitzer" said Thomas Gradgrind. "Your definition of a horse." "Quadruped. Graminivorous. Forty teeth, namely twenty-four grinders, four eye teeth, and twelve incisive. Sheds coat in the spring; in marshy countries shed hoofs, too. Hoofs hard, but requiring to be shod with iron. Age known by marks in mouth." That (and much more) Bitzer. "Now girl number twenty," said Mr. Gradgrind, "you know what a horse is."

Although Bitzer has certainly done an admirable job of listing some of the necessary requirements of the concept "horse," it is unlikely that "girl number twenty" has any better idea of what a horse is than she did before.

These kinds of definitions are often not very helpful unless we already know what the concept means. A more concrete way of communicating the concept "horse" would be to point out various animals that qualify as horses and other animals that do not. You could also explain why they do not. (E.g., That can't be a horse because it has two humps and its legs are too long and skinny.)

Although examples do not take the place of a clearly understood definition, they are often very useful in clarifying, supplementing, and expanding such a definition. If someone asked you "What is a horse?" and you replied by giving examples of different kinds of horses (thoroughbred racing horses, plow horses for farming, quarter-horses for cowboys, hunter horses for fox hunting, circus horses, etc.), you certainly would be communicating a good portion of the meaning of "horse." Giving examples of a concept complements and clarifies the necessary requirements for the correct use of that concept.

---

➤•◄

For each of the following concepts,

a. give a "dictionary" definition.

b. describe ways you could supplement and expand this definition.

*Example:* smile

      a. A facial expression characterized by an upward curving of the corners of the mouth and indicating pleasure, amusement, or derision.

      b. Smiling at someone or drawing a picture of a smiling face.

1. *cry*

   a. _____

     _____

     _____

   b. _____

     _____

2. *music*

   a. _____

     _____

     _____

   b. _____

     _____

3. *art*

   a. _____

     _____

     _____

   b. _____

     _____

4. *learning*

   a. _____

     _____

     _____

   b. _____

     _____

5. *work*

   a. _____

     _____

     _____

   b. _____

     _____

6. *create*

   a.  _____

      _____

      _____

   b.  _____

      _____

Giving an effective definition of a concept thus means both

1. identifying the general qualities of the concept, which determine when it can be correctly applied.
2. using representative examples to demonstrate actual applications of the concept—examples that embody the general qualities of the concept.

The process of providing definitions of concepts is thus the same process we use to develop concepts. As we discovered in this chapter, we develop our concepts through the interactive process of

> *generalizing* the essential requirements of the concept by focusing on the common characteristics of a group of things.
>
> *interpreting* the concept by finding specific examples to illustrate it, based on applying the requirements of the concept.

The definitions that we normally find in dictionaries tend to focus on the first of these activities—namely, providing some of the necessary requirements of the concept. As a result, dictionaries only sketch the outermost boundaries of the concept, as we saw with Bitzer's definition of a horse on page 323. In order for us to really get a sense of how that concept can and should be used, we have to engage in the interactive process of generalizing and interpreting.

---

Select a concept from a field you know well. First describe how you came to understand that concept. Does this description reflect the processes of generalizing and interpreting that we have been discussing in this chapter? Then define that concept, providing both the requirements and examples.

---

Let us review the ideas we have been exploring in this chapter by analyzing the concept "responsibility." "Responsibility" is a complex idea that has an entire network of meanings. The word comes from the Latin word *respondere*, which means "to pledge or promise."

A. *Generalizing*

1. Describe two important responsibilities you have in your life.
2. Did these responsibilities originate with yourself or with others? Explain.
3. In reflecting on these responsibilities, identify the qualities they embody that lead you to think of them as "responsibilities."

When we encounter responsibilities in our lives, we can either accept them and act on them, or we can resist them and refuse to act on them. The manner in which we react to our responsibilities helps determine whether we are seen as being "responsible" or being "irresponsible."

4. Describe a person in your life who you think is very responsible.
5. Describe a person in your life who you think is very irresponsible.
6. In reflecting on these individuals, identify the qualities they embody that lead you to think of them as "responsible" and "irresponsible."

B. *Interpreting*

Consider the following situations. In each case, describe what you consider to be examples of responsible behavior and irresponsible behavior. Be sure to explain the reasons for your answer.

7. You are a member of a group of three students who are assigned the task of writing a report on a certain topic. Your life is very hectic and in addition you find the topic dull. What is your response?
8. You and a friend made plans over a month ago to attend a concert this Friday night. Monday night you get a call from a man/woman you've been wanting to date for a long time, asking you to a party on Friday. What is your response?
9. Describe a situation of your own to illustrate these concepts, and describe examples of responsible and irresponsible behavior in response to it.
10. Describe an area in which you think the government has a responsibility to its citizens and explain the reasons why.

C. *Defining*

Using these activities of generalizing and interpreting as a foundation, give definitions of each of the following concepts by

listing the qualities that make up the boundaries of the concept.

identifying the key examples that embody and illustrate the qualities of the concept.

11. Responsible
12. Irresponsible

D. *Relating*

The concept of responsibility is related to many other important concepts, including a number we have been considering in this book.

13. Review the qualities of the concept "thinking critically," which are detailed in Chapter 3. Explain how the concept "thinking critically" is related to the concept "responsibility."

14. Review the qualities of the concept "maturity" that is examined in the selection from Gail Sheehy's *Passages* (p. 299). Explain how the concept "maturity" is related to the concept "responsibility."

E. *Composing*

15. Using the concept "responsibility" as a starting point, create a map that generates ideas related to this concept and shows their various relationships. (Mapping guidelines, see Chapter Eight "Symbolizing & Map-Making")

16. Using this map as a reference, write a passage that explores one aspect of the concept "responsibility."

# Chapter Ten
# Composing

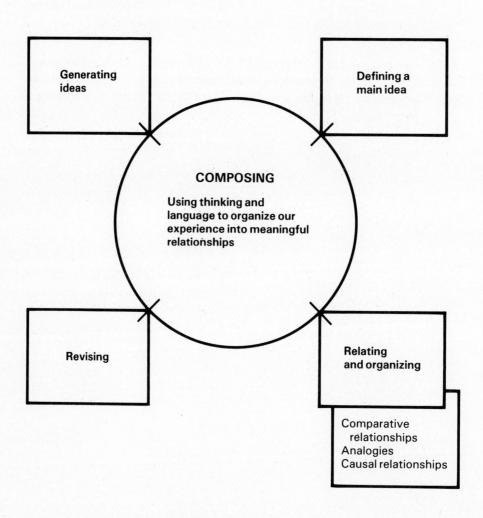

Generating ideas

Defining a main idea

COMPOSING

Using thinking and language to organize our experience into meaningful relationships

Revising

Relating and organizing

Comparative relationships
Analogies
Causal relationships

THROUGHOUT THIS BOOK we have been considering and experiencing the insight that each one of us is a "creator." Each of us is actively shaping—as well as discovering—the world that we live in. Our world does not exist as a finished product, waiting for us to perceive it, think about it, and describe it with words and pictures. Instead, we are *active participants* in composing the world that seems so familiar to us.

The goal of this composing process is to organize our world into meaningful patterns that will help us figure out what is going on and what we ought to do. Composing our world involves all the activities that we have been exploring, including

| | | |
|---|---|---|
| perceiving | symbolizing | generalizing |
| believing | describing | interpreting |
| knowing | classifying | conceptualizing |
| solving problems | analyzing | defining |

The purpose of these thinking activities is to shape and organize our experience in order to make sense of it. Although we are usually unaware that we are performing these activities, our ability to think critically gives us the means to examine the different ways by which we are making sense of the world so that we can develop and sharpen our understanding. As we actively discover and compose various patterns, what we are really doing is exploring the ways in which different aspects of our experience *relate* to each other. Let us investigate this idea further.

In the last chapter we found that the process of forming and applying concepts is one of the primary ways that we organize and make sense our world. On pages 330–333 is a list that details major kidnapings since 1900.[1] Review the list carefully, and then explore the information presented by using concepts to classify the information in various ways. For example, you might want to use concepts such as

age of victim

sex of victim

reason for kidnaping

outcome of kidnaping

---

[1] I am indebted for the idea of this exercise to Mina Shaughnessy, *Errors and Expectations: A Guide for the Teacher of Basic Writing* (New York: Oxford University Press, 1977).

*Major Kidnapings*

**Edward A. Cudahy Jr.,** 16, in Omaha, Neb., **Dec. 18, 1900.** Returned Dec. 20 after $25,000 paid. Pat Crowe confessed.

**Robert Franks,** 13, in Chicago, **May 22, 1924,** by 2 youths, Richard Loeb and Nathan Leopold, who killed boy. Demand for $10,000 ignored. Loeb died in prison, Leopold paroled 1958.

**Charles A. Lindbergh Jr.,** 20 mos. old, in Hopewell, N.J., **Mar. 1, 1932;** found dead May 12. Ransom of $50,000 was paid to man identified as Bruno Richard Hauptmann, 35, paroled German convict who entered U.S. illegally. Hauptmann passed ransom bill and $14,000 marked money was found in his garage. He was convicted after spectacular trial at Flemington, and electrocuted in Trenton, N.J., prison, Apr. 3, 1936.

**William A. Hamm Jr.,** 39, in St. Paul, **June 15, 1933.** $100,000 paid. Alvin Karpis given life, paroled in 1969.

**Charles F. Urschel,** in Oklahoma City, **July 22, 1933.** Released July 31 after $200,000 paid. George (Machine Gun) Kelly and 5 others given life.

**Brooke L. Hart,** 22, in San Jose, Cal. Thomas Thurmond and John Holmes arrested after demanding $40,000 ransom. When Hart's body was found in San Francisco Bay, **Nov. 26, 1933,** a mob attacked the jail at San Jose and lynched the 2 kidnappers.

**George Weyerhaeuser,** 9, in Tacoma, Wash., **May 24, 1935.** Returned home June 1 after $200,000 paid. Kidnappers given 20 to 60 years.

**Charles Mattson,** 10, in Tacoma, Wash., **Dec. 27, 1936.** Found dead Jan. 11, 1937. Kidnaper asked $28,000, failed to contact.

**Arthur Fried,** in White Plains, N.Y., **Dec. 4, 1937.** Body not found. Two kidnapers executed.

**Robert C. Greenlease,** 6, taken from school **Sept. 28, 1953,** and held for $600,000. Body found Oct. 7. Mrs. Bonnie Brown Heady and Carl A. Hall pleaded guilty and were executed.

**Peter Weinberger,** 32 days old, Westbury, N.Y., **July 4, 1956,** for $2,000 ransom, not paid. Child found dead. Angelo John LaMarca, 31, convicted, executed.

**Cynthia Ruotolo,** 6 wks old, taken from carriage in front of Hamden, Conn. store **Sept. 1, 1956.** Body found in lake.

**Lee Crary,** 8 in Everett, Wash., **Sept. 22, 1957,** $10,000 ransom, not paid. He escaped after 3 days, led police to George E. Collins, who was convicted.

**Eric Peugeot,** 4, taken from playground at St. Cloud golf course, Paris, **Apr. 12, 1960.** Released unharmed 3 days later after payment of undisclosed sum. Two sentenced to prison.

**Frank Sinatra Jr.,** 19, from hotel room in Lake Tahoe, Cal., **Dec. 8, 1963.** Released **Dec. 11** after his father paid $240,000 ransom. Three men sentenced to prison; most of ransom recovered.

**Barbara Jane Mackle,** 20, abducted **Dec. 17, 1968,** from Atlanta, Ga., motel, was found unharmed 3 days later, buried in a coffin-like wooden box 18 inches underground, after her father had paid $500,000 ransom; Gary Steven Krist sentenced to life, Ruth Eisenmann-Schier to 7 years; most of ransom recovered.

**Anne Katherine Jenkins,** 22, abducted **May 10, 1969,** from her Baltimore apartment, freed 3 days later after her father paid $10,000 ransom.

**Mrs. Roy Fuchs,** 35, and 3 children held hostage 2 hours, **May 14, 1969,** in Long Island, N.Y., released after her husband, a bank manager, paid kidnapers $129,000 in bank funds; 4 men arrested, ransom recovered.

**C. Burke Elbrick,** U.S. ambassador to Brazil, kidnaped by revolutionaries in Rio de Janeiro **Sept. 4, 1969;** released 3 days later after Brazil yielded to kidnaper's demands to publish manifesto and release 15 political prisoners.

**Patrick Dolan,** 18, found shot to death near Sao Paulo, Brazil, **Nov. 5, 1969,** after he was kidnaped and $12,500 paid.

**Sean M. Holly,** U.S. diplomat, in Guatemala **Mar. 6, 1970;** freed 2 days later upon release of 3 terrorists from prison.

**Lt. Col. Donald J. Crowley,** U.S. air attache, in Dominican Republic **Mar. 24, 1970;** released after government allowed 20 prisoners to leave the country.

**Count Karl von Spreti,** W. German ambassador to Guatemala, **Mar. 31, 1970;** slain after Guatemala refused demands for $700,000 and release of 22 prisoners.

**Pedro Eugenio Arambaru,** former Argentine president, by terrorists **May 29, 1970;** body found July 17.

**Ehrenfried von Holleben,** W. German ambassador to Brazil, by terrorists **June 11, 1970;** freed after release of 40 prisoners.

**Daniel A. Mitrione,** U.S. diplomat, **July 31, 1970,** by terrorists in Montevideo, Uruguay; body found Aug. 10 after government rejected demands for release of all political prisoners.

**James R. Cross,** British trade commissioner, **Oct. 5, 1970,** by French Canadian separatists in Quebec; freed Dec. 3 after 3 kidnapers and relatives flown to Cuba by government.

**Pierre Laporte,** Quebec Labor Minister, by separatists **Oct. 10, 1970;** body found Oct. 18.

**Giovanni E. Bucher,** Swiss ambassador **Dec. 7, 1970,** by revolutionaries in Rio de Janeiro; freed Jan. 16, 1971, after Brazil released 70 political prisoners.

**Geoffrey Jackson,** British ambassador, in Montevideo, **Jan. 8, 1971,** by Tupamaro terrorists. Held as ransom for release of imprisoned terrorists, he was released Sept. 9, after the prisoners escaped.

**Ephraim Elrom,** Israel consul general in Istanbul, **May 17, 1971.** Held as ransom for imprisoned terrorists, he was found dead May 23.

**Mrs. Virginia Piper,** 49 abducted **July 27, 1972,** from her home in suburban Minneapolis; found unharmed near Duluth 2 days later after her husband paid $1 million ransom to the kidnapers.

**Victor E. Samuelson,** Exxon executive, **Dec. 6, 1973,** in Campana, Argentina, by Marxist guerrillas, freed Apr. 29, 1974, after payment of record $14.2 million ransom.

**J. Paul Getty 3d,** 17, grandson of the U.S. oil mogul, released **Dec. 15, 1973,** in southern Italy after $2.8 million ransom paid.

**Patricia (Patty) Hearst,** 19, taken from her Berkeley, Cal., apartment **Feb. 4, 1974.** Symbionese Liberation Army demanded her father, Randolph A. Hearst, publisher, give millions to poor. Hearst offered $2 million in food; the Hearst Corp. offered $4 million worth. Kidnapers objected to way food was distributed. Patricia, in message, said she had joined SLA; she was identified by FBI as taking part in a San Francisco bank holdup, **Apr. 15;** she claimed, in message, she had been coerced. Again identified by FBI in a store holdup, **May 16,** she was classified by FBI as "an armed, dangerous fugitive." **FBI, Sept. 18, 1975,** captured Patricia and others in San Francisco; they were indicted on various charges. Patricia for bank robbery. A San Francisco jury convicted her, **Mar. 20, 1976.** She was released from prison under executive clemency, **Feb. 1, 1979.** In 1978, William and Emily Harris were sentenced to 10 years to life for the Hearst kidnaping.

**J. Reginald Murphy,** 40, an editor of *Atlanta* (Ga.) *Constitution,* kidnaped **Feb. 20, 1974,** freed **Feb. 22** after payment of $700,000 ransom by the newspaper. Police arrested William A. H. Williams, a contractor; most of the money was recovered.

**J. Guadalupe Zuno Hernandez,** 83, father-in-law of Mexican President Luis Echeverria Alvarez, seized by 4 terrorists **Aug. 28, 1974;** government refused to negotiate; he was released **Sept. 8.**

**E. B. Reville,** Hepzibah, Ga., banker, and wife Jean, kidnaped **Sept. 30, 1974.** Ransom of $30,000 paid. He was found alive; Mrs. Reville was found dead of carbon monoxide fumes in car trunk **Oct. 2.**

**Jack Teich,** Kings Point, N.Y., steel executive, seized **Nov. 12, 1974;** released **Nov. 19** after payment of $750,000.

**Samuel Bronfman,** 21, heir to Seagram liquor fortune, allegedly abducted **Aug. 9, 1975,** in Purchase, N.Y.; $2.3 million ransom paid. FBI and N.Y.C. police found Samuel **Aug. 17** in Brooklyn, N.Y., apartment, recovered ransom, and arrested Mel Patrick Lynch and Dominic Byrne. Two found not guilty of kidnap, but convicted of extortion after they claimed Sam masterminded ransom plot.

**Hanns-Martin Schleyer,** a West German industrialist, was kidnaped in Cologne, **Sept. 5, 1977** by armed terrorists. Schleyer was found dead, **Oct. 19,** in an abandoned car shortly after 3 jailed terrorist leaders of the Baader-Meinhof gang were found dead in their prison cells near Stuttgart, West Germany.

**Aldo Moro,** former Italian premier, kidnaped in Rome, **Mar. 16, 1978,** by left-wing terrorists. Five of his bodyguards killed during abduction. Moro's bullet-ridden body was found in a parked car, **May 9,** in Rome. Six members of the Red Brigades arrested, charged, June 5, with complicity in the kidnaping.

**James L. Dozier,** a U.S. Army general, kidnapped from his apartment in Verona, Italy, **Dec. 17, 1981,** by members of the Red Brigades terrorist organization. He was rescued, **Jan. 28, 1982,** by Italian police.

**Dr. Hector Zevalloses,** owner of an abortion clinic, and his wife were kidnapped in Edwardsville, Ill., **Aug. 13, 1982,** by the Army of God, an anti-abortion group. The Zevalloses were released unharmed, Aug. 20.

After classifying the information in a variety of ways, examine your classifications and think about what conclusions you can come to. Asking questions like those below might lead you to some conclusions about the information.

1. Who are the typical kidnap victims? (age, sex, occupation, etc.)

    *Conclusion:* _____

    _____

2. What are the typical reasons for kidnapping?

    *Conclusion:* _____

    _____

3. Has there been any change over time regarding the type of victims usually kidnapped?

    *Conclusion:* _____

    _____

    _____

4. _____

   *Conclusion:* _____

   _____

   _____

5. _____

   *Conclusion:* _____

   _____

   _____

6. _____

   *Conclusion:* _____

   _____

   _____

## The composing process

Let us reflect on the way our thinking process worked through this exercise. We were presented with a list of information, and we made an active effort to identify and organize this information into patterns that made sense to us. In so doing, we were trying to discover and compose relationships that would connect the information we were exploring. As we established these various relationships, what began simply as a list of information was shaped into patterns that had meaning for us. As a result of this composing activity, we were able to understand the information in new ways.

This is the heart of the thinking process. When we think, we are making sense of our world by discovering and composing patterns that we understand. We do so by *identifying* aspects of our experience (with symbols) and *relating* these aspects to one another in various patterns. The relationships that we compose and discover are reflected in our thinking and in our language. In the pages ahead, we will be exploring in some detail the composing process as it is expressed in our thinking and in our use of language. Our examination will include the following composing activities:

   Generating ideas

   Defining a main idea

   Organizing our ideas

   Revising our ideas

# Generating ideas

Ideas are not created in isolation but are almost always related to a particular subject. We develop them by exploring that subject. Listed below are the annual salaries of various individuals and professions in the United States during 1983. Carefully examine the list and then explore the information presented by using concepts to classify it in different ways. You might want to use concepts such as

> amount of salary
>
> type of occupation (e.g., entertainment, business, athletic, etc.)
>
> level of education

*National Average Starting Salaries*

Accountant  $14,500

Accountant (Tax)  $33,000

Actor  $5,000

Advertising Manager  $21,000

Air Traffic Controller  $29,374

Airplane Inspector  $34,930

Airplane Flight Attendant  $12,000

Anesthesiologist  $100,000

Announcer  $14,300

Architect  $17,100

Armed Forces:

   General/Admiral  $62,000

   1st Lieutenant  $18,000

   Private  $7,200

Assembler (Production)  $9,720

Astronomer  $18,000

Athlete (Professional)  $54,000

Athletic Trainer  $15,000

Attorney (Tax)  $24,508

Attendant (Service Station)  $9,568

Bagger  $7,920

Baker  $12,272

Bank Officer (Operations)
   $20–29,000

Bank Officer (Corporate Controller)
   $50–95,000

Barber  $7,200

Bartender  $9,734

Beekeeper  $14,580

Bellhop  $6,739

Biologist  $22,486

Bookkeeper  $11,440

Bricklayer  $20,384

Botanist  $22,165

Box Maker  $9,072

Boat Builder  $17,546

Boat Loader  $29,120

Butcher  $30,912

Cabinetmaker  $25,480

Carpenter  $19,670

Caseworker (Child Welfare)
   $12,000

Cashier  $9,152

Chef  $19,800

*National Average Starting Salaries*

Chauffeur   $12,480

Chemist   $21,360

Child Care Attendant (School)
   $7,696

Chiropractor   $30,000

Clergy Member   $25,000

Clerk (Accounting)   $9,575

Clerk (File)   $6,760

Clerk (Post-Office)   $21,840

Clerk-Typist   $11,596

Collector (Toll)   $9,990

Composer (Music)   $21,320

Conductor (Orchestra)   $23,860

Conductor (Passenger Car)   $36,000

Construction Worker   $13,208

Cook   $10,400

Correction Officer   $15,000

Counselor   $15,000

Counter Attendant (Coffee-Shop)
   $4,816

Dancer   $17,107

Dental Assistant   $13,408

Dentist   $57,517

Derrick Operator   $21,840

Designer (Clothes)   $18,900

Detective   $21,060

Die Maker (Bench)   $20,744

Dining Room Attendant   $5,850

Disc Jockey   $12,636

Dog Groomer   $16,200

Donut Machine Operator   $9,072

Dragline Operator   $21,760

Driver (Bus)   $17,264

Driver (Tractor-Trailer Truck)
   $27,581

Driver (Taxi)   $10,530

Driver (Concrete Mixing Truck)
   $27,581

Economist   $30,000

Editor (Newspaper)   $17,000

Electrician   $22,404

Engineer (Mechanical)   $25,500

Engineer (Nuclear)   $18,900

Engraver   $18,900

Envelope Machine Operator
   $9,990

Executive Secretary   $17,628

Exterminator   $11,880

Faculty Member (College)   $22,734

Farmer (General)   $15,120

Farmworker   $7,137

Financial Analyst   $18,900

Fire Chief   $32,500

Firefighter   $11,000

Fire Inspector   $15,768

Fisherman (Net)   $11,880

Food Service Worker   $8,788

Forest Worker   $11,880

Funeral Director   $15,500

Garbage Collector   $12,116

Doctor (General Practioner)
   $71,900

Geologist   $22,000

Government:

   President   $200,000

   Vice-President   $91,000

*National Average Starting Salaries*

Senators/Representatives
$72,600

Governor $35–100,000

Guard (Security) $12,532

Home Attendant $6,968

Horse Trainer $16,848

Host/Hostess (Restaurant) $10,530

Housecleaner $7,500

Humorist $50,000

Illustrator $22,356

Interpreter $24,300

Janitor $11,908

Jockey $18,900

Judge $40,500

Keypunch Operator $12,480

Knitting Machine Operator $8,532

Laborer (Construction) $19,110

Lathe Operator $17,550

Lawyer (Corporation) $24,300

Librarian $13,127

Library Assistant $8,951

Lithographic Plate Maker $26,389

Loan Officer $32,000

Locksmith $12,636

Locomotive Engineer $39,300

Logger $13,364

Machinist $19,292

Mail Carrier $21,840

Manager (Fast Foods) $20,000

Manager (Systems Analyst)
$35,247

Manicurist $11,000

Mason (Cement) $25,609

Mate (Ship) $28,632

Mechanic (Aircraft) $15,538

Mechanic (Automobile) $15,964

Mechanic (Data Processing)
$22,308

Medical Assistant $9,612

Meteorologist $14,375

Meter Reader $16,484

Milling Machine Operator $20,520

Miner $20,800

Model $23,760

Narcotics Investigator $16,416

Newswriter $15,120

Nurse's Aide $9,464

Nurse (Licensed Practical)
$13,160

Nurse (Midwife) $18,360

Obstetrician $100,000

Occupational Therapist $17,300

Office Manager $17,524

Optometrist $20,754

Ordinary Seaman $13,296

Painter (Construction) $15,288

Paper Hanger $25,272

Park Ranger $13,247

Parole Officer $14,580

Pattern Maker $14,338

Pediatrician $70,300

Pharmacist $23,004

Personnel Manager $21,800

Photographer $18,096

Photograph Finisher $9,477

Photo Journalist $8,541

Physicist $18,241

Piano Tuner $7,800

*National Average Starting Salaries*

Pilot (Airplane, commercial) $57,240

Pilot (Test) $29,374

Plasterer (Construction) $25,272

Police Captain $25,731

Police Officer $21,060

Postmaster $24,300

Power-Shovel Operator $24,856

Principal $33,480

Private Investigator $21,600

Programmer (Information System) $22,152

Proofreader $9,720

Psychologist (Clinical) $25,000

Psychologist (Industrial, Organizational) $36,000

Rancher (Livestock) $14,580

Receptionist $12,116

Repairer (Appliance) $10,530

Repairer (Instrument) $23,348

Retail Store Manager $18,900

Ring Maker (Jewelry) $13,163

Rock-Drill Operator $23,166

Sales Agent (Real Estate) $17,628

Scientist (Animal) $30,000

Scientist (Soil) $14,500

Secretary $13,468

Security Sales:

  Junior Trader $24,200

  Broker $62–150,400

Set Decorator $15,120

Sewer Worker $8,632

Sheriff (Deputy) $15,200

Singer $11,440

Social Worker (School) $15,900

Stage Director $24,300

Sports Instructor $17,000

Stenographer $14,872

Stonemason $20,384

Steelworker (Structural) $27,821

Stunt Performer $32,400

Surgeon $100,000

Surgical Technician $7,200

Systems Analyst $18,500

Tailor $10,800

Taxidermist $11,880

Teacher's Aide $7,826

Teacher $14,250

Tool-and-Die Maker $22,724

Trapper (Animal) $11,880

Tree Surgeon $11,880

Typist $11,596

Umpire $5,940

Urban Planner $16,000

Veterinarian $20,000

Vice-President (Data Processing) $50,469

Waiter/Waitress $8,216

Weaver (Hand Loom) $8,532

Welder (Arc) $17,940

Word Processing Operator $13,156

Writer (Editorial) $23,760

Writer (Screen) $32,940

Writer (Technical Publications) $9,720

Zoologist $16,416

After classifying the salary information in a variety of ways, examine your classifications and see what conclusions you can come to. Questions such as the following might lead to some conclusions about the information.

1. How do the salaries from the various occupations compare with one another?

   *Conclusion:* _____

   _____

2. In what ways do the salaries reflect the level of education? The amount of experience?

   *Conclusion:* _____

   _____

3. What factors determine the amount of a salary?

   *Conclusion:* _____

   _____

4. _____

   *Conclusion:* _____

   _____

5. _____

   *Conclusion:* _____

   _____

6. _____

   *Conclusion:* _____

   _____

Now let us develop our ideas about salaries further. To do so, we will use the mapping strategy that we examined in Chapter Eight. At that time we identified the following mapping guidelines:

1. Begin with what you consider to be the most important idea as the "center" of the map and then branch out from it to related ideas.
2. Your ideas should be written on lines that are connected to other lines, in order to express clearly the relationships between the various ideas.
3. Print the ideas in capital letters so that they can be easily read and referred to.

In constructing your map, you might want to begin with the questions and conclusions that you just described. For example, the beginning of a map might look something like the one below:

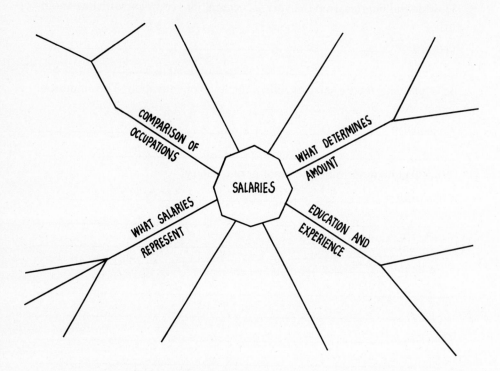

After working on your map for a while, you may find that you have exhausted your ideas. When this happens, use the following questions to help stimulate additional ideas and connections[1]:

*Can you give examples of the subject?*
e.g., What are the salaries of people that you know?

*How do you respond to it or feel about it?*
e.g., What is your reaction to a counter attendant earning $4,816? an obstetrician earning $100,000?

---

[1]I have adapted this list of questions from Jack Blum, Carolyn Brinkman, Elizabeth Hoffman, and David Peck, *A Guide to the Whole Writing Process* (Boston: Houghton Mifflin Co., 1984).

*Why is it valuable or important?*
e.g., Why do people focus so much attention on salaries? What do salaries symbolize in our society?

*What are the causes or reasons for this attention?*
e.g., What factors determine the amount of salaries?

*What results from it?*
e.g., What results occur based on the amount people earn?

*How does it compare to other things?*
e.g., How do different professions compare in terms of salary?

*What is my interpretation?*
e.g., Am I for or against the way salaries are established? Why?

*Have there been changes in the subject?*
e.g., What changes have occurred in salary levels over time?

*What ought to be done?*
e.g., What factors should determine what salary someone earns?

As you think through these questions, return to your map to generate new ideas and form different relationships. For example, further development of the map may look like the one on page 342.

## Defining a main idea

The next step in composing is to define a *working* main idea suggested by the information and ideas you have been considering. Once selected, your main idea—known as a *thesis*—will act to focus your thinking on a central theme. It will also guide your future explorations and suggest new ideas and other relationships. Of course, a variety of main ideas can usually develop out of any particular situation. And, your initial working idea will probably need redefining as you explore your material further. Here are some potential main ideas based on the map pictured on page 342.

1.  The amount of money a person earns is an important factor in determining a person's social status.
2.  Both high-paying and low-paying jobs have psychological hazards. However, the types of hazards are different.

Using your map as a reference, identify some of the main ideas you could use to focus your thinking on the topic of salaries.

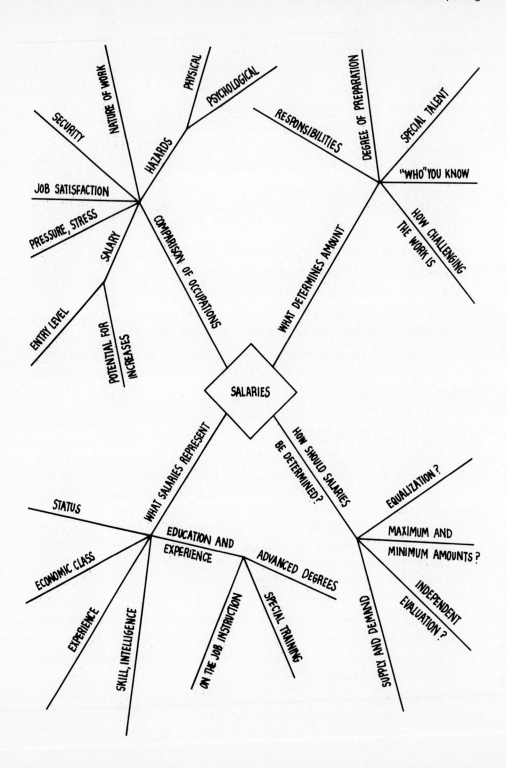

3. _____
_____

4. _____
_____

5. _____
_____

Once you have generated a number of main ideas, select the one that interests you most. In our example, the main idea selected was the following:

*Main Idea:*   Both high-paying and low-paying jobs have psychological hazards. However, the types of hazards are different.

Think carefully about the main ideas you have identified and select the one that you would like to pursue further:

*Main Idea:* _____

_____

After you decide on a main idea, the next step is to return to the map you created on page 341 and identify all the ideas and relationships connected to this central theme. In our example, the map on page 342 was used to identify the following ideas and relationships:

1. The amount of salary is related to the amount of responsibility a person has.
2. Occupations differ in terms of the type and amount of stress.
3. The amount of salary is related to how challenging the work is.

Exploring a topic is a process of moving back and forth between the various composing activities. This type of interactive exploration stimulates the most comprehensive and deepest thinking about the subject. To this end, create a map that uses the main idea you identified above as the starting point and the related ideas you just identified as the initial branches. This map should enable you to further develop and refine your thinking about your particular thesis. In terms of our example, the diagram on page 344 illustrates a further mapping activity based on ideas previously identified.

The map you have just created represents your initial thinking about a central idea related to the subject of salaries. Now we need to turn our attention to how we can shape and organize the results of these explorations. This shaping and organizing will enable us to refine our thinking further and aid us in presenting our ideas to others in written or spoken form.

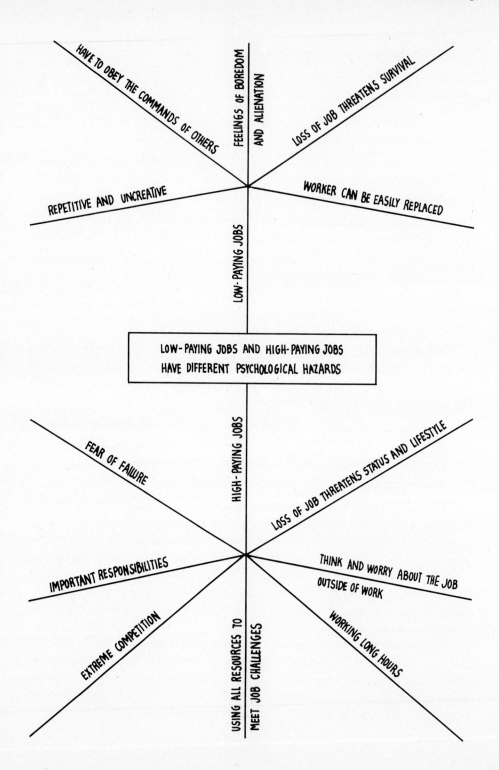

LOW-PAYING JOBS

HAVE TO OBEY THE COMMANDS OF OTHERS

FEELINGS OF BOREDOM AND ALIENATION

LOSS OF JOB THREATENS SURVIVAL

REPETITIVE AND UNCREATIVE

WORKER CAN BE EASILY REPLACED

LOW-PAYING JOBS AND HIGH-PAYING JOBS HAVE DIFFERENT PSYCHOLOGICAL HAZARDS

HIGH-PAYING JOBS

FEAR OF FAILURE

LOSS OF JOB THREATENS STATUS AND LIFESTYLE

IMPORTANT RESPONSIBILITIES

THINK AND WORRY ABOUT THE JOB OUTSIDE OF WORK

EXTREME COMPETITION

USING ALL RESOURCES TO MEET JOB CHALLENGES

WORKING LONG HOURS

# Relating and organizing

Ideas, things, and events in the world can be related and organized in a variety of ways. All of these different ways of relating and organizing reflect basic thinking patterns that we rely on constantly when we think and when we use language to write, speak, and read. For example, the ideas and information regarding salaries and work that we have been considering can be related and organized in many different patterns. This fact becomes obvious if you compare the map that you have just developed with those of other class members. These basic thought patterns are an essential part of the way that we continually compose and make sense of our world. They include the following ways of relating:

*Chronological relationships*    relating things in a time sequence

*Part/whole relationships*       relating the individual parts of something to each other and to the whole

*Process relationships*          relating aspects of the growth, development, or change of something

*Interactive relationships*      relating things in terms of the back and forth influences between them

*Comparative relationships*      relating things in the same general category in terms of their similarities and dissimilarities

*Analogical relationships*       relating things belonging to different categories in order to illuminate our understanding of the things being related

*Cause/Effect relationships*     relating events in terms of the way some event(s) are responsible for bringing about other event(s)

All of these basic thinking patterns (and others besides) play an active role in the way we perceive, shape, and organize—in other words, compose—our world in order to make it understandable to us. The particular patterns that we use to organize our ideas in writing depend on (1) the subject we are exploring; (2) the type of writing we are doing; (3) the main ideas we want to emphasize; (4) the audience who will be reading our work; and (5) the ultimate purpose we are aiming for. In most cases, our writing will use a variety of basic thinking patterns in order to organize and relate the ideas being considered.

In this chapter we will be examining the thinking patterns expressed in the following relationships:

Comparative relationships
Analogical relationships
Cause and effect relationships

As we examine these thinking patterns, we will also be seeing how they help us relate and organize the ideas about salaries and work that we have been developing.

### Comparative relationships

We have seen how we describe, classify, conceptualize, and define through a process of organized *comparing* (looking for similarities) and *contrasting* (looking for differences). Comparing and contrasting is integral to the thinking process, and we are constantly engaging in this activity as we attempt to organize and make sense of the world.

---

➤•◄      Think of a time during the last month when you went shopping for a particular item, which you ended up buying. It might have been an article of clothing, a good book or new record, a radio, etc. List the thing that you have selected, noting as much specific information about it as you can remember—brand, color, size, cost, and so on.

*Item Purchased:*   Levi's jeans, size 31 × 31, blue, straight cut, $18.00

*Item Purchased:* _____

_____

When you went shopping, you probably spent a fair amount of time examining other items of the same type, things that you looked at but *did not buy.* List one of these competing items below:

*Item Not Purchased:* _____

As you made your decision to purchase the item you did, you probably compared and contrasted the various brands before making your selection. In the space below, list some of the factors you took into consideration in comparing the different items. For example:

| *Item Purchased* | *Comparative Factors* | *Item Not Purchased* |
|---|---|---|
| Levi's jeans | brand | Bon Jour jeans |
| blue | color | blue |
| $18.00 | price | $28.00 |

| Item Purchased | Comparative Factors | Item Not Purchased |
|---|---|---|
| straight cut | style | designer cut |
| regular denim | material | stretch denim |
| 31" × 31" | size | 31" × 31" |

| Item purchased | Comparative Factors | Item Not Purchased |
|---|---|---|
| _____ | _____ | _____ |
| _____ | _____ | _____ |
| _____ | _____ | _____ |
| _____ | _____ | _____ |
| _____ | _____ | _____ |
| _____ | _____ | _____ |

We compare and contrast in this way all the time, usually without even realizing it. Whenever we select an item on a menu, a purchase from the grocery store, or a seat in a theater or on a bus, we are automatically looking for similarities and differences among the various items from which we are selecting, and these similarities and differences will guide us in making our decision.

Of course, we do not always engage in a systematic process of comparison and contrast. In many cases, the selections and decisions we make seem to be unconscious. This may be so because we have already performed an organized comparison and contrast some time in the past and already know what we want and why we want it (e.g., "I always choose an aisle seat so I don't have to climb over people").

However, we sometimes make decisions impulsively, without any thought or comparative examination. Maybe someone told us to, maybe we were influenced by the commercial we saw, or maybe we simply said, "What the heck, let's take a chance." Sometimes these impulsive decisions work out for us, but often they do not because they are simply a result of rolling the dice. On the other hand, when we engage in a critical and comparative examination, we gain information that can help us make intelligent decisions.

**_Standards for comparison_**  Naturally, not all the factors we use in comparing and contrasting are equally important in our decision making. In any comparison, some similarities and differences outweigh others. How do we determine which factors are more important than others, and which information is more relevant than other information? Unfortunately, there is no simple formula or pat answer to these questions.

➤•◄       Review the lists you completed on page 347 and place a check next to those factors that played an important part in your decision.

The factors you just selected represent the comparative information you found to be most important and relevant and probably reflect your needs and purposes. If you are on a limited budget, price differences may play a key role in your decision. If money is no object, your decision may have been based solely on the quality of the item or on some other consideration.

➤•◄       List the factors you checked and then explain why each was important or relevant to your comparative analysis and subsequent decision.

1. _____

2. _____

3. _____

Even though there is no hard and fast way to determine which areas of comparison are most important, it does help us to become *aware* of the factors that are influencing our perceptions and decisions. These areas of comparison represent the standards we use to come to conclusions, and a critical and reflective examination of them can help us sharpen, clarify, and improve them.

➤•◄       For each of the subjects listed below, describe the areas of comparison that you think are most important in making informed and intelligent choices.

1. Selecting the most competent doctor to perform an operation on you.

a. _____

b. _____

c. _____

2. Selecting the best philosophy teacher to study with.

a. _____

b. _____

c. _____

3. Selecting the most reliable friend to ask an important favor of.

a. _____

b. _____

c. _____

4. Selecting a major course of study at college.

a. _____

b. _____

c. _____

5. Deciding in what geographical area to live.

a. _____

b. _____

c. _____

When making comparisons, there are pitfalls we should try to avoid:

1. *Incomplete comparisons.* This difficulty arises when we focus on too few points of comparison. For example, in looking for a competent surgeon to cut us open and sew us up, we might decide to focus only on the prices that each doctor charges. However, even though this may be an important area for comparative analysis, we would be foolish to overlook other areas of comparison, such as medical training, experience, recommendations, and success rates.

2. *Selective comparisons.* This problem occurs when we take a one-sided view of a comparative situation—when we concentrate on the points favoring one side of the things being compared but overlook the points favoring the other side. For example, in selecting a dependable friend to perform a favor for you, you may focus on "Bob," because he is your best friend and one you have known the longest but overlook the fact that, the last few times you asked him to do something for you, he let you down.

---

Review the responses you gave in the comparison exercise on page 348. Do the areas of comparison you selected reflect either incomplete or selective comparisons? If so, see if you can find additional areas of comparison to balance the two sides better. ►•◄

Comparative relationships are a useful way for us to relate and explore ideas we are trying to understand. In the following essay by Margaret Mead, entitled "From Popping the Question to Popping the Pill," notice how the author has used comparisons and contrasts to organize her thinking and writing. After you have read the essay, answer the questions which follow it.

# From Popping the Question to Popping the Pill
*by Margaret Mead*

There have been major changes in attitudes toward courtship and marriage among those middle-class, educated Americans who are celebrated in the media and who are style setters for American life. Courtship was once a regular part of American life; it was a long period, sometimes lasting for many years, and also a tentative one, during which a future husband or wife could still turn back but during which their relationship became more and more exclusive and socially recognized. Courtship both preceded the announcement of an engagement and followed the announcement, although a broken engagement was so serious that it could be expected to throw the girl into a depression from which she might never recover.

There were definite rules governing the courtship period, from the "bundling" permitted in early New England days, when young couples slept side by side with all their clothes on, to strict etiquette that prescribed what sort of gifts a man might give his fiancée in circles where expensive presents were customary. Gifts had to be either immediately consumable, like candy or flowers, or indestructible, like diamonds—which could be given back, their value unimpaired, if there was a rift in the relationship. Objects that could be damaged by use, like gloves and furs, were forbidden. A gentleman might call for a lady in a cab or in his own equipage, but it was regarded as inappropriate for him to pay for her train fare if they went on a journey.

How much chaperoning was necessary, and how much privacy the courting couple was allowed, was a matter of varying local custom. Long walks home through country lanes after church and sitting up in the parlor after their elders had retired for the night may have been permitted, but the bride was expected to be a virgin at marriage. The procedure for breaking off an engagement, which included the return of letters and photographs, was a symbolic way of stating that an unconsummated relationship could still be erased from social memory.

The wedding day was the highest point in a girl's life—a day to which she looked forward all her unmarried days and to which she looked back for the rest of her life. The splendor of her wedding, the elegance of dress and veil, the cutting of the cake, the departure amid a shower of rice and confetti, gave her an accolade of which no subsequent event could completely rob her. Today people over 50 years of age still treat their daughter's wedding this way, prominently displaying the photographs of the occasion. Until very recently, all brides' books prescribed exactly the same ritual they had prescribed 50 years before. The etiquette governing wedding presents—gifts that were or were not appropriate, the bride's maiden initials on her linen—was also specified. For the bridegroom the wedding represented the end of his free, bachelor days, and the bachelor dinner the night before the wedding symbolized this loss of freedom. A woman who did not marry—even if she had the alibi of a fiancé who had been killed in war or had abilities and charm and money of her own—was always at a social disadvantage, while an eligible bachelor was sought after by hostess after hostess.

Courtship ended at the altar, as the bride waited anxiously for the bridegroom who might not appear or might have forgotten the ring. Suppliant gallantry was replaced overnight by a reversal of roles, the wife now becoming the one who read her husband's every frown with anxiety lest she displease him.

This set of rituals established a rhythm between the future husband and wife and between the two sets of parents who would later become co-grandparents. It was an opportunity for mistakes to be corrected; and if the parents could not be won over, there was, as a last resort, elopement, in which the young couple proclaimed their desperate attraction to each other by flouting parental blessing. Each part of the system could be tested out for a marriage that was expected to last for life. We have very different ways today.

Since World War I, changes in relationships between the sexes have been occurring with bewildering speed. The automobile presented a challenge to chaperonage that American adults met by default. From then on, except in ceremonial and symbolic ways, chaperonage disappeared, and a style of premarital relationship was set up in which the onus was put on the girl to refuse inappropriate requests, while each young man declared his suitability by asking for favors that he did not expect to receive. The disappearance of chaperonage was facilitated by the greater freedom of middle-aged women, who began to envy their daughters' freedom, which they had never had. Social forms went through a whole series of rapid changes: The dance with formal partners and programs gave way to occasions in which mothers, or daughters, invited many more young men than girls, and the popular girl hardly circled the dance floor twice in the same man's arms. Dating replaced courtship—not as a prelude to anything but rather as a way of demonstrating popularity. Long engagements became increasingly unfashionable, and a series of more tentative commitments became more popular. As college education became the norm for millions of young people, "pinning" became a common stage before engagement. The ring was likely to appear just before the wedding day. And during the 1950's more and more brides got married while pregnant—but they still wore the long white veil, which was a symbol of virginity.

In this conservative, security-minded decade love became less important than marriage, and lovers almost disappeared from parks and riverbanks as young people threatened each other: "Either you marry me now, or I'll marry someone else." Courtship and dating were embraced by young people in lower grades in school, until children totally unready for sex were enmeshed by the rituals of pairing off. Marriage became a necessity for everyone, for boys as well as for girls: Mothers worried if their sons preferred electronic equipment or chess to girls and pushed their daughters relentlessly into marriage. Divorce became more and more prevalent, and people who felt their marriages were failing began to worry about whether they ought to get a divorce, divorce becoming a duty to an unfulfilled husband or to children exposed to an unhappy marriage. Remarriage was expected, until finally, with men dying earlier than women, there were no men left to marry. The United States became the most married country in the world. Children, your own or adopted, were just as essential, and the suburban life-style—each nuclear family isolated in its own home, with several children, a station wagon and a country-club membership—became the admired life-style, displayed in magazines for the whole world to see.

By the early sixties there were signs of change. We discovered we were running out of educated labor, and under the heading of self-fulfillment educated married women were being tempted back into the labor market. Young people began to advocate frankness and honesty, rebelling against the extreme hypocrisy of the 1950s, when religious and educational institutions alike connived to produce pregnancies that would lead to marriage. Love as an absorbing feeling for another person was rediscovered, as marriage as a goal for every girl and boy receded into the background.

A series of worldwide political and ecological events facilitated these changes. Freedom for women accompanied agitation for freedom for blacks, for other minorities, for the Third World, for youth, for gay people. Zero-population growth became a goal, and it was no longer unfashionable to admit one did not plan to have children, or perhaps even to marry. The marriage age rose a little, the number of children fell a little. The enjoyment of pornography and use of obscenity became the self-imposed obligation of the emancipated women. Affirmative action catapulted many unprepared women into executive positions. Men, weary of the large families of the '50s, began to desert them; young mothers, frightened by the prospect of being deserted, pulled up stakes and left their suburban split-levels to try to make it in the cities. "Arrangements," or public cohabitation of young people with approval and support from their families, college deans and employers, became common.

By the early 1970s the doomsters were proclaiming that the family was dead. There were over 8,000,000 single-parent households, most of them headed by poorly paid women. There were endless discussions of "open marriages," "group marriages," communes in which the children were children of the group, and open discussion of previously taboo subjects, including an emphasis on female sexuality. Yet most Americans continued to live as they always had, with girls still hoping for a permanent marriage and viewing "arrangements" as stepping-stones to marriage. The much-publicized behavior of small but conspicuous groups filtered through the layers of society, so that the freedoms claimed by college youth were being claimed five years later by blue-collar youth; "swinging" (mate swapping) as a pastime of a bored upper-middle-class filtered down.

Perhaps the most striking change of all is that courtship is no longer a prelude to consummation. In many levels of contemporary society, sex relations require no prelude at all; the courtship that exists today tends to occur between a casual sex encounter and a later attempt by either the man or the woman to turn it into a permanent relationship. Courtship is also seen as an act in which either sex can take the lead. Women are felt to have an alternative to marriage, as once they had in the Middle Ages, when convent life was the choice of a large part of the population. Weddings are less conventional, although new conventions, like reading from Kahlil Gibran's *The Prophet,* spread very quickly. There is also a growing rebellion against the kind of town planning and housing that isolate young couples from the help of older people and friends that they need.

But the family is not dead. It is going through stormy times, and millions of children are paying the penalty of current disorganization, experimentation and discontent. In the process, the adults who should never marry are sorting themselves out. Marriage and parenthood are being viewed as a vocation rather than as the duty of every human being. As we seek more human forms of existence, the next question may well be how to protect our young people from a premature, pervasive insistence upon precocious sexuality, sexuality that contains neither love nor delight.

The birthrate is going up a little; women are having just as many babies as before, but having them later. The rights of fathers are being discovered and placed beside the rights of mothers. Exploitive and commercialized abortion mills are being questioned, and the Pill is proving less a panacea than was hoped. In a world troubled by economic and political instability, unemployment, highjacking, kidnapping, and bombs, the preoccupation with private decisions is shifting to concern about the whole of humankind.

Active concern for the world permits either celibacy *or* marriage, but continuous preoccupation with sex leaves no time for anything else. As we used to say in the '20s, promiscuity, like free verse, is lacking in structure.

1.  Identify the two key ideas being compared that Margaret Mead uses to develop her thinking about the subject of courtship.

    A. _____

    B. _____

2. Analyze the points of similarity and dissimilarity between the ideas being
   compared.

| virginity | A. bride expected to be a virgin | B. bride not usually expected to be a virgin |
|---|---|---|
| _____ | _____ | _____ |
| _____ | _____ | _____ |
| _____ | _____ | _____ |
| _____ | _____ | _____ |

➤•◄    Return to the ideas about salaries that you generated and mapped on pages
340–344. Select two key ideas that you think might be compared and contrasted
in order to further your understanding of the topic. After identifying those key
ideas, analyze the relationships between them by setting up and completing a
comparative list.

Return to the ideas about salaries that you generated and mapped on pages

The following comparative list evolved from the map on page 344.

| Low-Paying Occupations | High-Paying Occupations |
|---|---|
| 1. work is often repetitive | work is rarely repetitive--usually demands a high level of functioning |
| 2. major hazards are feeling bored and alienated | major hazards are stress and pressure |
| 3. workers have specific duties and have to obey the directives of others | workers have more responsibilities, authority, autonomy |
| 4. the work does not usually involve competition with others | work usually involves intense competition with others |
| 5. fear of losing job is a major concern | fear of failure is a major concern |
| 6. workers usually have fixed hours | workers often work long hours and take work home |
| 7. loss of job threatens survival | loss of job threatens status and life-style |

### Analogical relationships

Comparisons come in many forms. So far, we have been focusing on the
comparisons we make between things that are basically *similar*. In each of the
cases we examined, the things being compared were either drawn from the

same general category (e.g., doctors, philosophy classes, or friends) or related to the same general area of experience (e.g., deciding where to live).

As we noted, we are making comparisons between similar things all the time, whether they are items on a menu or methods of birth control. However, there is another kind of comparison that does *not* focus on basically similar things. Such comparisons are known as *analogies,* and their goal is to illuminate a concept from one category by comparing it with another concept from a different category. Consider the following example:

> Life's but a walking shadow, a poor player
> That struts and frets his hour upon the stage
> and then is heard no more.
>
> —William Shakespeare

In this famous quotation, Shakespeare is comparing two things which at first glance don't seem to have anything in common at all: life and an actor. Yet as we look closer at the comparison, we begin to see that even though these two things are unlike in many ways, there are also some very important similarities between them. What are some of these similarities?

1. _____

2. _____

3. _____

As we can see from this example, the purpose of an analogy is not the same as the purpose of the comparisons we considered in the last section. At that time, we noted that the goal of comparing similar things is usually to make a choice and that the process of comparing can provide us with information on which we can base an intelligent decision. In the case of analogies, however, the main goal is not to choose or decide; it is to illuminate our understanding. Identifying similarities between very different things can often stimulate us to see these things in a new light, from a different perspective than we are used to. This can result in a clearer and more complete understanding of the things being compared.

**Analogy** • A comparison between things that are basically dissimilar made for the purpose of illuminating our understanding of the things being compared.

We ourselves often create and use analogies to get a point across to someone else. Used appropriately, analogies can help us illustrate and explain what we are trying to communicate. This is particularly important when we have difficulty in finding the right words to represent our experiences. Powerful or complex emotions can make us speechless, or make us say things like "words cannot describe what I feel." Imagine that you are trying to describe your feelings of love and caring for another person. In order to illustrate and clarify the feelings that you are trying to communicate, you might compare your feelings of love to "the first rose of spring," noting the following similarities:

> Like the rose, this is the first great love of your life.
>
> Like the fragile yet supple petals of the rose, your feelings are tender and sensitive.
>
> Like the beauty of the rose, the beauty of your love should grow with each passing day.

Can you think of other comparisons of love to a rose?

> Like the color of the rose, _____.
>
> Like the fragrance of the rose, _____.
>
> Like the thorns of the rose, _____.

➤•◀    Name another thing that you could compare your love to in order to help explain it to someone else and note the points of similarity between the two.

My love is like a _____.

1. _____

2. _____

3. _____

➤•◀    Another favorite subject for analogies is the idea of the meaning or purpose of life, which the simple use of the word *life* does not communicate. We have just seen Shakespeare's comparison of life to an actor. Here are some other popular analogies involving life. What are some points of similarity in each of those comparisons?

1. Life is just a bowl of cherries.

   a. _____

   b. _____

2. Life is a football game.

   a. _____

   b. _____

3. Life is a tale told by an idiot, full of sound and fury, signifying nothing.

   a. _____

   b. _____

Now create analogies for life that represent some of your feelings.

1. Life is _____.

2. Life is _____.

3. Life is _____.

Create your own analogies for the following emotionally charged symbols: ➤•◀

1. Friendship is _____.

2. Fear is _____.

3. God is _____.

4. Evil is _____.

5. Beauty is _____.

In addition to communicating experiences that resist simple characterization, analogies are also useful when we are trying to explain something that is very complicated. For instance, we might compare the eye to a camera lens or the immunological system of the body to the National Guard (corpuscles are called to active duty when undesirable elements threaten the well-being of the organism and rush to the scene of danger).

Analogies possess the power to bring things to life by invoking images that illuminate the points of comparison. Consider the following analogies and explain the points of comparison that the author is trying to make.

1. "Laws are like cobwebs, which may catch small flies, but let wasps and hornets break through."—Jonathan Swift

   _____

   _____

2. "I am as pure as the driven slush."—Tallulah Bankhead

_____

_____

3. "He has all the qualities of a dog, except its devotion."—Gore Vidal

_____

_____

_____

➤•◄        Create analogies to help illuminate two subjects of your own selection, and
list the points of similarity between the things being compared.

1. _____ is like _____.

   a.  _____

   b.  _____

   c.  _____

2. _____ is like _____.

   a.  _____

   b.  _____

   c.  _____

***Implicit and explicit analogies***   From the examples discussed so far,
we can see that analogies have two parts: an *original subject* and a *compared subject* (what the original is being likened to). In comparing your love to the first
rose of spring, the *original subject* is your feelings of love and caring for someone
whereas the *compared subject* is what you are comparing those feelings to in
order to illuminate and express them—namely, the first rose of spring.

In creating analogies, the connection between the original subject and the
compared subject can be either obvious (explicit) or implied (implicit). For example, we can echo the lament of the great pool hustler, "Minnesota Fats," and
say:

A pool player in a tuxedo *is like* a hotdog with whipped cream on it.

This is an obvious analogy (known as a *simile*) because we have explicitly noted
the connection between the original subject (man in tuxedo) and the compared
subject (hotdog with whipped cream) by using the comparative terms "is like."

We could also have used other forms of explicit comparison, such as "is similar to," "reminds me of," or "makes me think of."

On the other hand, we could say:

A pool player in a tuxedo *is* a hotdog with whipped cream on it.

In this case, we are making an implied comparison (known as a *metaphor*), because we have not included any words that point out that we are making a comparison. Instead, we are stating that the original subject *is* the compared subject. Naturally, we are assuming that most people will understand that we are making a comparison between two different things and not describing a biological transformation.

---

Create *similes* (explicit analogies) for two subjects of your own choosing,  ➤•◄
noting the points of comparison.

1. _____

   a. _____

   b. _____

2. _____

   a. _____

   b. _____

---

Create *metaphors* (implicit analogies) for two subjects of your own choos-  ➤•◄
ing, noting the points of comparison.

1. _____

   a. _____

   b. _____

2. _____

   a. _____

   b. _____

***Extended analogies*** The analogies considered so far have been of a fairly simple sort, designed for limited purposes and displaying relatively few points of resemblance. However, we also use analogies for more ambitious purposes, such as extended discussions of a subject. In these cases, an analogy can provide the framework for the discussion as we try to explain an idea by comparing it in some detail to something else.

Consider the following essay by Dr. Lewis Thomas, a noted physician and science writer, in which he uses an extended analogy to illuminate human social behavior.

## On Societies as Organisms
*by Lewis Thomas*

Viewed from a suitable height, the aggregating clusters of medical scientists in the bright sunlight of the boardwalk at Atlantic City, swarmed there from everywhere for the annual meetings, have the look of assemblages of social insects. There is the same vibrating, ionic movement, interrupted by the darting back and forth of jerky individuals to touch antennae and exchange small bits of information; periodically, the mass casts out, like a trout-line, a long single file unerringly toward Childs's.[1] If the boards were not fastened down, it would not be a surprise to see them put together a nest of sorts.

It is permissible to say this sort of thing about humans. They do resemble, in their most compulsively social behavior, ants at a distance. It is, however, quite bad form in biological circles to put it the other way round, to imply that the operation of insect societies has any relation at all to human affairs. The writers of books on insect behavior generally take pains, in their prefaces, to caution that insects are like creatures from another planet, that their behavior is absolutely foreign, totally unhuman, unearthly, almost unbiological. They are more like perfectly tooled but crazy little machines, and we violate science when we try to read human meanings in their arrangements.

It is hard for a bystander not to do so. Ants are so much like human beings as to be an embarrassment. They farm fungi, raise aphids as livestock, launch armies into wars, use chemical sprays to alarm and confuse enemies, capture slaves. The families of weaver ants engage in child labor, holding their larvae like shuttles to spin out the thread that sews the leaves together for their fungus gardens. They exchange information ceaselessly. They do everything but watch television.

What makes us most uncomfortable is that they, and the bees and termites and social wasps, seem to live two kinds of lives: they are individuals, going about the day's business without much evidence of thought for tomorrow, and they are at the same time component parts, cellular elements, in the huge,

---

[1]A local restaurant.

writhing, ruminating organism of the Hill, the nest, the hive. It is because of this aspect, I think, that we most wish for them to be something foreign. We do not like the notion that there can be collective societies with the capacity to behave like organisms. If such things exist, they can have nothing to do with us.

Still, there it is. A solitary ant, afield, cannot be considered to have much of anything on his mind; indeed, with only a few neurons strung together by fibers, he can't be imagined to have a mind at all, much less a thought. He is more like a ganglion on legs. Four ants together, or ten, encircling a dead moth on a path, begin to look more like an idea. They fumble and shove, gradually moving the food toward the Hill, but as though by blind chance. It is only when you watch the dense mass of thousands of ants, crowded together around the Hill, blackening the ground, that you begin to see the whole beast, and now you observe it thinking, planning, calculating. It is an intelligence, a kind of live computer, with crawling bits for its wits.

At a stage in the construction, twigs of a certain size are needed, and all the members forage obsessively for twigs of just this size. Later, when outer walls are to be finished, thatched, the size must change, and as though given new orders by telephone, all the workers shift the search to the new twigs. If you disturb the arrangement of a part of the Hill, hundreds of ants will set it vibrating, shifting, until it is put right again. Distant sources of food are somehow sensed, and long lines, like tentacles, reach out over the ground, up over walls, behind boulders, to fetch it in.

Termites are even more extraordinary in the way they seem to accumulate intelligence as they gather together. Two or three termites in a chamber will begin to pick up pellets and move them from place to place, but nothing comes of it; nothing is built. As more join in, they seem to reach a critical mass, a quorum, and the thinking begins. They place pellets atop pellets, then throw up columns and beautiful, curving, symmetrical arches, and the crystalline architecture of vaulted chambers is created. It is not known how they communicate with each other, how the chains of termites building one column know when to turn toward the crew on the adjacent column, or how, when the time comes, they manage the flawless joining of the arches. The stimuli that set them off at the outset, building collectively instead of shifting things about, may be pheromones[2] released when they reach committee size. They react as if alarmed. They become agitated, excited, and then they begin working, like artists.

Bees live lives of organisms, tissues, cells, organelles, all at the same time. The single bee, out of the hive retrieving sugar (instructed by the dancer:

[2]Hormones secreted by insects when communicating with other insects.

''south-southeast for seven hundred meters, clover—mind you make corrections for the sundrift'') is still as much a part of the hive as if attached by a filament. Building the hive, the workers have the look of embryonic cells organizing a developing tissue; from a distance they are like the viruses inside a cell, running off row after row of symmetrical polygons as though laying down crystals. When the time for swarming comes, and the old queen prepares to leave with her part of the population, it is as though the hive were involved in mitosis. There is an agitated moving of bees back and forth, like granules in cell sap. They distribute themselves in almost precisely equal parts, half to the departing queen, half to the new one. Thus, like an egg, the great, hairy, black and golden creature splits in two, each with an equal share of the family genome.

The phenomenon of separate animals joining up to form an organism is not unique in insects. Slime-mold cells do it all the time, of course, in each life cycle. At first they are single amebocytes swimming around, eating bacteria, aloof from each other, untouching, voting straight Republican. Then, a bell sounds, and acrasin[3] is released by special cells toward which the others converge in stellate ranks, touch, fuse together, and construct the slug, solid as a trout. A splendid stalk is raised, with a fruiting body on top, and out of this comes the next generation of amebocytes, ready to swim across the same moist ground, solitary and ambitious.

Herring and other fish in schools are at times so closely integrated, their actions so coordinated, that they seem to be functionally a great multi-fish organism. Flocking birds, especially the seabirds nesting on the slopes of offshore islands in Newfoundland, are similarly attached, connected, synchronized.

Although we are by all odds the most social of all social animals—more interdependent, more attached to each other, more inseparable in our behavior than bees—we do not often feel our conjoined intelligence. Perhaps, however, we are linked in circuits for the storage, processing, and retrieval of information, since this appears to be the most basic and universal of all human enterprises. It may be our biological function to build a certain kind of Hill. We have access to all the information of the biosphere, arriving as elementary units in the stream of solar photons. When we have learned how these are rearranged against randomness, to make, say, springtails, quantum mechanics, and the late quartets, we may have a clearer notion how to proceed. The circuitry seems to be there, even if the current is not always on.

The system of communications used in science should provide a neat, workable model for studying mechanisms of information-building in human

---

[3]Chemical attractant named after the class (Acrasiae) to which these special slime molds belong.

society. Ziman, in a recent *Nature* essay, points out, "the invention of a mechanism for the systematic publication of *fragments* of scientific work may well have been the key event in the history of modern science." He continues:

> A regular journal carries from one research worker to another the various . . . observations which are of common interest. . . . A typical scientific paper has never pretended to be more than another little piece in a larger jigsaw—not significant in itself but as an element in a grander scheme. *This technique, of soliciting many modest contributions to the store of human knowledge, has been the secret of Western science since the seventeenth century, for it achieves a corporate, collective power that is far greater than any one individual can exert* [italics mine].

With some alternation of terms, some toning down, the passage could describe the building of a termite nest.

It is fascinating that the word "explore" does not apply to the searching aspect of the activity, but has its origins in the sounds we make while engaged in it. We like to think of exploring in science as a lonely, meditative business, and so it is in the first stages, but always, sooner or later, before the enterprise reaches completion, as we explore, we call to each other, communicate, publish, send letters to the editor, present papers, cry out on finding.

1.  Describe the two members of the analogy that Thomas uses to organize his thinking in this essay.

    *Original subject:* _____

    *Compared subject:* _____

2.  Identify the points of similarity (and *dis*-similarity which Thomas discovers between the original subject and the compared subject.

    *Points of similarity*

    a.  _____

    b.  _____

    c.  _____

    d.  _____

    *Points of dissimilarity*

    a.  _____

    b.  _____

3.  Describe what you believe is the main point that Thomas is illustrating by means of this extended analogy.

_____

_____

_____

►•◄     Return to the ideas about salaries, which you generated and mapped on
page 343. Create an analogy that might help illuminate your ideas and organize
your thinking. Then analyze your analogy by identifying the points of similarity
and dissimilarity between your original subject and your compared subject.
The following analogy relates to the map on page 344.

Various occupations can have psychological hazards associated
with them in the same way that other occupations can have physical hazards. Coal miners are susceptible to Black Lung disease;
dentists are vulnerable to lower back pain; dancers are prone to
foot and ankle problems; singers often have throat and voice
difficulties. In the same way, people in certain professions are
susceptible to various psychological hazards. For instance,
assembly-line workers may become bored and depressed because
their work has little meaning for them; policemen have an unusually high divorce rate and a suicide rate that is exceeded only
by doctors, who also have a high drug addiction and alcoholism
rate; people in high-pressure business positions often develop
migraine headaches, ulcers, high blood pressure, and heart disease.

Original Subject: the relation between occupations and psychological
                  hazards

Compared Subject: the relation between occupations and physical
                  hazards

Similarities:

1.  Certain professions seem to be associated with certain hazards--physi-
    cal and/or psychological.

2.  The particular hazard--whether physical or psychological--seems to be
    the result of certain characteristic qualities of the occupation.

Dissimilarities:

1.  Physical ailments are usually more easily observed and verified than
    psychological ailments.

2.  The relationship between certain occupations and corresponding physi-
    cal hazards is more easily verified than that between occupations and
    psychological hazards.

### Causal relationships

As we have seen in this chapter, the activity of thinking is the activity of forming and interpreting relationships—figuring out exactly how all the things in our experience relate to each other. This thinking activity is what enables us to compose meaningful maps of our world, giving us the means to make sense of things and arrive at intelligent decisions.

Another of the fundamental relationships we use to organize and make sense of our world is the relationship of *cause and effect*. If you were right now to pinch yourself hard enough to feel it, you would be demonstrating a cause and effect relationship. Stated very simply, a *cause* is anything that is responsible for bringing about something else—usually termed the *effect*. The *cause* (the pinch) brings about the *effect* (the feeling of pain). When we make a causal statement, we are merely stating that a causal relationship exists between two or more things:

The pinch *caused* the pain in my arm.

Of course, when we make (or think) causal statements, we do not always use the word *cause*. For example, the following statements are all causal statements. In each case, identify the cause and the effect.

1. Since I was the last person to leave, I turned off the lights.

    *Cause:* _____

    *Effect:* _____

2. The guard at the door prevented me from re-entering the theater, even though I had my ticket stub.

    *Cause:* _____

    *Effect:* _____

3. Taking lots of vitamin C really cured me of that terrible cold I had.

    *Cause:* _____

    *Effect:* _____

4. I accidently toasted my hand along with the marshmallows, by getting too close to the fire.

    *Cause:* _____

    *Effect:* _____

In these statements, the words *turned off, prevented, cured,* and *toasted* all point to the fact that something has caused something else to take place. Our language contains thousands of these causal "cousins."

➤•◄     Create three sentences that express a causal relationship without actually using the word *cause*.

1. _____

   _____

   _____

   *Cause:* _____

   *Effect:* _____

2. _____

   _____

   _____

   *Cause:* _____

   *Effect:* _____

3. _____

   _____

   _____

   *Cause:* _____

   *Effect:* _____

***Causal thinking***   We make causal statements all the time, and we are always thinking in terms of causal relationships. In fact, the goal of much of our thinking is to figure out *why* something happened or *how* something came about. For if we can figure out how and why things occur, we can then try to predict what will happen in the future. These predictions of anticipated results form the basis of many of our decisions. For example, the experience of toasting our hand along with the marshmallows might lead us to choose a longer stick for toasting—simply because we are able to figure out the causal relationships involved and then make predictions based on our understanding (namely, a longer stick will keep my hand further away from the fire, which will prevent it from getting toasted).

➤•◄     Consider the following activities, which you probably performed today. Each activity assumes that certain causal relationships exist, which influenced your decision to perform them. Explain one such causal relationship for each activity.

1. Setting the alarm clock
   *Causal relationship:* Setting the alarm will cause a noise at a certain time, which will then wake me up.
2. Brushing your teeth
   *Causal relationship:* _____

   _____

3. Eating breakfast
   *Causal relationship:* _____

   _____

4. Putting on shoes
   *Causal relationship:* _____

   _____

5. Locking the door
   *Causal relationship:* _____

   _____

***Causal chains***   Although we tend to think of causes and effects in isolation—A caused B—in reality causes and effects rarely (if ever) appear by themselves. Causes and effects generally appear as parts of more complex patterns, including two that we will examine here:

1. Causal chains
2. Contributory causes

Consider the following scenario:

Your paper on the topic "Is there life after death?" is due on Monday morning. You have reserved the whole weekend to work on it, and are just getting started when the phone rings—your best friend from your childhood is in town, and wants to stay with you for the weekend. You say yes. By Sunday night, you've had a great weekend, but have made little progress on your paper. You begin writing, when suddenly you feel stomach cramps—it must have been those raw oysters that you had for lunch! Three hours later, you are ready to continue work. You brew a pot of coffee and get started. At 3:00 A.M. you are too exhausted to continue. You decide to get a few hours of sleep, and set the alarm clock for 6:00 A.M., giving you plenty of time to finish up. When you wake up, you find that it's nine o'clock—the alarm failed to go off! There is only forty minutes to class, and you have no chance of getting the paper done on time. As you ride to school, you go over the causes for this disaster in your mind. You are no longer worried about life after death—you are now worried about life after this class!

1. What are the causes you can identify in this situation that are responsible for the paper not being completed on time?

   a. _____

   b. _____

   c. _____

   d. _____

2. What do you think is the single most important cause?

   _____

3. What do you think your teacher will identify as the most important cause? Why?

   _____

   _____

➤•◄   Create a similar scenario of your own, detailing a chain of causes that result in one of the following effects:

1. Being late for class
2. Standing someone up for a date
3. Failing an exam

A *causal chain,* as we can see from these examples, is a situation in which one thing leads to another, which then leads to another, and so on. There is not just *one* cause for the resulting effect; there is a whole string of causes. Which cause in the string is the "real" cause? Our answer often depends on our perspective on the situation. In the example of the unfinished paper on the topic "Is there life after death?" the student might see the cause as a faulty alarm clock. The teacher, on the other hand, might see the cause of the problem as an overall lack of planning. Proper planning, he or she might say, does not leave things until the last minute, when unexpected problems can prevent us from reaching our goal.

➤•◄   Review the scenario you created above. Explain how the "real" cause of the final effect could vary depending on your perspective on the situation.

**Contributory causes**   In addition to operating in causal chains over a period of time (A leads to B → C → D → etc.), causes can also act simultaneously to produce an effect. When this happens (as it often does), we have a situation in which a number of different causes are instrumental in bringing something about. Instead of working in isolation, each cause *contributes* to bringing about the final effect. When this situation occurs, each cause serves to support and reinforce the action of the other causes.

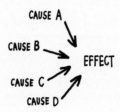

Consider the following situation:

> It is the end of the term, and you have been working incredibly hard at school—writing papers, preparing for exams, finishing up course projects. You haven't been getting enough sleep, and you haven't been eating regular or well-balanced meals. To make matters worse, you have been under intense pressure in your personal life, having serious arguments with your boyfriend or girlfriend. You find that this is constantly on your mind. It is the middle of the flu season and many of the people you know have been sick with various bugs. Walking home from school one evening, you get soaked by an unexpected shower. By the time that you get home, you are shivering. You soon find yourself in bed with a thermometer in your mouth—you are sick!

What was the "cause" of your getting sick? In this situation, you can see it probably was not just *one* thing that brought about your illness. It was probably a *combination* of different factors that led to your physical breakdown: low resistance, getting wet and chilled, being exposed to various germs and viruses, physical exhaustion, lack of proper eating, etc. Taken by itself, no one factor might have been enough to cause your illness. Working together, they all contributed to the final outcome.

---

Create a similar scenario of your own, detailing the contributory causes ➤•◄ that might work together in bringing about one of the following effects:

1. A break-up with your boyfriend or girlfriend
2. Failing a course
3. Losing or winning a game you played in

*Causal persuasion*   Not only do we actively organize our world in terms of cause and effect relationships in order to make sense of it, but there are many people who want us to see the cause and effect relationships that they believe exist. For example:

> Politicians assure us that a vote for them will result in "a chicken in every pot and a car in every garage."
>
> Advertisers tell us that using this detergent will leave our wash "cleaner than clean, whiter than white."
>
> Doctors tell us that eating a balanced diet will result in better health.
>
> Educators tell us that a college degree is worth an average of $300,000 additional income over an individual's life.
>
> Scientists inform us that nuclear energy will result in a better life for all of us.

In each of these cases, certain causal claims are being made about how the world operates, in an effort to persuade us to adopt a certain point of view. As critical thinkers, it is our duty to evaluate these various causal claims in an effort to figure out whether they are sensible ways of organizing the world.

---

➤ • ◄        Consider the following causal claims, and explain how you might go about evaluating whether they make sense.

*Example:*   Taking the right vitamins can improve your health.

*Evaluation:*   Review the medical research that examines the effect of taking vitamins on our health; speak to a nutritionist; speak to our doctor.

1. Sweet Smell deodorant will keep you drier all day long.

   *Evaluation:* _____

   _____

   _____

2. Allure perfume will cause men to be attracted to you.

   *Evaluation:* _____

   _____

   _____

3. Natural childbirth will result in a more fulfilling birth experience.
   *Evaluation:* _____

   _____

   _____

4. Aspirin Plus will give you faster, longer-lasting relief from headaches.
   *Evaluation:* _____

   _____

   _____

5. Radial tires will improve the gas mileage of your car.
   *Evaluation:* _____

   _____

   _____

6. I think that he is the real father of the child, even though he denies it.
   *Evaluation:* _____

   _____

   _____

7. Talking to your house plants will contribute to their health.
   *Evaluation:* _____

   _____

   _____

***Extended causal discussions***   Many of the discussions that we engage
in and the essays that we write are based on an extended analysis of a cause and
effect situation. When this happens, the concept of causality is used both to
help us explain our viewpoint and to give us a means of organizing and
structuring the topic we are examining. Consider the following essay on the
topic of teen-age pregnancies:

# Teen Pregnancies Involve More Than Sex
*By Caryl Rivers*

A virtual epidemic of pregnancies is under way in this nation's teen-age
population; in 1979 alone, 262,700 babies were born to unwed teens. Predict-
ably, educators, parent groups and editorial writers have responded to this

news with a clamor for more and better sex education. Indeed, that is urgently necessary, but sex education alone is not the answer. We need to take a clear-eyed look at how we are bringing up young girls in this culture; otherwise, we won't come anywhere near understanding the psychological dynamics that lead little girls into unwed teen-age motherhood.

We tend to see teen-age pregnancy in terms of sexuality, which we start worrying about when girls reach puberty. In fact, that is a dozen years too late. The lessons that little girls learn when they are 2 or 5 or 7 have a direct bearing on the issues they will confront when they reach adolescence. The girl who receives early training in independence and assertiveness has a good chance of not falling into the trap of premature motherhood.

Why is this so? If you examine the sexual behavior of teen-agers, you find that, for girls, the driving force is not libido but the need for love and acceptance. When you read the letters that teen-agers send to advice columnists, one theme emerges with great frequency: "I don't want to have sex, but I'm afraid I'll lose my boyfriend."

It is very hard for a teen, at an age when peer pressure and the desire for male attention is intense, to insist that she will set her own timetable for when she will engage in sex. And, if she decides that she is ready for sex, she probably has to take the initiative in insisting on contraception. To do this requires a sense that she can and must control her own destiny. The ability to make demands, handle conflict, plan ahead—these are not qualities that a girl can develop overnight at puberty. Yet too often we do not train our girls early in these traits.

When psychologists Grace Baruch and Rosalind Barnett of the Wellesley Center for Research on Women and I surveyed the scientific literature on women and young girls, we found a number of troublesome currents. We found that girls tend to underestimate their own ability, and that they do so in pre-school and when they are seniors in college. We also found that the closer girls got to adulthood, the less they valued their own sex.

Psychologist Lois Hoffman of the University of Michigan, a specialist in this field, says that girls' undeveloped self-confidence causes them to cling to an infantile fear of abandonment and a belief that their safety lies only in their dependence on others.

I saw a demonstration of this when I was a chaperone on a Girl Scout camping trip. The girls, age 9 to 12, repeatedly ran to the troop leader, seeking her approval before deciding where to put a sleeping bag or whether to put on bug spray. They needed far more help and approval in making even simple decisions than would a group of boys the same age—even though many girls of that age are bigger and stronger than boys.

One reason for this behavior is that girls get more approval when they ask for help than boys do. When psychologist Bevery Fagot studied parents of 2-year-olds, she found more expressions of approval given to girls seeking help than to boys. This was true even when the parents said they believed in treating both sexes alike.

Girls receiving such messages are less likely to take risks, to test their own abilities. Instead, they try to figure out what it is that adults want from them and concentrate on being "good little girls." They never learn to handle conflict or even temporary lack of approval.

At adolescence, too often they transfer this dependency from parents to boyfriends. They get pregnant "by accident," not really understanding that they have any responsibility for or control over what happens in their lives.

If we care, not only about teen-age pregnancy but also about the psychological health of girls, we must be on guard against the viruses of self-devaluation and dependence. We must be sure that girls are not given permission to fail because of "those little eyes so helpless and appealing."

Unfortunately, many of the school programs designed to enhance the development of girls' skills—encouraging them to try science and math, sharpening their athletic abilities—are falling by the wayside in an era of budget-cutting. It may not be easy to see how a girl's ability to do calculus or sink a free throw relates to the pregnancy statistics, but the link is there. If we help girls develop confidence and self-esteem, then perhaps they can deal with issues of sexuality as strong individuals, not merely as victims.

All the sex education in the world will not put a real dent in the pregnancy rate if we can't persuade young girls that they can—and must—control their future, not merely collide with it.

In analyzing this essay, we should ask ourselves the following questions:

1. What is the basic cause and effect relationship that the author is presenting?

   *Cause:* _____

   *Effect:* _____

2. What evidence does the author offer to support her belief in this cause and effect relationship?

   _____

   _____

   _____

3. Can you think of other causes of teen-age pregnancy that the author has overlooked?

_____

_____

_____

4. Do you think that the author has fallen into any of the causal pitfalls that we explored? Explain why or why not.

_____

_____

_____

➤•◄     Return to the ideas about salaries that you generated and mapped on page 343. Describe some of the cause and effect relationships that you believe might exist between the key ideas you have identified.

For example, the following description of cause-and-effect relationships is based on the ideas mapped on page 344.

The psychological hazards of low-paying occupations are often different from the psychological hazards of high-paying occupations because of different causes. For example, imagine occupations like assembly-line workers, typists, manual laborers, and so on. In these types of occupations the tasks are specifically delineated and the workers' responsibilities are limited. However, workers must cope with the tedium of doing the same thing over and over again. In addition, since they are performing only one small part of the overall process in which they are engaged, workers have little sense of connection with what they are producing. In most of these occupations workers are not challenged to use their creative or critical thinking abilities and so do not have the opportunity to develop a sense of fulfillment in what they are doing. Also, in many low-paying jobs workers are at the mercy of their supervisors, having either to follow their commands without question or to risk getting dismissed. It's clear that this sort of situation can result in boredom, depression, feelings of alienation, and eroded sense of self-worth.

In contrast, high-paying occupations often embody different factors that result in other psychological hazards. For example, occupations like highly placed business executives, successful athletes, airline pilots, the President, movie stars, and so on have a number of qualities in common. In most cases these jobs involve tremendous responsibility. People have high expectations of performance; actions are carefully scrutinized; and people in these positions are expected to deliver. In trying to meet this challenge, workers are forced to use as many of their creative and critical thinking abilities as possible, to push themselves in order to maintain or improve their high level of performance, and to work long hours so that they can stay on top of things. These occupations are often extremely competitive, forcing workers to think about their jobs even when they go home. And since the stakes are so high, the fear of failing is proportionally large. It's obvious that these types of stresses and pressures can result in tension, anxiety, headaches, ulcers, high-blood pressure, and other psychological ailments.

## Composing an essay

Thus far in this chapter, we have explored a sequential process of composing:

> Generating and mapping ideas
>
> Defining a main idea
>
> Organizing ideas

For most people, these steps rarely take place in such a neat, orderly sequence. Instead, there is usually a continual back and forth (interactive) movement among these activities as we gradually develop and sharpen our ideas.

One purpose of the composing process is to present our ideas to others in spoken or written form. We want them to understand our thinking, to further develop the ideas we are exploring, and to ask intelligent questions. In order to attain this goal, it is useful for us to organize our ideas in a way that will aid others in making sense of our thinking. The form normally used to organize ideas in a written essay reflects the basic questions that we raise when discussing ideas with others[1]:

> What is your point? (stating the main idea)
>
> I don't quite get your meaning (explaining the main idea)

---

[1] From Mina Shaughnessy, *Errors and Expectations: A Guide for the Teacher of Basic Writing* (New York: Oxford University Press, 1977), p. 273.

Prove it to me (providing examples, evidence, and arguments to support
the main idea)

So what? (drawing a conclusion)

By using the work you have been doing in this chapter concerning the topic of
salaries, you can organize your thinking into a basic essay format.

### Stating the main idea

The first part of your essay should introduce the specific topic you will be
exploring. Review your work in this area on page 343 and then write a paragraph introducing your main idea.

### Explaining the main idea

The next part of your essay should give a further elaboration of your main
idea, describing it more fully and with more detail. Review your work on page
343 and then write a paragraph explaining your main idea in more detail.

### Providing examples, evidence, and arguments to support the main idea

Once you have stated and explained your main point, your next task is to
offer evidence supporting the point you are making. The evidence you provide
can take a number of different forms:

1. You can *compare and contrast* various ideas, a thinking pattern we explored
   on pages 346–354.

2. You can suggest *analogies* to illustrate your points, a thinking pattern we
   explored on pages 354–364.

3. You can suggest *cause and effect* relationships, a thinking pattern we
   explored on pages 365–375

4. You can give *examples* to illustrate your general ideas, a thinking process
   we explored in Chapter Nine (pp. 322–325).

5. You can identify *reasons* that support your point of view, a thinking strategy we explored in Chapter Three (pp. 72–83).

6. You can present *arguments* that attempt to persuade readers that your
   thinking is accurate and complete, a thinking process we will be exploring
   in Chapter Twelve (pp. 411–456).

Review your work on pages 340–344 and then write two to three paragraphs that provide examples, evidence, and arguments supporting your main
point.

### Drawing a conclusion

The purpose of a conclusion is to summarize the main idea you have been considering in the paper, along with the central reasons, evidence, and arguments that support your thinking. You might want to suggest further questions that need to be answered or new directions for pursuing further the ideas you have been exploring.

Review the paragraphs you have already written and then compose a paragraph that summarizes the points you have been addressing.

The following essay evolved from the ideas mapped on page 344.

Psychological Hazards on the Job

Most occupations have psychological hazards for the people performing the work. In general, the psychological hazards in high-paying jobs are different from those in low-paying jobs. This is because different jobs have qualities that create their own unique kinds of stress and pressure.

Psychological hazards are as much a part of an occupation as physical hazards. For example, we know that coal miners are susceptible to Black Lung disease; dentists are vulnerable to lower back pain; dancers are prone to foot and ankle problems; singers often have voice and throat difficulties. In the same way, people in different professions are susceptible to various psychological hazards. For instance, assembly-line workers may become bored and depressed because their work has little meaning for them; policemen have an unusually high divorce rate and a suicide rate that is exceeded only by doctors; doctors also have a high drug addiction and alcoholism rate; people in executive-level business positions often develop migraine headaches, ulcers, high blood pressure, and heart disease. When we consider the various psychological hazards of individual professions, we can see that in general the pressures and stress of high-paying occupations are different from the pressures and stress of low-paying occupations.

Consider, for example, some of the low-paying occupations in our society such as assembly-line worker, manual laborer, typist, and short order cook. In all of these positions the tasks are very specific and the responsibilities are limited. People in these occupations must cope with the tedium of doing the same thing over and over again. Because people are following detailed instructions, they have little opportunity to use their creative and critical thinking abilities. Since people in these jobs are performing only one small part of the overall project they are involved in, they do not really feel connected to what they are producing. This diminishes their chance to develop a sense of satisfaction or personal fulfillment in what they are doing. Also, in many low-paying jobs, people are at the complete mercy of their supervisors, having to follow their commands without questions or risk getting fired. Taken as a whole, it's easy to see how these factors can create significant psychological hazards such as boredom, depression, a feeling of alienation, and an eroded sense of self-worth.

In contrast, high-paying occupations often embody different qualities that result in different psychological hazards. For example, consider some of the high-paying occupations in our society such as senior business executives, successful athletes, airline pilots, the President, movie stars, and so on. These occupations have a number of qualities in common. In most cases these jobs involve significant responsibilities--failure usually results in very serious consequences. There are high expectations of people in these positions. Their actions are carefully scrutinized and they are expected to deliver. In trying to meet these challenges, people are usually forced to use as many of their creative and critical thinking abilities as they can, to work long hours, and to push themselves in order to maintain or improve their high level of performance. These occupations are typically extremely competitive, and people involved in them usually continue to think and worry about them after they go home. And since the stakes are so high, the fear of failing is proportionally greater. Looked at together, it is clear how these factors can create significant psychological hazards such as extreme tension, anxiety, and stress that can lead to migraine headaches, high-blood pressure, ulcers, heart conditions, and a variety of other psychological ailments.

In summary, it seems apparent that most occupations have certain psychological hazards associated with them, and that the hazards for low-paying jobs tend to be different than for high-paying jobs. Of course, no occupation by itself causes stress, pressure, alienation, or depression. These and other ailments are a result of the way individuals in these occupations react to the demands of their particular job. Some people are able to deal

much more effectively with the job demands than others. In the
years ahead, it would be a significant advancement if our society
would identify the psychological hazards for various occupations
just as physical hazards have been identified and then help employers and employees devise strategies for minimizing and coping
with these hazards.

## Revising

In the last few chapters, we have been emphasizing the notion that thinking is
an interactive process, constantly moving back and forth between various
activities in order to make sense of things—forming and applying concepts,
defining and exemplifying key terms, generating and developing ideas. This
same interactive process is a part of the writing process, a conclusion that
makes sense since our writing expresses our thinking and uses all the thinking
activities we have been examining. Most writers find it natural to move back
and forth between the various aspects of the writing process as they follow out
the line of their thinking. In fact, you will probably discover that the process of
writing does not merely express your thinking: it also *stimulates* your thinking,
suggesting ideas and ways to explore them.

Because thinking and writing are interactive in nature, in a sense we are
continually revising our thinking and writing. The first draft of our writing is
usually just that—a first draft. Having expressed our thinking in language, it is
important for us to go back and "re-see" (the origin of the word *revise*) our writing from a fresh perspective. In addition, it is helpful to have others read what
we have written and give us their reactions.

Improving sentence structure and correcting spelling and punctuation are
of course part of the revising process. However, we also want to take a fresh
look at the *thinking* that is being expressed. One useful strategy is to create an
outline or map of the first draft because it enables us to identify the main ideas
and express their relationships. This in turn may suggest ways we can clarify
our thinking by rearranging different parts, developing certain points further,
or deleting what is repetitious or not central to the main ideas of the paper. And
remember, revising is an ongoing process that can occur at any of the stages we
have been exploring.

You have probably been revising all along as you explored, mapped, and
drafted your essay on salaries and work. After completing a draft of your essay,

you should re-view how you have developed and organized your ideas and information by following these steps:

1. Create a map that expresses the main points and their various relationships being considered in your paper.
2. Examine your map carefully, looking for ways to clarify and improve your ideas. Determine whether you should
   a. rearrange the sequence of your ideas.
   b. develop certain ideas further.
   c. delete points that are repetitious or not central to the subject.
      Revise your map (or create a new one) to reflect these changes
3. Compose a revised draft of your paper, using your revision map as a guide.

# Chapter Eleven
# Reporting, Inferring, Judging

**REPORTING**

Describing information that can be verified through investigation.

**INFERRING**

Going beyond factual information to describe what is not currently known.

**JUDGING**

Expressing an evaluation based on certain criteria

THE MAIN GOAL of our thinking is to identify and organize the world in ways that will enable us to understand what is going on and then to make reasoned decisions based on our understanding. As we actively compose our world, language is the most powerful tool we have to identify aspects of our experience (with symbols) and relate these aspects to one another. The relationships that we compose and discover express the basic thinking patterns we use to make sense of the world. In the last chapter, we critically examined a number of these basic thinking patterns, including

> comparing and contrasting.
>
> relating by analogy.
>
> relating by cause and effect.

In this chapter we will be thinking critically about some other thinking patterns that we use to organize and make sense of our world, including

> reporting.
>
> inferring.
>
> judging.

Just like the other thinking patterns we have explored, these ways of organizing and relating are expressed in both our thinking and in our use of language.

Describe what you think is the type of statement made by the following sentences:

1. My bus was late today.

    *Type of statement:* _____

2. My bus will probably be late tomorrow.

    *Type of statement:* _____

3. The bus system is unreliable.

    *Type of statement:* _____

Let us try this activity again with a different set of statements.

1. Each modern atomic warhead has over one hundred times the explosive power of the bomb dropped on Hiroshima.

    *Type of statement:* _____

2. With all of the billions of planets in the universe, the odds are that there are other forms of life in the cosmos.

    *Type of statement:* _____

3. In the long run, the energy needs of the world will best be met by solar energy technology, rather than nuclear energy or fossil fuels.

   *Type of statement:* _____

As we examine these various statements, we can see that they are providing us with different types of information about the world. For example, the first statements in each list both report aspects of the world that we can verify—that is, check for accuracy. By doing the appropriate sort of investigating, we can determine whether the bus was actually late today and whether modern atomic warheads really have the power attributed to them. When we describe the world in ways that can be verified through investigation, we are said to be *reporting* factual information about the world.

**Reporting Factual Information** • Describing the world in ways that can be verified through investigation.

Looking at the second statements in each list, we can see immediately that they provide a different sort of information from the first ones. Here the statements that are being made about the world cannot be verified. There is no way to investigate and determine with certainty whether the bus will indeed be late tomorrow or whether there is in fact life on other planets. Although these conclusions may be based on factual information, they go beyond factual information to make statements about what is not currently known. When we describe the world in ways that are based on factual information yet go beyond this information to make statements regarding what is not currently known, we are said to be *inferring* conclusions about the world.

**Inferring** • Describing the world in ways that are based on factual information yet go beyond this information to make statements about what is not currently known.

Finally, as we examine the third statements in both lists, it is apparent that they are different from both factual reports and inferences. They describe the world in ways that express the speaker's evaluation—of the bus service and of energy sources. These evaluations are based on certain standards (criteria) that the speaker is using to judge the bus service as unreliable and solar energy as more promising than nuclear energy or fossil fuels. When we describe the world in ways that express our evaluation based on certain criteria, we are said to be *judging*.

**Judging** • Describing the world in ways that express our evaluation based on certain criteria.

We are continually using these various ways of describing and organizing our world—reporting, inferring, judging—to make sense of our experience. In most cases, we are not aware that we are actually performing these activities, nor are we usually aware of the differences between them. Yet these three activities work together to help us see the world as a complete picture.

---

➤•◄     Carefully examine the photograph on page 385. Write five statements based on your observations. Then identify each of your statements as *reporting, inferring,* or *judging,* and explain why you classified them as such.

*Reporting* factual information by describing the world in ways that can be verified through investigation.

*Inferring* information by describing the world in ways that are based on factual information yet go beyond to make statements regarding what is not currently known.

*Judging* by describing the world in ways that express our evaluation, based on certain criteria.

---

➤•◄     Carefully read the following selection, taken from Patricia Cayo Sexton's book *Spanish Harlem.* After completing your reading, identify (on the basis of the article) whether the following statements are *reporting, inferring,* or *judging,* and then explain why you are classifying them as such.

## Backdrop of Poverty
*by Patricia Cayo Sexton*

At 6:30 A.M., while silk-stocking Manhattan is asleep, East Harlem is starting to bustle. The poor are early risers. They have the jobs others don't want: the early-hour jobs, the late-hour jobs. Many rise early because it is a rural habit.

Along about 7:30 the streets are filled with fast-moving people: men, women, and swarms of children of all sizes. The parochial school children can be seen in clusters, with their togetherness identity tag—a school hat, a blouse, a uniform.

You may be able to buy a *New York Times* at the corner newsstand in the morning, but you probably will not be able to buy a cup of coffee. The poor drink their coffee and eat their breakfasts, such as they are, at home. Few eat out.

Some will stand at the bus stops, but most will crowd into the downtown subways that speed them to jobs in commercial or silk-stocking areas: to serve

the affluent, or work in their stores or small industrial shops. Many of the
Negro women will go to domestic service; and the Puerto Rican women, to their
sewing machines in the garment shops.

Later in the day, if it is warm, the men who have no jobs will come out and
stand on the sidewalks and talk together. They will watch the street and the
passers-by and kibitz with one another. The old people, and from time to time
the housewives, will sit at the window and join the watchers. And those with
leisure may call them idle. Later, when the children return from school, the
sidewalks and streets will jump with activity. Clusters of men, sitting on orange
crates on the sidewalks, will play checkers or cards. The women will sit on the
stoop, arms folded, and watch the young at play; and the young men, flexing
their muscles, will look for some adventure. Vendors, ringing their bells, will
hawk hot dogs, orange drinks, ice cream; and the caressing but often jarring
noise of honking horns, music, children's games, and casual quarrels, whistles,
singing, will go on late into the night. When you are in it you don't notice the
noise, but when you stand away and listen to a taped conversation, the sound
suddenly appears as a background roar. This loud stimulation of the senses may
produce some of the emotionalism of the poor.

East Harlem is a busy place, night and day, filled with the joyous and
troubled lives of residents—rather than the heavy commercial traffic of mid-
Manhattan. New York's street life is unique. So much action, so much
togetherness. The critics who lament its passing have a point. The middle class
who disdain life conducted so openly in the streets might compare its satisfac-
tions to the sometimes parched and estranged quality of their own backyards.

| *Statements* | *Factual Report* | *Inference* | *Judgment* |
|---|---|---|---|
| 1. The residents of Spanish Harlem tend to rise early in the morning. | | | |
| *Explanation:* _____ | | | |
| _____ | | | |
| _____ | | | |
| 2. Not many people eat out because they can't afford to. | | | |
| *Explanation:* _____ | | | |
| _____ | | | |
| _____ | | | |

*Statements*                                      *Factual   Inference   Judgment*
                                                  *Report*

3. Many of the people in Spanish Harlem are
   lazy.

   *Explanation:* _____

   _____

   _____

4. Harlem is a very noisy place to live in.

   *Explanation:* _____

   _____

   _____

5. Living in the midst of so much noise contributes to the very emotional nature of
   the residents.

   *Explanation:* _____

   _____

   _____

6. There is more social togetherness in
   Harlem than in middle-class neighborhoods.

   *Explanation:* _____

   _____

   _____

7. Many of the people going to work are in
   the service of the wealthy.

   *Explanation:* _____

   _____

   _____

Now create three statements of your own (one report, one inference, and one judgment) that are related to the article. Explain why you are classifying each statement a *report,* an *inference,* or a *judgment.*

8. _____

   _____

*Statements*                                          *Factual Inference Judgment*
                                                      *Report*
*Explanation:* _____

_____

9. _____

*Explanation:* _____

_____

10. _____

_____

*Explanation:* _____

_____

As you worked through these two exercises, you probably became aware of the way that we continually use the activities of reporting, inferring, and judging to organize and make sense of our world. In addition, you probably experienced some difficulty in distinguishing these different kinds of activities. This is because we rarely make an effort to try to separate them. Instead, our reporting, inferring, and judging tend to be woven together, organizing our world into a seamless fabric. Only when we make a special effort to reflect and think critically are we able to recognize these activities as being distinct. Let us examine each of them in more detail.

## Reporting factual information

The statements that result from the activity of reporting express the most accurate beliefs we have about the world. Factual beliefs have earned this distinction because they are verifiable, usually with one or more of our senses. For example, consider the following factual statement:

That young woman is wearing a brown hat in the rain.

This statement about an event in the world is considered to be factual because it can be verified by our immediate sense experience—what we can (in principle or in theory) see, hear, touch, feel or smell. It is important to say *in principle* or *in theory*, because we often do not use all of our relevant senses to check out what we are experiencing. Look again at our example of a factual statement:

That young woman is wearing a brown hat in the rain.

We would normally be satisfied to *see* this event, without insisting on touching or smelling the hat or giving the person a physical examination. But if necessary, we could perform these additional actions—in principle or in theory.

We use the same reasoning when we believe factual statements from other people that we are not in a position to check out immediately. For instance:

> The Great Wall of China is over 1,500 miles long.
>
> There are large mountains and craters on the moon.
>
> Our skin is covered with germs.

We consider these to be factual statements because, even though we cannot verify them with our senses at the moment, we could in principle or in theory verify them with our senses

> *if* we were flown to China.
>
> *if* we were rocketed to the moon.
>
> *if* we were to examine our skin with a powerful microscope.

---

Identify three of your factual beliefs about the world that are *not* based on your personal experience. Explain how you could in principle verify these beliefs.

1. *Statement:* _____

   *How to verify:* _____

2. *Statement:* _____

   *How to verify:* _____

3. *Statement:* _____

   *How to verify:* _____

We communicate factual information to each other by means of *reports*. A report is a description of something that we have experienced, given in a way that is as accurate and complete as possible. Through reports, we can share our sense experiences with other people, and this mutual sharing enables us to learn much more about the world than if we were confined to knowing only what we experience. The *recording* (making records) of factual reports also makes possible the accumulation of knowledge learned by previous generations.

Because factual reports play such an important role in our exchange and accumulation of information about the world, it is important that they be as accurate and complete as possible. This brings us to a problem. We have already seen in Chapter Five, "Perceiving," that our perceptions and observations are often *not* accurate or complete. What this means is that often when we think we are making true factual reports, our reports are actually inaccurate or incomplete. For instance, consider our earlier "factual statement":

That young woman is wearing a brown hat in the rain.

Here are some questions we could ask concerning how accurate our statement really is:

Is the woman really young, or does she merely look young?

Is the woman really a woman, or a man (or alien creature)
    disguised as a woman?

Is that really a hat the woman/man/creature is wearing, or something else
    (e.g., a paper bag) being used to keep her/his/its head dry?

Of course, there are methods that we could use to clear up these questions with more detailed observations. Can you describe some of these methods?

Besides difficulties with observations, the "facts" that we see in the world actually depend on more general *beliefs* that we have about how the world operates. Consider the question:

Why did the man's body fall from the top of the building to the sidewalk?

If we have had some general science courses, we might say something like "The body was simply obeying the law of gravity," and we would consider this to be a "factual statement." But how did people account for this sort of event before Newton formulated the law of gravity? Some popular responses might have included the following:

Things always fall down, not up.

The spirit in the body wanted to join with the spirit of the earth.

When people made statements like these and others, such as "Humans can't fly," they thought that they were making "factual statements." Increased knowledge and understanding have since shown these "factual beliefs" to be inaccurate, and so they have been replaced by "better" beliefs. These "better beliefs" are able to explain the world in a way that is more accurate and predictable. Will many of the beliefs that we now consider to be factually accurate also be replaced in the future by beliefs that are *more* accurate and predictable? If history is any indication, this will most certainly happen. (Already Newton's formulations have been replaced by Einstein's, based on his theory of relativity. And in the opinions of some scientists, Einstein's have been replaced as well.)

From the following list of statements, select the statements that you be- ►•◄ lieve to be "factual." Then explain briefly how you might try to verify these statements.

1. Bill has season tickets to see the New York Yankees.

   *How to verify:* _____

   _____

2. Sandra is a baseball fanatic.

   *How to verify:* _____

   _____

3. It's very stuffy in here.

   *How to verify:* _____

   _____

4. The thermometer reads over 100 degrees!

   *How to verify:* _____

   _____

5. Many students drop out of college and don't graduate.

   *How to verify:* _____

   _____

6. America is a democracy.

   *How to verify:* _____

   _____

7. Real men don't cry.

   *How to verify:* _____

   _____

8. Rome wasn't built in a day.

   *How to verify:* _____

   _____

9. America is the land of opportunity.

   *How to verify:* _____

   _____

10. Smoking cigarettes will shorten your life.

    *How to verify:* _____

    _____

11. Automobiles pollute the air we breathe.

    *How to verify:* _____

    _____

12. We are destroying the enviroment.

*How to verify:* _____

_____

When people report factual information, we expect that their report is giving accurate information. This information is usually based on experience (theirs or someone else's) and can be verified by others such as ourselves.

►•◄   Select a neighborhood that you are familiar with and write a list of ten to twelve factual statements that describe it and the people who live there. Be sure to include the following information:

1. Description of the physical appearance of the neighborhood—what it looks like, sounds like, smells like, etc. *Be specific.*

   *Example:* Many of the small businesses in Greenwich Village—mom and pop groceries, tailors, coffee shops with soda fountains—have been replaced with expensive restaurants and exclusive boutiques.

2. Description of some of the individuals or types of people who live in the neighborhood and with their usual activities. *Be specific.*

   *Example:* The residents of Greenwich Village form a richly diverse parade each morning: young professionals moving brusquely off to work; children in Osh-Kosh overalls and parochial school plaids skipping energetically to a day of education; mothers with strollers mingling with the self-employed, the unemployed, and the retired, easing into the day at a leisurely pace; and finally, the shopkeepers, hard-working and friendly people from six continents preparing for a day of business.

3. Comparison and contrast of this neighborhood with another neighborhood that you are familiar with. *Be specific.*

   *Example:* One of the striking differences between Greenwich Village and other parts of Manhatten is the size of the buildings. Instead of towering structures that blot out the sky and diminish your sense of significance, the architecture of the Village is human scale, creating the distinct impression that this is a neighborhood in which people are considered to be more important than the buildings that they occupy.

Make sure that your statements are accurate and verifiable. After you complete your list of factual statements, have someone else in the class review it, using the criteria of accuracy and verifiability.

# Inferring

Imagine yourself in the following situations:

1.  It is 2:00 A.M. and your roommate comes crashing through the door into the room. He staggers unsteadily to his bed and falls across it, dropping (and breaking) a nearly empty whiskey bottle. You rush over and ask "What happened?" With alcoholic fumes blasting from his mouth, your roomate mumbles: "I juss wanna hadda widdel drink!" What do you conclude?

    _____

    _____

2.  Your roommate has just learned that she passed a math exam for which she had done absolutely no studying. Happily humming the song "I did it my way," she comes bouncing over to you, and with a huge grin on her face, she says: "Let me buy you dinner to celebrate!" What do you conclude about how she is feeling?

    _____

    _____

3.  It is midnight and the library is about to close. As you head for the door, you spy your roommate shuffling along in an awkward waddle. His coat is bulged out in front like he's pregnant. When you ask "What's going on?" he gives you a glare and hisses, "Shhh!" Just before he reaches the door, a pile of books slides from under his coat and crashes to the floor. What do you conclude?

    _____

    _____

In these examples, it would certainly seem reasonable to conclude that

1.  my roommate is drunk.
2.  my roommate is happy.
3.  my roommate is stealing library books.

Although these conclusions are reasonable, they are *not* factual reports; they are *inferences*. We have not actually experienced our roommate's "drunkenness," "happiness," or "stealing." Instead, we have *inferred* it based on his or her behavior and the circumstances. What are the clues in these situations that might lead to these conclusions?

1. _____

_____

2. _____

_____

3. _____

_____

One way of understanding the inferential nature of these views is to ask yourself the following questions:

1. Have you ever pretended to be drunk when you weren't? Could other people tell?
2. Have you ever pretended to be happy when you weren't? Could other people tell?
3. Have you ever been accused of stealing something when you were perfectly innocent? How did this happen?

From these examples we can see that whereas factual beliefs can in principle be verified by direct observation, *inferential beliefs* go beyond what can be directly observed. Thus inferences are beliefs about unknown or unobserved events, that are based on known or observed events.

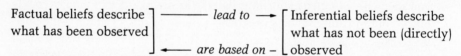

For instance, in the examples above, it was the fact that we observed certain actions of our roommate that led us to infer things that we were *not* observing directly—"He's drunk," "She's happy," "He's stealing books." Making such simple inferences is something that we do all of the time. It is so automatic that usually we are not even aware that we are going beyond our immediate observations, and we have difficulty in drawing a sharp line between what is *observed* and what is *inferred.* Making such inferences enables us to see the world as a complete picture, to fill in the blanks and round out what is actually being presented to our senses. In a sense, we become artists, painting a picture of the world that is consistent, coherent, and predictable. However, this picture is actually based on observations that are often fragmentary and incomplete.

➤•◄       Identify two inferences you made today and describe the factual observations that led you to them.

1.  *Inference:* _____

    *Factual observation:* _____

2.  *Inference:* _____

    *Factual observation:* _____

We do not use inferences just to round out, or complete, the picture of what we are observing. Our picture also includes *predictions* of what will be taking place in the near future. (For example, in a few minutes, the teacher will stop talking and you will get up and leave the room.) These predictions and expectations are also inferences, as we attempt to determine what is currently unknown from what is already known.

---

Examine the situation you are currently in as you read this passage, and ➤•◄ identify the expectations and predictions that are a part of your perception of the situation.

Of course, our inferences may be mistaken, and in fact they frequently are. For example, you may infer that the woman sitting next to you is wearing two earrings and then discover that she has only one. Or you may expect the class to end at noon and find that the teacher lets you go early—or late.

In the last section we concluded that not even factual beliefs are ever absolutely certain. Compared to factual beliefs, however, inferential beliefs are a great deal more uncertain. This difference in certainty makes it crucial for us to distinguish factual beliefs from inferential beliefs.

For example, do you ever cross streets with cars heading toward you, expecting them to stop for a red light or because you have the right of way? Is this a factual belief or an inference? Considered objectively, are you running a serious risk when you do this? In evaluating the risk, think of all the motorists that may be in a hurry, not paying attention, drunk, ill, and so on.

---

Consider the following situations. Then analyze each by asking the ques- ➤•◄ tions given below.

Placing your hand in a closing elevator door to reopen it.

Taking an unknown drug at a party.

Jumping out of an airplane with a parachute on.

Riding on the back of a motorcycle.

Taking a drug prescribed by your doctor.

1. Is this action based on a factual belief or an inference?
2. In what ways might the inference be mistaken?
3. What is the degree of risk involved?

Having an accurate picture of the world depends on our being able to evaluate how *certain* our beliefs are. Therefore it is crucial that we

> *distinguish* inferences from factual beliefs and then
>
> *evaluate* how certain or uncertain our inferences are.

This is known as "calculating the risks," and it is one of the key skills in successfully solving problems and deciding what to do.

The distinction between what is observed and what is inferred is paid particular attention in courtroom settings, where defense lawyers usually want witnesses to describe *only what they observed*—not what they *inferred* as part of the observation. When a witness includes an inference such as "I saw him steal it," the lawyer may object that the statement represents a "conclusion of the witness" and move to have the observation stricken from the record.

Finally, we should be aware that even though *in theory* facts and inferences can be distinguished, *in practice* it is almost impossible to communicate with others by sticking only to factual observations. A reasonable approach is to state our inference *along with* the observable evidence upon which the inference is based (e.g., John *seemed* happy because . . .) Our language has an entire collection of terms (*seems, appears, is likely,* etc.) that signal that we are making an inference and not expressing an observable fact.

---

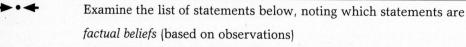

Examine the list of statements below, noting which statements are

*factual beliefs* (based on observations)

*inferential beliefs* (conclusions that go beyond observations)

For each factual statement, describe how you might go about verifying the information. For each inferential statement, describe a factual observation on which the inference could be based.

> *Note:* Some statements may contain *both* factual beliefs and inferential beliefs.

1. This is the hottest day in twenty years.

_____

_____

_____

2.  When my leg starts to ache, that means snow is on the way.

_____

_____

3.  The team was pleased by the outcome of the game.

_____

_____

4.  The grass is wet—it must have rained last night.

_____

_____

5.  I know that she's going to make a mistake—she always finds a way to mess things up.

_____

_____

6.  Drinking too much alcohol is bad for your health.

_____

_____

7.  Look at him sweat and shake—he must be terribly nervous.

_____

_____

8.  There's a policeman coming this way, and he's pretty angry.

_____

_____

9.  I think that it's pretty clear that the accident was caused by that person driving too fast.

_____

_____

_____

10. John F. Kennedy was the first U.S. president who was a Catholic.

_____

_____

_____

11. Mary has been depressed for days.

_____

_____

_____

12. Look at the sand in your shoes—you went to the beach instead of school today!

_____

_____

_____

13. Fifty men lost their lives in the construction of the Queensboro Bridge.

_____

_____

_____

14. Nancy said she wasn't feeling well yesterday—I'll bet that she's out sick today.

_____

_____

_____

15. Two ball in the side pocket.

_____

_____

_____

➤•◄        In the space below, write three inferential statements of your own creation.

1. _____

_____

2. _____

_____

3. _____

_____

For each of the inferential statements you just created, describe the *observational clues* that have led you to make these statements.

1. _____

_____

2. _____

_____

3. _____

_____

Consider the following situations. What inferences might you be inclined to make based on what you are observing?

1. You see your boyfriend or girlfriend leaving a restaurant with someone you have never seen before.

_____

_____

2. A student in your class is consistently late for class.

_____

_____

3. You see a friend of yours driving a new car.

_____

_____

4. A teacher asks the same student to stay after class several times.

_____

_____

5. You don't receive a birthday card from your parents.

_____

_____

6. When you call up a friend, the person hangs up on you.

_____

_____

7. You enter a room full of people you know and all conversation stops.

_____

_____

8. Driving on the highway, you observe an area of the road containing broken glass and skid marks.

_____

_____

▶•◀     Imagine that you are a defense attorney listening to the following testimony. At what points would you make the objection: "This is a conclusion of the witness"?

I saw Harvey running down the street, right after he knocked the old lady down. He had her purse in his hand and was trying to escape as fast as he could. He was really scared. I wasn't surprised because Harvey has always taken advantage of others. It's not the first time that he's stolen either, I can tell you that. Just last summer he robbed the poor box at St. Anthony's. He was bragging about it for weeks.

**Complicated inferences**

So far we have been exploring relatively simple inferences. However, many of the inferences that people make are much more complicated. In fact, much of our knowledge about the world rests on the ability to make complicated inferences in a systematic and logical way. Consider the following story and explain what inferences each person is making. However, keep in mind that just because an inference is more complicated does not mean that it is more accurate; in fact, the opposite is often the case.

*The Kiss and the Slap*

In a railroad compartment, an American grandmother with her young and attractive granddaughter, a Romanian officer and a Nazi officer were the only occupants. The train was passing through a dark tunnel, and what was heard was a loud kiss and a vigorous slap. After the train emerged from the tunnel nobody spoke, but the grandmother was saying to herself: "I am proud of her." The granddaughter was saying to herself: "Well, grandmother is old enough not to mind a little kiss. Besides, the fellows are nice, I am surprised what a hard wallop grandmother has." The Nazi officer was meditating, "How clever those Romanians are! They steal a kiss and have the other fellow slapped." The Romanian officer was chuckling to himself: "How smart I am! I kissed my own hand and slapped the Nazi!"[1]

List the observations of each of the individuals and describe the inference each makes based on his or her observation.

| Individual | Observation | Inference |
| --- | --- | --- |
| Grandmother | Loud kiss and vigorous slap | One of the men kissed the granddaughter and she slapped him |
| Granddaughter | _____ | _____ |
|  | _____ | _____ |
| Romanian officer | _____ | _____ |
|  | _____ | _____ |
| Nazi officer | _____ | _____ |
|  | _____ | _____ |

One of the masters of inference is the legendary Sherlock Holmes. In the following passage, Holmes makes an astonishing number of inferences on meeting Dr. Watson. Study carefully the conclusions he comes to. Are they reasonable? Can you explain how he reaches these conclusions?

## Holmes Meets Watson

"You appeared to be surprised when I told you, on our first meeting, that you had come from Afghanistan."

"You were told, no doubt."

[1]Alfred Korzybski, "The Role of Language in Perceptual Processes," in *Perception—An Approach to Personality,* edited by Robert R. Blake and Glenn V. Ramsey (New York: The Ronald Press Co., 1951), pp. 170–171.

"Nothing of the sort. I *knew* you came from Afghanistan. From long habit the train of thoughts ran so swiftly through my mind that I arrived at the conclusion without being conscious of intermediate steps. There were such steps, however. The train of reasoning ran, 'Here is a gentleman of a medical type, but with the air of a military man. Clearly an army doctor, then. He is just come from the tropics, for his face is dark, and that is not the natural tint of his skin, for his wrists are fair. He has undergone hardship and sickness, as his haggard face says clearly. His left arm has been injured. He holds it in a stiff and unnatural manner. Where in the tropics could an English army doctor have seen much hardship and got his arm wounded? Clearly in Afghanistan?' The whole train of thought did not occupy a second. I then remarked that you came from Afghanistan, and you were astonished."[1]

Describe the observations that lead Sherlock Holmes to the following inferences

| *Inference* | *Observations* |
|---|---|
| 1. Watson was "an army doctor." | _____ |
| | _____ |
| 2. Watson "has undergone hardship and sickness." | _____ |
| | _____ |
| 3. Watson has come from Afghanistan. | _____ |
| | _____ |

➤ • ◄     Return to the list of factual statements you created on page 392 to describe a neighborhood that you are familiar with. For *each* factual statement you listed, create an inferential statement that is based on that particular factual statement. For example:

*Factual statement:* Many of the small businesses in Greenwich Village—mom and pop groceries, tailors, coffee shops with soda fountains—have been replaced with expensive restaurants and exclusive boutiques.

*Inferential statement:* There has been a significant increase in the commercial rents, driving out the small businesses that can't pay these rents.

---

[1]From "A Study in Scarlet," in *The Complete Works of Sherlock Holmes*, by Sir Arthur Conan Doyle (New York: Doubleday, 1930).

## Judging

In the space provided below, identify and describe a friend that you have, a course you have taken, and the school that you attend. Be sure that your descriptions are specific and include what you think about the friend, the course, and the school.

1. _____ is a friend that I have.

   He/she is _____

   _____

   _____

   _____

2. _____ is a course I have taken.

   It was _____

   _____

   _____

   _____

3. _____ is the school I attend.

   It is _____

   _____

   _____

   _____

   Now review your responses. Do they include *factual* descriptions? For each response, describe in the space below the factual information that can be verified.

1. _____

   _____

2. _____

   _____

3. _____

   _____

In addition to factual reports, your descriptions may contain *inferences* about them based on factual information. Can you identify any inferences? Describe them below.

1. _____
   _____
2. _____
   _____
3. _____
   _____

In addition to inferences, your descriptions may also include *judgments* about them. When we judge, we express *our evaluation* of what we are observing or experiencing based on certain criteria. So while facts and inferences are designed to help us figure out what is actually happening (or will happen), the purpose of judgments is to express our evaluation about what is happening (or will happen). For example:

My new car has broken down three times in the first six months. (Fact)

My new car will probably continue to have difficulties. (Inference)

My new car is a lemon. (Judgment)

When we pronounce our new car a "lemon," we are making a judgment based on certain criteria we have in mind. For instance, a "lemon" is usually a newly purchased item with which we have repeated problems—generally an automobile.

To take another example of judging, consider the following statements:

Carla always does her work thoroughly and completes it on time. (Fact)

Carla will probably continue to do her work in this fashion. (Inference)

Carla is a very responsible person. (Judgment)

By judging Carla to be responsible, we are evaluating her on the basis of the criteria that we believe indicate a responsible person. One such criterion is completing assigned work on time. Can you identify additional criteria for judging someone to be responsible? (You may want to review our discussion of the concept of responsibility in Chapter Nine, page 325.)

*Criteria for Judging Someone as Responsible:*

1. Completing assigned work on time
2. _____
3. _____
4. _____

Review your descriptions of a friend, a course, and your school (p. 403). ➤•◄
Can you identify any judgments in your descriptions? If so, list them below.

1. *Friend:* _____

    *Judgment(s):* _____

    _____

2. *Course:* _____

    *Judgment(s):* _____

    _____

3. *School:* _____

    *Judgment(s):* _____

    _____

For each judgment you have listed, identify the criteria on which the judgment
is based.

1. *Judgment:* _____

    *Criteria:*
    a. _____

    b. _____

2. *Judgment:* _____

    *Criteria:* _____
    a. _____

    b. _____

3. *Judgment:* _____

    *Criteria:* _____
    a. _____

    b. _____

When we judge, we are often expressing our feelings of approval or disapproval. However, sometimes we make judgments that conflict with what we
personally approve of. For example:

> I think a woman should be able to have an abortion if she chooses to, al-
> though I don't believe it's right.

> I can see why you think that person is very beautiful, even though he or she
> is not the type that appeals to me.

In fact, at times it is essential to disregard our personal feelings of approval or disapproval when we judge. The judges in our justice system, for instance, should render evaluations based on the law, not on their personal preferences.

---

➤ • ◄        Consider the judgments you stated on page 405. Do they express evaluations of which you personally approve, or are they independent of your personal preferences?

### Discussing differences in judgments

Many of our disagreements with other people focus on differences in judgments. For example:

> That is a very professional musical group.

> That is a very amateurish musical group.

As critical thinkers, we need to approach such differences in judgments intelligently. We can do so by following these guidelines:

1. *Making explicit* the criteria being used as a basis for the judgment
2. Trying to *establish the reasons* that justify these criteria

For instance, if I make the judgment "That's a beautiful Alaskan malamute," I am basing my judgment on certain criteria of malamute beauty. Once these standards are made explicit, we can discuss whether they make sense and what is the justification for them. If we rely on observing and describing the physical characteristics of the dog—height, weight, shape, coat, etc.—we will never determine whether our judgment ("That's a beautiful malamute.") makes sense. Our idea of what makes for a beautiful malamute may be completely different from someone else's idea of malamute beauty. Our only hope for resolving the issue is to

1. make explicit the standards we are using to judge malamute beauty.
2. give reasons that justify these criteria. E.g., "These are the criteria established by the American Kennel Club, and they reflect an overall sense of strength, balance, and proportion. In addition these criteria evaluate the physical qualities needed for the sled-pulling tasks of the malamute."

Understanding how judgments function is also important in order to encourage us to continue thinking critically about a situation. For instance, the judgment "This course is worthless!" does not encourage further exploration and critical analysis. In fact, it may prevent such an analysis by *discouraging* further exploration. Judgments seem to summarize the situation in a final sort of way. And because judgments are sometimes made *before* we have a clear and complete understanding of the situation, they can serve to *prevent* us from seeing that situation as clearly and completely as we might. Of course, if we understand that all judgments are based on criteria that may or may not be adequately justified, we can explore these judgments further by making the criteria explicit and examining the reasons that justify them.

## Distinguishing reports, inferences, and judgments

Although the activities of reporting, inferring, and judging tend to be woven together in our experience, it is important for us to be able to distinguish them. Each of these activities plays a different role in helping us make sense of our world, and we should be careful not to confuse these roles. For example, although people may appear to be reporting factual information, they may actually be expressing personal evaluations, which are not factual. Consider the statement: "New York City is a filthy and dangerous pigpen." While seeming to be reporting factual information, the speaker is really expressing his or her personal judgment. Of course, speakers can identify their judgments with such phrases as "In my opinion" or "My evaluation is," etc. Sometimes, however, speakers do not identify their judgments because they want us to treat their judgments as factual information. Confusing the activities of reporting, inferring, and judging can be misleading and even dangerous.

Confusing factual information with judgments can be personally damaging as well. For example, there is a big difference between the statements:

I failed my exam today. (Fact)

I am a failure. (Judgment)

Stating the fact "I failed my exam today" describes our situation in a concrete way, enabling us to see it as a problem we can hope to solve through reflection and hard work. On the other hand, if we make the judgment "I am a failure," this sort of general evaluation does not encourage us to explore solutions to the problem or improve our situation.

Finally, another important reason for distinguishing the activities of reporting, inferring, and judging concerns the accuracy of our statements. For instance, we noted that factual statements tend to be reasonably accurate since they are by nature verifiable whereas inferences are usually much less certain. As a result, it is crucial for us to know what type of belief we are dealing with so that we can accurately evaluate the probability of its being true. If we treat an inference—for instance, "I don't think that this exam will be very difficult so I'm not going to bother to study "—as if it had the certainty of a factual statement, we may find ourselves in an unexpected predicament.

---

➤•◄        In the list of statements below, identify the factual reports, the inferences, and the judgments.

a.   For every *factual report* you identify, describe how you might go about verifying the information.

b.   For every *inference* you identify, describe a factual report on which it could be based.

c.   For every *judgment* you identify, list the criteria on which the judgment is based.

1.  He's the best athlete on the team.

_____

_____

_____

2.  Look at the syllabus for this course—it's going to involve a lot of reading.

_____

_____

_____

3.  My mother is a saint.

_____

_____

_____

4.  People on welfare are lazy because they're not working.

_____

_____

_____

5.  You shouldn't waste your time in college when you could be earning real money.

_____

_____

_____

6.  Only the strong survive.

_____

_____

7. Look at the size of those tracks in the snow—there's a very large deer around here.

_____

_____

_____

8. That book is nothing but trash—and I love it!

_____

_____

_____

9. Women's bodybuilding is ridiculous.

_____

_____

_____

10. We all agreed that it was a very exciting movie.

_____

_____

_____

11. That was the dullest lecture I've ever had the displeasure of listening to.

_____

_____

_____

12. She's a beautiful person.

_____

_____

_____

Review the list of factual statements and inferential statements you made concerning your neighborhood (pp. 392 and 402). Using these statements as a basis, develop a list of ten to twelve statements that express judgments about your neighborhood.

*Example:*

*Factual statement:* Many of the small businesses in Greenwich Village—mom and pop groceries, tailors, coffee shops with soda fountains—have been replaced with expensive restaurants and exclusive boutiques.

*Inferential statement:* There has been a significant increase in the commerical rents, driving out the small businesses that can't pay these rents.

*Judgment:* I think that the trend away from small, privately owned businesses is unfortunate because it reduces the diversity of the neighborhood, it makes residents walk further for needed services, and it decreases our sense of being a member of a social community.

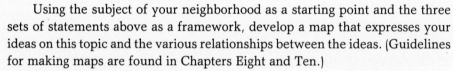

Using the subject of your neighborhood as a starting point and the three sets of statements above as a framework, develop a map that expresses your ideas on this topic and the various relationships between the ideas. (Guidelines for making maps are found in Chapters Eight and Ten.)

Using this map as a guide, write an essay about your neighborhood.

# Chapter Twelve
# Constructing Arguments

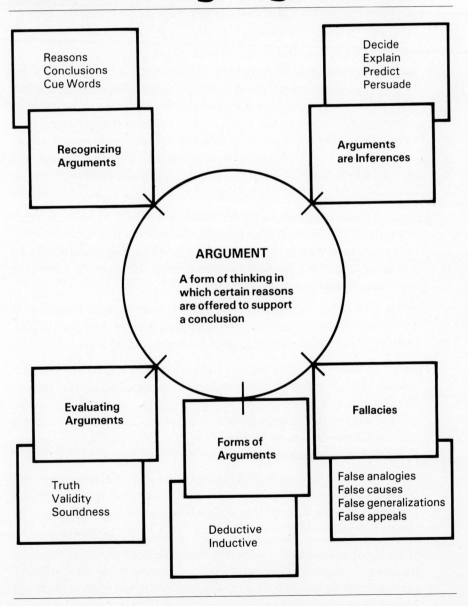

Reasons
Conclusions
Cue Words

Recognizing
Arguments

Decide
Explain
Predict
Persuade

Arguments
are Inferences

ARGUMENT

A form of thinking in
which certain reasons
are offered to support
a conclusion

Evaluating
Arguments

Truth
Validity
Soundness

Forms of
Arguments

Deductive
Inductive

Fallacies

False analogies
False causes
False generalizations
False appeals

CONSIDER CAREFULLY the following discussion regarding whether marijuana should be legalized:

*Dennis:*  Did you hear about the person who was sentenced to fifteen
years in prison for possessing marijuana? I think this is one of the most
outrageously unjust punishments I've ever heard of! In most states, people who are convicted of armed robbery, rape, or even murder don't receive fifteen-year sentences.

*Caroline:*  I agree that this is one case in which the punishment doesn't
seem to fit the crime. But you have to realize that drugs pose a serious
threat to the young people of our country. Look at all the people who are
addicted to drugs, who have their lives ruined, and who often die at an
early age of overdoses. And think of all the crimes that are committed
by people in order to support their drug habits. As a result, sometimes society has to make an example of someone—like the person you
mentioned—in order to convince people of the seriousness of the situation.

*Dennis:*  That's ridiculous. In the first place, it's not right to punish someone unfairly just to provide an example. At least not in a society that believes in justice. And in the second place, smoking marijuana is nothing
like using drugs such as heroin or even cocaine. It follows that smoking
marijuana should not be against the law.

*Caroline:*  I don't agree. Although marijuana might not be as dangerous as
some other drugs, smoking it surely isn't good for you. And I don't think
that anything that is a threat to your health should be legal.

*Dennis:*  What about cigarettes and alcohol? We *know* that they are dangerous. Medical research has linked smoking cigarettes to lung cancer,
emphysema, and heart disease, while alcohol damages your liver. No
one has proved that marijuana is a threat to our health. And even if it
does turn out to be somewhat unhealthy, it's certainly not as dangerous
as cigarettes and alcohol.

*Caroline:*  That's a good point. But to tell you the truth, I'm not so sure that
cigarettes and alcohol should be legal. And in any case, they are already
legal. Just because cigarettes and alcohol are bad for your health is no
reason to legalize another drug that can cause health problems.

*Dennis:*  Look—life is full of risks. We take chances every time we cross
the street or climb into our car. In fact, with all of those loonies on the
road, driving is a lot more hazardous to our health than any of the drugs
around. And many of the foods we eat can kill. For example, red meat

and artificial sweeteners can cause cancer. The point is, if people want to take chances with their health, that's up to them. And many people in our society like to mellow out with marijuana. Even people like Jimmy Carter say it probably should be legalized. I read somewhere that over 70 percent of the people in the United States think that marijuana should be legalized.

*Caroline:* There's a big difference between letting people drive cars and letting them use dangerous drugs. Society has a responsibility to protect people from themselves. People often do things that are foolish if they are encouraged or given the opportunity to. Legalizing something like marijuana encourages people to use it, especially young people. It follows that, if it were legalized, many more people would use it. It's like society saying "This is all right—go ahead and use it."

*Dennis:* I still maintain that marijuana isn't dangerous. It's not addictive—like heroin is—and there is no evidence that it harms you. Consequently, anything that is harmless should be legal.

*Caroline:* Marijuana may not be physically addictive like heroin, but I think that it can be psychologically addictive, because people tend to use more and more of it over time. I know a number of people who spend a lot of their time getting high. What about Carl? All he does is lie around and get high. This shows that smoking it over a period of time definitely affects your mind. Think about the people you know who smoke a lot—don't they seem to be floating in a dream world? How are they ever going to make anything of their lives? As far as I'm concerned, a pothead is like a zombie—living but dead.

*Dennis:* Since you have had so little experience with marijuana, I don't think that you can offer an informed opinion on the subject. And anyway, if you do too much of anything it can hurt you. Even something as healthy as exercise can cause problems if you do too much of it. But I sure don't see anything wrong with toking up with some friends at a party or even getting into a relaxed state by yourself. In fact, I find that I can even concentrate better on my schoolwork after taking a little smoke.

*Caroline:* If you really believe that, then marijuana really has damaged your brain. You're just trying to rationalize your drug habit. Smoking marijuana doesn't help you concentrate—it takes you away from reality. And I don't think that people can control it. Either you smoke and surrender control of your life, or you don't smoke because you want to retain control. There's nothing in between.

*Dennis:* Let me point out something to you. Because marijuana is illegal, organized crime controls its distribution and makes all the money out of it. If marijuana were legalized, the government could tax the sale of it—like cigarettes and alcohol—and then use the money for some worthwhile purpose. For example, many states have legalized gambling and use the money to support education. In fact, the major tobacco companies have already copyrighted names for different marijuana brands —like "Acapulco Gold." Obviously they believe that marijuana will soon become legal.

*Caroline:* Just because the government can make money out of something doesn't mean that they should legalize it. We could also legalize prostitution or muggings, and then tax the proceeds. Also, simply because the cigarette companies are prepared to sell marijuana doesn't mean that it makes sense to. After all, they're the ones who are selling us cigarettes.

---

➤•◄     Complete this dialogue, incorporating other views on the subject of legalizing marijuana.

*Dennis:*  _____

_____

_____

_____

*Caroline:*  _____

_____

_____

_____

*Dennis:*  _____

_____

_____

_____

*Caroline:*  _____

_____

_____

_____

# Recognizing arguments

The preceding discussion is an illustration of two people engaging in dialogue, which we have defined (in Chapter Three) as the systematic exchange of ideas. Participating in this sort of dialogue with others is one of the keys to thinking critically because it stimulates us to develop our minds by carefully examining the way we make sense of the world. Discussing issues with others encourages us to be mentally active, to ask questions, to view issues from different perspectives, and to develop reasons to support our conclusions. It is this last quality of thinking critically—supporting our conclusions with reasons—that we will focus on in this final chapter.

When we offer reasons to support a conclusion, we are considered to be presenting an *argument*. For instance, at the beginning of the previous discussion, Dennis presents the following argument concerning the person who was given a fifteen-year sentence for possessing marijuana:

*Reason:*   Possessing marijuana is not a serious offense.

*Reason:*   There are many other more serious offenses—such as armed robbery, rape, and murder—that don't receive such stiff sentences.

*Conclusion:*   Therefore this fifteen-year sentence is an unjust punishment.

Can you identify an additional reason that supports this conclusion?

*Reason:*   _____

_____

From this example, we can see that an argument is a form of human thinking in which certain statements (reasons) are offered in support of another statement (a conclusion).

**Argument** • A form of thinking in which certain statements (reasons) are offered in support of another statement (a conclusion).

This definition of *argument* is somewhat different from the meaning of the concept in our ordinary language. In common speech, "argument" usually refers to a dispute or quarrel between people, often involving intense feelings. (For example: "I got into a terrible argument with the idiot who hit the back of my car.") Very often these quarrels involve people presenting arguments in the sense we have defined the concept, although the arguments are usually not carefully reasoned or clearly stated because the people are so angry. Despite this common meaning of argument as a quarrel among people, we are going to maintain our more technical meaning of it as a form of human thinking in which certain statements (reasons) are offered in support of some other statement (a conclusion).

Based on this concept of argument, we can define the main ideas that make up an argument:

**Reasons** • Statements that support another statement (known as a conclusion), justify it, or make it more probable.

**Conclusion** • A statement that explains, asserts, or predicts on the basis of statements (known as reasons) that are offered as evidence for it.

The type of thinking that uses argument—reasons in support of conclusions—is known as *reasoning,* and it is a type of thinking that we have been doing throughout this book, as well as in much of our lives. We are continually trying to explain, justify, and predict things by reasoning in this way.

Of course, our reasoning—and the reasoning of others—is not always correct. For example, the reasons someone offers may not really support the conclusion they are supposed to. Or the conclusion that is stated may not really follow from the reasons stated. These difficulties are illustrated in a number of the arguments contained in the discussion on marijuana. Nevertheless, whenever we accept a conclusion as likely or true based on certain reasons or whenever we offer reasons to support a conclusion, we are using arguments to engage in reasoning—even if our reasoning is weak or faulty and needs to be improved. In this chapter we will be carefully exploring both the way that we construct effective arguments and the way that we evaluate arguments in order to develop and sharpen our reasoning ability.

Let us return to the discussion about marijuana to look at another argument. After Dennis presents the argument ending with the conclusion that the fifteen-year prison sentence is an unjust punishment, Caroline considers that argument. Although she acknowledges that "In this case the punishment doesn't seem to fit the crime," she goes on to offer reasons that lead to a conflicting conclusion:

*Reason:* Drugs pose a very serious threat to the young people of our country.

*Reason:* Many crimes are committed in order to support drug habits.

*Conclusion:* As a result, sometimes society has to make an example of someone in order to convince people of the seriousness of the situation.

Can you identify an additional reason that supports this conclusion?

*Reason:* _____

_____

## Cue words for arguments

Our language provides guidance in our efforts to identify reasons and conclusions. There are certain key words, known as *cue words,* which signal that a reason is being offered in support of a conclusion or that a conclusion is being announced on the basis of certain reasons. For example, in response to Caroline's conclusion that society sometimes has to make an example of someone in order to convince people of the seriousness of the situation, Dennis gives the following argument:

*Reason:* In the first place, it's not right to punish someone unfairly just to provide an example.

*Reason:* In the second place, smoking marijuana is nothing like using drugs such as heroin or even cocaine.

*Conclusion:* It follows that smoking marijuana should not be against the law.

In this argument, the phrases "In the first place" and "In the second place" signal that reasons are being offered in support of a conclusion. Similarly, the phrase "It follows that" signals that a conclusion is being announced on the basis of certain reasons. Here is a list of the most commonly used cue words for reasons and conclusions:

### Cue Words Signaling Reasons

| | |
|---|---|
| since | in view of |
| for | first, second |
| because | in the first (second) place |
| as shown by | may be inferred from |
| as indicated by | may be deduced from |
| given that | may be derived from |
| assuming that | for the reason that |

### Cue Words Signaling Conclusions

| | |
|---|---|
| therefore | then |
| thus | it follows that |
| hence | thereby showing |

*Cue Words Signaling Conclusions*

| | |
|---|---|
| so | demonstrates that |
| (which) shows that | allows us to infer that |
| (which) proves that | suggests very strongly that |
| implies that | you see that |
| points to | leads me to believe that |
| as a result | allows us to infer that |
| consequently | allows us to deduce that |

Of course, identifying reasons, conclusions, and arguments involves more than looking for cue words. The words and phrases just listed do not always signal reasons and conclusions, and in many cases arguments are made without the use of cue words. However, cue words do help to alert us that an argument is being made.

---

►•◄     Review the discussion on marijuana and underline any cue words signaling that reasons are being offered or that conclusions are being announced.

---

►•◄     With the aid of cue words, identify the various arguments contained in the discussion concerning marijuana. For each argument describe

a.   the *reasons* that are being offered in support of a conclusion.
b.   the *conclusion* that is being announced on the basis of the reasons.

Before you get started, review the three arguments we have examined so far in this chapter.

---

►•◄     Review the arguments that you have identified and see if you can name any additional reasons that could support the various conclusions.

---

►•◄     Construct two additional arguments, one in favor of legalizing marijuana and one opposed to it. Clearly identify your reasons as well as the conclusion you draw from those reasons. Also, explain how your reasons support your conclusion.

# Arguments are inferences

When we construct arguments, we are composing and relating the world by means of our ability to infer. As we saw in the last chapter, inferring is a thinking process that we use to reason from what we already know (or believe to be the case) to new knowledge or beliefs. This is usually what we do when we construct arguments. We work from reasons that we know or believe in to conclusions that are based on these reasons.

Just as inferring can be used to make sense of different types of situations, so we can also construct arguments for different purposes. In a variety of situations, we construct arguments to make sense of what is taking place and to decide, explain, predict, and persuade. An example of each of these different types of arguments is listed below. After each example, construct an argument of the same type.

### We construct arguments to decide
A. *Reason:*  Throughout my life, I've always been interested in all different kinds of electricity.

   *Reason:*  There are many attractive job opportunities in the field of electrical engineering.

   *Conclusion:*  I think that I will work toward becoming an electrical engineer.

B. *Reason:* _____

   _____

   *Reason:* _____

   _____

   *Conclusion:* _____

   _____

### We construct arguments to explain
A. *Reason:*  I was delayed leaving my house because my dog needed an emergency walking.

   *Reason:*  There was an unexpected traffic jam caused by motorists slowing down to view an overturned chicken truck.

   *Conclusion:*  Therefore I was late for our appointment.

B.  *Reason:*  _____

_____

*Reason:*  _____

_____

*Conclusion:*  _____

_____

## We construct arguments to predict

A.  *Reason:*  People often do foolish things if they are given the opportunity.

*Reason:*  Legalizing something like marijuana encourages people to use it.

*Conclusion:*  It follows that, if marijuana is legalized, many more people would use it.

B.  *Reason:*  _____

_____

*Reason:*  _____

_____

*Conclusion:*  _____

_____

## We construct arguments to persuade

A.  *Reason:*  If criminals think that killing someone will result in their own death, then they will be more likely to think twice about it.

*Reason:*  The Old Testament of the Bible endorses revenge when it states "An eye for an eye and a tooth for a tooth."

*Conclusion:*  This leads me to believe that we should practice capital punishment. Don't you agree?

B.  *Reason:*  _____

_____

*Reason:*  _____

_____

*Conclusion:*  _____

_____

# Evaluating arguments

In order to be able to construct effective arguments, we must be skilled in evaluating the effectiveness of arguments already constructed. There are two aspects of each argument that must be investigated independently in order to determine the effectiveness of the argument as a whole.

1. How true are the reasons being offered to support the conclusion?
2. To what extent do the reasons support the conclusion or to what extent does the conclusion follow from the reasons offered?

We will first examine each of these ways of evaluating arguments separately and then see how they work together.

### How true are the reasons being offered to support the conclusion?

This aspect of evaluating arguments deals with trying to determine the truth of the reasons that are being used to support a conclusion. Does the reason make sense? What evidence is being offered as part of the reason? Do I know the reason to be true based on my experience? Is the reason based on a source that can be trusted? We use these questions and others like them to analyze the reasons offered and to determine how true they are. As we saw in Chapter Six, "Believing and Knowing," evaluating the sort of beliefs that are usually found as reasons in arguments is a complex and ongoing challenge. Let us evaluate the truth of the reasons presented in our initial discussion.

*Argument 1*

*Reason:* Possessing marijuana is not a serious offense.

*Evaluation:* As it stands, this reason needs further evidence to support it. The major issue of the discussion is whether or not possessing (and using) marijuana is in fact a serious offense or no offense at all. This reason would be strengthened by stating: "Possessing marijuana is not as serious an offense as armed robbery, rape, and murder." Most people would probably agree that this reason is true.

*Reason:* There are many other more serious offenses—such as armed robbery, rape, and murder—that don't receive such stiff sentences.

*Evaluation:* The accuracy of this reason is highly doubtful. It is true that there is wide variation in the sentences handed down for the same offense. The sentences vary from state to state and also vary within states and even within the same court. Nevertheless, on the whole, serious offenses like armed robbery, rape, and murder do receive long prison sentences. The real point here is that a fifteen-year sentence for possessing marijuana is extremely unusual when compared to other sentences for marijuana possession.

## Argument 2

*Reason:*  Drugs pose a very serious threat to the young people of our country.

*Evaluation:*  As the later discussion points out, this statement is much too vague. "Drugs" cannot be treated as being all the same. Some drugs are beneficial (such as aspirin) while other drugs are highly dangerous (such as heroin). In order to strengthen this reason, we would have to be more specific, stating "Drugs like heroin, amphetamines, and angel dust pose a very serious threat to the young people of our country." We could increase the accuracy of the reason even more by adding the qualification "*some of* the young people of our country" since there are many young people not involved with dangerous drugs.

*Reason:*  Many crimes are committed in order to support drug habits.

*Evaluation:* _____

_____

_____

_____

_____

_____

## Argument 3

*Reason:*  It's not right to punish someone unfairly just to provide an example.

*Evaluation:*  This reason raises an interesting and complex ethical question that has been debated for centuries. The political theorist Machiavelli stated that "The ends justify the means," which implies that if we bring about desirable results it does not matter how we go about doing it. He would therefore probably disagree with this reason, since using someone as an example might bring about desirable results, even though it might be personally unfair to the person being used as an example. However, in our society, which is based on the idea of fairness under the law, most people would probably agree with this reason.

*Reason:*  Smoking marijuana is nothing like using drugs such as heroin or even cocaine.

*Evaluation:* _____

_____

_____

_____

_____

_____

Review the other arguments from the discussion on marijuana that you identified on page 418. Evaluate the truth of each of the reasons contained in the arguments.

**To what extent do the reasons support the conclusion or to what extent does the conclusion follow from the reasons offered?**

In addition to determining whether the reasons are true, evaluating arguments involves investigating the *relationship* between the reasons and the conclusion. When the reasons support the conclusion, so that the conclusion follows from the reasons being offered, the argument is *valid*.[1] However, if the reasons do *not* support the conclusion so that the conclusion does *not* follow from the reasons being offered, the argument is *invalid*. One way to focus on the concept of validity is to *assume* that all the reasons in the argument are true, and then try to determine how probable they make the conclusion. Let us explore some examples of valid and invalid arguments.

*Valid Argument*

*Reason:*  Anything that is a threat to our health should not be legal.

*Reason:*  Marijuana is a threat to our health.

*Conclusion:*  Therefore marijuana should not be legal.

*Explanation:*  This is a valid argument because, if we assume that the reasons are true, then the conclusion necessarily follows. Of course, we

---

[1]In formal logic, the term *validity* is reserved for deductively valid arguments in which the conclusions follow necessarily from the premises. For our purposes, we will be using *validity* in its more common sense to refer to the degree to which our reasons support our conclusion. Arguments that are valid in this sense are those in which the premises provide strong support for the conclusions. Although such arguments may be deductively valid, they are not necessarily so.

may not agree that either or both of the reasons are true and so not agree with the conclusion. Nevertheless, the *form* of the argument is valid. This particular form of thinking is known as *deduction,* and we will examine deductive reasoning more closely in the pages ahead.

### Valid Argument

*Reason:*   As part of a project in my social science class, we selected 100 students in the school to be interviewed. We took special steps to insure that these students were representative of the student body as a whole (total students, 4,386). We asked the selected students whether they thought that the United States should actively try to overthrow foreign governments that the United States disapproves of. Of the 100 students interviewed, 88 students said the United States should definitely *not* be involved in such activities.

*Conclusion:*   We can conclude that most students in the school believe that the United States should not be engaged in attempts to actively overthrow foreign governments that the United States disapproves of.

*Explanation:*   This is a valid argument because, if we assume that the reason is true, then it provides strong support for the conclusion. In this case, the key part of the reason is the statement that the 100 students selected were representative of the entire 4,386 students at the school. In order to evaluate the truth of the reason, we might want to investigate the procedures used to select the 100 students in order to determine whether this sample was in fact representative of all the students. This particular form of thinking is known as *induction*, and we will explore inductive reasoning more fully in the sections that follow.

### Invalid Argument

*Reason:*   Former President Jimmy Carter believes that marijuana should be legalized.

*Reason:*   Jimmy Carter is an intelligent person.

*Conclusion:*   Therefore marijuana should be legalized.

*Explanation:*   This argument is *not* valid because even if we assume that the reasons are true, the conclusion does not follow. Although Jimmy Carter is an intelligent person and served as president, these facts do not give him any special expertise on the question of legalizing marijuana, nor is this a question that should be based on any one person's opinion, no matter who that person is. This particular form of thinking illustrates a type of *fallacy,* and we will be investigating fallacious reasoning later on in this chapter.

## The soundness of arguments

When an argument includes both true reasons and a valid structure, the argument is considered to be *sound*. However, when an argument has either false reasons or an invalid structure, the argument is considered to be *unsound*.

True reasons

Valid structure ⟩ ————————————————→ Sound argument

False reasons

Valid structure ⟩ ————————————————→ Unsound argument

True reasons

Invalid structure ⟩ ————————————————→ Unsound argument

False reasons

Invalid structure ⟩ ————————————————→ Unsound argument

From this chart, we can see that, in terms of arguments, "truth" and "validity" are not the same concepts. An argument can have true reasons and an invalid structure or false reasons and a valid structure. In both cases the argument is *unsound*. To be sound, an argument must have *both* true reasons and a valid structure. For example, consider the following argument:

*Reason:*  In order for a democracy to function most effectively, the citizens should be able to think critically about the important social and political issues.

*Reason:*  Education plays a key role in developing critical thinking abilities.

*Conclusion:*  Therefore education plays a key role in insuring that a democracy is functioning most effectively.

A good case could be made for the soundness of this argument because the reasons are strong and the argument structure is valid. Of course, someone might contend that one or both of the reasons are not completely true, which illustrates an important point about the arguments we construct and evaluate. Many of the arguments we encounter in life fall somewhere in between complete soundness and complete unsoundness.

First, we are often not sure if our reasons are completely true. Throughout this book we have found that developing accurate beliefs is an ongoing process and that our beliefs are subject to clarification and revision. As a result, the conclusion of any argument can be only as certain as the reasons supporting the conclusion. Second, this same idea applies to the concept of validity, which reflects the degree to which our reasons support our conclusion. In addition to being completely valid or completely invalid, many of the arguments we deal with fall in between these extremes. As we have noted, one helpful strategy for evaluating the degree of validity of an argument is to assume that the reasons offered are true and then try to determine how probable the reasons make the conclusion.

To sum up, evaluating arguments effectively involves both the truth of the reasons and the validity of the argument structure. The degree of soundness an argument has depends on how accurate our reasons turn out to be and how valid the argument's structure is.

## Forms of arguments

There are a number of basic argument forms that we normally use to organize, relate, and make sense of the world. Two of the major types of argument forms are *deductive arguments* and *inductive arguments*.

### Deductive arguments

The deductive argument is the one most commonly associated with the study of logic. Though it has a variety of valid forms, they all share one characteristic: if you accept the supporting reasons (also called *premises*) as true, then you must necessarily accept the conclusion as being true.

**Deductive Argument** • Reasoning from premises which are known or assumed to be true to a conclusion which follows logically from these premises.

For example, consider the following famous deductive argument:

*Reason/Premise:*   All men are mortal.

*Reason/Premise:*   Socrates is a man.

*Conclusion:*   Therefore Socrates is mortal.

In this example of deductive thinking, accepting the premises of the argument as true means that the conclusion necessarily follows; it cannot be false. Many deductive arguments, like the argument above, are structured as *syllogisms,* an argument form that consists of two supporting premises and a conclusion. However, there is also a large number of *invalid* deductive forms, one of which is illustrated in Woody Allen's syllogism:

*Reason/Premise:*   All men are mortal.

*Reason/Premise:*   Socrates is a man.

*Conclusion:*   Therefore all men are Socrates.

In the next several pages, we will briefly examine some common valid deductive forms.

***Applying a general rule***   Whenever we reason by using the form illustrated by the valid Socrates syllogism, we are using the following argument structure:

*Premise:*   All A (men) are B (mortal).

*Premise:*   S is an A (Socrates is a man).

*Conclusion:*   Therefore S is a B (Socrates is mortal).

This basic argument form is valid, no matter what terms are included. For example:

*Premise:*   All politicians are untrustworthy.

*Premise:*   Bill White is a politician.

*Conclusion:*   Therefore, Bill White is untrustworthy.

Notice again that, with any valid deductive form, *if* we assume that the premises are true, then we must accept the conclusion. Of course, in this case there is considerable doubt that the first premise is actually true.

When we diagram this argument form, it becomes clear why it is a valid way of thinking:

The *first premise* states that classification A (men) falls within classification B (mortal).

The *second premise* states that S (Socrates) is a member of classification A (men).

The *conclusion* simply states what has now become obvious—namely, that S (Socrates) must fall within classification B (mortal).

Although we are usually not aware of it, we use this basic type of reasoning whenever we apply a general rule in the form *All A is B.* For instance:

*Premise:*   All children eight years old should be in bed by 9:30 P.M.

*Premise:*   You are an eight-year-old child.

*Conclusion:*   Therefore you should be in bed by 9:30 P.M.

---

►•◄     Review the discussion at the beginning of this chapter and see if you can identify any deductive arguments that use this form.

*Premise:*  _____

*Premise:*  _____

*Conclusion:*  _____

---

►•◄     Describe an example from your own experience in which you use this deductive form.

*Premise:*  _____

*Premise:*  _____

*Conclusion:*  _____

**Modus ponens**   Another valid deductive form that we commonly use in our thinking goes by the name *modus ponens*—that is, "affirming the antecedent"—and is illustrated in the following example:

*Premise:*   If I have prepared thoroughly for the final exam, then I will do well.

*Premise:*   I prepared thoroughly for the exam.

*Conclusion:*   Therefore I should do well on the exam.

When we reason like this, we are using the following argument structure:

*Premise:*   If A (I have prepared thoroughly), then B (I will do well).

*Premise:*   A (I have prepared thoroughly).

*Conclusion:*   Therefore B (I will do well).

Like all valid deductive forms, this form is valid no matter what specific terms are included. For example:

*Premise:*   If the Democrats are able to register 20 million new voters, then they will win the presidential election.

*Premise:*   The Democrats were able to register more than twenty million
   new voters.

*Conclusion:*   Therefore the Democrats will win the presidential election.

As with other valid argument forms, the conclusion will be true *only if* the reasons are true. Although the second premise in this argument expresses information which can be verified, the first premise would be more difficult to establish.

---

Review the discussion at the beginning of this chapter and see if you can   ➤•◄
identify any deductive arguments that use this form.

*Premise:*   _____

_____

*Premise:*   _____

_____

*Conclusion:*   _____

_____

---

Describe an example from your own experience in which you have used   ➤•◄
this deductive form.

*Premise:*   _____

_____

*Premise:*   _____

_____

*Conclusion:*   _____

_____

***Modus tollens***   A third commonly used valid deductive form has the
name *modus tollens*—that is, "denying the consequence"—and is illustrated in
the following example:

*Premise:*   If Michael were a really good friend, he would lend me his car
   for the weekend.

*Premise:*   Michael refuses to lend me his car for the weekend.

*Conclusion:*   Therefore Michael is not a really good friend.

When we reason in this fashion, we are using the following argument structure:

*Premise:*   If A (Michael is a really good friend) then B (He will lend me his car).

*Premise:*   Not B (He won't lend me his car).

*Conclusion:*   Therefore not A (He's not a really good friend).

Again, like other valid reasoning forms, this form is valid no matter what subject is being considered. For instance:

*Premise:*   If the Soviet Union were genuinely interested in nuclear disarmament, it would participate in the arms reduction talks.

*Premise:*   The Soviet Union refuses to participate in the arms reduction talks.

*Conclusion:*   Therefore the Soviet Union is not genuinely interested in nuclear disarmament.

This conclusion—and any other conclusion produced by this form of reasoning—can be considered accurate only if the reasons are true. In this case, the second premise would probably be easier to verify than the first.

---

►•◄        Review the discussion at the beginning of this chapter (pp. 412–414) and see if you can identify any deductive arguments that use this reasoning form.

*Premise:*   _____

_____

*Premise:*   _____

_____

*Conclusion:*   _____

_____

---

►•◄        Describe an example from your own experience in which you used this deductive form.

*Premise:*   _____

_____

*Premise:* _____

_____

*Conclusion:* _____

_____

***Disjunctive syllogism***   A fourth common form of a valid deductive argument is known as a *disjunctive syllogism.* The term *disjunctive* means presenting several alternatives, and in this context the alternatives are exclusive—that is, either one or the other of the alternatives is true, but not both. This form is illustrated in the following example:

*Premise:*   Either I left my wallet on my dresser or I have lost it.

*Premise:*   The wallet is not on my dresser.

*Conclusion:*   Therefore I must have lost it.

When we reason in this way, we are using the following argument structure:

*Premise:*   Either A (I left my wallet on my dresser) or B (I lost it).

*Premise:*   Not A (I didn't leave it on the dresser).

*Conclusion:*   Therefore B (I have lost it).

This valid reasoning form can be applied to any number of different situations and still yield valid results. For example:

*Premise:*   Either your stomach trouble is due to what you are eating or it is due to nervous tension.

*Premise:*   You tell me that you have been taking special care with your diet.

*Conclusion:*   Therefore your stomach trouble is due to nervous tension.

In order to determine the accuracy of the conclusion, it is necessary to determine the accuracy of the premises. If they are true, then the conclusion must be true.

Review the discussion at the beginning of this chapter and see if you can ➤•◄ identify any deductive arguments that use this reasoning form.

*Premise:* _____

_____

*Premise:* _____

_____

*Conclusion:* _____

_____

➤•◄     Describe an example from your own experience in which you used this deductive form.

*Premise:* _____

_____

*Premise:* _____

_____

*Conclusion:* _____

_____

All these basic argument forms—applying a general rule, *modus ponens, modus tollens,* and disjunctive syllogism—are found not only in our everyday conversations, but are used at every level of thinking. They appear in academic disciplines, in scientific inquiry, in debates on social issues, and so on. In addition to these common examples, there are many other argument forms that constitute human reasoning. By sharpening our understanding of these ways of thinking, we are better able to make sense of the world by constructing and evaluating effective arguments.

### Inductive arguments

Much of our reasoning is inductive. We saw in the previous section that deductive arguments are designed to provide conclusions that are certain. If we know the premises to be true and if the argument is organized into a valid deductive form, then the conclusion necessarily follows; it cannot be false. In contrast, inductive arguments rarely provide conclusions that are totally certain. This is because the process of reasoning by induction involves arriving at a conclusion based on incomplete evidence. For example, answer the following questions:

1. Identify a professor or a class that you decided to take on the recommendations of others.

_____

2.  Describe how you went about making your decision.

_____

_____

_____

This experience illustrates how you used the process of induction to reason from some incomplete information (known as a *sample*) to a conclusion based on this information.

Let us consider another example. Imagine that you have been assigned the task of finding out the class's views on legalizing marijuana. In the course of your investigation, you interview five students from the class of twenty-five. You discover that each of the five students interviewed favors legalization. At this point you might reason: if these five students support legalization, then it is likely that the rest of the class supports legalization as well. This conclusion is the product of induction, as you reasoned from a limited sample to a more general conclusion regarding the group from which the sample was taken.

**Inductive Argument**  •  Reasoning from a limited sample to a general conclusion based on this sample.

In this example it is obvious that your conclusion may not be correct. When evaluating our inductive arguments—and those of others—we should always ask ourselves the following questions:

*Is the sample known?*  It is important that we know what individuals constitute the sample that we are generalizing from. If someone begins an argument with a phrase like "People are saying" or "Everyone knows," we have a right to determine who these people actually are in order to evaluate the inductive conclusion that follows. In the case of the class interviews, the members of the sample *are* known.

*Is the sample sufficient?*  If an inductive conclusion is to be probable, the sample from which we are generalizing must be large enough to give an accurate sense of the group as a whole. For instance, if we interview only one class member from whom we then generalize to the class as a whole, our sample is clearly too small. This one view probably does not fairly represent the views of the other twenty-four class members. From this standpoint, interviewing five class members is probably not a sufficient number either. Naturally, the larger our sample, the better the chance that the sample will accurately reflect the group as a whole.

**_Is the sample representative?_**   In order for an inductive conclusion to be probable, the sample must fairly represent the various views found in the larger group. For instance, you might discover in your class project that the first five people you interviewed were friends of yours, who also happened to hold similar views on legalization. As a result, this initial sample may not fairly represent the group as a whole, which probably includes views that differ from yours and those of your friends. When scientific polling is done in order to determine political preferences, television viewing, and so on, great care is normally taken to make the sample as representative as possible. The more representative our sample, the more valid our conclusion.

---

   Listed below are a number of inductive arguments. In each case evaluate the probability of the conclusion by answering the following questions:

Is the sample known?

Is the sample sufficient?

Is the sample representative?

1. Young people really are dangerous drivers. Both of the accidents I've been involved in were with people under twenty-one. And my friends say the same thing.

   *Evaluation:* _____

   _____

   _____

2. "Four out of five dentists surveyed recommend Trident gum for their patients who chew gum."

   *Evaluation:*  _____

   _____

   _____

3. *The Hite Report* produced some surprising statistics regarding female sexuality. Its conclusions were based on the responses contained on three thousand questionnaires (one hundred thousand questionnaires were distributed). Questionnaires were mailed to various women's groups and abortion-rights groups. Additional questionnaires were sent to readers of

magazines like *Mademoiselle, Bride,* and *Ms.* who responded to notices
he project.

*tion:* _____

_____

_____

_____

Describe an example of inductive reasoning from your own experience,   ➤•◄
and then evaluate your conclusion by answering the three questions listed in
the preceding exercise.

## Pitfalls and fallacies

In this book we have been focusing our attention on the qualities of critical
thinking. Along the way we have explored some of the pitfalls in thinking that
we are all susceptible to. For example, in Chapter Three, "Thinking Critically,"
our analysis of the qualities of critical thinking involved looking at the qualities
of *un*critical thinking.

| *Critical Thinking* | *Uncritical Thinking* |
|---|---|
| Thinking actively | Thinking passively |
| Thinking for ourselves | Imitating the thinking of others |
| Carefully exploring a situation or issue | Reacting superficially or impulsively |
| Being open to new ideas and different viewpoints | Being closed-minded and stubborn |
| Supporting our ideas with reasons and evidence | Adopting and stating ideas without a supporting foundation |
| Being able to discuss our ideas in an organized way | Telling others what we believe without being able to listen and exchange views |

In Chapter Seven, "Language," we carefully examined the concepts of *ambiguity* and *vagueness*, exploring some of the ways that these qualities can interfere
with clear thinking and precise expression.

In this section we will be investigating some additional pitfalls in thinking—ways of making sense of the world that are not logical and, as a result, usually not effective. In particular, we will focus on *fallacies,* arguments that are

not sound because of various errors in reasoning. Although the reasoning of fallacious arguments is unsound, the arguments are often persuasive because they can appear to be logical; they usually appeal to our emotions and prejudices; and they often support conclusions that we want to believe are accurate.

**Fallacies** • Unsound arguments that are often persuasive because they can appear to be logical; they usually appeal to our emotions and prejudices; and they often support conclusions that we want to believe are accurate.

Fallacious reasoning is typically used to influence others and seeks to persuade not on the basis of sound arguments and critical thinking but rather on the basis of emotional and illogical factors.

Aristotle, a Greek philosopher, established the science of studying arguments (logic) in the fourth century B.C., and he was the first to classify the major types of fallacious reasoning. Let us explore some of the key fallacies that have been a part of human thinking for over two thousand years.

### False analogies

As we saw in Chapter Ten, "Composing," analogies can serve a number of useful purposes in relating and organizing our experience and ideas. However, they can be easily misused. Consider someone who urges the persecution of a group of people because "they are like infections spreading through a healthy organism." Or the salesman who urges you to buy a costly encyclopedia set so that "your children can climb the mountain of knowledge and gaze down from its towering heights." Or the government leaders who advocate beginning a war so that "we can stamp out this international plague," "show the world who is boss," and "be able to look at ourselves in the mirror again."

Analogies can be very illuminating. However, as these examples suggest, they can also be very dangerous. Analogies are often used to persuade at any cost, and when this occurs, they are working against the goals of critical thinking. As a result, when we create and evaluate analogies we have to be aware not only of the points of comparison or similarity but also to take into account the points of *dis*similarity. If we find that these points of dissimilarity are significant, we may have to reject the analogy as being misleading.

 Review the following analogies. Do you think they are misleading? If so, can you think of another compared subject that retains the points of comparison while eliminating the points of dissimilarity?

1. Being a student is like being a sponge—the less you know, the more you can soak up.
2. The relationship of a wife to her husband is like the relationship of a blocker to a running back—she creates the opportunities for his success.
3. The human mind is like a computer.
4. Getting married is like hitching two oxen to the same yoke.
5. The President of the United States is like the father of a family.

### False causes

Because causality plays such a dominant role in the way that we make sense of the world, there are many mistakes and errors in judgment made in connection with it. Let us look at some of the most common pitfalls associated with causality.

**Questionable cause**   The pitfall of *questionable cause* occurs when someone presents a causal relationship for which there is no real evidence. Superstitious beliefs often fall into this category, for instance, "Break a mirror and you are guaranteed seven years bad luck." Some people feel that the statements of astrology fall into this category.

---

Consider the following passage from St. Augustine's *Confessions*. Does it seem to support or deny the causal assertions of astrology? Why?

Firminus had heard from his father that when his mother had been pregnant with him, a slave belonging to a friend of his father's was also about to bear....It happened that since the two women had their babies at the same instant, the men were forced to cast exactly the same horoscope for each newborn child down to the last detail, one for his son, the other for the little slave....Yet Firminus, born to wealth in his parents' house, had one of the more illustrious careers in life...whereas the slave had no alleviation of his life's burden.

**Misidentification of the cause**   Very often in a causal situation we are not certain about what is causing what—in other words, what is the cause and what is the effect.

---

Examine the following pairs of items. Which are the causes and which are the effects? Why?

1. Poverty—lack of success
2. Headaches—tension

3. Failure in school—personal problems

4. Shyness—lack of confidence

5. Drug dependency—emotional difficulties

***Post hoc ergo propter hoc***   The translation of this Latin phrase is "After it, therefore because of it." It refers to those situations in which, because two things occur close together in time, we assume that one caused the other. For example, imagine that each time that you wore our favorite shirt, your team won the game. You might be tempted to conclude that the one event (wearing your favorite shirt) had some influence on the other event (winning the game). As a result, you might continue to wear this shirt "for good luck." It is easy to see how this sort of mistaken thinking can lead to all sorts of superstitious beliefs.

Consider the following causal conclusion arrived at by the fictional character Huckleberry Finn in the following passage. How would you analyze the conclusion that he comes to?

> I've always reckoned that looking at the new moon over your left shoulder is one of the carelessest and foolishest things a body can do. Old Hank Bunker done it once, and bragged about it; and in less than two years he got drunk and fell off a shot tower and spread himself out so that he was just a kind of layer. . . . But anyway, it all come of looking at the moon that way, like a fool.

➤•◄   Can you identify any of your own superstitious beliefs or practices that might have been the result of "post hoc" thinking? List two and explain how they originated.

1. _____

_____

2. _____

_____

***Slippery slope***   This causal pitfall is illustrated in the following advice:

Don't smoke that first marijuana cigarette. If you do, it won't be long before you are smoking hashish. Then you will soon be popping pills and snorting cocaine. Before you know it, you will be hooked on heroin, and you will end your life with a drug overdose in some rat-infested hotel room.

"Slippery slope" thinking asserts that one undesirable action will lead to a worse action, which will lead to a worse one still, all the way down the "slippery slope," until we reach some terrible disaster at the bottom. Although this progression may indeed happen, there is certainly no causal guarantee that it will.

---

Create "slippery slope" scenarios for the following warnings:

1. If you take that first drink...
2. If you fail that first test...
3. If the United States lets El Salvador go to the Communists...

---

Identify and explain the causal pitfalls illustrated in the following examples.

1. The person who won the lottery says that she dreamt the winning number. I'm going to start writing down the numbers in my dreams.

2. Yesterday I forgot to take my vitamins, and I immediately got sick. That mistake won't happen again!

3. I'm warning you—if you start missing classes, it won't be long before you fail out of school and ruin your future.

4. I always take the first seat in the bus. Today I took another seat, and the bus broke down. And you accuse me of being superstitious!

5. I think the reason I'm not doing well in school is because I'm just not interested. Also, I simply don't have enough time to study.

### False generalizations

In Chapter Nine, "Forming Concepts," we explored the way that we form concepts through the interactive process of generalizing (identifying the common qualities that define the boundaries of the concept) and interpreting (identifying examples of the concept). This is similar to the generalizing process involved in constructing inductive inferences, as we seek to reach a general conclusion based on a limited number of examples and then apply this conclusion to other examples. Each of these two activities—generalizing and interpreting—can give rise to fallacious ways of thinking, including the three we will examine in this section:

Hasty generalization
Sweeping generalization
False dilemma

***Hasty generalization***     Consider the following examples of reasoning. Do you think that the arguments are sound? Why or why not?

> My boyfriends have never shown any real concern for my feelings. My conclusion is that men are insensitive, selfish, and emotionally superficial.

> My mother always gets upset over insignificant things. This leads me to believe that women are very emotional.

In both of these cases, a general conclusion has been reached that is based on a very small sample. As a result, the reasons provide very weak support for the conclusions that are being developed. It just does not make good sense to generalize from a few individuals to all men or all women. Our conclusion is hasty because our sample is not large enough to provide adequate justification for our generalization.

Of course, many generalizations are more warranted because the conclusion is based on a sample that is larger and more representative of the group as a whole. For example:

> I've had many different teachers and I have spoken to other students about the teachers they have had. Based on these experiences I would conclude that the most effective teachers involve the students in the learning process instead of simply lecturing to them.

> I have done a lot of research on the relation between the size of cars and the gas mileage which they get. In general, I think that it makes sense to conclude that large cars tend to get fewer miles per gallon than smaller cars.

In both of these cases, the conclusions are generalized from samples that are larger and more representative than the samples in the preceding two arguments. As a result, the reasons of these latter arguments provide much stronger support for the conclusions.

Unfortunately, many of the general conclusions that we reach about the world are not legitimate because they are based on samples that are too small or not representative. In these cases, the generalization is a distortion because it creates a false impression of the group that is being represented. These illegitimate generalizations sometimes result in *stereotypes*—general conclusions about a group that are negative and destructive. Stereotypes affect our perception of the world because they encourage us to form an inaccurate idea of an entire group based on insufficient evidence ("Men are insensitive and selfish"). Even if we have experiences that conflict with our stereotype ("This man is not insensitive and selfish"), we tend to overlook the conflicting information in favor of the stereotype ("All men are insensitive and selfish—except for this one").

Review the discussion about legalizing marijuana offered at the beginning  of this chapter. Can you identify any hasty generalizations? If so, explain why you think a given generalization is not warranted.

Have you ever been the victim of a stereotyped generalization? Describe  the experience and explain why you believe that you were subjected to this kind of generalization.

There are many stereotypes in our culture—in advertising, in the movies, on television, in literature, and so on.

1. Describe one such stereotype.
2. Identify some specific examples of places where this stereotype is found.
3. Explain the reasons why you think that this stereotype developed.

**_Sweeping generalizations_**    While the fallacy of hasty generalization deals with errors in the process of generalizing, the fallacy of sweeping generalization focuses on difficulties in the process of interpreting. Consider the following examples of reasoning. Do you think that the arguments are sound? Why or why not?

> Vigorous exercise contributes to overall good health. Therefore vigorous exercise should be practiced by recent heart attack victims, people who are out of shape, and women who are about to give birth.

> People should be allowed to make their own decisions, providing that their actions do not harm other people. Therefore people who are trying to commit suicide should be left alone to do what they want.

In both of these cases, generalizations that are true in most cases have been deliberately applied to instances that are clearly intended to be exceptions to the generalizations because of special features that the exceptions possess. Of course, the use of sweeping generalizations stimulates us to clarify the generalization, rephrasing it to exclude instances that have special features like those above. For example, the first generalization above could be reformulated as "Vigorous exercise contributes to overall good health, _except for_ recent heart attack victims, people out of shape, and women who are about to give birth." Sweeping generalizations become dangerous only when they are accepted without critical analysis and reformulation.

► • ◄      Review the following arguments and identify those that you believe are examples of sweeping generalizations.

For each sweeping generalization you identify,

a.   explain *why* you believe it is a sweeping generalization.

b.   reformulate the statement so that it becomes a legitimate generalization.

1.   A college education stimulates you to develop as a person and prepares you for many professions. Therefore, everyone should attend college, no matter what career they are interested in.

2.   Drugs such as heroin and morphine are addictive and therefore dangerous drugs. This means that they should never be used, even as pain killers in medical situations.

3.   Once criminals have served time for the crimes they have committed, they have paid their debt to society and should be permitted to work at any job they choose.

*False dilemma*      The fallacy of the false dilemma—also known as the either/or fallacy or the black-or-white fallacy—occurs when we are asked to choose between two extreme alternatives without being able to consider additional options. For example, we may say, "Either you're for me or against me," meaning that a choice has to be made between these alternatives. Sometimes giving people only two choices on an issue makes sense ("If you decide to swim the English Channel, you'll either make it or you won't.") At other times, however, viewing situations in such extreme terms may be a serious oversimplification—for it would mean viewing a complicated situation in terms that are too simple.

► • ◄      Review the dialogue about legalizing marijuana at the beginning of the chapter and see if you can identify any false dilemma fallacies. Once you have identified the fallacies, suggest different alternatives than those being presented.

► • ◄      The following statements are examples of false dilemmas. After analyzing the fallacy in each case, suggest different alternatives than those being presented.

*Example:*   "Everyone in Germany is a National Socialist—the few outside the party are either lunatics or idiots." (Adolf Hitler, quoted by *The New York Times,* 5 April 1938.)

*Analysis:*   This is an oversimplification. Hitler is saying that if you are not a Nazi, then you are a lunatic or an idiot. By limiting the population to these two groups, Hitler was simply ignoring all the people who did not qualify as either Nazis or lunatics.

1. "America—Love it or Leave it!"

2. "She loves me; she loves me not."

3. "Live free or die"

4. "If you're not part of the solution, then you're part of the problem." (Eldridge Cleaver)

5. "If you know about BMW, you either own one or you want to."


**False appeals**

Many fallacious arguments appeal for support to factors that have little or nothing to do with the argument being offered. In these cases, false appeals are substituted for sound reasoning and a critical examination of the issues. Such appeals, known also as fallacies of relevance, include the following kinds of fallacious thinking:

Appeal to authority
Appeal to pity
Appeal to fear
Appeal to ignorance
Appeal to personal attack


***Appeal to authority***   In Chapter Six, "Believing and Knowing," we explored the ways in which we sometimes appeal to various authorities to establish our beliefs or prove our points. At that time, we noted that, in order for authorities to serve as a basis for beliefs, they must have legitimate expertise in the area they are advising on—like an experienced mechanic diagnosing a problem with our car. However, people often appeal to authorities who are not qualified to give an expert opinion. Consider the reasoning in the following arguments. Do you think that the arguments are sound? Why or why not?

Hi. You've probably seen me out on the football field. After a hard day's work crushing halfbacks and sacking quarterbacks, I like to settle down with a cold, smooth Maltz beer.

SONY. Ask anyone.

Over 11 million women will read this ad. Only 16 will own the coat.

Each of these arguments is intended to persuade us of the value of a product through the appeal to various authorities. In the first case, the authority is a well-known sports figure; in the second, the authority is large numbers of people; and in the third, the authority is a select few, appealing to our desire to be exclusive ("snob appeal"). Unfortunately, none of these authorities offers legitimate expertise about the product. Football players are not beer experts; large numbers of people are often misled; and exclusive groups of people are frequently mistaken in their beliefs. In order to evaluate authorities, we have to ask:

What is the expertise of the authorities based on?

Is their expertise in the area they are commenting on?

---

➤•◄    Review the discussion on legalizing marijuana at the beginning of the chapter. Can you locate any examples of false appeal to authority? If so, explain why you believe that the authority is not an expert in the area with which he/she is being linked.

---

➤•◄    Locate an example that illustrates a false appeal to authority. Explain why you think that the appeal is not warranted.

***Appeal to pity***    Consider the reasoning in the following arguments. Do you think that the arguments are sound? Why or why not?

I know that I haven't completed my term paper, but I really think that I should be excused. This has been a very difficult semester for me. I caught every kind of flu that came around. In addition, my brother has a drinking problem, and this has been very upsetting to me. Also, my dog died.

I admit that my client embezzled money from the company, your honor. However, I would like to bring several facts to your attention. He is a family man, with a wonderful wife and two terrific children. He is an important member of the community. He is active in the church, coaches a little league baseball team, and has worked very hard to be a good person who cares about people. I think that you should take these things into consideration in handing down your sentence.

In each of these arguments, the reasons being offered to support the conclusions may indeed be true. However, they are not relevant to the conclusion. Instead of providing evidence that supports the conclusion, the reasons offered are designed to make us feel sorry for the person involved and so agree with the conclusion out of sympathy. Although these appeals are often effective, the arguments are not sound. The probability of a conclusion can only be established by reasons that support and are relevant to the conclusion.

---

Locate or develop an example of an argument that commits the fallacy of  appealing to pity.

**_Appeal to fear_**   Consider the reasoning in the following arguments. Do you think that the arguments are sound? Why or why not?

> I'm afraid I don't think you deserve a raise. After all, there are many people who would be happy to have your job at the salary you are currently receiving. I would be happy to interview some of these people if you really think that you are underpaid.

> The reason that you are doing poorly in my class is that you do not seem to make enough effort. If you don't work harder, then you will not meet the course requirements and you will not pass.

In both of these arguments, the conclusions being suggested are supported by an appeal to fear, not by reasons that provide evidence for the conclusions. In the first case, the threat is: if you do not forgo your salary demands, your job may be in jeopardy. In the second case, the threat is: if you do not appear to work harder, then you will fail the course. In neither instance are the real issues being discussed.

Is a salary increase deserved?

Is the student actually making an effort?

People who appeal to fear to support their conclusions are interested only in prevailing, regardless of which position might be more justified.

---

Locate or develop an example of an argument that commits the fallacy of appealing to fear.

**_Appeal to ignorance_**   Consider the reasoning in the following arguments. Do you think that the arguments are sound? Why or why not?

> You say that you don't believe in God. But can you prove that He doesn't exist? If not, then you have to accept the conclusion that He does in fact exist.

> Greco Tires are the best. None have been proved better.

> With me, abortion is not a problem of religion. It's a problem of the Constitution. I believe that until and unless someone can establish that the unborn child is not a living human being, then that child is already protected by the Constitution, which guarantees life, liberty, and the pursuit of happiness to all of us. (Ronald Reagan, 8 October 1984)

When this argument form is used, the person offering the conclusion is asking his or her opponent to *disprove* the conclusion. If the opponent is unable to do so, then the conclusion is asserted to be true. This argument form is not valid because it is the job of the person proposing the argument to prove the conclusion. Simply because an opponent cannot *dis*prove the conclusion offers no evidence that the conclusion is in fact justified. For instance, in the first example above, the fact that someone cannot prove that God does not exist provides no persuasive reason for believing that he does.

---

►•◄    Review the discussion on legalizing marijuana at the beginning of the chapter. Can you identify arguments that are based on an appeal to ignorance? Describe any examples and explain why.

---

►•◄    Locate or develop an example of an argument that commits the fallacy of appealing to ignorance.

**Appeal to personal attack**    Consider the reasoning in the following arguments. Do you think that the arguments are valid? Why or why not?

> Your opinion on this issue is false. It's impossible to believe anything you say.

> How can you have an intelligent opinion about abortion? You're not a woman, so this is a decision that you'll never have to make.

> "Well, I guess I'm reminded a little bit of what Will Rogers once said about Hoover. He said it's not what he doesn't know that bothers me, it's what he knows for sure just ain't so." (Walter Mondale characterizing Ronald Reagan, 8 October 1984)

This argument form has been one of the most frequently used fallacies through the ages. Its effectiveness results from ignoring the issues of the argument and focusing instead on the personal qualities of the person making the argument. By trying to discredit the other person, the effort is being made to discredit the argument—no matter what reasons are offered. This fallacy is also referred to as the *ad hominem* argument, which means "to the man" rather than to the issue, and *poisoning the well*, because we are trying to insure that any water drawn from our opponent's well will be treated as undrinkable.

The effort to discredit can take two forms, as illustrated in the examples above. The fallacy can be *abusive* in the sense that we are directly attacking the credibility of our opponent (as in the third example). In addition, the fallacy can also be *circumstantial* in the sense that we are claiming that the person's circumstances, not character, render his or her opinion so biased or uninformed that it cannot be treated seriously (as in the second example). Other examples of the circumstantial form of the fallacy would include disregarding the views on nuclear plant safety given by an owner of one of the plants, or ignoring the views of a company comparing a product it manufactures with competing products.

---

Review the discussion on legalizing marijuana at the beginning of the chapter. See if you can identify any arguments which are based on an appeal to personal attack. Describe any examples and explain why they illustrate this fallacy.

---

Locate or develop examples of arguments that commit the abusive and circumstantial forms of this fallacious reasoning.

---

Our ability to detect and analyze fallacious arguments is an important part of our efforts to make sense of the world. Review the following article entitled "Heroin, Marijuana, and LSD," and then analyze it in the following manner:

1. Identify and describe the arguments being offered
2. Evaluate the accuracy of the reasons presented in support of the conclusions.
3. Evaluate the validity of the arguments offered by determining the degree to which the reasons support the conclusions (or the conclusions follow from the reasons).
4. Identify and analyze any fallacious reasoning that is being offered.

## Heroin, Marijuana, and LSD
*by David A. Noebel*

Narcotics, of course, are dangerous even when administered under the care of a physician. Both heroin and marijuana are exceedingly dangerous. Heroin is the strongest and most addictive opium derivative and is either sniffed into the nasal passages through the nose or mixed in water and heated to form a

solution and injected intravenously with a hypodermic directly into the bloodstream. Marijuana is a derivative from the hemp weed, which affects the nervous system and the brain of the user, causing mental unbalance for varying
periods of time and in which a sufficient dose of the active substance—tetrahy-
drocannabianol—is capable of producing all the hallucinatory and psychotic effects relative to LSD (which is conceded to be one of the most powerful drugs
known).

Repeated use of heroin produces psychological and physical dependence
in which the user has an overwhelming compulsion to continue using the drug.
Under heroin the body develops a tolerance for it in the bloodstream and
virtually all bodily functions are attuned to that presence. Of course, once the
victim has the habit, he stops at nothing to satisfy it, and since heroin is considered incurably addictive, when the narcotic is no longer in the body, death can
result even during the withdrawal process.

Marijuana, on the other hand, is no less to be desired. In a timely article on
narcotics, Dr. Susan Huck, in a personal interview with the noted geneticist,
Dr. Louis Diaz de Souza (who has spent 18 years investigating the effects of
marijuana on the human body) found that "even one smoke of marijuana does
calamitous damage to the chromosomes." The doctor told her that damage to
one chromosome, "may mean that the child will be hemophilian, or mongo-
loid, or afflicted with leukemia. The chromosome may pass from one generation to another. The child of the marijuana user may show this damage or his
child may show it."[1]

Unfortunately, a semantical argument has developed over the usage of the
word "addictive" and "dependent." Some argue the drug is not addictive, but
rather the user only becomes dependent on it. Others, e.g., Dr. Hardin Jones, of
the Donner Laboratory at the University of California (Berkeley), maintains
that marijuana is habit-forming and with continued use it is addictive. Naturally, the argument makes little difference since (1) few are so sophisticated as to
see any difference between "addictive" and "dependent" and (2) since it takes
the user away from reality and removes his normal inhibitions, marijuana is
harmful apart from either word. Smith, Kline & French Laboratories, in a special report prepared primarily for educators, found marijuana not only impair-
ing the user's ability to drive an automobile, but producing such physical effects as dizziness, dry mouth, dilated pupils and burning eyes, urinary
frequency, diarrhea, nausea and vomiting.[2]

---

[1]*American Opinion*, May 1969, p. 58.
[2]*Tulsa Daily World*, May 5, 1967, p. 8.

Dr. Hardin Jones in his research found marijuana not only habit-forming and addictive with continued use, but also reported (1) that although it does not lead to the use of harder narcotics through chemical addiction, it promotes a curiosity about the harder drugs; (2) that its effect is cumulative, witness that a neophyte needs several joints to "turn on," whereas a professional can get high on one; (3) that it interferes with normal perceptions; (4) that its cumulative impact brings repeated hallucinations that disturb the reference memory, causing (5) wholesale abandonment of goals and ambitions.

Jones goes on to say that marijuana and other drugs are in a very real sense sexual stimulants. Marijuana is a mild aphrodisiac. "It enhances sensitivity and makes a person more receptive to sensual stimuli," he says, "but this condition only lasts a short period of time and chronic marijuana users find that sex activities without the drug are difficult and confusing."[3]

And the world-famous authority on marijuana, Dr. Constandinos J. Miras, of the University of Athens, who has been studying man and marijuana for over twenty-five years, found marijuana users to have abnormal brain wave readings and marked behavioral changes. Longtime users, for example, revealed chronic lethargy and loss of inhibitions for two years after their last usage. Many of his subjects were slipping into less demanding jobs as the habit got a firmer grip on them and were variously depressed and exalted, not always sure when they were having hallucinations. Others went through a rapid succession of physical changes—crying, laughing, sluggishness, hunger for sugar, hallucinating. The idea of the so-called harmless use of marijuana is either ignorance or deception. And one State official in Maryland remarked that marijuana not only induces a lethargy in most people, but a dangerous attitude toward the community.

The hallucinogens which are popularly known as psychedelics (since they produce sensations distorting time, space, sound and color) include LSD, STP and DMT. All hallucinogens create hallucinations which lessen the user's ability to discriminate between fact and fancy, and studies indicate that LSD may cause chromosome damage which could result in mental deficiencies and blood diseases in children born to users. One of the foremost authorities in the United States on LSD is Dr. J. Thomas Ungerleider. He states that, "LSD has been called a consciousness-expanding drug. In fact, it is quite the reverse. It decreases one's ability to select and pay attention. Therefore, it decreases conscious functions. Sensations do become intensified. Perception, however, is not enhanced, and visual and auditory acuteness are not revolutionized, but rather

---

[3]*Tulsa Daily World,* September 25, 1969, p. 16A.

are distorted." Since LSD dulls the user's objective judgment, which is replaced by purely subjective values, Dr. Ungerleider says, "LSD seems to affect a person's value system."[4]

Then, too, both the amphetamines and barbiturates are danger drugs. Amphetamines, often called pep pills, produce a feeling of excitation which usually manifests itself in appetite loss with an increasing ability to go without sleep for long periods of time. The most common amphetamines are Benzedrine (called Bennies), Dexedrine (called Dexies) and Methadrine (referred to as crystal or speed). The danger, of course, with amphetamines as well as barbiturates is the psychological desire to continue using the drugs. The most common barbiturates are Amytal (referred to as Blue Heavens), Nembutal (or Yellow Jackets) and Seconal (called Red Devils or Red Birds). In the jargon of drug addicts, barbiturates in general are referred to as "goofballs" and affect the central nervous system and the brain by slowly depressing the mental and physical functions of the body. A person under the influence of a barbiturate will be disoriented to time, place and person and may experience delusions and hallucinations.

Obviously, such drugs cannot be equated with apple pie and vanilla ice cream. And any drug—marijuana, for example, which at one moment makes a person feel so tiny he is not able to step off an eight-inch curb, and yet an hour later makes him feel so huge he could step off a ten-story building—is dangerous. Any individual, who under the influence of marijuana can barrel down the highway at 80 mph and assume he is only traveling 20 mph, or drive through a red light which appears to be green and smash into a row of cars which appeared to be a mile away, is dangerous. And, any drug—LSD, for example, which makes a person feel he can fly like a bird and so take off from a four-story building only to discover he is flying to his death—is not safe.

## Constructing extended arguments

For most of this chapter, we have focused our attention on individual arguments, which, seen in isolation, may appear to be neat, logical packages that exist apart from our general thinking activities. This is clearly not the case. The reasoning expressed in arguments is a fundamental aspect of the thinking process we use to make sense of the world. Reasoning is an integral part of the way we organize and relate our experience, enabling us to solve problems, work to-

---

[4]*Tulsa Tribune*, February 24, 1967, p. 14.

ward our goals, make sense of information, understand others, explain and predict events, and so on. In order to reason effectively, we have to utilize all the thinking and language skills that we have been developing in this book. Sharpening our reasoning abilities does not simply involve learning certain argument forms; it means developing ways of thinking so that we can understand our world and make effective decisions.

As a result, our ability to construct effective arguments reveals the degree to which we have become critical thinkers. When we argue effectively for a conclusion, we are thinking actively, developing reasons to support our position, analyzing the issues from multiple perspectives, exchanging our views with others in a thoughtful fashion, and critically reflecting on the entire process on an ongoing basis. As you complete the final exercise in this chapter, make an effort to become aware of the way you are using the thinking and language abilities we have been exploring in this book.

---

In the following article, the psychologist Robert Coles examines the moral awareness of children. Coles claims that our society clings to the idea of children as pure innocents and does not see the ethical decisions that they make or the complicated moral issues that they confront. Through examples of the many children he has met, Coles argues for the need for parents to teach their children moral values.

## I Listen to My Parents and I Wonder What They Believe
*by Robert Coles*

Not so long ago children were looked upon in a sentimental fashion as ''angels'' or as ''innocents.'' Today, thanks to Freud and his followers, boys and girls are understood to have complicated inner lives; to feel love, hate, envy and rivalry in various and subtle mixtures; to be eager participants in the sexual and emotional politics of the home, neighborhood and school. Yet some of us parents still cling to the notion of childhood innocence in another way. We do not see that our children also make ethical decisions every day in their own lives, or realize how attuned they may be to moral currents and issues in the larger society.

In Appalachia I heard a girl of eight whose father owns coal fields (and gas stations, a department store and much timberland) wonder about ''life'' one day: "I'll be walking to the school bus, and I'll ask myself why there's some who are poor and their daddies can't find a job, and there's some who are lucky like me. Last month there was an explosion in a mine my daddy owns, and everyone became upset. Two miners got killed. My daddy said it was their own fault, because they'll be working and they get careless. When my mother asked if there was anything wrong with the safety down in the mine, he told her no and she shouldn't ask questions like that. Then the Government people came and they said it was the owner's fault—Daddy's. But he has a lawyer and the lawyer is fighting the Government and the union. In school, kids ask me what I think, and I sure do feel sorry for the two miners and so does my mother—I know that. She told me it's just not a fair world and you have to remember that. Of course, there's no one who can be sure there won't be trouble; like my daddy says, the rain falls on the just and the unjust. My brother is only six and he asked Daddy awhile back who are the 'just' and the 'unjust,' and Daddy said there are people who work hard and they live good lives, and there are lazy people and they're always trying to sponge off others. But I guess you have to feel sorry for anyone who has a lot trouble, because it's poured-down, heavy rain.''

Listening, one begins to realize that an elementary-school child is no stranger to moral reflection—and to ethical conflict. This girl was torn between her loyalty to her particular background, its values and assumptions, and to a larger affiliation—her membership in the nation, the world. As a human being whose parents were kind and decent to her, she was inclined to be thoughtful and sensitive with respect to others, no matter what their work or position in society. But her father was among other things a mineowner, and she had already learned to shape her concerns to suit that fact of life. The result: a moral oscillation of sorts, first toward nameless others all over the world and then toward her own family. As the girl put it later, when she was a year older: ''You should try to have 'good thoughts' about everyone, the minister says, and our teacher says that too. But you should honor your father and mother most of all; that's why you should find out what they think and then sort of copy them. But sometimes you're not sure if you're on the right track.''

*Sort of copy them.* There could be worse descriptions of how children acquire moral values. In fact, the girl understood how girls and boys all over the world ''sort of'' develop attitudes of what is right and wrong, ideas of who the just and the unjust are. And they also struggle hard and long, and not always with success, to find out where the ''right track'' starts and ends. Children need encouragement or assistance as they wage that struggle.

In home after home that I have visited, and in many classrooms, I have met children who not only are growing emotionally and intellectually but also are trying to make sense of the world morally. That is to say, they are asking themselves and others about issues of fair play, justice, liberty, equality. Those last

words are abstractions, of course—the stuff of college term papers. And there
are, one has to repeat, those in psychology and psychiatry who would deny
elementary-school children access to that "higher level" of moral reflection.
But any parent who has listened closely to his or her child knows that girls and
boys are capable of wondering about matters of morality, and knows too that
often it is their grown-up protectors (parents, relatives, teachers, neighbors)
who are made uncomfortable by the so-called "innocent" nature of the questions children may ask or the statements they may make. Often enough the
issue is not the moral capacity of children but the default of us parents who fail
to respond to inquiries put to us by our daughters and sons—and fail to set
moral standards for both ourselves and our children.

Do's and don't's are, of course, pressed upon many of our girls and boys.
But a moral education is something more than a series of rules handed down,
and in our time one cannot assume that every parent feels able—sure enough of
her own or his own actual beliefs and values—to make even an initial explana-
tory and disciplinary effort toward a moral education. Furthermore, for many
of us parents these days it is a child's emotional life that preoccupies us.

In 1963, when I was studying school desegregation in the South, I had extended conversations with Black and white elementary-school children caught
up in a dramatic moment of historical change. For longer than I care to remember, I concentrated on possible psychiatric troubles, on how a given child was
managing under circumstances of extreme stress, on how I could be of
help—with "support," with reassurance, with a helpful psychological observation or interpretation. In many instances I was off the mark. These children
weren't "patients"; they weren't even complaining. They were worried, all
right, and often enough they had things to say that were substantive—that had
to do not so much with troubled emotions as with questions of right and wrong
in the real-life dramas taking place in their worlds.

Here is a nine-year old white boy, the son of ardent segregationists, telling
me about his sense of what desegregation meant to Louisiana in the 1960s:
"They told us it wouldn't happen—never. My daddy said none of us white
people would go into schools with the colored. But then it did happen, and
when I went to school the first day I didn't know what would go on. Would the
school stay open or would it close up? We didn't know what to do; the teacher
kept telling us that we should be good and obey the law, but my daddy said the
law was wrong. Then my mother said she wanted me in school even if there
were some colored kids there. She said if we all stayed home she'd be a 'nervous wreck.' So I went.

"After a while I saw that the colored weren't so bad. I saw that there are
different kinds of colored people, just like with us whites. There was one of the

colored who was nice, a boy who smiled, and he played real good. There was another one, a boy, who wouldn't talk with anyone. I don't know if it's right that we all be in the same school. Maybe it isn't right. My sister is starting school next year, and she says she doesn't care if there's 'mixing of the races.' She says they told her in Sunday school that everyone is a child of God, and then a kid asked if that goes for the colored too and the teacher said yes, she thought so. My daddy said that it's true, God made everyone—but that doesn't mean we all have to be living together under the same roof in the home or the school. But my mother said we'll never know what God wants of us but we have to try to read His mind, and that's why we pray. So when I say my prayers I ask God to tell me what's the right thing to do. In school I try to say hello to the colored, because they're kids, and you can't be mean or you'll be 'doing wrong,' like my grandmother says.''

Children aren't usually long-winded in the moral discussions they have with one another or with adults, and in quoting this boy I have pulled together comments he made to me in the course of several days. But everything he said was of interest to me. I was interested in the boy's changing racial attitudes. It was clear he was trying to find a coherent, sensible moral position too. It was also borne in on me that if one spends days, weeks in a given home, it is hard to escape a particular moral climate just as significant as the psychological one.

In many homes parents establish moral assumptions, mandates, priorities. They teach children what to believe in, what not to believe in. They teach children what is permissible or not permissible—and why. They may summon up the Bible, the flag, history, novels, aphorisms, philosophical or political sayings, personal memories—all in an effort to teach children how to behave, what and whom to respect and for which reasons. Or they may neglect to do so, and in so doing teach their children *that*—a moral abdication, of sorts—and in this way fail their children. Children need and long for words of moral advice, instruction, warning, as much as they need words of affirmation or criticism from their parents about other matters. They must learn how to dress and what to wear, how to eat and what to eat; and they must also learn how to behave under X or Y or Z conditions, and why.

All the time, in 20 years of working with poor children and rich children, Black children and white children, children from rural areas and urban areas and in every region of this country, I have heard questions—thoroughly intelligent and discerning questions—about social and historical matters, about personal behavior, and so on. But most striking is the fact that almost all those questions, in one way or another, are moral in nature: Why did the Pilgrims leave England? Why didn't they just stay and agree to do what the king wanted them to do?. . . Should you try to share all you've got or should you save a lot for yourself?. . . What do you do when you see others fighting—do you try to break up the fight, do you stand by and watch or do you leave as fast as you can?. . . Is it right that some people haven't got enough to eat?. . .I see other kids cheating and I wish I could copy the answers too; but I won't cheat, though sometimes I feel I'd like to and I get all mixed up. I go home and talk with my parents, and I ask them what should you do do if you see kids cheating—pay no attention, or report the kids or do the same thing they are doing?

Those are examples of children's concerns—and surely millions of American parents have heard versions of them. Have the various "experts" on childhood stressed strongly enough the importance of such questions—and the importance of the hunger we all have, no matter what our age or background, to examine what we believe in, are willing to stand up for, and what we are determined to ask, likewise, of our children?

Children not only need our understanding of their complicated emotional lives; they also need a constant regard for the moral issues that come their way as soon as they are old enough to play with others and take part in the politics of the nursery, the back yard and the schoolroom. They need to be told what they must do and what they must not do. They need control over themselves and a sense of what others are entitled to from them—co-operation, thoughtfulness, an attentive ear and eye. They need discipline not only to tame their excesses of emotion but discipline also connected to stated and clarified moral values. They need, in other words, something to believe in that is larger than their own appetites and urges and, yes, bigger than their "psychological drives." They need a larger view of the world, a moral context, as it were—a faith that addresses itself to the meaning of this life we all live and, soon enough, let go of.

Yes, it is time for us parents to begin to look more closely at what ideas our children have about the world; and it would be well to do so before they become teen-agers and young adults and begin to remind us, as often happens, of how little attention we did pay to their moral development. Perhaps a nine-year-old girl from a well-off suburban home in Texas put it better than anyone else I've met:

"I listen to my parents, and I wonder what they believe in more than anything else. I asked my mom and my daddy once: What's the thing that means most to you? They said they didn't know but I shouldn't worry my head too hard with questions like that. So I asked my best friend, and she said she wonders if there's a God and how do you know Him and what does He want you to do—I mean, when you're in school or out playing with your friends. They talk about God in church, but is it only in church that He's there and keeping an eye on you? I saw a kid steal in a store, and I know her father has a lot of money—because I hear my daddy talk. But stealing's wrong. My mother said she's a 'sick girl,' but it's still wrong what she did. Don't you think?''

There was more—much more—in the course of the months I came to know that child and her parents and their neighbors. But those observations and question—a ''mere child's''—reminded me unforgettably of the aching hunger for firm ethical principles that so many of us feel. Ought we not begin thinking about this need? Ought we not all be asking ourselves more intently what standards we live by—and how we can satisfy our children's hunger for moral values?

1. a. Describe the arguments Coles uses to support the idea that each of us—beginning as children—has a need to make sense of the moral dimension of our experience.

   b. Evaluate the accuracy of the reasons supporting Coles's conclusions.

   c. Evaluate the validity of the arguments he presents.

2. a. Develop at least one additional argument to support Coles's view.

   b. Develop at least one argument that conflicts with his view.

3. Using the Coles article as a resource, define your own understanding of the concept of *moral awareness.*

   a. Describe one or more examples from your own experience that illustrate the concept of *moral awareness.*

   b. Based on these examples, identify the necessary requirements of the concept of *moral awareness.*

4. At the end of the article, Coles calls for the need to think about how we teach moral awareness:

   . . . those observations and questions—a ''mere child's''—reminded me unforgettably of the aching hunger for firm ethical principles that so many of us feel. Ought we not begin thinking about this need? Ought we not all be asking ourselves more intently what standards we live by—and how we can satisfy our children's hunger for moral values?

   Explain what you see as the connections between developing moral awareness and our ability to think critically, as suggested by Coles.

5. a. Identify a moral issue that you feel strongly about, and describe your beliefs about this issue.

   b. Describe how you developed your beliefs about this moral issue, based on your experience (education, family, friends, critical reflection, etc.).

   c. Explain how you would teach this moral issue to someone else. Be sure to support your views with well-reasoned arguments. (You may want to review the analysis of the composing process in Chapter Ten.)

Robert Coles, "I Listen to My Parents and I Wonder What They Believe": This article appeared in *Redbook,* February 1980. Reprinted by permission of Dr. Robert Coles.

The author would like to thank the following students for permission to reprint their work: Maggie Collazo, Ertha Keitt, Martin Stroud, Sandy Serra, Eddy Polanco, Kathryn Collazo, Patricia Valdez, Carmen Garcia, Sophia Iffla, Lynn Whalen, Jackie Gabriellini, Debra White, Emil Figueroa, Barbara Messer, Mayra Suero, Bartolome Medina, Frankie Rouse, Freda Daniel.

# Index